The State of the Parties

Second Edition

*The Changing Role
of Contemporary American Parties*

Edited by
JOHN C. GREEN
DANIEL M. SHEA

ROWMAN & LITTLEFIELD PUBLISHERS, INC.
Lanham • Boulder • New York • London

ROWMAN & LITTLEFIELD PUBLISHERS, INC.

Published in the United States of America
by Rowman & Littlefield Publishers, Inc.
4720 Boston Way, Lanham, Maryland 20706

3 Henrietta Street
London WC2E 8LU, England

British Cataloging in Publication Information Available

Library of Congress Cataloging-in-Publication Data

The state of the parties : the changing role of contemporary American
    parties / edited by John C. Green, Daniel M. Shea. — 2nd ed.
        p.   cm.— (People, passions, and power)
    Includes bibliographical references and index.
        ISBN 0-8476-8265-X (alk. paper). — ISBN 0-8476-8266-8 (alk. paper)
        1. Political parties—United States. I. Green, John Clifford, 1953– .
    II. Shea, Daniel M. III. Series.
JK2261.S824   1996
324.273—dc20   96-29110
                                                           CIP

ISBN 0–8476-8265-X (cloth : alk. paper)
ISBN 0–8476–8266-8 (pbk. : alk. paper)

Printed in the United States of America

⊖™ The paper used in this publication meets the minimum requirements of American
National Standard for Information Sciences—Permanence of Paper for Printed Library
Materials, ANSI Z39.48–1984.

The State of the Parties

People, Passions, and Power: Social Movements, Interest Organizations, and the Political Process
John C. Green, Series Editor

This new series explores the people, activities, and institutions that animate the political process. The series emphasizes recent changes in that process—new actors, new movements, new strategies, new successes (or failures) to enter the political mainstream or influence everyday politics—and places these changes in context with the past and the future. Books in the series combine high quality scholarship with accessibility so that they may be used as core or supplementary texts in upper division political science, sociology, and communication studies courses. The series is consciously interdisciplinary and encourages cross-discipline collaboration and research.

The State of the Parties, Second Edition: The Changing Role of Contemporary American Parties (1996) edited by John C. Green and Daniel M. Shea

Social Movements and American Political Institutions (forthcoming) edited by Anne Costain and Andrew S. McFarland

After the Boom: The Politics of Generation X (forthcoming) edited by Stephen C. Craig and Stephen Earl Bennett

Dedicated to

Brendan and Darcy Green
and
Abigail Shea

Contents

PART FOUR
Party Policy and Values

PART FIVE
Reconceptualizing Parties

Illustrations

Tables

Figures

Preface

The first edition of this book originated from research coordinated at the Ray C. Bliss Institute of Applied Politics in 1993. Our goal was to bring together party scholars from around the nation to discuss changes in party politics and new avenues of research. These efforts were an enormous success, boasting a "dream team" of scholars whose work was published in the fall of 1994.

While it might seem odd that a second edition would follow just two years later, we felt compelled to move in this direction for a number of reasons. First, the 1994 midterm election had a dramatic impact on party politics. Rarely has our system undergone such a massive partisan turnover at all levels of government. Second, several of the conditions touched upon in the first volume have continued in the last two years, for instance, the growing import of third party candidates and the flow of party money. Finally, the debate over the precise role of parties in American politics has taken on a new quality of late. National, state, and local party organizations are more active than in the recent past, but at the same time seem less germane to the average citizen—and in some ways to the political process itself. So, we compiled this new edition with the goal of providing students and scholars of American parties with some of the most timely, innovative research available. Because we believe the party system is in a period of profound transformation, we anticipate a continuing flow of new editions.

The development of this volume was greatly aided by the staff of the Bliss Institute. Kimberly Haverkamp was not only instrumental in corresponding with authors, compiling the chapters, and managing layout, but has honed the unique skill of putting up with the editors—no simple task, to be sure. Also giving a hand at the Institute were Heather Milota and Heather Starr. We owe a debt of thanks to Jon Sisk, Jennifer Knerr, and Julie Kirsch at Rowman & Littlefield. They were more than accommodating on a number of tough calls, and bent over backward to help finish the book on time. Finally, we would surely be remiss if we did not acknowledge our families, principally Lynn Green and Christine Gatto-Shea. Without their unwavering support and encouragement this book would not have been possible.

Paths and Crossroads: The State of the Parties and Party Scholarship

John C. Green
Daniel M. Shea

The 1992 and 1994 elections raise daunting questions about the state of American political parties. The rise of Ross Perot, deep divisions within governing coalitions, and the continued decline of voter partisanship all point to a weakened state of the parties. These patterns are confused, however, by countertrends suggesting a strengthened state: moves toward party government, first by the Democrats in 1992 and then the Republicans in 1994, and the continued expansion of party organizations at all levels. Overall, the parties appear to be in a state of flux. This situation would be challenge enough for scholars, but there is the added burden that party scholarship is in flux as well.

Political scientists trained in the paradigms of the 1950s and 1960s increasingly find themselves questioning the ability of political parties to link the governed with the government and, perhaps, in their quieter moments, the desirability of such linkages. Meanwhile, scholars trained in the 1970s and 1980s find it difficult to teach the old virtues of party government. But even those who view party decline as the norm are confronted by the increased vitality of many party organizations. Indeed, the enterprise that many of us have chosen—learning and teaching about parties—seems increasingly alienated from real-world politics. The question of how best to think about parties is being raised precisely when the parties have provided a lot to think about.

At one level, this book does little to resolve the situation. It is only honest to admit that the state of contradiction and paradox that bedevils the study of parties is amply displayed here, and the value of these essays stems as much from the portrait of work in progress as from the picture of the parties presented. Yet, taken as a whole, these essays outline new understandings of parties and new directions for party scholarship. The parties themselves confront divergent paths and it is unclear which direction they will follow. And not coincidentally, party scholarship also stands at a crossroads, uncertain of what should be studied and how. The good news is that there is no shortage of effort on either front. These efforts can be usefully organized around three broad topics: party systems, party activities, and party values.

The focus on party systems involves crucial questions regarding the role of parties in the political system, including their relationship to citizens, public officials, and social processes, and then the question of what these relationships should be. Attention to the party activities raises narrower, but no less important, queries: what do the parties actually do, and what difference does it make? A focus on party values highlights parallel concerns: what do parties care about, and how do these concerns matter? These are not new questions, of course, and a brief review of the path of previous scholarship will help set the present dilemmas in context.

Historic Paths: The Tripod and Responsible Party Models

Much of the puzzlement surrounding parties comes from the confrontation of time-honored postulates with present realities. Chief among these is the "tripod" view of parties, which conceives of parties as party-in-the-electorate, party-in-government, and party-as-organization. This distinction has been used skillfully by students and teachers for better than half a century. When combined with another venerable concept, the "responsible" party model, the results offer a set of empirical and normative expectations about the operation of parties that once gave persuasive answers to the questions now posed.

Party was seen as the most important link between voters and government officials. Voter preferences, the raw material for public policy in a democracy, were assumed to be the core source of partisanship. Party organizations sought to use these affections in order to mobilize votes on behalf of their candidates. If those candidates were successful at the polls, the preferences of the people who voted for them would then be extended to the government. As such, the activities and values of party organizations bore a direct relationship to the party's linkage role in the political system. The engine of this process was electoral competition, and the American constitutional arrangements imposed a two-party structure on the task.

For advocates of responsible parties, this linkage was accomplished when a party's candidates offered clear policy stands to the voters, carried out their promises when elected, and faced the wrath or reward of the voters in the next election. Alliances of copartisans in government could overcome the separation of powers and federalism. Accordingly, policy formulation was the key feature of well-functioning parties. Other scholars doubted the practicality and/or wisdom of strict policy responsibility and assumed that parties had narrower goals, namely, winning elections, and that public policy was only one means of appealing to voters. But this "conventional," "rational-efficient," or "pluralist-organizational" view of parties still largely accepted the tripod model. Of course, party organizations often failed to perform as expected, but there was reason to expect they could do better. The "state of the parties" thus took on great significance, and proposals for improving the major party organizations became a staple of the literature.

The debate over party responsibility aside, the elements of the tripod were once well supported by large bodies of research. In many areas this is no longer the case. For example, studies of the electorate once showed that citizens' partisanship was the dominant influence on vote choice. Tying partisanship to generational change and dramatic events, scholars identified critical elections, the "mainsprings" of American politics, that marked the transition from one period of stable partisanship and public policy to another. However, recent research suggests a sharp decline in partisanship, and the theory of critical elections is under serious reconsideration. A similar pattern occurred for party-in-government: partisanship was once a dominant factor in legislative and executive behavior, but divided-government and candidate-centered politics has reduced its importance. Changes of a different sort have occurred for party organizations. Once-potent local parties have atrophied, being replaced by stronger state and national organizations that are more active, capable, and sophisticated than ever before, yet more distant from the citizenry.

The net effect of these changes has been to simultaneously cast doubt on the usefulness of the tripod and to intensify the debate over party responsibility. Indeed, advocates and critics of responsible parties, including some in this volume (chapter 23), have attacked the tripod. The crucial problem is the ruptured link between partisans in the electorate and government, which some critics lay at the feet of the parties themselves. Other scholars point to the vitality of party organizations and argue that the tripod misspecified parties by the inclusion of voters and candidates. A renewed demand for responsible parties has become a potent crosscurrent in these disputes. Other scholars still find the tripod useful in descriptive terms at least, and others wait with increasing frustration for the development of an alternative.

It is these considerations that produce the new focus on party systems, activities, and values. In some respects these topics represent an extension and abstraction of the tripod, but in other respects they are a narrowing of concerns and a return to basic questions. And chief among these is the role that parties can and should play in the democratic process.

Divergent Paths: The Party System under Stress

The first section of this book confronts the role of parties in the political system. All three authors agree that the state of the parties is poor, but each offers a different understanding of the problem and possible sources of improvement. In order, they find the problems outside the party system, outside of the parties, and within the parties themselves, and argue, respectively, for renewed partisanship, better partisanship, and a new kind of partisanship in the electorate and elsewhere. James Reichley (chapter 2) argues that the American two-party system is likely to weather its current woes, but there is no guarantee that the present parties will survive, or if they do, that they will maintain recognizable coalitions. He suggests that the party system operates on sixty- to seventy-year "super cycles" and that we are nearing the end of the present one. Parties are performing poorly because the polity is confused by the massive societal transformations of our era. As in the past, these changes may conclude with political settlements of which strengthened parties and renewed partisanship will be a part.

In partial contrast, Ralph Goldman (chapter 3) finds that the weakened state of the parties comes from within the political system itself. He argues that the vital functions performed by parties have been misunderstood and deprecated by political elites. Unless public opinion toward parties is improved, the major parties will continue to decline, even if the political situation changes or new reforms are instituted. Goldman proposes a thoroughgoing public relations campaign and a "bill of rights" for the parties. All told, the broader linkage role of parties requires the creation of better partisans, committed to party organizations as instruments of democracy.

Theodore Lowi (chapter 4) departs sharply from the previous essays by arguing that the two-party system has outlived its usefulness and that modern America needs a "responsible three-party system." The parties are performing poorly because they are old, entrenched institutions unwilling and unable to confront the problems of the day, to the detriment of the government and the disgust of the governed. He argues that it is unlikely that societal transformations will renew the party system (as Reichley suggests) or that the system can be salvaged from within (as Goldman proposes). Thus, a new system is required with a genuine "third" party as its centerpiece. Lowi details how such a new party might arise and how it would improve the performance of the government, as well as the obstacles to its development.

A Well-Traveled Path: Party Activities

Whether the present party system can be renewed from the outside, from within, or must be replaced, there remains the crucial question of what parties actually do and the impact of their activities. The twelve essays in the second section address this topic with a close eye on the 1992 and 1994 elections. Overall, these essays suggest a more positive state of the parties than the essays in the previous section: parties are shown to be active organizations, and poor performance is certainly not due to lack of effort. Most of these chapters draw inspiration from the party organizational studies of the last decade, which have proved to be one of the most productive research paths in the field.

Anthony Corrado (chapter 5) provides a detailed portrait of the activities of the Democratic and Republican National Committees in the 1992 election. Even jaded observers will be impressed by the efforts of the national organizations to encourage strong candidacies, develop party unity, and deploy resources effectively. In fact, the success of Bill Clinton owes much to the efforts of national Democratic leaders, while George Bush suffered from confusion among the Republicans. The national committees may be catching up with their congressional counterparts, the efforts of which are detailed by Paul Herrnson (chapter 6). In 1992, "hill committees" were challenged by scandals, retirements, and redistricting. Although facing more demands than they could meet, both parties were able to effectively deploy a vast array of resources. The Republicans appear to have been somewhat more effective in these efforts, in contrast to the presidential campaign. Overall, the much discussed growth of the national party organizations continues unabated. This growth included extensive financial links between the national, state, and local party organizations, which are reported on by Robert Biersack (chapter 7). Using newly available data on "soft money," Biersack argues that the strategic deployment of these resources may represent an important step toward the integration of national, state, and local party committees. The Republican made even further gains in 1994.

The next three chapters offer some evidence on the role played by major party organizations in the 1994 campaign. Andrew Appleton and Dan Ward (chapter 8) report on a survey of Democratic and Republican state party chairs in regard to the 1994 elections, including evidence on how they developed electoral expectations, understood the outcomes, and planned to respond with changes to their organizations. These findings are complemented by John Green's essay (chapter 9) on local Republican officials' assessments of the sources of the GOP victory in 1994. According to these data from four key states, Republican party organizations played a small but crucial role in the outcome of the election. Finally, John Frendreis, Alan Gitelson, Gregory Flemming, and Anne Layzell (chapter 10) detail the activities of county party committees in state legislative races in 1992 and 1994. As with their national and state counterparts, local parties displayed considerable structural capacity and provided assistance to local campaigns, particularly traditional grassroots activities such as recruiting campaign volunteers and get-out-the-vote efforts.

The following three chapters are case studies of party activities at the subnational level, beginning with Anne Hildreth and Dan Shea (chapter 11) on legislative campaign committees (LCC) in New York State. Frequently hailed as prime evidence of revitalized parties, these authors cast a critical eye on the relationship of the New York LCCs with the traditional state and county party committees. They find the LCCs to be driven by electoral concerns and less interested in working with other party organizations on other matters, thus reducing the scope of their impact on state politics. A similar situation is reported in Michael Margolis and David Resnick's account of local parties in Cincinnati, Ohio (chapter 12). Following a well-known pattern, they find the local parties uninterested in the most important local issue, urban economic development. A sharp contrast to this story of party decline is described by William Binning, Melanie Blumberg, and John Green (chapter 13) in Youngstown, Ohio, where the local Democratic Party was revitalized and made an instrument of economic redevelopment.

The third part of the book reports on the activities of independent candidacies and minor parties. Randall Partin, Lori Weber, Ronald Rapoport, and Walter Stone report on the Perot activities in 1992 and 1994 (chapter 14). As one might expect, the Perot following was characterized by a combination of disgust with the major parties and attraction to Perot, but, surprisingly, many of his followers had been previously involved in party and interest group activities. Perot drew substantially from the existing activist corps, but also expanded that group for future campaigns, as is amply demonstrated by their involvement in the 1994 campaign. Minor party activity was by no means limited to the Perot activists, as Chrisrtian Collet and Jerrold Hansen (chapter 15) show in their essay on minor party candidates, and James Guth and John Green (chapter 16) show in their work on minor party activists. Indeed, the size and diversity of minor party activity is part of the contemporary flux in party politics.

The Path Less Traveled: Party Values

One difference between major and minor parties is the greater policy orientation of the latter. Of course, the lack of clear-cut policy stands among the major parties is an ancient complaint. The responsible party model demanded that parties develop and proclaim distinct values, particularly in the form of detailed legislative programs. Such parties have been rare in the United States—the disappointment with party programs has taken on a legendary quality. The lack of progress on policy making, paralleling the expansion of other kinds of programmatic activities, has surely made the situation worse. Perhaps as a consequence, there has been less research on the policy-oriented qualities of party organizations that fall short of the responsible ideal.

The chapters in part four contribute to the study of party values in a number of provocative ways. First, Laura Berkowitz and Steve Lilienthal (chapter 17) describe the recent policy-making initiatives of the Democratic and Republican National Committees. Motivated by the results of the 1992 and 1994 elections, both parties set about encouraging the development of new ideas. These initiatives are unprecedented in their use of modern communications technology, but, as the authors point out, the interests of officeholders and candidates may eventually limit them. Sandy Maisel's (chapter 18) work on the major party platforms in 1992, and Robin Kolodny's (chapter 19) report on the Republican Contract with America is 1994 illustrate the impact of candidate-centered politics on the expressions of party values. Both authors find that party values are best expressed through the party's candidates, and not the other way around. However, one should not conclude that the major parties do not differ on matters of policy. As John Jackson and Nancy Clayton (chapter 20) amply document, there had been significant differences between major party elites and identifiers on a host of issues. Comparing elite and mass opinion from 1980 to 1992, they conclude that the major parties really do "stand for something."

The 1992 election was widely billed as the "year of the Democratic woman in politics" and 1994 produced significant gains for Republican women. Barbara Burrell and J. Cherie Strachan (chapter 21) take a careful look at how parties aided female candidates. They find that while women have made considerable gains as activists and leaders, women candidates often have had to bypass the party to gain nominations and get elected to office. Now that it has become clear that women are strong candidates, the party organizations are more supportive.

Party Concepts at a Crossroads

One might conclude from the foregoing chapters that the poor state of the party system results from a disjunction between new party activities and weakened party values. This situation has produced a debate on the focus of party scholarship, which closely resembles the original debate over the responsible parties. The watchwords of this disagreement are party "decline" versus "revival." Not surprisingly, scholars most interested in party values and impressed by the apparent rupture between voters and elected officials find parties in decline, while those most interested in party activities and impressed by the recent growth of party organizations find them undergoing revival. This debate is joined in part five.

John Coleman (chapter 22) offers a critique of the party revival camp and organizational studies in particular. What difference does it make, he asks, if party organizations are stronger and more complex, if voters disdain them and elected officials ignore them? He argues for integrating the various party components with changes in the economy, echoing in many respects Reichley's arguments about cycles in the party system (chapter 2). John Frendreis (chapter 23) offers a rebuttal to Coleman's critique. Writing at the request of the editors of this volume, he produces a concise response to the issues raised. While also arguing that the tripod model of parties should be abandoned, he offers a model of parties using firms in the marketplace as a metaphor, in language reminiscent of Lowi (chapter 4). Frendreis points out, for instance, that party voters and party organizations are as separate as customers and the firms that sell them products; there is a similar distinction between parties and elected officials. The behavior of voters and officials should not be seen *as* the behavior of parties, but as a *function of* the behavior of parties.

New Directions in Party Scholarship

Just as the parties are in a state of flux, party scholarship is in a state of transition. It is unclear at this juncture whether a new paradigm lies over the horizon or if a slow accumulation of research will gradually fill the present void. Improving upon the tripod and responsible party models is by no means a simple task. But clearly these essays raise important questions worthy of more attention.

The broader role of parties in the political system is open to new scrutiny. Does economic change underlie the party system? And if so, what other equally dynamic aspects of social life, such as demographic transitions, value shifts, and technological transformations shape party dynamics? Conceivably, "the state of the parties" is a reflection of the state of American society. In this regard, the "privileged position" of the two-party system in scholarly discourse is increasingly open to question. Is it inevitable in the American context, and is it desirable under present circumstances? These questions lie at the foundation of party scholarship.

Party activities are clearly central to such an understanding, and there is much more to learn about them. Scholars are now in a position to move beyond documenting the activities of parties, which generally implies that more is better, to exploring their quality and impact. Overall, what impact do party activities have on elections, the quality of government, and the party system itself? Party values are also certainly pivotal to understanding party change. Will new mechanisms develop for making party policy? These questions lead us back to a basic question: do organizational adjustment and growth produce more responsible parties?

These topics are sufficient, of course, to fill a generation of research. All should rejoice that efforts to answer these and other questions are well under way; the state of the parties is in flux, inspiring new directions in scholarship.

PART ONE

The Party System Under Stress

2

The Future of the American Two-Party System after 1994

A. James Reichley

Predicting the future of the American two-party system initially requires answers to two questions: Will parties of any kind continue to play an important role in structuring American politics? If so, will we continue to have a predominantly two-party system, which, of course, is unusual in most democratic polities? If the answer to both of these questions is affirmative, there remain the questions, with which this chapter will principally deal, of whether the two major parties will be the Republicans and the Democrats, as they have been since the Civil War, and whether one party or the other will normally be dominant, as has sometimes occurred in our history (though not recently).

On the question of the survival of any kind of party system, I have elsewhere argued that the parties are in trouble (Reichley 1992: 411–33) but that nevertheless it is difficult to imagine democratic politics completely without parties, and that given effective leadership and some changes in laws regulating parties and the ways they function, it is possible and even likely that before the end of this decade parties will achieve at least a modest revival. Some thoughtful analysts disagree. They have concluded that the current phenomenon of dealignment, in which more and more Americans feel little or no connection to either major party, will continue to the point that parties will be almost irrelevant to either politics or government (Phillips 1993: 233; Ginsberg and Shefter 1990: 37–75; Shafer 1991).

There is much evidence on their side. About one-third of those interviewed by pollsters now say they regard themselves as independents. Analysis has shown that about two-thirds of those calling themselves independents are about as regular in their support of one party in national elections as the so-called weak party identifiers (Keith et al. 1992). The true lesson of this finding, however, seems to me to be not that most declared independents are closet partisans, but rather that many who nominally identify with a party are in fact behavioral independents. Certainly the remarkable 19 percent showing of the independent candidate Ross Perot in the 1992 presidential elections shows that there are a great many voters in the national electorate who are quite prepared to cast their presidential ballots for someone other than the Republican or Democratic candidate.

The old patronage-based state and local machines that used to provide foot soldiers for the parties are almost everywhere in ruins. The media perform much of the role of screening candidates that used to be carried out by the party organizations. Presidential nominees are chosen through state primaries and caucuses in which party organizations play little part. Candidates for state, congressional, and local offices rely more on personal organizations and backing from interest groups than on party organizations. Many voters think nothing of splitting their tickets between parties in voting for president and members of Congress.

We are not going back to the times in the late nineteenth and early twentieth centuries when the major parties were like great popular armies, almost churches, which fought in well-drilled and enthusiastic ranks in each campaign. Other forces—the media, interest groups, citizen watchdog organizations, professional campaign consultants—will continue to rival the parties for influence in our politics. There is little reason for complacency among those of us who believe that strong parties make an essential contribution to democracy. But parties are likely to continue playing a major role in national politics for the foreseeable future. Actually, during the 1980s there were some signs of party revival. National party organizations, including the congressional campaign committees, which used to be relatively weak, raised more money and were more active than ever before in our history. Party unity in Congress trended upward. The major parties were more ideologically distinct than at any time since the early 1930s. All of these trends have continued into the 1990s.

A Durable System

Will the United States, however, continue to maintain a predominantly two-party system? Most democratic polities, even in relatively homogeneous countries like Sweden and the Netherlands, have tended to divide into three or more parties. Maurice Duverger pointed out long ago (in his formulation known as Duverger's law) that polities which maintain single-member, first-past-the-post systems of election, principally the United States and the British dominions, tend to foster the development of two major parties. Systems including two rounds of elections or using some form of proportional representation tend to produce a multiplicity of parties (Duverger 1954: 217).

Even polities like Britain, Canada, and Australia, however, which like the United States, use the first-past-the-post system, have generally had at least one significant minor party represented in parliament alongside two major ones. Why have enduring minor parties with significant impact been so rare in the United States?

I have argued that American politics has usually been formed, at least loosely, around two great ideological traditions, which I have called the republican tradition and the liberal tradition. These are, roughly, the tradition descended from Alexander Hamilton and represented since the Civil War by the Republican Party on the one side, and the competing tradition descended from Thomas Jefferson and represented since the time of Andrew Jackson by the Democratic Party on the other (Reichley 1992: 3–6). In this sense, a two-party system is thus natural to our politics.

I do not doubt, however, that without the shaping influence of electoral institutions the political system of a nation so large and so economically and culturally diverse as the United States would long since have produced a substantial number of competing parties. The first-past-the-post system helps push us toward a two-party system. But the thing that has really kept this system locked in place has been the institution of the electoral college for selecting presidents.

Quite contrary to the Founders' intention, the electoral college, as long as most states retain the at-large system for choosing electors (not required by the Constitution), effectively limits the presidential candidates with a real chance of winning to the nominees of the two major parties (or at least has done so since 1860). Ross Perot won 19 percent of the popular vote but did not receive a single vote in the electoral college. It even makes it unlikely that a minor party can hold the balance of power between the two major parties, as has sometimes occurred in Britain and Canada. Strom Thurmond in 1948 and George Wallace in 1968, running as candidates of states' rights parties opposing racial integration, were able to win the electoral votes of several southern states. But the tendency of the electoral college to magnify the margin of the major party candidate with the larger popular vote usually produces a safe electoral vote majority for the popular vote winner. Constitutional change to eliminate the electoral college, which a majority of voters tell pollsters they favor, would entail a political effort that is unlikely to be forthcoming—at least until the winner in the popular vote loses in the electoral college, as occurred several times in the nineteenth century and almost happened in 1976.

Thus the high visibility of presidential elections shapes our entire political system. As long as the institution of the electoral college confines the real presidential competition to the candidates of the two major parties, the United States will continue to have a two-party system in most congressional and state elections.

Support for Change

Of course, we live in changing times. Two states, Maine and Nebraska, now elect some of their presidential electors at the congressional district level. If this trend were to continue, minor party candidates could pick up electoral votes from specialized constituencies here and there across the country, preventing either major party candidate from winning the required absolute majority in the electoral college and throwing the presidential election into the House of Representatives.

Even if the electoral college remains with little change, modern communications and transportation technology enables independent or minor party candidates to assemble formidable national followings for a single election. If party ties continue to weaken, Perot or some successor might cross the threshold at which he or she would have a realistic chance of winning, overcoming the objection that voting for an independent is "throwing your vote away." Significantly, when asked by a Lou Harris poll in 1992 whether "the two-party system is serving this country well," 59 percent of the participants answered no. Nevertheless, the institutional supports provided by the electoral college as now constituted and the first-past-the-post system make the emergence of a multiparty system, as both called for and predicted by Theodore Lowi and other political scientists and commentators, improbable any time soon (see chapter 4 in this volume).

This does not, however, necessarily mean that the two major parties will continue to be the Republicans and the Democrats. Even in countries with institutionally fortified two-party systems, new parties have at times displaced one of the major existing parties, as the Republicans did the Whigs in the United States in the 1850s, and the Labour party did the Liberals in Britain in the 1920s.

It has seemed anomalous to many observers that the United States has never had a true left-wing party in the European sense, and some have predicted that the Democrats will eventually break up and give way to a socialist successor. The worldwide decline of socialism in recent years has perhaps made this less likely, but there is still the possibility that intraparty revolt against an unpopular centrist Democratic president might produce a significant break-away party on the left. On the other side, at low ebbs of the Republican Party, such as 1964 and 1976, some conservatives have proposed abandonment of the Republican label and creation of a new national conservative party. And there is recurring sentiment among the electorate that what we really need is a new centrist party, divorced from the extremes of the Republicans and Democrats, which Perot to some extent tapped in 1992.

The difficulties of forming a new major party, nevertheless, are formidable—as Perot himself discovered. It is no accident that no enduring new major party has emerged in American politics for more than 130 years. The existing major parties have proven adept at picking up the issues attracting support to new parties, as did the Democrats with the Populists in the 1890s, the Republicans and the Democrats with the Progressives in the 1910s, the Democrats with various liberal and socialist minor parties, and the Republicans with various states' rights parties.

The representatives of the two major parties have taken pains to enact election laws that strongly favor major party candidates. Public financing of presidential election campaigns heavily advantages the Republican and Democratic nominees. At the state level, barriers against third-party candidates are even more severe. In Pennsylvania, for example, Republican or Democratic candidates for the state senate need only one thousand signatures on petitions to get their names on the ballot while minor party candidates require twenty-nine thousand (reduced from fifty-six thousand by court order).

A major national disaster or conflict might lead to the creation of a new major party, as the struggle over slavery gave birth to the Republicans in the 1850s. Barring such a catastrophe, it is probable not only that we will continue to have a two-party system, but also that the Republicans and the Democrats will be the main competitors. After all, even the Great Depression of the 1930s failed to put enduring cracks in the existing two-party system, though for a time it spawned some successful third parties at the state level, such as the Farmer-Labor party in Minnesota and the Progressives in Wisconsin.

Throwing the Rascals Out

Let us, then, concentrate on the two-party system as we know it and consider what appear to be its electoral characteristics, particularly those that may give some clue to our likely political future. We still really do not have very extensive spans of experience for studying the long-range behavior of party systems (two-party or otherwise): about two centuries in the United States and Britain; somewhat less in France, some countries of northwestern Europe, and the British dominions; only since the Second World War in most of the other democracies; and only five or six years in Eastern Europe and the countries of the former Soviet Union.

Nevertheless, some characteristics of the electoral effects of party competition seem to appear. First, there seems to be a tendency for voters to grow disenchanted with a party in power, even if no major disasters occur, after about ten years. The normal result is for the incumbent party to be voted out, often by a large majority, and the former opposition installed. This tendency may be countered or outweighed by special circumstances, as when the fear of including communist parties in government in France and Italy kept conservative parties in power for extended periods; or when voters' distrust of the opposition or lack of a fully developed party system produced long-lasting dominance by one party, such as the Socialists in Sweden from the

1930s to the 1970s, Labor in Israel from independence to the early 1970s, the Congress Party in India from the 1940s to the 1970s, and the Liberal-Democrats in Japan from the 1950s to 1993. Even in these instances, however, accumulation of voter discontent and stagnation or corruption within the old majority party eventually led to change of party control.

The operation of the ten-year cycle appears particularly pronounced in countries with two-party systems, probably because this system inhibits formation of new coalitions through which incumbent parties sometimes are able to hold onto power under multiparty systems. In the United States, the ten-year cycle translates into two or three presidential terms. From the early 1950s to the 1990s, the Republicans and Democrats regularly alternated in control of the White House, with three two-term cycles, one three-term (the Reagan-Bush years), and one that was confined to a single term (the Carter administration).

Going back somewhat further, since the present party system was formed in the 1850s, the average duration of party control of the White House has been eleven years. The only markedly longer periods of party dominance were the twenty-four-year tenure of the Republicans during and after the Civil War, and the twenty-year period of Democratic supremacy during and after the Great Depression.

Similar cycles appear to operate for the governorship in states with competitive two-party systems. In the seven most populated states with truly competitive systems, the average period of party control of the governorship from 1950 to 1990 was 8.5 years. This average conceals some extended periods when one party or the other was dominant in New York and Michigan, and some long stretches of uninterrupted control by the Republicans in Illinois and the Democrats in New Jersey. But in Pennsylvania, Ohio, and California, the two parties exchanged control of the governor's office with almost rhythmic regularity. Cyclical party turnover now seems to be developing in some of the southern states where the Democrats used to enjoy one-party dominance, such as Texas and North Carolina.

The impulse of voters to "throw the rascals out" by changing party control at regular intervals is both understandable and rational. After two or three terms of one party in control of a nation or state, enough things are likely to have gone wrong to give voters a taste for change. This tendency may sometimes be unjust to the party in power, but it at least keeps incumbent parties on their toes, seeking to come up with policies and solutions that will cause voters to relent and give them "four more years." Moreover, under conditions of modern government, a party team that has held office for two terms or more is likely to be run-down, reduced to petty bickering, and bereft of new ideas. Henry Kissinger used to say that an administration begins to use up its intellectual capital from the day it takes office.

Since the 1950s, regular shifts in party control have not occurred in Congress. From the Civil War to the Eisenhower administration, control of

Congress normally accompanied, or slightly preceded, the presidential cycle. In only three two-year periods did the president's party not control at least one house of Congress (under Hayes 1879–80, Cleveland 1895–96, and Wilson 1919–20). From 1954 to 1994, however, the Democrats controlled the House of Representatives without interruption and held the Senate except for a six-year stretch from 1981 through 1986. As a result, Republican presidents during this forty-year span regularly confronted Congresses controlled by their partisan opposition, producing the famous deadlock that has wreaked havoc with the policy-making process. After the 1994 election the shoe was on the other foot, with a Democratic president facing a Republican Congress—creating even more spectacular instances of deadlock. David Mayhew has offered evidence to support his claim that the effects of divided control have not been so bad (Mayhew 1991). This may be true in some policy areas, but in crucial areas of budget making and foreign policy the liabilities seem clear.

In any case, the failure of cyclical turnover in Congress seemed to have damaging effects on the entire political system. Even apart from the policy results of deadlock, the long dominance of Congress by the Democrats produced an impression among many voters that the system was impervious to electoral change, and this impression probably played a part in the long-term decline in voter participation. It was probably also bad for the congressional Democrats themselves (as a political force, though not of course in terms of individual members). The effects of long duration in power by one party that special circumstances have produced in the politics of, for example, Japan, Italy, and Mexico, were all too evident in recent years in Congress: arrogance, preoccupation with "perks," outright corruption, and stagnation of ideas. Whether the Republicans' success in 1994 will significantly alter voter perceptions and institutional vitality remains to be seen.

Cyclical Theories

Beyond the normal two- or three-term cycle in party control of the presidency, the existence of party cycles (or ideological cycles) in national politics becomes speculative. Such cycles, if they exist, however, are important and require inclusion in any overall consideration of parties. Probably the best known of the theories of long-term political cycles is that of the historian Arthur Schlesinger Jr. (1986: 32–33), carrying on work begun by his father. Schlesinger's theory is more closely related to ideology than to party, but it also has party manifestations.

According to Schlesinger, throughout American history there have been regular alterations between cycles of liberalism and conservatism, each lasting about sixteen years or four presidential terms. Liberalism is defined as commitment to "public purpose," and conservatism as defense of "private interest." The most recent cycles have been the liberal one, launched by John

Kennedy in 1960, and its conservative successor that began in the late 1970s. Right on time, Schlesinger claimed after the 1992 election, a new liberal cycle began with Bill Clinton's victory.

This theory—like almost all cyclical theories—requires some nimble tucking. The Civil War Republicans, "liberal" under Lincoln, somehow become "conservative" under Grant (though in many cases they were the same people) and hang on long beyond their allotted cycle; Theodore Roosevelt, Taft, and Wilson are lumped together in a liberal cycle, despite the bitter interparty and intraparty battles of the time; Nixon and Ford become part of the liberal cycle that began in 1960; and Carter becomes the harbinger of a return to conservatism. The primary identifications of conservatism with private interest and liberalism with public purpose are somewhat suspect, given conservatism's commitment to publicly maintained moral standards and liberalism's defense of private choice on questions of personal behavior. Still, the theory has sufficient resonance in history to suggest the presence of a real phenomenon. What Schlesinger is on to, I think, is the succession of phases in a much longer cycle, which I will describe below.

The most widely discussed cyclical theory developed in political science was introduced by V. O. Key (1955), linking cycles to "realigning" or "critical" elections, which, it is claimed, have periodically purged American politics and government of accumulated detritus and opened the way to new growth. Key's work has been carried on in recent years by, among others, Walter Dean Burnham (1970), James Sundquist (1983), Gerald Pomper (1970), and Paul Allen Beck (1974: 199–21). In most versions of this theory, realigning elections, ending the dominance of one political party and ushering in normal majority control by another, have occurred every twenty-eight to thirty-six years. The root of these cycles appears to be policy upheaval, coupled with generational change.

There is some dispute over which were the actual realigning elections, but general agreement places realignments at or just before the elections of Thomas Jefferson in 1800, Andrew Jackson in 1828, Abraham Lincoln in 1860, William McKinley in 1896, and Franklin Roosevelt in 1932. (Some theorists drop the elections of Jefferson and Jackson, on the ground that the party system did not achieve mature development until the 1830s.)

A puzzle for believers in the theory of realigning elections is the apparent failure of one to occur on schedule in the 1960s. Burnham deals with this problem by arguing that a realignment *did* occur with the election of Richard Nixon as president in 1968 and the creation of a new Republican majority in presidential politics. Certainly the shift of the South away from the Democrats at the presidential level after 1968 was a major change in national politics. But if this was a realignment, why did it not produce a change in control of Congress or of most of the major states, as previous realignments had done? Everett Carll Ladd (1991) and Byron Shafer (1991), among others, have argued that realignment theory, whatever utility it may once have had for political science, has been made obsolete by technological and social change.

Supercycles

The elections usually identified as critical to realignments—1800, 1828, 1860, 1896, and 1932—were clearly times when something important happened in American politics. But were all of these major realignments in the sense of changing one majority party for another? The victories of the (Jeffersonian) Republicans in 1800, the Republicans in 1860, and the Democrats in 1932 certainly were. But what of the 1828 and 1896 elections, which are needed to maintain the thirty-six-year cycle?

Jackson won in 1828 after a period of about ten years in which national politics had been in flux and the old hegemony of Jefferson's party appeared shaken. But Jackson was clearly in the line of the Jeffersonians, and was so recognized at the time. Martin Van Buren, one of Jackson's principal lieutenants and his successor as president, wrote, "The two great parties of this country, with occasional changes in their names only, have, for the principal part of a century, occupied antagonistic positions upon all important political questions. They have maintained an unbroken succession. . . ." (Van Buren 1967: 2). Jackson carried every state Jefferson carried in 1800 and lost every state Jefferson lost. Jefferson's narrow victory over John Adams in 1800 was converted into Jackson's landslide triumph over John Quincy Adams in 1828 by the addition of new western states in which the Democrats were strong. So the 1828 election *restored* the dominance of the Democrats (under their new name) instead of bringing in a new majority party.

Similarly, McKinley's victory in 1896 followed a period in which Republicans and Democrats had taken turns controlling the federal government, or dividing control, and in which there had been no clear majority party. The 1896 election represented a rallying of the forces, temporarily in eclipse, that had made the Republicans the clear majority party from 1860 to 1876. McKinley won through renewal of the coalition of northeastern and midwestern states on which the Republican Party had been founded. William Jennings Bryan, his Democratic opponent, swept the South, the Democrats' principal stronghold since the end of Reconstruction. Bryan also tapped the farmers' revolt and the silver issue in the West to win some of the normally Republican western states that had been admitted to the Union since the Civil War. But within a few years most of these were back in the Republican column where they normally remained until the Great Depression of the 1930s. The 1896 election, therefore, did not displace the former majority party, but renewed and strengthened the party that became dominant after the last major realignment—a point also made by Pomper (1970).

What, then, do we have? Not five or six major realigning elections but three: 1800, 1860, and 1932. Each of these began a cycle in which one party was generally dominant, lasting not thirty-six years, but *sixty to seventy years*. The climactic elections won by Jackson and McKinley, which I identify as 1832 (rather than 1828) and 1896, were in this scheme elections in which the dominant force of the cycle that had begun about thirty years before met and decisively defeated a force trying to turn back the clock to the prevailing ethos of the preceding cycle (the conservative opposition directed by Nicholas Biddle in 1832 and the populist crusade championed by Bryan in 1896).

The mystery of why no true realignment occurred in the 1960s is thus explained: it was not due. What actually happened in the 1960s was the climax of the cycle dominated by liberalism and the Democratic Party that had begun in the 1930s. In 1964, Lyndon Johnson decisively defeated Barry Goldwater, representing a radical version of the laissez-faire economic doctrine that had prevailed during the preceding cycle. The movement of the South away from the Democrats at the end of the 1960s was an early sign of the breakup of the New Deal cycle—similar to the move of the Northeast away from the Democrats in the 1840s and the swing of major northern cities away from the Republicans in the era of Woodrow Wilson.

As shown schematically in figure 2.1, each of the sixty- to seventy-year-long cycles moved through roughly similar phases: (1) a breakthrough election in which the new majority gained power under a charismatic leader (Jefferson, Lincoln, F. D. Roosevelt), followed by an extended period during which the new majority party changed the direction of government and enacted much of its program; (2) a period of pause in which the new majority lost some of its dynamism and the forces that dominated the preceding cycle staged a minor comeback (J. Q. Adams, Cleveland, Eisenhower); (3) a climactic victory by the majority party over a more radical expression of the ethos of the preceding cycle (Jackson over Biddle, McKinley over Bryan, Johnson over Goldwater), followed by enactment of remaining items in the majority party's program; and, finally, (4) the gradual decline and ultimate collapse of the majority party, opening the way for a new realignment and a new majority. There have been only three such fully developed cycles in our national history, though, as figure 2.1 shows, the outline of an earlier cycle can be seen in the nation-building process that reached its climax with the American Revolution and went through its declining, though still fruitful, phase during the Federalist era.

The phases of the sixty- to seventy-year-long cycles correspond roughly to some of Schlesinger's sixteen-year cycles. The long-cycle theory, however, explains why the Jeffersonians after 1800, the Republicans after 1860, and the Democrats after 1932 held onto power for longer than Schlesinger's theory would predict. Those were all periods covered by the initial phase of the long cycle, during which the new majority is fresh and holds the support of the public through an extended series of elections. The separate cycles posited in

Figure 2.1 American Political Cycles

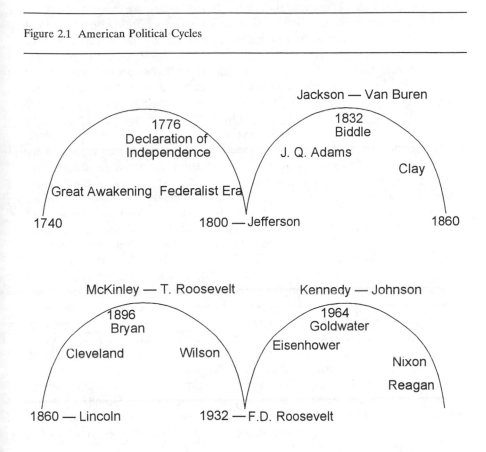

the twenty-eight- to thirty-six-year theory correspond neatly to the rise and decline segments of the long cycle.

The Next Major Change

The possibility of a sixty- to seventy-year cycle has occasionally been glimpsed by political scientists and historians. It was first discussed, to my knowledge, by the political scientist Quincy Wright in 1942 (1942: 143–145). In recent years, William Riker (1982: 214–16) and Jerome Mileur (1989: 1–3) have suggested the possibility of a sixty- to seventy-year cycle. Political scientists have generally been reluctant to consider the possibility of sixty- to seventy-year party dominance cycles, largely, I think, because the limited time over which democracies have so far extended gives us little material against which to test such a hypothesis. Such skepticism is understandable and even reasonable. But the long-cycle theory fits the evidence we have better than any of the other cyclical schemes. There is also some indication that long cycles have been at work in Britain and France, although this requires further study.

If such long cycles exist, what causes them? Perhaps to some extent they reflect cycles in the underlying economic system, such as the "long wave" cycles suggested in the 1920s by the Russian economist Nikolai Kondratieff (1984: 32ff.) and discussed often since by futurist economists. Kondratieff and his followers have claimed to detect cycles lasting about fifty years in which market economies swing between booms and major depressions caused by "overbuilding of the capital sector." Kondratieff long waves correspond roughly to the long party dominance cycles in American history. The economic expansion that started in the 1790s petered out through the 1840s and 1850s, and the expansion that began in the 1860s, though interrupted by several pauses, did not truly collapse until the depression of the 1930s. According to Kondratieff theorists, we are now in the down swing of the expansion that began in the 1940s. For more than a decade, many of them have been predicting that a new economic collapse is just around the corner.

Political cycles are also probably rooted to some extent in generational change. Schlesinger argues that his sixteen-year cycles reflect the succession of political generations. Members of the political generation of John Kennedy, for example, were putting into effect values and attitudes acquired during their youth in the liberal environment of the 1930s. The Reaganites of the 1980s were applying views they had developed during the relatively conservative 1950s (though many of the Reaganites regarded themselves as revolting *against* Eisenhower moderate Republicanism). Members of the generation of the 1990s, in this theory, are prepared to reintroduce the liberal values with which Kennedy inspired them during their college years in the 1960s (Schlesinger 1986: 33–34).

Schlesinger's analysis, like his larger cyclical theory, captures part of the truth. Truly major changes in political direction, however, seem to occur only after persons whose political values and party loyalties were formed by a major realignment, including many who were in childhood at the time, have largely passed from the political scene. So long as generations whose party ties were shaped by the Civil War remained politically active, even voting in substantial numbers, the normal Republican majority in national elections was hard to shake. Similarly, party loyalties formed by the Great Depression and the New Deal have been exceptionally durable. In the 1990s, the generations whose attitudes were most deeply marked by the Depression and the New Deal, roughly those born from 1905 to 1930, have included a sharply declining share of the total electorate—already in 1996 less than 15 percent. This, I think, is a major reason for the increasing segment of voters who feel no particular loyalty to either major party.

The last two major realignments, in the 1860s and the 1930s, came at the time of massive traumas within the larger social system, respectively the Civil War and the Great Depression. The first realignment, in the 1800s, coincided with huge territorial growth and migration of population. Probably a major realignment requires *both* extraordinary social upheaval *and* an electorate in which ties to the existing party system have grown weak. We certainly now have the latter. If the Kondratieff theorists are correct, we will probably soon encounter severe economic turmoil. But the causes of social upheaval need not be primarily economic—those of the 1800s and 1860s were not. Possibly an ecological crisis could trigger the next political realignment. Or continuation of current trends toward moral and social disorder and decay could bring it on. The point is that the political system is now open, as it was not in the 1960s when the hold of the New Deal alignment remained strong, for transformation by a major economic or social shock. If the precedent of earlier long cycles holds, the 1990s may correspond not to the 1960s, but to the 1850s and late 1920s.

Another factor holding up major realignment during most of the 1970s and 1980s was divided government. While one party controlled the White House and the other Congress, the voters found it difficult to fix responsibility for the conduct of government and therefore to take out discontent on one party or the other. After one term of united government under the Democrats at the end of the 1970s, the Republicans won the White House and the Senate and made substantial gains in the House in 1980. Having failed to gain complete control of Congress at the time of Ronald Reagan's first election, however, it was unlikely they would do so thereafter during the Reagan or Bush administrations—the voters tending to take out resentments against the party controlling the White House by voting for the opposition in congressional elections.

In an earlier edition of this book, I concluded this chapter with the following prediction, written in the fall of 1993: "The *most* likely next major change in national politics, probably in a term or two, is a strong swing to the Republicans, potentially for an extended period." Events moved more rapidly than I had expected. One year later in November, 1994, the voters, after only two years of united Democratic control of the federal government, swept the Republicans to majorities in both houses of Congress for the first time in forty years.

The 1994 election was something that at the national level has become very rare in American politics: a truly party election. All over the country voters were casting ballots for Republicans—or against Democrats, which in governmental terms comes to the same thing. Not only did the Republicans win control of Congress, they also made advances all across the ballot at the state and local levels. The Republican surge in the once solidly Democratic South has been widely noted. No less remarkably, Republicans won huge, though perhaps more ephemeral, victories in gubernatorial contests in midwestern industrial states like Ohio, Michigan, Illinois, and Wisconsin.

Was the 1994 election the critical realignment that the sixty- to seventy-year cycle would lead us to expect? In itself, probably not. More likely, it was the beginning of the final phase of the part of the cycle that precedes realignment. Critical realignments are complex phenomena, and while they are in motion one should not pretend to be sure how they will turn out. The massive victory by the nativist Know Nothing Party in the 1854 election was not itself the realignment, but in retrospect can be seen to have been a crucial step in the process that finally produced the Republican realignment of the 1860s. The Democratic victory in the 1930 congressional elections led more directly to the New Deal realignment two years later.

I also wrote in 1993: "If the Democrats fail to make good on their current opportunity, and the Republicans on their next one, the continued dealignment predicted by many analysts may well take place. National politics will then increasingly be built around personalities, campaign cosmetics, and interest group pressures.

"There is another possibility. Public disaffection with both major parties and the entire party system is now so great that a new political force, promising to transcend all parties and return to something like the nonpartisan system the Founders intended, might be able to break through the barriers protecting the existing party system and get control of the national government, at least for a term or two. The floodgates to major constitutional change might then be opened, leading to—who knows what? A parliamentary system? Government by electronic referenda? Or a truly imperial presidency?"

Realignment, then, is not written in the stars. A successful realignment will require a party that provides creative solutions to the nation's major problems and opportunities—as Jefferson, Lincoln, and Roosevelt did after their parties took control of government at the start of three earlier cycles. Achievement of such realignment during the next few years, at least by the beginning of the twenty-first century, seems to me vital to the good health of our entire governmental system.

3

Who Speaks for the Political Parties or, Martin Van Buren, Where Are You When We Need You?

Ralph M. Goldman

Congress and the Clinton administration have committed themselves to major electoral reform. With a surprise handshake during a June 1995 meeting in New Hampshire, President Clinton and Speaker Gingrich agreed to form a commission to recommend electoral reform. Subsequently (November 2, 1995), Speaker Gingrich, in testimony before the House Oversight Commission, broadened the proposal beyond campaign finance reform to include the political party system.

In the past, reforms have been little more than tinkerings with one of the nation's most vital institutions, namely, its party system. The most usual changes include new but circumventable limits on campaign contributions, a modicum of public financing, and slightly more demanding disclosure requirements. Amidst all the current interest in reform, *little mention is made regarding the principals themselves*, namely, the executives of the nation's political parties. Their failure to make a serious contribution to the public debate is perceived by many citizens as an admission of guilt for unnamed sins.

Institutional rationalization of the American party system is certainly long overdue, but it is difficult to achieve in an atmosphere of suspicion and hostility. After two centuries of wear and tear, it is certainly reasonable to discuss overhauling the party system. Structural components need to be better connected. Desirable functions need to be better protected and nurtured. Essential activities need to be explained and conducted more openly. The entire system needs to be subject to rules and practices that increase efficiency and effectiveness, with full organizational accountability for management and outcomes. These are significant and legitimate matters for citizens, legislators, media, and party executives to examine. The political parties are, after all, legitimate associations whose services to the community include implementation of popular sovereignty, the formulation of the public agenda, and the advancement of a democratic way of life.

The Parties' Systematic and Persistent Bad Rap

Unfortunately, a strong, and sometimes justifiable, antiparty tradition has taken hold in the United States, making a candid and constructive approach to party organization, management, and accountability extraordinarily difficult. "Antipartyism," especially as articulated by the media, by practicing politicians, and by competitors for political influence, has produced a collection of dubious assumptions and unfriendly attitudes that come into play with occasional revelations of scandal, such as bribes, excessive campaign contributions, or unethical use of public resources. Such revelations are usually accompanied by righteous calls for harnessing party "monsters" or, at least, cutting off one or another of their functional limbs.

This bad rap started a long time ago. The British party system, the first modern party system, was barely a century old when Viscount Henry St. John Bolingbroke (1982) pronounced parties *obsolete*. As a Tory leader during the early decades of the eighteenth century, Bolingbroke wrote the best contemporary analysis of party as an institution. Almost always in the opposition and himself a master of machination, Bolingbroke vented his frustrations in his analysis, decrying parties as "corrupt," Parliament as "enslaved" by the parties, and party debate generally "nasty." Bolingbroke failed to understand that the British party system was the institutional alternative to English civil wars of the preceding millennia, hence, by definition, the arena for nonmilitary political nastiness (Goldman 1990 chap. 3).[1]

A half century later, another notable, President George Washington, added his antiparty commentary. In his message to the Third Congress of the United States on November 19, 1794, the president specifically condemned the activities of "certain self-created societies." His reference was to the highly partisan county and city political associations that, at that time, provided support to the Jeffersonian Democratic-Republican Party. Washington's statement led to a resolution offered by the Federalists in Congress strongly supporting the denunciation. James Madison, the Democratic-Republican leader in the House of Representatives, worked diligently to water down the resolution and succeeded only when the Speaker broke the tie vote.

Ironically, the Federalists refused to acknowledge that they were a political party. One Federalist—Alexander Hamilton—knew better. In 1802, soon after the Jeffersonians captured the presidency, Hamilton offered his colleagues a plan to establish a national Federalist association to be called "The Christian Constitutional Society." This society was to be headed by a president and a twelve-member national council. There would be "sub-directing Councils" of thirteen members for each state and as many local branches as possible. Financed by a five dollar annual fee, this association would diffuse information about "fit" men and promote their election. The association would also pursue "charitable and useful" activities, particularly in the growing cities, through relief societies for immigrants and vocational schools for workers (Hamilton 1851: 540-43). These were precisely the activities that political parties performed at that time. Hamilton's Federalist colleagues would have none of it. The Federalists disappeared as a party during the next decade.

The nineteenth century was a time of flux, factionalism, and failure in the party system. Factions came and went with ease and frequency. Party failure to deal with the slavery issue led to the Civil War and radical Republicanism produced a vindictive Reconstruction Era. Tammany Hall and Boss Tweed became the model for urban machines, whose dominance was contested from time to time by wealthy merchants and other civic-minded citizens. State machines became prominent toward the latter part of the century, their alliances influencing national politics and the distribution of federal patronage. The press was sharp-tongued and partisan. Protest movements arose, sometimes became "third" parties, then disappeared. Corruption made its appearance at state legislatures. Paradoxically, despite a high level of voter loyalty to their own party at election time, by the end of the century citizens in general had little confidence in the party system.

The opening of the twentieth century brought in muckrakers and progressives, the former to expose partisan evil and the latter to reconstruct the party system with the direct primary, nonpartisan elections, an expanding civil service, and a host of other antiparty measures. The credibility of the parties was further undermined by the emergence of a racist one-party South, presidential nominations engineered in "smoke-filled rooms," corporate bribery scandals, and the like. At times, if newspapers and commentary journals were to be believed, logic demanded the outlawing of parties.

In the reality beyond the media, however, party organizations somehow managed to nominate and elect distinguished citizens to public offices, welcome and Americanize millions of immigrants, keep voter participation at a high level, distribute jobs and assistance to the needy, transform street gangs into civic safety patrols, and maintain a close watch and an attentive ear for signs of popular discontent. In general, Americans seemed willing, for a long time, to pay for these positive civic functions by tolerating urban and state party machines, various forms of patronage, and the winner-take-all principle. At the turn of the century, however, the aforementioned excesses and corruption, together with the perennial bad rap, brought constraints to the party process.

Deprecating Assumptions and Tongue-Tied Defenders

Progressive factions in both major parties, defectors to third parties, massive immigration and virulent nativism, the one-party South, and the antiparty predispositions of newly admitted western states kept the parties in stress during the first third of the twentieth century. The stress was aggravated by the enduring antiparty assumptions. Some are quite familiar. Money in politics is presumed to be either intrinsically evil or a source of evil. Contributions to political campaigns are invariably deemed excessive. Party executives are presumed to be power-hungry, self-aggrandizing "slickers" and "bosses." Corruption, rather than public service, is considered the principal product of party activism. Money or patronage for maintenance of party organizations is thought to be wasteful, if not immoral. These are the more prominent hostile assumptions.

Those who agree with these assumptions rarely, if ever, acknowledge parties as the principal instruments of several fundamental extraelectoral functions: the implementers of popular sovereignty in a democracy; the institutional alternative to civil war; the principal recruiters of public servants; the nation's most influential civic educator; the nation's most important agenda setter. These critics, perhaps for lack of knowledge about the history of political institutions, are the last to recognize that failure to nourish these vital functions could cost a nation its democracy. The case for these profoundly important extraelectoral functions can be readily and briefly made.

Popular Sovereignty

Mass participation in the election of national leaders and the making of public policies was, for the most part, a nineteenth-century development spurred by theories of popular sovereignty and representative government. Various election systems were designed to give an authoritative "voice" to the people, but it was political parties and the many organized interest groups that coalesced within and around the parties that formulated the arguments about political issues, legislated the rules of popular participation, and mobilized voters to exercise their sovereignty at the polls. In the twentieth century, whether in totalitarian or democratic states, popular sovereignty, as manifest in election outcomes, has been assumed and has been the event that legitimizes the holding of government office. In dictatorships as in competitive party systems, under conditions of duress or in free and fair elections, party organizations have turned out the votes that give leaders their mandate from the popular sovereigns, that is, from the parties-in-the-electorate.

Alternative to War

England's centuries of civil war ended when a viable party system emerged in the seventeenth century. The United States' Civil War began when its party system collapsed in the late 1850s—Whigs disappearing, Republicans trying to take their place, and Democrats splitting asunder. Recently, El Salvador, Nicaragua, South Africa, the Philippines, the Russian Federation, and a host of other nations have struggled to establish competitive party systems to replace defunct dictatorships and inconclusive civil wars. The process that makes these critical transitions possible is observable: the principal architects are party leaders, and the end products are the institutional rules that make for an enduring party system (Goldman 1990).

Recruiters of Public Servants

In one way or another, the parties are principal recruiters of citizens willing to render public service. Through nomination for election and job patronage in victory, early U.S. parties found and "preselected" the persons to fill the offices of government. Jefferson and Madison actively sought out candidates for Congress in order to challenge the Federalist hold on that institution, and national party leaders continue to do so. Despite occasional excesses and corruption, early urban and rural bosses and party machines played a major role in electing or appointing "their people" to the local and state jobs that performed the operations of government. With the adoption of nonpartisan elections by many communities, party labels have been made opaque for the election day occasion, but fool hardly anyone. In recent times, with the diminution of party patronage, much recruitment flows through lobbying and legislative channels, but almost always with a partisan orientation.[2]

Civic Educators

Totalitarian parties are resolute in matters of ideological and civic education. They organize thoroughly for this purpose and teach aggressively. In the American context, civic education can be described as indirect, casual, and negligible. Family and religious sources transmit basic values, many of them indirectly political and partisan in consequence. Schools deal lightly with political history, symbols, rituals, and broad structures of government, usually avoiding discussion of parties and partisanship. Most information about politics and government comes to the citizenry, again indirectly, by way of the contests between the parties and the media reports about this competition. The gross inadequacy of this information is confirmed in survey after survey. Lack of information is perhaps the major reason for the low esteem in which U.S. political institutions are held.

Agenda Setters

Gaining public attention, getting on the policy-making agenda, and obtaining a favorable policy decision are difficult and extremely competitive work. This is a principal factor for the parties at different stages and levels of government. For the most part, the national agenda is found in the decisions of party leaders in Congress, the rhetoric of candidates in the heat of election contests, the unread platforms of the parties, and the headlines and pictures in the media. Whereas organized interests and the media have been increasingly influential at the early stages of gaining public attention and setting up popular attitudes, in the last analysis it is party leaders who must negotiate the subject matter and the priorities of the agenda.

Administering the System

By ignoring these many significant extraelectoral functions, the negative assumptions about parties have led to faulty questions about real pathologies of the party system and its functions. In a Gresham's Law of analysis, these poorly framed questions drive out the significant ones. In turn, this tends to produce reforms that put into place unworkable panaceas with unintended and unfortunate consequences. In such an environment, it becomes unthinkable, for example, to argue that money, when given in a public manner and disclosed on the public record, is a legitimate source of political influence in competitive politics. Limitations on campaign contributions do not limit; they merely challenge campaigners' ingenuity to invent new circumventions and subterfuges for giving.

Where is the party executive who will take the time and effort to explain that political parties are organizations which, like other organizations, must have staff and funds if they are to render public service?   Let us suppose that the parties were perceived and structured as ordinary stock-issuing corporations (not that they could or should be). How differently the party organization, management, financing, and other operational and management needs would be treated!   The party name and symbols would be legally protected for their good-will value, a protection currently reserved for corporate names and trademarks in the commercial arena. The party's nominations would probably take on the character of an explicit contract, with the nominee making a binding promise to represent the party's program and constituencies in exchange for acquiring the legitimacy and good will inherent in the party's name and the promotional effort of the party's organization. The party's financial operations and records would become public accounts subject to periodic professional audit and publication. In other words, if the parties were treated as public utility corporations, perceptions, assumptions, issues, attitudes, and solutions would be radically altered, and for the good of American democracy (Epstein 1989: 239).

However, these are *not* the perspectives from which the ills of the U.S. party system are diagnosed. Consequently, those who are dedicated to party renewal and party development rush in with suggestions for fixing *the parties*: a reorganization here, a reform there, a panacea elsewhere. Yet the problem may have more to do with political culture than political organization. The approach should be *to fix the political and attitudinal context in which the parties must live.*

There are examples in the world of business. When poisoned capsules were found in Tylenol™ containers, what did executives of that corporation do to recover the reputation of their company and product? They explained in detail the circumstances of the problem, they countered accusations of production negligence, and they proclaimed once again the wonders of their products. PepsiCola™ executives acted similarly when people claimed that they were finding medical syringes in soda cans.

These comparisons may be somewhat overdrawn, but they make the point that corporate executives have a responsibility to explain problems and defend their enterprise. Political party executives should have exactly the same responsibility: explaining party functions in general; exposing the details of a bad situation in particular instances; countering the validity of negative charges; and proclaiming the wonders of their organization and the party system. When was the last time a national party chairman performed such civic education? Perhaps Jim Farley and Ray Bliss come to mind.

The independent presidential candidacy of Ross Perot in 1992 brought into sharp focus serious questions about the viability of the U.S. party system. A *Washington Post*-ABC News Poll[3] asked, "Do you agree or disagree with the following statement: Both political parties are pretty much out of touch with the American people." The responses revealed that 82 percent agreed, 15 percent disagreed, and 3 percent didn't know. A second question was asked: "Thinking about both the Republican and Democratic parties, do you generally think that political parties are playing a bigger role or a smaller role in people's lives today than they did in the past?" A total of 41 percent chose "bigger role," 50 percent thought a "smaller role," 4 percent the same role, and 5 percent didn't know.

Although these data suggest overwhelming disappointment in the two major parties, total disenchantment with parties in general was not evident. Sixty-six percent thought it would be good for the country if there were a new major party to compete with the Democrats and Republicans; only 24 percent thought adding a new party would be bad. Although the situation seemed ripe for a Ross Perot third-party effort, there was an even 44 to 44 percent split on the question of whether Perot should be the one to start his own independent political party. The most intense anger against the two major parties appeared among the Perot supporters who, when asked what the term "political party" meant to them, responded with such phrases as "corruption," "rich, wealthy," "self-serving," "good-old-boy networks," "liars," and the like (Morin and Dionne 1992).

David S. Broder, one of the pundits who is a serious student of parties, has more than once issued a call for "the rediscovery of political parties." But Broder acknowledges that "it will not be easy to persuade people that this [the need for parties] is the case" (1993). He continues:

Parties are almost invisible in the public dialogue today—especially on television. On the tube, conflicts are always personal, not institutional—Clarence Thomas v. Anita Hill, not a Republican president against a Democratic Senate. Individualistic office-seekers ignore or camouflage their party labels. Federal and state laws impede the parties' operations.

Broder concludes with a note of urgency and an assignment of responsibility for "the rediscovery of parties."

One reason that people don't vote along party lines any longer is that the media on which they depend don't tell them that parties make a difference.
But this is not a task for the press alone. The men and women of learning —especially the historians and political scientists—need to be heard on these issues. Our experiment in republican government is faltering today. Quack remedies such as term limits are being successfully hawked to the public. Scholarly detachment, at such a moment, is a crime. Either we will begin the rescue of responsible politics and effective government this year or hasten their disappearance.[4]

The Functional Competitors to Parties

Over the past half century, institutional competitors have emerged and have arrogated to themselves many of the functions traditionally performed by the political parties. These competitors include the bureaucracies that administer the welfare state, the political entrepreneurs who become members of Congress, community service groups, campaign consultants, organized interests, and the mass media.

Bureaucracies

It was no coincidence that urban and rural political machines began to disintegrate soon after the New Deal brought in the welfare state. Federal civil servants were assigned many of the functions previously handled by party personnel. The job-finding work of precinct and ward captains was taken over by the United States Employment Service, thus diminishing job patronage, which, like profit for a business enterprise, is among the major motivations for seeking party victory. The Social Security Administration provided benefits to the destitute, the unemployed, and the elderly to a far greater extent and more reliably than any party organization ever did. Additional government agencies took over other party activities.

Members of Congress

Rich or poor, citizens used to turn to their local party leaders for guidance and help in dealing with government agencies. The modest "fee" for such assistance was usually party loyalty during election campaigns and at the ballot box. The past half century has seen individual members of Congress increasingly render the constituent services formerly provided by party executives. Today, about 50 percent of congressional staff effort is devoted to constituency service. This transfer of function is undoubtedly correlated with the decline in the role of the parties in the nomination and election of members of Congress and senators. In previous times, local party leaders, meeting in caucus or committees, played the leading role in placing nominees for Congress on the ballot. In recent decades, running for Congress has been a personal entrepreneurial exercise. Candidates are self-selected. Nominations are made in primary elections, with or without party endorsement. Campaigns are self-directed, with little party support and little obligation to adhere to party platforms (Center for Party Development 1993). This disengagement of members of Congress from party has been facilitated in part by congressional appropriation of funds for maintaining members' district offices. Why should a constituent go to local party headquarters for help when he or she can go directly to the district office of the more influential member of Congress for faster and better service?

Community Service Groups

For a century and a half the parties provided the energy that kept the melting pot warm and welcoming. The Americanization of millions of immigrants, the political management of ethnic ghettos and enclaves, and the ladder of upward mobility for many of the new citizens were the work of party organizations. Today, however, local party figures no longer welcome arrivals at the dock or the airport. These activities are conducted by community groups, organized principally by ethnic leaders, educators, social workers, or the staffs of candidates for office.

Campaign Consultants

Ever since public opinion polling became a relatively exact science in the 1930s, voters have been asked about their party affiliation, social characteristics, eligibility to vote, probability of voting, attitudes toward different ideological labels and current political issues, perceptions of candidates, responses to different messages, and so on. As polling technology improved, so has the precision and marketability of findings. In the course of this evolution, opinion pollsters have displaced precinct captains as the principal empiricists in matters of local demography, political issues, partisan attitudes, voting preferences, and other information about the party-in-the-electorate. Moreover, with this technology have come the experts; traditional party intelligence operations have been converted into the merchandise of public relations consultants.

Organized Interests

Freedom of association and the right of petition under the Constitution have given rise to thousands of organized interest groups, many of which have spawned "political action committees" (PACs). In order to maximize their influence, interest groups and PACs give major attention to party nominations, platforms, and election campaigns. They exercise influence in several ways: informationally, by testimony during legislative and party platform hearings; organizationally, by supporting voter registration and turnout campaigns; and financially, by contributing funds principally to candidate campaigns.

Financial contributions have increased in recent decades in part because election campaigns have become increasingly competitive and expensive. The average cost of a campaign for a member of Congress is $600,000 and for senator, $7,000,000. Almost everyone agrees that campaign costs and contributions have become exorbitant, but few suggest meaningful alternatives. Whenever this apparent excess reaches the "outrageous" level, Congress passes legislation placing new constraints on contributions. Within one or two elections thereafter, however, it becomes clear that money, like water, finds its way through unnoticed cracks, with party organizations the least benefited. Major contributors would rather give to individual candidates than to a party agency. The PACs pay attention to candidates' official status, incumbency record, and issue commitments, regardless of party affiliation. This practice confounds the fundraising efforts of the parties.

Media

Another class of functional competitors of the parties is the mass media: newspapers, news and commentary magazines, radio, and, above all, television. Prior to the 1960s, a candidate for public office usually needed to convince party peers of his political skills and electability. For example, in the 1960 Humphrey–Kennedy contest for the Democratic presidential nomination, Jack Kennedy challenged Hubert Humphrey in the West Virginia primary, thought to be "Humphrey country." Kennedy won, and the party's leaders, particularly Mayor Richard Daley and other urban bosses, were convinced that their national nominating convention delegations should vote for Kennedy.

With the arrival of radio and television into nearly every American home, it became possible for a candidate, particularly a rich one, to circumvent the assessments of party peers. A self-selected candidate can win a party's nomination without a word of endorsement from the leadership or rank-and-file of the party. Several candidates for the Senate were soon doing just this. In the striking case of Ross Perot, his wealth permitted him to run for the presidency without a party. A couple of million dollars worth of television exposure coupled with perhaps excessive "free" media coverage made his name a household word within a few weeks.[5]

But the media are more than a technology and a campaign tool. They are also publishers, editors, pundits, and reporters with a special opportunity to determine the perceptions and attitudes of their audiences, the content and strategy of political campaigns, and, often enough, the outcome of elections. For example, in presidential election campaigns it is common for television and newspaper commentators to complain that the candidates are failing to address substantive issues. Yet each party has a platform and each candidate's headquarters distributes elaborate policy statements on almost every issue. The campaigns are "issueless" mainly because the media fail to report and analyze these policy statements, preferring to report campaigns like horse races.

As these competitors take over traditional party functions, what is left for the parties to do? There are, of course, those "invisible functions" for which parties were created in the first place: the implementation of the concept of popular sovereignty; the search for social and governing consensus; the recruitment and experiential training of political leaders; the articulation of dissent; and the harnessing of conflict to nonviolent methods of disagreement. These are hardly small tasks. Political philosophers would probably applaud these invisible functions and argue that they are worth everything a democratic community can contribute to their sustenance. How, then, should party executives and devotees of the party system attack the problem of fixing the political and attitudinal context in which the parties must operate?

A Public Relations Campaign for the Parties

We are dealing with an antiparty ethic, that is, a long-term, deeply ingrained attitudinal pattern. This pattern is debilitating, if not destructive, of a precious political institution. How may we go about fixing the political and attitudinal context in which the parties must live? Behavioral scientists will warn how difficult it is to change attitudes. Advertising executives are much more optimistic and bet their livelihoods on public relations campaigns. The public relations campaigns defending Tylenol™ and PepsiCola™ were brief, reasonable, and successful. But a PR campaign on behalf of the party system? Sounds foolish and gimmicky. We may expect that the concept of a public relations campaign on behalf of the party system will evoke ridicule and controversy.

By separating out the principal negative beliefs in the pattern of attitudes about parties, the pro-party themes of a public relations program may be reasonably constructed. Each of the negative beliefs requires exposure, rebuttal, or reformulation, tasks that are common in public relations campaigns. The following is a short list of negative beliefs that would need to be targeted.

- Money and related resources are always a negative influence in public affairs.
- Limits on campaign contributions and expenditures will prevent corruption and the exercise of undue influence.
- Party activity should be voluntary rather than a normal cost of democracy.
- Party reform or change of any kind is likely to benefit one side in the competition between parties and also destabilize the work of incumbents.
- It is a good thing that functional competitors—bureaucrats, members of Congress, community groups, political consultants, organized interest groups, candidates' personal organizations, and the media—have benefited from the disablement of party function and influence.

What would be some of the elements of a continuing public relations campaign on behalf of the U.S. party system? Some suggestions follow.

Revive Civic Education

Survey after survey during the last several decades reports that most parents would *not* want their children to make a career of politics, that is, party politics. We also know that children from ages as young as ten and eleven begin to be aware of and interested in political phenomena. Half of all young adults from eighteen to twenty-four years of age voted for president in the early 1970s; only a third participated in the most recent elections. At some period between childhood and parenthood, civic education in the United States is failing miserably.

Elementary and secondary schools are in great need of civic education programs that are realistic, exciting, informative, and legitimating of our communal lives as a democratic nation. Textbooks and lectures alone will not do it. Simulations, field trips, internships, computer-assisted games and simulations, charismatic party leaders, and inventive teachers have roles to play. The disagreements and self-interests that manifest themselves in our party system and other political institutions should be characterized as legitimate and, if conducted in keeping with the "rules of the game," honorable. The nature of professionalism in public service should be fully and fairly described. Above all, skepticism and inquiry should replace cynicism and condemnation in what we teach our young and our new citizens about our party system.

Political Parties Day

Americans commemorate innumerable occasions and causes, from Ground Hog Day in February to Sadie Hawkins Day in November. A

Political Parties Day[6] celebrated annually in an enlightening fashion on an appropriate day could become a salutary ritual. Perhaps the day chosen should be the one traditionally associated with the parties, namely, July 4, a day for patriotic feelings. Name the day and the rest of the celebratory arrangements can be left to American ingenuity.

Monitor the Media

"Except as a way to hand out patronage, 'the political party' went out with the icebox and the running board." This is the view of the executive producer of CBS's highly influential *60 Minutes* (Hewitt 1992). A distinguished political commentator (Drew 1993) stated the following: "The need to reform the system by which politicians raise money for their campaigns is by now pretty well understood. The current system is one of legalized corruption." George Will, in support of term limits, offers these words on the idea of public funding of campaigns: "True, public finance would eliminate fundraising, the most tiresome aspect of careers devoted to politics. But there should not be such careers. And until the political class will accede to term limits . . . nothing should be done to make the life of the political class less disagreeable" (1993).

Such antiparty punditry is pervasive and hardly helps improve a precious institution that is in trouble. Most media references to the parties, unfortunately, are loaded with innuendos and unsupported charges. Politicians portrayed on television dramatizations tend to be purchasable, sexist, slick, and/or dim-witted. Print media seem unable to describe campaign activities, expenditures, and financial contributions without implying theft, corruption, and other evils. Party leaders attending party fundraisers are almost invariably reported as guilty-by-association, implicitly auctioning off their less-than-sacred honor. And the White House aide who accepts a gift watch had better pack his bags the next day. The targets of these ad hoc media-generated ethical standards are, consistently, party leaders. The standards are applied by the media "guardians."

Unquestionably, the media set the perceptions, the attitudes, and the tone with which the people of the United States see and respond to their political parties. It does not require a First Amendment scholar to recognize that the media serve a vital function in our politics. The performance of this function should be of the highest quality and accountability, particularly as it relates to the operations of our party system and the work of its leaders. The situation calls for creation of a commission, a professional group, an ombudsman, or some other body to monitor, call to account, and promote the objectivity and fairness with which the media in specific instances treat the parties and the party system. We should never censor the media, but we need not acquiesce to their perceptions and behavior, particularly if these are tearing down our party system.

A Bill of Rights Statute

All bills of rights are agendas for focusing attention, provoking debate, and legitimizing reinterpretation of concepts and principles. Consider the two centuries of attention, debate, and reinterpretation of each of the first ten amendments to the United States Constitution. There could hardly have been invented a better device to keep such fundamental principles as free speech, freedom of association, and right of petition close to the lives and minds of Americans. A legislated Bill of Rights for Political Parties may render similar sociopsychological as well as political purposes.

A good model for setting forth the mutuality of rights *and* responsibilities of parties is the U.S. Bill of Rights. The provisions, which would be applicable to all party systems, might include the following:

1. Political parties shall be protected from violence and the threat of violence. They shall themselves refrain from acts of and incitements to violence and harassment.
2. Political parties shall share in the rights of freedom of association. They shall accordingly abide by the constitutional and statutory rules of association.
3. Political parties shall enjoy the rights of free speech and be assured fair communication access to the entire citizenry. The parties, in turn, shall refrain from disruption of communication channels and presentation of false information.
4. The name of a political party, its symbols, its declarations, and its endorsements shall be protected under the laws of copyright. Parties shall abide by these same laws and their own published regulations regarding these matters.
5. The nominating prerogatives of legally established parties and the opportunity for new parties to enter the nomination and election processes shall be protected under the law. For their part, political parties shall refrain from frivolous nominations, secret nominating procedures, and disruption of nonpartisan nominating and election activities.
6. In recognition of the public services rendered by political parties, selected organizational, campaign, nomination, and election functions of duly established parties shall be financed from public revenues. In order to remain qualified for public funding, the parties must adhere to the laws governing ethical uses of private as well as public funds and related resources and abide by rules of public disclosure of all private and public receipts and expenditures of funds.
7. In order that parties may pursue their nomination, campaign, and election functions with maximum safety, they shall be assured secrecy of the ballot, security of voting places and ballots cast, and opportunity

for their chosen agents to observe the administration of the election laws and procedures. The parties shall respect the security of all polling places, election officials, and authorized observers.

8. Military personnel on active duty and practicing clergy of any denomination may not be nominated by political parties for any elective public office. The parties shall refrain from employing clergy or military personnel in election campaigns and other activities related to the pursuit of elective office.

9. Political parties may organize in an overt and legally prescribed manner across geographical and political boundaries, whether within a nation or transnationally among nations. These transcommunal party associations shall abide by the laws of the subnational or national entities among which they operate or associate. They shall refrain from subversion, violence, or secret organizing activity that may jeopardize the host community.

10. The elections and other legal outcomes of party effort shall be acknowledged by the prompt and peaceful installation of elected party nominees into the public offices won. The parties shall submit disputed nominations and elections to an independent judiciary or a nonpartisan third-party agency for resolution.

Although most of these provisions seem to be already in place and respected here and in other democracies, upon closer inspection the United States still has a distance to go to meet some of the standards. With respect to provision 2, for example, do U.S. parties really share all the rights of freedom of association? From time to time, this question comes before the courts. As recently as 1986, the Supreme Court, on appeal, affirmed that the state of Connecticut could not prevent unaffiliated voters from voting in certain Republican primary elections when the Republican Party invited them to do so (*Tashjian v. Republican Party of Connecticut* 1986). Connecticut argued that it was protecting the two-party system by confining registered party voters to their own party's primary. The Court declared Connecticut's attempt to prevent participation to be an infringement of freedom of association. In this and other cases, the courts have had to be called upon in order to clarify freedom of association as it applies to political parties.

Provision 6 concerns the public funding of parties. This would probably be the most loudly debated provision. Is it proper to ask U.S. citizens to pay the parties a "fee" for rendering public services? It costs money to open and maintain party headquarters. Minimal communication with the citizenry—more during campaign periods—requires funds or free access to public channels. If nominating procedures must be conducted in a public manner, as in primary elections, parties must expend funds and other resources. The presentation of programs of public policy cannot be done without financial cost. Participation in election administration is expensive. The principle of public funding of party functions is already established for such activities as the conduct of national nominating conventions, primary elections, and general elections. Yet, the decline in one-dollar check-offs for the parties told us that the citizens would rather not pay for these services. Surprisingly, politicians themselves share this attitude.[7] Is the problem one of ethics, ignorance, or institutional procedure?

Provision 9 alludes to cross-boundary party collaborations. Americans know of such collaborations from their experience with federalism and the coalition of state parties into national parties. However, they know very little about transnational party collaborations such as those of the Christian Democratic, Socialist, Liberal, Conservative, and Green internationals. If anything, many Americans continue to believe that the defunct Communist International is still among us, largely because the Comintern received heightened press coverage in the years when it seemed to threaten American security. Transnational parties are likely to have a substantial role in U.S. and global politics in the not-too-distant future, but few are prepared to deal with the emerging challenge to the concept of national sovereignty that transnational parties pose (Goldman 1983). With the arrival of the Internet and the World Wide Web, however, this lack of awareness is likely to change rapidly and confront Americans with the problem of creating a party system for the world, let alone acknowledging the importance of their own party system.

In sum, the citizens and leaders of the United States could profit from a thoughtful debate generated by a proposed bill of rights and responsibilities for the parties. A statement of institutional rights and responsibilities such as a Bill of Rights for Political Parties could reformulate public consideration of the parties and their problems, emphasizing positive goals and change rather than negative attributions and constraints. Talk of improvement would replace condemnation as the content of public discussion about the debilities of the parties.

These suggestions for a continuing public relations campaign on behalf of the party system are just that, suggestions rather than panaceas. Any response to the bad rap needs popular involvement and creative thought. We need to hear again the words of a somewhat forgotten president of the United States, Martin Van Buren (1967):

> But knowing, as all men of sense know, that political parties are inseparable from free governments, and that in many and material respects they are highly useful to the country, I never could bring myself for my part to deprecate their existence. . . . The disposition to abuse power, so deeply planted in the human heart, can by no other means be more effectively checked; and it has always struck me as more honorable and manly and more in harmony with the character of our People and of our Institutions to deal with the subject of Political Parties in a sincere and wiser spirit.

Notes

1.   Two hundred and sixty years later, E. J. Dionne (1993) asked, "Why has [party] politics become such a nasty and often inhumane business?" Dionne offers several possible explanations, among them the inclination of politicians to "pound each other, often viciously" when they are mandated to but cannot find real answers to real crises. "Name-calling is especially widespread on emotive issues," particularly since adversaries feel that they must demonize each other. What Dionne—and Bolingbroke—did not recall is the historical fact that party systems often take the place of more violent, hence even nastier, forms of political controversy.

2.   There is an ample political science literature describing the motivations of persons choosing a career in politics and public service and the avenues of their entry into the system.

3.   A *Washington Post*-ABC News Poll conducted June 24–28, 1992

4.   Apropos term limits, a recent survey of former members of Congress (Center for Party Development 1993: 17) asked whether term limits would, in their opinion, increase or decrease the influence of the political parties in the recruitment of [candidates for Congress]. Party influence would increase according to 45.3 percent of the former members, decrease in the view of 12.6 percent, and make no difference in the opinion of 37.9 percent. Comparisons were made to term-limit practices in Latin America, where party leaders frequently play musical chairs in high offices, but, as a group, maintain control. Term-limit legislation may well become a panacea with unintended consequences, such as strengthening rather than weakening the role of the parties.

5.   Bertram Gross has speculated how a totalitarian future may emerge in the United States (1980). Some of the tendencies identified by him appear in the Perot "phenomenon."

6.   The implication of this title is that Americans would prefer to celebrate their respective parties, major and minor, rather than a party *system*.

7.   The survey of former members of Congress (Center for Party Development 1993) found that 75–80 percent of the former members, as do most of their fellow citizens, oppose public funding of organizational units of the parties.

4

Toward a Responsible Three-Party System:
Prospects and Obstacles

Theodore J. Lowi

One of the best kept secrets in American politics is that the two-party system has long been brain-dead—kept alive by support systems like state electoral laws that protect the established parties from rivals and by public subsidies and so-called campaign reform. The two-party system would collapse in an instant if the tubes were pulled and the IVS were cut. The current parties will not, and cannot, reform a system that drastically needs overhauling. The extraordinary rise of Ross Perot in the 1992 election and the remarkable outburst of enthusiasm for his ill-defined alternative to the established parties removed all doubt about the viability of a broad-based third party. It now falls to others to make a breakthrough to a responsible three-party system.[1]

At the same time, any suggestion of the possibility of a genuine third party receives the cold shoulder from the press and bored ridicule from academics. This reaction should surprise no one. Like the established parties themselves, social scientists are rarely given to innovation; they are almost always on the side of conventional wisdom, proven methodology, and the prevailing canon of their disciplines. Political scientists may call two-party doctrine a paradigm rather than canon, but they are no less loyal to it. With almost religious zeal, the high priests of the two-party system have preached the established faith, and their students who became leading journalists have perpetuated the two-party dogma. Thus, impetus for reform is about as unlikely to come from professors as from precinct captains.

To be sure, a great deal of scholarly analysis has been advanced to explain why third parties quickly disappear and why the two-party system is both natural and virtuous. Political scientists who believe this hold that the traditional Anglo-Saxon electoral system—based on first-past-the-post, single member districts—produces the two-party system by routinely discouraging new parties. They reason that since there can be only one victor in each district, even voters who strongly favor the candidate of a third or fourth party will ultimately vote for one of the two major candidates to avoid wasting their vote and also to avoid contributing to the victory of the least preferred of the major candidates. (This has been elevated to the status of a physical law, called "Duverger's Law" after its most prominent purveyor.) A two-party system is the best of all possible worlds, they hold, because it produces automatic majorities, enabling the victorious party to govern effectively for its full term of office.

Interestingly enough, although many scholars present the two-party system as being inevitable, it has never been left to accomplish its wonders alone. It has been supplemented by primary laws, nomination laws, campaign-finance laws, and electoral rules that are heavily biased against the formation and maintenance of anything other than the two-party system. And even with all that nourishment, two-party systems have prevailed in only a minority of all electoral districts in the United States since 1896. Most of the districts, from those that elect members of state legislatures up to the state as a whole in presidential elections, have in fact been dominated by one-party systems. During the past century, most of our larger cities and many counties, especially those governed by political machines, were admired by social scientists for their ability to overcome governmental fragmentation and to integrate immigrants into electoral politics even as they preached the gospel of the two-party system. While crusading reformers attacked the machines, most political scientists continued to defend them, even while they criticized specific abuses. Although academics are often aware of the deficiencies and strengths of parties, their commitment to the present system prevents them from considering a new one.

It is now time for a frank, realistic discussion of alternatives. No amount of tinkering, adjustment, reorganization, or aggressive public relations campaigns can bring back to life a party system that on its own devices would surely have crumbled a long time ago and that remains vibrant only in the hearts of party practitioners and political scientists. It is becoming increasingly clear that the usual scapegoats—divided government, campaign practices, scandals—are not the problem. The problem is, and always was, to be found within the two-party system itself.

The Constituent Function of American Parties

Much of the reluctance on the part of scholars to jettison myths surrounding the two-party system stems from a fundamental misconception regarding the true function of American parties. As I have argued elsewhere and at some length,[2] parties perform a *constituent* or *constitutional* role in the American polity. Because this notion bears directly on my argument concerning the need for a responsible three-party system, a brief summary is in order.

By stating that parties perform constituent functions, I am not suggesting simply that they represent certain groups or individuals—all parties at least try to represent some segment of the public. Instead, I am using the term in a much broader sense, meaning "necessary in the formation of the whole; forming; composing; making as an essential part." Constituent means that which constitutes. Constitution is the setting up of the way in which a political regime is organized and the laws that govern its organization. Parties have played a crucial role—intended or not—in "constituting" the American political regime by providing much of the organization and rules by which it is structured, staffed, and operated.

This view of party rests upon the distinction between constituent processes on the one hand and policy processes on the other. Political parties may perform both constituent and policy functions; such parties have been labeled as "responsible." American parties have almost never been responsible, policy-making parties, and most reform efforts to make them so have failed. On the other hand, political parties may perform only constituent functions; such parties have been variously called "pragmatic" or "rational-efficient." American parties have nearly always been constituent based, and attempts to improve their organizational capacity in this regard have often succeeded. Indeed, the genius of the American party system, if genius is the right word, is that it has split the regime from policy, keeping the legitimacy of the government separate from the consequences of governing.

One important effect of constituent parties has been the lack of development of American political institutions, even as the society grew and modernized dramatically. A careful review of American history reveals several important regularities of the two-party system. First, the formation of new parties (or the dissolution or reorganization of existing ones) produces changes in the nature of the regime, while the functioning of established parties does not. In fact, the shift from new to established parties has been accompanied by a parallel shift in the effects of party, from liberal to conservative, from innovation to consolidation, or from change to resistance to change.

Second, new ideas and issues develop or redevelop parties, but parties, particularly established ones, rarely develop ideas or present new issues on their own. Party organizations are thus vehicles for changes in policy originating in other places, but they are not often incubators of policy alternatives. Once a system of parties is established, the range and scope of policy discussion is set, until and unless some disturbance arises from other quarters. Third, the key feature of the functioning of constituent parties has been the existence of competition and not so much what the competition was about. The more dynamic and intense the level of competition, the more democratic parties become, often in spite of themselves. But the more regularized and diffuse the competition, the more conservative the parties become. The key to understanding the two-party system, and the current necessity of a genuine third party, lies in understanding these regularities.

During the first party period, roughly from 1789 to 1840, parties served a liberating, democratic role. To begin with, the new parties helped democratize the presidency. The first great organized effort to carry an opposition candidate, Thomas Jefferson, into office in the campaign of 1800 was a giant step toward the plebiscitary presidency—namely, the pledging of electors. By such means the election of the president was decentralized and popularized by the parties. The growth of parties directly checked or reversed tendencies toward a "fusion of powers" at the national level, mainly through the influence that the new parties exerted upon recruitment and succession of leaders.

The new parties also helped disperse national power by encouraging the formation of local organizations. The election of Andrew Jackson, the first rank "outsider," and the nominating, organizing, and campaigning of professional politicians around Martin Van Buren increased participation in the regime. The existence of vibrant organizations dedicated to the pursuit of many offices provided the raw material for opposition and debate. Grand alliances of these organizations made it possible to coordinate the activities of officeholders in a fragmented governmental system. Finally, the new parties helped democratize the electorate. This effect is easiest to document by the sheer expansion of political activity at local levels. As a result of the expansion of organized political activity, individual involvement also spread greatly and mass participation in nominations and elections became highly visible at all levels of public office. The spread of political activity helped increase the size of the electorate and produced increasingly large turnouts. None of these consequences of the emerging parties were particularly policy oriented, of course, but the process of party development linked elites to masses around the key issues of the day.

By the 1840s, however, the national party system seemed to pause in its development. Parties would henceforth monopolize all important elections and party machinery would dominate, if not monopolize, all nominations. Parties would also monopolize the procedures and administration of Congress as well as virtually all of the state legislatures. The schemes of party organization and procedure were to remain about the same for decades to come. Parties no longer served a liberating or democratic role, but rather a constricting, conservative one. With a few exceptions, the two-party system has functioned this way ever since.

The tendencies of established parties were as nearly opposite to those of new parties as is possible in a dynamic, modernizing society. For one thing, the established parties contributed to the status quo in government structure. For example, they helped maintain the centrality of federalism, even as the national government and the Constitution expanded to meet the problems of a nationally integrated country. Political leaders, including members of Congress, developed a fundamental stake in the integrity of the state boundary because it was the largest unit for electoral office. This force has had a powerful impact on the substance of much important national legislation throughout the last century, from social insurance to environmental protection. Parties have participated in a silent conspiracy to prevent policy innovations from departing too far from eighteenth-century constitutional structure.

The established parties also made elective offices less democratic by resisting leadership change and policy innovation. From the courthouse to the White House, the parties have not of their own accord brought new elites to the fore or offered powerful checks on existing elites. Neither do they regularly bring new issues to the fore. It has been rare for the two major parties to take opposite stands on new controversies; it is much more common for new cleavages to develop within the existing parties, providing incentives to avoid addressing these controversies.

Finally, there is little evidence to suggest partisan competition has any real impact on electoral mobilization. In many instances closely balanced parties appear to have actively resisted further democratization of the electorate. Expanding the franchise to new voters and mobilizing existing ones often threatens existing party coalitions, and thus established parties have reasons to ignore or actively oppose such expansions. Along these lines, established parties have an investment in existing social cleavages and no real interest in building a consensus across the myriad of ethnic, religious, and regional groupings that characterize American society.

Of course, there have been a few important instances since the 1840s when the established parties have been programmatic and innovative. At such times—most clearly in 1856–60, 1896–1900, 1912–14, and 1933–35—significant differences appeared between the parties and they became innovative rather than conservative. Each period was ushered in by the "redevelopment" of one of the established parties after an earlier political disaster. Such reorganization made the party oligarchies more susceptible to direction from interest groups with strong policy commitments. Party leaders also became more susceptible to mass opinion, partly as the result of the mobilization of new social movements, but also due to increased competition from rivals. And in these periods, the appearance of a third party was a powerful force in implementing these changes. Of course, these third parties eventually faded, once the major parties stole their message and followers, and reestablished a new, conservative equilibrium.

The Two-Party Impasse

Back when the federal government was smaller and less important, the two-party system could carry out its constituent functions without much regard to ideology or policy. Its unresponsiveness produced major political blunders from time to time, but the system was able to right itself after a brief period of reorganization. But with the New Deal and the rise of the welfare state, the federal government became increasingly vulnerable to ideological battles over policy. Even then, such problems were not particularly noticeable while the government and the economy were expanding, but in the early 1970s class and ideological conflicts began to emerge more starkly, and the two-party system was increasingly unable to offer productive competition.

Thus were born the familiar "wedge" issues—crime, welfare, prayer, economic regulation, social regulation, taxes, deficits, and anticommunism. No matter what position party leaders took on such issues, they were bound to alienate a substantial segment of their constituency. While the Democrats were the first to feel the cut of wedge issues, particularly concerning race, Republicans are now having their own agonies over abortion, crime, foreign policy, and budget deficits. Wedge issues immobilize party leadership, and once parties are immobilized the government is itself immobilized.

Party leaders have responded to this gridlock not with renewed efforts to mobilize the electorate but with the strategy of scandal. An occasional exposure of genuine corruption is a healthy thing for a democracy, but when scandal becomes an alternative to issues, leaving the status quo basically unaltered, it is almost certain that all the lights at the intersection are stuck on red. In fact, the use of scandal as a political strategy has been so effective that politicians have undermined themselves by demonstrating to the American people that the system itself is corrupt.

The established parties have atrophied because both have been in power too long. In theory, a defeated party becomes vulnerable to new interests because it is weaker and therefore more willing to take risks. But for nearly forty years, both parties have in effect been majority parties. Since each party has controlled a branch of government for much of that time, neither is eager to settle major policy issues in the voting booth. Voters find it difficult to assess blame or praise, making accountability judgments and partisan affiliation difficult. A very important aspect of the corruption of leadership is the tacit contract between the two parties to avoid taking important issues to the voters and in general to avoid taking risks.

Even a brief look at the two established parties reveals the urgency of the need for fundamental reform, and any remaining doubt will be removed before the end of the Clinton administration. The established parties do not lack for leadership, and with briefing books a foot thick and plenty of economists-for-rent, they certainly do not lack for programs. Here Ross Perot certainly was right: Washington is full of plans, good plans, that the two parties turn into useless parchment. The Republican and Democratic parties are immobilized by having to promise too many things to too many people.

Republicans say that they consider government to be the problem, not the solution, particularly in economic matters. Yet, to attract enough voters to win elections, they have also pushed measures designed to make moral choices for all citizens; for example, restrictions on abortions are hardly the mark of a party that distrusts government action.

The Democrats like government action: the commitment of government to new programs with grandiose goals and generous budgets is, for them, tantamount to solving problems. President Clinton, for example, took bold stands on a multitude of issues during the campaign, but he conveyed no sense of priority among them. Once in office, Clinton quickly conceded the impossibility of the task he had defined. As *The New York Times* put it in a headline on its front page: "Clinton, after raising hope, tries to lower expectations."

As in the past, the present two-party system functions to keep leadership, succession, and governmental structure separate from the actual settlement of issues. The tendencies of the established parties to preserve institutional structure, avoid issues, and stifle competition are too far advanced for easy reversal. It is time for a new party organization, championing new ideas, to make the party system more competitive, as the original American parties did. A genuine third party would shatter this conservative alliance, jump-start the development process, and once again make parties agents of liberation, democracy, and innovation.

The Impact of a Genuine Third Party

Predictably, defenders of the two-party system have devoted considerable energy to shooting down any suggestion that the status quo can be improved upon. They have produced all sorts of scenarios about how a third party could throw presidential elections into the Congress, with the House of Representatives choosing the president and the Senate choosing the vice president. Worse yet, if it survived to future elections, a third party would hold the balance of power and, as a result, wield an influence far out of proportion to its electoral size. It might, by its example, produce a fourth or a fifth party. And if it elected members to Congress, it might even inconvenience congressional leaders in their allocation of committee assignments. There is a great deal of truth in these scenarios: a genuine third party might well cause such things and as a consequence help reconstitute the American regime.

With three parties, no party needs to seek a majority or pretend that it is a majority. What a liberating effect this would have on party leaders and candidates, to go after constituencies composed of 34 percent rather than 51 percent of the voters. When 51 percent is needed, a party or candidate has to be all things to all people—going after about 80 percent of the voters to get the required 51 percent. A three-party system would be driven more by issues, precisely because parties fighting for pluralities can be clearer in their positions. Third parties have often presented constructive and imaginative programs, which have then been ridiculed by leaders of the two major parties, who point out that third-party candidates can afford to be intelligent and bold since they cannot possibly win. But that is the point. In a three-party system, even the two major parties would have stronger incentives to be more clearly programmatic, since their goal would be more realistic and their constituency base would be simpler. Thus, each party could be a responsible party.

Two factors would help prevent the fragmentation that multiparty systems sometimes cause abroad, as in Israel. First, the American electoral system is not based on pure proportional representation. That system, allowing a party garnering a small number of votes to send at least one representative to the legislature, benefits the smallest of parties. Second, the fact that voters formally elect the chief executive provides incentives for splinter parties to coalesce behind one candidate. In a classic parliamentary system, even a party that has elected only a few representatives can exert a disproportionate influence on the selection of a premier.

Flowing directly from three-party competition, voting would increase, as would other forms of participation. Virtually our entire political experience tells us that more organized party competition produces more participation. And we already know that genuine three-party competition draws people into politics—not merely as voters but as petition gatherers, door knockers, envelope lickers, and $5 contributors—making the three-party system an antidote to the mass politics that virtually everybody complains about nowadays.

Even defenders of the two-party system criticize the candidates' reliance on television, computerized voter lists, mass mailings, and phone banks—which dehumanize politics, discourage participation, replace discourse with ten-second sound bites, and reduce substantive alternatives to subliminal imagery and pictorial allusion. And the inordinate expense of this mass politics has led to a reliance on corporate money, particularly through political action committees, destroying any hope of collective party responsibility.

These practices and their consequences cannot be eliminated by new laws—even if the laws did not violate the First Amendment. A multiparty system would not immediately wipe out capital-intensive mass politics, but it would eliminate many of the pressures and incentives that produce its extremes because third parties tend to rely on labor-intensive politics. Third parties simply do not have access to the kind of financing that capital-intensive politics requires. But more than that, there is an enthusiasm about an emerging party that inspires people to come out from their private lives and to convert their civic activity to political activity.

Finally, the existence of a genuine third party would parliamentarize the presidency. As noted above, once a third party proves that it has staying power, it would increase the probability of presidential elections being settled in the House of Representatives, immediately making Congress the primary constituency of the presidency. Congress would not suddenly "have power over" the presidency. It has such power already, in that the Constitution allows it complete discretion in choosing from among the top three candidates. But if Congress were the constituency of the president, the president would have to engage Congress in constant discourse. The president might under those circumstances have even more power than now, but he would have far less incentive to go over the head of Congress to build a mass following. Even now, with two parties based loosely on mythical majorities, a president cannot depend on his party to provide a consistent congressional majority. The whole idea of an electoral mandate is something a victorious president claims but few members of Congress accept, even for the length of the reputed honeymoon. Thus, current reality already forces the president to bargain with members of the opposition party.

Confronting three parties in Congress, each of whose members were elected on the basis of clear policy positions, the president's opportunities for bargaining for majority support would be more fluid and frequent. In our two-party environment, issues are bargained out within the ranks of each party and often never see the light of day, particularly during the session prior to a presidential election. A third party with a small contingent of members of Congress would insure a more open and substantive atmosphere for bargaining to take place—after the election.

A genuine third party would play the role of honest broker and policy manager because it would hold a balance of power in many important and divisive issues. There would be little fear of the tail wagging the dog because, unlike European parties, Democrats and Republicans are not ideologically very far apart—they have simply not been cooperating with each other. The presence of a third-party delegation gives the president an alternative for bargaining, but if the new party raised its price too high it would simply give the president a greater incentive to bargain with the other major party. Another important myth in the United States is that policy making is a matter of debate between the affirmative and the negative. But simple yea versus nay on clearly defined alternatives is a very late stage in any policy-making process.

Over time, a three-party system would alter the constitution of the American regime. Very quickly and directly, the entire pattern of recruitment and succession would change. The separation of powers would begin to recede until the presidency and both houses of Congress had become a single institution. The function of the cabinet and the very purpose of cabinet officers would change. These patterns would develop whether the lead issues were crime, economic development, health care, or foreign affairs. The parties would inevitably be more policy oriented and responsive to the public will.

The point here is that the third party is a liberating rather than a confining force, a force for open debate on policies. Just as the rise of the two-party system fundamentally altered the constitutional structure of our government appropriately for the nineteenth century, so a three-party system would alter the structure appropriately for the twenty-first century.

Toward a Genuine Third Party

Immediately, one must add an important proviso: A genuine third party must be built from the bottom up. It must be an opportunistic party, oriented toward the winning of elections. It must nominate and campaign for its own candidates at all levels and not simply run someone for president. Of course, building such a party will be difficult. It will require mobilizing a large number of people and resources. And it must attract regular Democrats and Republicans by nominating some of them to run as candidates with the third-party nomination as well as that of their own party. Joint sponsorship has been practiced by the Liberal and Conservative parties in New York for decades. Being listed on two lines on the ballot is a powerful incentive for regular Democrats and Republicans to cooperate with a new party, if not to switch over. About forty states have laws preventing or discouraging this practice, but their provisions will probably not stand up to serious litigation.

Although a genuine third party will not be able to elect a president, it must elect enough legislators to make a difference. This was a big error for Ross Perot when he ran for president. Not only did he mistakenly assume he could win, but even if he had won, he would not have had a majority in Congress; in fact, he would have faced a very hostile Congress. Perot would have been able to carry out none of his programs. Thus, a third party may present voters a clear set of policy alternatives but it must be clear on what it can accomplish. It is not a governing party; it must pursue means other than taking over the government in order to implement programs.

Here history provides some good examples. While genuine third parties have been infrequent in the United States, whenever they have organized from the bottom up they have had significant and generally positive effects on the regime. One of these is providing a halfway house for groups "wedged" out of the two larger parties. In 1924, the progressive movement succeeded in forming the Progressive Party in Wisconsin and other midwestern states, which nominated Robert M. La Follette for president. In the 1930s, the Farmer-Labor Party flourished in Minnesota, where it eventually fused with an invigorated Democratic Party. In the process, both of these third parties provided the channel through which many dissident and alienated groups found their way back into politics, and their influence lingered long after the parties themselves. Similarly, wherever the Dixiecrats organized as a party, that state was later transformed to a genuinely competitive two-party state.

Of course, many third parties in American history have not built from the bottom up, including left- and right-wing splinter factions, protest movements, candidate caucuses, and single-issue interest groups, most of which sought merely to use a presidential campaign to advance their substantive message. Few of these groups have wanted or tried to play a continuing role in the American political system. Here again, Ross Perot provides an instructive example and a warning. After the election, he chose not to institutionalize his campaign by building a genuine third party, but chose instead to found a "citizens lobby," United We Stand America. Our system hardly needs another sophisticated lobby stirring up the grassroots to pressure the established parties, particularly one that is dominated by its celebrity founder. The resources available in the Perot campaign—plentiful money, a dynamic leader, thousands of committed volunteers, and millions of disenchanted citizens—are wasted on such an effort. Just imagine where a third party would be today if a fraction of Perot's expenditures had gone to organizing efforts at the grassroots level to field candidates from municipal elections on up.

There are, however, numerous efforts under way to exploit this opportunity. A national Independence Party was founded in 1992, drawing on many former Perot activists but operating on a party principle rather than a group principle. In 1993, the party's name was changed to the Federation of Independent Parties to accommodate the several affiliated state parties operating under different names. Some predated our national effort, and others were operating in states that do not permit the use of party labels, such as Independent, that have been used before or might tend to misrepresent the size or character of the membership. But as with most such efforts, the national party began to founder in 1994, when at its organizing convention it was split apart by integration with the New Alliance Party. The party changed its name to the Patriot Party and the leaders of the New Alliance Party dropped their name and separate identity in an effort to indicate that they are no longer a fringe party. Although the future of the national party was left very much in doubt, the elements of a real national candidacy were in place. And meanwhile, genuine centrist parties were forming in more than twenty states, some affiliated with the national party and some not. Candidates for governor and Congress and other offices were nominated in 1994, and there was the beginning of real progress toward three-way electoral contests—and also two-way contests where the third party candidate offered at least some opposition to an otherwise uncontested incumbent.

Such efforts that produce few if any electoral victories confirm to mainstream observers the futility of efforts to form a new electoral party. However, if the leaders, organizers, and activists within the new party maintain awareness that victory comes in more than one form—politics is not a game—the chance of persistence and growth is enhanced. So is the ultimate goal of transformation of American politics by turning the two-party system into a three-party system. The results of such a three-party system would be immediate, unlike the long and unintended developments of party reform within the context of the two-party system. The first definite possibility is that the two major parties would, in this three-party context, be able to realize more of their own virtues. The programs and goals of the established two parties are not inherently evil; it is their duopoly that is evil. Both operate as majority parties, both enjoy much of the satisfactions of majority parties and have for a long time. Because of that, they are decadent parties. If power, according to the philosopher, does corrupt, it is usually from having a lot of it for too long a time. The duopoly has to go.

A second consequence, again an immediate consequence flowing from the permanent establishment of a three-party system, is improvement in the legitimacy of political action and public objects. It is no figment of the imagination that the public is receptive to a new third-party organization. The results of the 1992 election reveal that millions of Americans are willing to vote for someone and some party other than the Democratic or Republican. Polls conducted during the most partisan season, the spring and summer of 1992, confirmed that nearly 60 percent of the American people were favorably disposed toward the creation of a new political party.

Meanwhile, personal commitment to the major parties continues to decline and public distrust of politicians continues to increase unabated. The high priests of the two-party system are looking for the explanation everywhere except where the explanation truly resides—in the present party itself. Since the two parties are a duopoly and operate as a duopoly, they have no incentive or will to break open and look publicly at the hundreds of thousands of established coalitions and networks that support the programs that give rise to the deficit and the impossibility of reducing it. There is no way these party leaders can reduce the deficit by screaming at the deficit figure itself and by passing legislation like Gramm-Rudman or constitutional amendments to promise some kind of ceiling on the aggregate figure itself. That is akin to howling at the moon. The gridlock over the deficit and the growing national debt was never attributed to divided government. It was attributed to the two-party duopoly and its primordial stake in the maintenance of the networks of support for existing programs, whether they are still useful or completely outmoded. A third party with no stake in those networks will not immediately bring honesty and integrity to government and will not immediately bring the budget into balance. But it will contribute to honesty in budgeting because it will have every incentive, every selfish incentive, to do so.

Finally, if this new effort to create a genuine third party in a new three-party system accomplishes nothing else, it will at least make a great contribution to political pedagogy and public education. It should be considered a great success if it jolts entrenched political journalism and academic political science toward a reconsideration of their myth-ridden conception of the prerequisite of democracy in general and American democracy in particular. And it can be considered a great success already to the extent that textbooks and classrooms are raising fresh and new curiosities about what really works in a democratic political system. We end as we begin, with the proposition that there is nothing in the universe that demands a two-party system, and therefore it is not sacrilegious to advocate an alternative.

Postscript 1996: The End of the Two-Party System?

The case for a three-party system is stronger today than ever. Popular support for a third party remains well above 50 percent, and even Ross Perot did a 180-degree turn in 1995, choosing to convert United We Stand America from a civic consciousness movement to a political party. This was an important commitment because Perot and associates were fully aware of how tedious, difficult, and expensive it is to gain ballot access for a political party rather than an independent candidate. As of the end of February, Perot's Reform Party had succeeded in gaining ballot access in twelve states, with strong prospects of seven or eight more during the spring.

Sifting the Recent Evidence

Yet, in many important respects, the United States today seems farther away than ever from the end of the two-party system. Here is some of the evidence:

- The 1994 congressional elections produced a spectacular reaffirmation of the party system. Burnham (1996) and others are already recognizing 1994 as the critical realignment election they had been expecting for many years.
- Even without a presidential election at stake, the 1994 election seemed to produce a mandate, in the form of the Contract with America.
- Party discipline has rarely been higher than it was in the first session of the 104th Congress. In fact, we have to reach back toward 1900 to find anything like the party discipline now seen regularly demonstrated in roll call after roll call.
- Divided government prevailed, but it seemed to be virtually an institutionalization of the two-party system, with one party dominating Congress and the other dominating the presidency. This can be seen as a form of party government, with each party being able to behave like a governing party, having control of at least one major branch of the national government.
- With realignment accompanied by institutionalization of the parties in governmental command posts, there was an unprecedented opportunity for "responsible party government" because a mandate plus institutional power contributed to the clarification, in almost laserlike precision, of the line of accountability between electorate and party.

- Finally, the priesthood within the political science and journalist professions generally embraces with renewed vigor their faith in the virtues of the two-party system as the only way America can be governed. If their faith in the two-party system remained strong despite the weaknesses of parties and the ambiguities of two-party confrontation, their faith can only be strengthened by the revival, indeed the renaissance, of party discipline and party responsibility.

But these facts do not sustain the brief for the two-party system when they are subjected to cross-examination by means of other facts:

- This is probably the most ideological era of American politics in the twentieth century, and yet the strongest and deepest political controversies are *within* the parties, not between them. Of course, this has been true for a long time, just as Samuel Lubell argued over forty years ago in his still useful book, *The Future of American Politics* (1952: 212): the key to the politics of any period in the United States will be found in the disputes taking place within the majority party.
- This is true now as in Lubell's time because the two-party system is still a duopoly, and like duopolies in the economy, the two competitors tend to move closer and closer toward each other as they discover there is more to be lost than gained from all-out competition. Whatever differences have existed between the Republican and the Democratic parties has practically disappeared during the past decade. They are like McDonald's and Burger King sitting close enough together to be able to share the same exit lane. Bill Clinton is the most recent Republican president, just as Richard Nixon was the last Democratic president.
- The intense and divisive controversies within the Republican Party are rich in policy content as well as ideology, but they are tearing the GOP apart even as they are mobilizing the Republican majority in the House of Representatives and only slightly less so in the Senate.
- The House Republicans led by Newt Gingrich met their Contract obligations and went beyond them. But since most of the items in the Contract and related bills were so consistently within the free market (or "moderate") wing of the Republican Party, every successful roll call contributed to the mobilization and further radicalization of the social issue (or "conservative") wing, inside Congress but also outside Washington at the grassroots.
- This polarization within the Republican Party almost literally destroyed the substantively innovative aspect of the Gingrich revolution. The boldest parts of the House's accomplishments were severely compromised and weakened in the Senate even before they reached the White House for possible veto. As energetic as the 104th Congress has been, the result has been incrementalism—full of sound and fury, but signifying little.

- As the Republican Revolution went beyond its 100 Days into its 300 Days and 400 Days, its program became less and less popular in the nation, and the popular rating of Congress, already low, declined along with the program. So did the public standing of Newt Gingrich. Few highly visible politicians have ever had the poll negatives to match those of Newt Gingrich.

- Early in the presidential nominating campaign of 1996, the astute David Broder (1996) observed that not only had "none of the Republican contenders [wanted] to embrace Speaker Newt Gingrich," but also that it was striking "that none of the surviving Republican presidential hopefuls is running on the 1994 Contract with America. In fact, the candidate who came closest to embracing the Contract, Senator Phil Gramm of Texas, withdrew after the first two tests, in Iowa and Louisiana."

- Another fundamental contribution to the decadence of the two-party system is the rise of the PACs, having swelled in numbers to more than forty-five hundred. Possibly the most significant contribution they make to politics is to reinforce incrementalism. Whatever impulse to substantive innovation there is in American politics is more than neutralized by the influence of the PACs, which are tied to individual members rather than to a party or to the nation. PACs use their influence to either obtain or protect a specialized law, agency, or decision. This helps explain why not a single major new national government program has been adopted or terminated since 1973—the year the reforms producing the PACs were first adopted.

- Since PACs finance elections, and PACs are found largely outside of the districts where most members are elected, PACs have helped implement a new system of *indirect representation*. Members are elected from geographic districts, but they have a fiduciary obligation to their financial sources outside their districts that at least competes with, if not displaces, their electoral obligations.

- The mischiefs of these particular factions can be appreciated all the more when we add the fact that PACs are a product, a *direct* product of the two-party system. Advertised as a major reform to strengthen political parties and to make them more honest in the wake of the Watergate scandal, PACs were a bipartisan reform. They were the result of an agreement to bring interest groups more directly into the electoral process by legalizing direct corporate financial support of legislative candidates.

All of the items above are not merely developments that have taken place *within* a two-party context; they are developments that have taken place *because* of the two-party duopoly. Thus, there appears to be nothing new in this most recent strengthening of party lines, except that Republican control of Congress after the 1994 election contributed to the equalization of PAC contributions between the two parties.

Since PACs are protected from abolition by the First Amendment and by the very power that PACs have over members of Congress, the best way to rid ourselves of the PAC scourge is by changing the party system. Moreover, the neutralization or downright obsolescence of the PACs will turn out to be only one of the many advantages to be gained in our democracy from a new multiparty system.

The way to start the process of genuine political reform is to take the present party system off life supports. Political scientists persist in predicting the failure of each and every effort to form a new political party, and the failure of each one is taken as confirmation of their predictions. It is as though "Duverger's Law" not only enjoyed the high status of a physical law but perhaps of natural or divine law because belief in the two-party system takes on the quality of a religion. But the truth of the matter is that third party efforts fail because that is the objective of the electoral laws of every state (where all the relevant electoral laws are made). The legal barriers to a new party and a new party system have proven far too strong for even the most dedicated, broadly based, and best financed new party movements. In response to an assertion made in the neoconservative *National Standard* that "American politics raises no significant technical bar against the existence of third parties," ballot access specialist Richard Winger listed nine formidable legal barriers. Space limitations permit identification here by label only: ballot access, campaign finance, government-funded primaries, timing of nominations, fusion, registration, voter information, representational election boards, and ballot order (*Ballot Access News*, January 14, 1966: 4).

Continued Signs of Change

There are some hopeful signs of change, however, in no small part because of the mobilization of multiculturalism and the legal challenges to make the electoral system more responsive to it. Whatever the challenge, each and every effort to make the present system appear more representative or more accessible only contributes further to the decline of its legitimacy. In other words, there appears to be no way to work out a legitimate and acceptable system of representation while preserving the single-member district system and all of the electoral laws supportive of it. For example, nothing is more likely to destroy the single-member district system than the benign gerrymandering of the districts in order to produce desired outcomes. The history of failed governments and short-lived republics in Europe and elsewhere is filled with clever efforts to redesign the electoral system to reach planned outcomes. This is why each effort at electoral engineering in the United States has been and will continue to be a national embarrassment. Even the Supreme Court has begun to recognize the practical impossibility of electoral engineering. As one electoral law expert put it: "There is nothing you can do in redistricting now that can keep you from getting sued." In its most recent effort, in the October 1995 term, the Supreme Court indicated that "bizarrely shaped" districts designed for prearranged political outcomes will be subjected to "strict scrutiny"—a status reserved for First and Fourteenth Amendment cases.

All such practices are in jeopardy of "strict scrutiny" because these new gerrymandering provisions are so often racial gerrymanders, albeit positive. Another reason is that "like the antifusion laws, they run afoul of the First Amendment." And for the latter reason alone, courts and parties will eventually have to confront the whole question of the constitutionality of the single-member district system. The beginning of the end rests on recognition of the fact that the single-member district system, especially when combined with two parties, will always systematically suppress *any definable minority*. The more identifiable and recognizable the minority, the more hurtful this suppression is to the legitimacy of democracy. Since there is absolutely no way to design single-member geographic districts that will obey the rules of continuity and numerical equality, and at the same time produce satisfactory minority representation, the constitutional support for the single member geographic system will continue to weaken until the courts will have to throw up their hands and give the states no alternative but to abandon districting altogether and go for at-large election of representatives. State-wide at-large election of representatives is not unknown in the United States. There have been a number of instances where states have had to turn temporarily to at-large elections when they were unable to reapportion following a decennial census. At-large election is coming soon, but not soon enough.[3]

The handwriting is already on other legal walls protecting the two-party system. Two lines of litigation are most relevant to the prospects of third party success in the future, but these are not the only constitutional challenges to the system. The first of these is the successful case involving "fusion" in Minnesota. Fusion is the original name for the practice of a minor party nominating another party's nominee, giving that nominee two places on the ballot. Fusion is permitted in only six or seven states. All other forbid it, either by state law or by major parties rules, providing that no candidate can occupy more than one spot on a ballot and can accept the nomination of one party, even if the candidate consents to the minor party's nomination and the other party does not object. Fusion is essential to the growth and durability of only a minor party, as is demonstrated not only by the four-party system in New York State, where fusion is permitted, but also confirmed by the fact that third parties flourished at the turn of the century until barriers to fusion were adopted.[4] In *Twin Cities Area New Party v. McKenna* (January 5, 1996) the United States Court of Appeals for the Eighth Circuit held that Minnesota's antifusion laws "are unconstitutional because the statutes severely burden the New Party's associational rights. . . ." The Court recognized that it was only invalidating provisions that prevented minor parties from joint nomination where the candidate and the relevant major party consented. It said explicitly that it was not confronting the broader Minnesota statute which states unconditionally that "no individual shall be named on any ballot as the candidate of more than one major political party" because this more general prohibition against fusion without the consent of the major party was not involved in this case.

Litigation in other states producing contrary results makes almost certain that the Supreme Court will in the near future take a leading case on the subject of fusion. In a 1991 Wisconsin case (*Swamp v. Kennedy*), the Seventh Federal Circuit voting three against two, handed down a decision inconsistent with the Minnesota decision. Meanwhile, litigation was under way in at least two other circuits, the Third in Pennsylvania and the Tenth in New Mexico. It is overwhelmingly probable that antifusion laws will not stand up under the strict scrutiny of the Supreme Court.

Another trace of handwriting on the wall against the two-party system is less directly applicable to third-party prospects, but it is still a strong indication of the darkening shadow over electoral laws that protect the two major parties. In late January 1996, the Federal Court of Appeals for the Second Circuit (Brooklyn) agreed with a ruling by a federal district judge that New York's ballot access rules are unconstitutional because they set an "undue burden" on presidential candidates not favored by the party. This meant that the forty-year-old ballot access rules of the state Republican Party, widely considered the most restrictive in the nation, were wiped out. This was another indication of the willingness of federal courts to confront biased electoral laws. In fact, between the ballot access cases and the districting cases, it begins to appear that few if any state protective electoral laws will stand up any longer to constitutional litigation.

Once the outmoded electoral system goes, so will go the two-party system in most of the states. And so will go the need for minority-oriented reforms, campaign and PAC reforms, and term-limit and electoral college reforms, since the multiparty system that would emerge would put to rest the myth of majority rule, without in any sense endangering the capacity of our legislatures to govern by majority rule. Minorities rule, or plurality rule, was always the American way. Even in the context of tight party discipline in the 104th Congress, virtually all roll calls on major legislation are the product of coalition building and caucus management. What is lacking is an appropriate mechanism for representing the minorities and pluralities that make up that electorate. And in a multiparty system, with easier means of forming and reforming parties, economic interest groups (as well as social groups and movements) will find it both necessary and desirable to seek to influence government through the political parties rather than devoting all their political resources to lobbying individual members or capturing relevant agencies.

The specter of a runaway ten- or twenty-party system where a tiny radical party with 2 percent of the representation can dictate policy for the country is the type of bogeyman device that every priest and parent uses to instill faith by fear. Constitutional change will almost certainly produce multimember districts, but these do not have to be statewide in populous states, nor do strict rules of proportional representation have to be adopted, nor will we be forced to convert to a parliamentary system of government. Once the necessity for multimember district representation is confronted, American legislatures will use their natural ingenuity to fashion electoral laws appropriate to our multicultural, plurality-rule country. Whatever system they fashion will be more hospitable to third and fourth parties, without eliminating the first and second parties. Indeed, one of the best features of a "responsible" multiparty system is that it will provide a much healthier environment for the major parties as well.

Notes

1. This chapter parallels arguments I have made elsewhere, including Lowi 1992a, 1992b, and 1994.

2. See Lowi 1975.

3. In 1995 alone, federal circuit courts were ruling on cases in at least five states arising out of challenges from white plaintiffs who contend that the districts as drawn infringe on their constitutional rights. By the end of 1995, a three-judge federal panel was devising a new map for all of Georgia's eleven congressional districts, following the failure of the Georgia legislature to do the job the previous summer. The Supreme Court threw out the Louisiana "racial gerrymander" case in 1994 on technical grounds, but will surely take it up again as soon as those objections are met by the Louisiana plaintiffs.

4. The Eighth Circuit opinion actually cited the leading article on the practice of fusion throughout the 1800s: Peter H. Argersinger, "A place on the Ballot: Fusion Politics and Antifusion Laws" (1980). This was reprinted as a chapter in Argersinger's book (1992).

PART TWO

Party Activities:
National, State, and Local

5

The Politics of Cohesion: The Role of the National Party Committees in the 1992 Election

Anthony Corrado

The last two decades have witnessed a resurgence of national party activity in electoral politics. Once cast as institutions of "politics without power" (Cotter and Hennessey 1964) in an increasingly candidate-centered political culture, the national party committees have responded to changes in their environment by expanding their institutional capacities and restructuring their operations to provide the services and resources candidates need in modern elections. They have improved their fundraising abilities, stabilized their staffs, and enhanced their technological capabilities, which, in turn, has revitalized their role in political campaigns and their relations with state and local parties.[1] As a result, the national party organizations have been able to recapture some of their former influence in the political process, especially in congressional elections, where they play a major role in providing campaign services and financial support to candidates (Herrnson 1988, 1989).

The extent to which this renewed level of national party activity has influenced presidential elections has been a more open question. Beginning in the late 1960s and early 1970s, the national party committees became more active and asserted their authority to formulate delegate selection rules and procedures for national nominating conventions (Ranney 1975; Shafer 1983; Price 1984; Wekkin 1984). But these rules changes have had the largely unintended effect of undermining the role of party organizations in the presidential nomination process (Crotty 1978; Ceasar 1982; Polsby 1983). Most important, the new rules opened up the selection process, which ended party control of the presidential nomination and produced more competitive, even divisive primaries. Competition was also encouraged by other reforms, especially the limitations and public funding provisions of the campaign finance reforms of the 1970s (H. Alexander 1992; Corrado 1993).

Consequently, presidential elections have become candidate-based contests in which contenders, relying on their own organizations and fundraising abilities, attempt to mobilize issue activists and other constituencies behind their individual candidacies. The national party organizations generally exercise little influence in this process. Yet, despite their declining influence, the party committees are still expected to carry out the difficult task of trying to unify partisan factions divided by the nomination contest. Their success in fulfilling this role constitutes an increasingly important electoral objective. As Martin Wattenberg has shown, the candidate with the most unified party has won every election since 1964. This has led him to conclude that "unified party support has become more crucial than ever to a presidential election victory" (1991b: 40) as the role of partisanship as a general determinant of voting behavior has declined (Stone 1984; Buell 1986).

This chapter examines some of the ways in which the revitalized national party organizations have tried to promote partisan cohesiveness in national elections.[2] In particular, it discusses the role of the Democratic National Committee (DNC) and Republican National Committee (RNC) in the 1992 presidential race and the use of resources designed to promote party integration and organizational strength in the general election campaign.

An Overview

Since the advent of the modern party reform movement, the national party committees have participated in the presidential selection process only to a limited extent. They are responsible for the rules that govern delegate selection. They organize the national conventions, which are technically part of the nominating process, and assist in the selection of members to the convention standing committees, which have the formal responsibility for drafting convention rules and writing the party's platform. They also provide indirect assistance to the party nominee through such activities as generic party advertising and the financing of voter registration and mobilization programs in the general election.

The DNC and RNC have generally taken a hands-off approach in the presidential nomination campaign and have eschewed expressing a candidate preference due to the prospect of an endorsed candidate losing the race. As Paul Herrnson has noted, such an outcome "would be disastrous . . . because the successful, unsupported candidate would become the head of the party's ticket and its titular leader" (1994a: 58). The parties have therefore, for political purposes, usually served as no more than honest brokers, allowing candidates to make their own decisions and form their own organizations in seeking the nomination.

The presidential race thus presents the party committees with two challenges that must be addressed in advance of the general election. First, nomination contests encourage party factionalism, particularly when the nomination is hotly contested, as in the 1976 Republican selection or the Democratic contests of the 1980s. But even in races in which the choice of a nominee is apparent relatively early, such as the 1988 Republican and 1992 Democratic contests, party divisions may result. Because the party platform and the convention are often used as vehicles for promoting party unification, unsuccessful candidates or issue activists within the party may continue to challenge the nomination in hopes of influencing the party's platform or being invited to address the convention (Polsby and Wildavsky 1984; Davis 1983; Shafer 1988). These efforts, regardless of their success, can serve to intensify splits within the party.

The incentive for candidates or issue activists to continue to mount a challenge for the party's standard is especially strong in the Democratic Party. The Democrats' rules mandate the proportional allocation of delegates based on voter preferences and a fairly open selection process for delegates and convention committee members, which tend to foster more prolonged contests, or at least provide certain groups within the party an opportunity to realize voting strength sufficient to have an effect on the platform or other convention decisions (Kirkpatrick 1976; Sullivan, Pressman, and Arterton 1976; Kamarck 1990; Corrado 1991). The Republicans have generally suffered less from long, divisive primary campaigns due to their greater reliance on winner-take-all delegate systems (Wattenberg 1991: 41). Despite this, the party has experienced in-fighting between candidate partisans and different wings of the party, as in the 1976 contest between President Ford and Ronald Reagan or the more recent struggles between party moderates and conservative activists. The second problem the national party organizations must confront is how to conduct a unified campaign effort. How are the activities of the two organizational structures, the party committees (national, state, and local) and the nominee's campaign, to be combined and coordinated? Usually this issue is resolved in a way that fails to promote party integration or organizational development; the nominee's campaign committee simply takes central responsibility for the general election and often seeks either to control the party organizations or to bypass them altogether.

In recent elections, presidential campaigns have increasingly relied on their own personnel to conduct state campaigns and often attempt to co-opt the party structure by shifting key campaign staff members to the party payroll. In 1984, Democratic nominee Walter Mondale even attempted to replace Charles Manatt as party chair during the Democratic National Convention, only to be rebuffed by members of the national committee (Germond and Witcover 1985: 381-85). Such actions diminish the value of party organizations and heighten tensions between party officials and presidential nominees. Indeed, concern among party officials about their role in national elections had become so pronounced by the beginning of the 1992 cycle that one of the Democratic presidential aspirants sought their support by promising that his campaign staff would not be sent into their states to manage the general election if he won the nomination.[3] So, despite their supposed revitalization, national party committees were not considered to be a vital institutional partner in the conduct of presidential campaigns through the 1980s.

Conventional wisdom argues that the party of the president has an advantage in resolving these problems and achieving party unity when the incumbent is seeking reelection. The national party chair is usually the hand-picked choice of the president, and the national committee functions as an extended political arm of the White House. The incumbent president normally lacks a serious challenger from within the party for the nomination. If he is challenged, the nomination is often decided early and his challenger concedes well before the convention, so there is plenty of time to ensure a harmonious convention. This is especially true if a Republican holds the Oval Office, since the Republicans tend to be more cohesive and less likely to divide over issue concerns (Wattenberg 1991).

In accordance with this view, George Bush was considered to have a substantial advantage entering the 1992 election cycle. Besides having the "traditional" edge presumed of an incumbent, Bush enjoyed an extraordinary level of public popularity in 1991 as a result of the end of the Cold War and the victory in the Gulf War. Many political observers thought that Bush could simply sit back and watch the Democrats "tear themselves up" in a primary campaign before undertaking a general election victory tour. Many Democratic Party leaders subscribed to this view as well, and some party officials and putative presidential candidates shifted their focus from 1992 to the possibilities in 1996. One Democrat who did not follow the pack was DNC Chair Ron Brown, who instead of conceding the election or shifting attention to the congressional and state races, took advantage of the Democrats' adverse position to harness the potential of a revitalized DNC and unite the party behind a common goal—recapturing the White House in 1992.

The Prenomination Campaign

The Democrats

When the late Ron Brown was elected chairman of the DNC, he took over a party organization in disarray. The Democrats had lost five of the past six presidential elections, including a humiliating loss in 1988 to George Bush. These elections had highlighted the Republican Party's superiority in resources and campaign planning. The Democrats' relative organizational weakness was made particularly clear in 1988, since the party seemed incapable of halting Michael Dukakis's descent from a double-digit lead in early August to a resounding defeat at the polls in November.

More importantly, the 1988 experience threatened to divide the Democratic coalition, since it rekindled the internal party debate concerning its strategy in national elections. In the aftermath of the election, some party leaders claimed that the key to future electoral success was to maintain the party's traditional liberal ideology and to focus on strategies designed to register and mobilize strongly partisan voting blocs, especially minorities and the poor. Others, especially the leaders of the Democratic Leadership Council (DLC), an institutionalized faction within the party, argued vehemently against this view (see chapter 21 in this volume). Instead, they advocated the need to recast the party's themes and programs to enhance their appeal to moderate, middle-class, and independent voters. Specifically, they advanced the need for a more populist, "progressive economic message" based on the values of upward mobility, individual responsibility, and equal opportunity that would recognize the interests of the middle class and the "moral sentiments of average Americans" rather than the liberal social views of the party elite (Galston and Kamarck 1989: 17).

The 1988 contest thus left the party confused as to its future, and the selection of Brown, a member of the party's liberal wing who had formerly assisted Senator Edward Kennedy and supported the Reverend Jesse Jackson, did not initially allay the concerns of many party members. But Brown quickly articulated a set of objectives that he hoped would bring the party together. First, he wanted to strengthen the DNC as a party institution and transform it "into a tough, aggressive, professional campaign organization" (Brown quoted in Ifill 1992b). Second, he wanted to strengthen relations between the national committee and state party affiliates, and assist in the modernization of state party organizations. Third, he felt the DNC should be devoted to one central goal: winning elections, especially the 1992 presidential election.

Brown's conception of the DNC and its electoral role was modeled on the RNC. As he saw it, the Democrats' problems in presidential races stemmed from an overemphasis on the nomination process; the party and its candidates had focused on party rules and divisive primary contests at the expense of general election planning (Ifill 1992b; Nagourney 1991). This left the party unprepared for the general election, forcing it to "reinvent the wheel" after each national convention. Conversely, the Republicans paid most attention to general election campaigns and applied strategies, which enabled them to provide substantial assistance to their nominee as soon as their convention was over. "There has been a mind set in the Democratic Party that you worry about the general election after you get past the nomination," Brown said. "We have to reverse that thinking" (Nagourney 1991). To achieve this purpose, Brown felt the party had to concentrate on the development of a political organization and a general election strategy that could be delivered to the party's nominee right after the convention. The role of the DNC would be to serve as the "designated agent" for general election planning (Germond and Witcover 1993: 87). While the presidential challengers competed in the primaries, the national committee would engage in such tasks as targeting, polling, issues research, and other activities geared toward the presidential election. Such an approach would highlight the party's objective of winning elections, as well as help secure an influential role for the party organization in the conduct of the general election campaign, since the DNC would be responsible for services that the presidential candidate would value.

As early as 1989, Brown set about the task of reorienting the party to his objectives. He began by strengthening the DNC institutionally. Although the general effect of recent party rules reforms had been to weaken the party's role in presidential campaigns, the DNC adopted two rules changes shortly after the 1988 election that served to enhance its role. The DNC overturned a rule adopted by the 1988 national convention and reinstated the members of the national committee as automatic, unpledged convention delegates (Corrado 1991). The committee also changed the term of the party chair to run from election to election, rather than convention to convention (Longley 1992). This change eliminated the prospect of a potentially disruptive leadership struggle or major turnover in the party hierarchy in the midst of the nominating convention.

Brown's primary institutional concern was the RNC's sizeable advantage in staff and resources (Longley 1992). The DNC embarked on an effort to enhance its organizational capacity, and gave priority to the improvement of its fundraising, media communications, and research staffs. Robert Farmer, who had directed Dukakis's successful 1988 fundraising effort and was chosen to serve as DNC treasurer in 1989, restructured the finance staff and developed programs for soliciting large gifts and soft money that could be used on party-building activities. The party developed new press operations, enhanced its capacity to tape "actualities" that could be transmitted to radio stations with the party's response to an issue of the day, and increased its ability to reach key constituencies through specialized publications such as minority and union newspapers (Barnes 1989b). The research staff, which in 1988 essentially consisted of two individuals largely responsible for speech-writing, was enlarged to a staff of six. This group was responsible for polls and focus groups, targeting analysis, issues research, and opposition candidate research. In addition, the DNC spent more than $30,000 to hire outside companies to investigate various activities of Bush and his family (Isikoff 1992). These investments in personnel and resources significantly improved the DNC's capabilities. Yet they still failed to compare to the RNC. For example, the RNC continued to raise significantly more money than the DNC (Federal Election Commission 1993b), and even after expanding the communications division, the DNC staff was still seven times smaller than its Republican counterpart (Barnes 1989b).

The DNC also focused on its relationship with the state party organizations. During the 1980s, the national committee had begun an effort to modernize some state party organizations by providing them with funds, usually raised in the form of "soft money" not subject to federal contribution limits, to build voter files and develop voter mobilization programs. Brown and Paul Tully, the DNC political director, dramatically expanded such efforts in order to strengthen the party's organizational ties and enhance its political efficacy. The vehicle for fulfilling this purpose was the "coordinated campaign." The DNC encouraged state party organizations to work with both the national committee and individual candidates to construct and finance a central political operation, independent of any particular candidate, that was responsible for building voter files, registering voters, and mobilizing the Democratic vote in each state (Longley 1992). These coordinated campaigns promoted cooperation between party organizations and candidates, and thus spurred working relationships between these actors, as well as the coordination of common organizational tasks. Party leaders felt that such efforts would create a "web of relationships" that would serve as an infrastructure designed to mobilize the vote in a presidential race (Barnes 1989b: 1104). The party would thus be able to offer the nominee a preexisting party organizational network that could be included as part of an overall general election campaign structure.

To demonstrate the potential benefit of coordinated campaign operations, the DNC initiated model programs in special congressional elections in 1989 and went on to establish coordinated programs in over thirty states in 1990 (Barnes 1989b; Longley 1992). Then, in 1991, Tully sold the concept to party officials and fundraisers at a series of party meetings, and convinced them to raise the funds needed for a more extensive coordinated campaign operation in 1992 (Germond and Witcover 1993: 87; Daley 1991a, 1991b; Edsall and Balz 1991).

In addition, the DNC research operation initiated a series of polls, focus groups, and targeting analyses designed to determine a national political strategy that would form the broader context of the DNC's electoral efforts and serve as a game plan for the presidential campaign. The DNC thus generated an approach that "would target key coastal, Midwestern and southern border states; revive efforts to mobilize black voters, who were generally neglected in 1988; and concentrate extraordinary resources in California, which, with 54 electoral votes, is assured of a pivotal role in any close presidential contest" (Edsall and Balz 1991). The party considered California, which would also be the site of two U.S. Senate races and fifty-two House contests, so important to its electoral success that the DNC held a meeting in the state in April of 1992, at which Brown asked party officials to sign an agreement to stage an $8 million effort to enhance research on state and local Republican candidates, voter registration, and get-out-the-vote programs (Ifill 1992b).

Besides these technical considerations, Brown sought to advance a message and issue agenda that could unify various groups within the party and serve as the foundation of a general election theme. Rather than have party officials debate such contentious issues as the death penalty, abortion, and budget policy, Brown attempted to focus the party on domestic concerns, including the economy, health care, and education. For example, even at the height of Bush's post-Gulf War popularity, Brown was arguing that the election would hinge on domestic concerns and that Democrats would benefit from a weak economy (Dillin 1991). He even encouraged the party leadership to draft policy resolutions on health care and trade to heighten attention to these areas (Shogan 1991).

Brown's efforts as chair to set an issue agenda for the party helped to increase the prospects for party unity. By increasing the salience of domestic concerns, the party highlighted Bush's weaknesses and steered away from the social issues and liberal policies that had become a source of tension within the party elite. It also linked the party to issues that appealed to the more populist, moderate Southern Democrats and middle-class voters, two groups the party was hoping to recapture in 1992 (see Edsall and Balz 1991; Germond and Witcover 1993: 87-89). Brown personally assisted in establishing these links by conducting a special meeting of Southern Democrats and by recognizing the DLC as an important group within the party (May and Drape 1991; see chapter 16 in this volume). On one occasion, he even left a DNC conference so that he could attend a simultaneous meeting of the DLC. Interestingly, Brown's actions drew little adverse response from the party's liberal wing; instead, he seemed to benefit from a general sense of pragmatism that permeated the party leadership, who were apparently willing to suppress ideological differences for the sake of winning an election.

One of the unique aspects of Brown's chairmanship was that he adopted a more interventionist approach to the presidential election than previous party leaders. He wanted the party in effect to nominate a candidate early in the primary campaign with minimal infighting so that the Democrats would not start the general election contest at a relative disadvantage. As the field of candidates began to emerge in late 1991, he intervened on a number of occasions to try to determine the field. One of his first actions in this regard was to approach Reverend Jesse Jackson and urge him not to enter the race so that the party could be relieved of the internal tensions it had experienced in the previous two elections (Ayres 1992). He ultimately persuaded Jackson to work with the party and play a leading role in the DNC's minority registration and mobilization programs (Broder 1992; Ifill 1992a; Wickham 1992). He also publicly prodded Governor Mario Cuomo of New York to make a decision concerning a presidential bid by late December so that the spectre of a Cuomo candidacy would not dominate the race and shift attention away from other candidates (Cook 1991).

As the campaign unfolded, Brown exerted his authority in an attempt to prevent bitter partisan bickering. He used his position as party spokesperson to warn presidential contenders to keep the debate civil, and specifically rebuked former California governor Jerry Brown in late March for personal attacks on Bill Clinton (with relatively little effect—Brown continued to contest the nomination through to the convention) (Berke 1992; Ifill 1992b).

Once it was clear that Clinton would be the nominee, Chairman Brown asked party leaders to unite behind him. Brown also ensured that representatives of key Democratic constituencies, such as labor, minority groups, and elected officials, would be included in the deliberations leading up to the convention. This latter goal was achieved in part through the twenty-five party leader and elected official positions (PLEOs) he controlled on each convention committee (platform, rules, and credentials), which are appointed by the party chair in accordance with national party rules.

The Republicans

The Republicans entered the 1992 election cycle with high hopes of another presidential victory. By March of 1991, President Bush's approval rating was soaring as a result of the Gulf War, as was support for his party. According to a Times-Mirror survey conducted at the time, 36 percent of the public identified themselves as Republicans, while only 29 percent identified themselves as Democrats. The survey also found that 50 percent of respondents wanted to see a Republican win in their congressional district, as opposed to 40 percent who hoped for a Democrat (Toner 1991a). The RNC planned to capitalize on this renewed level of support to expand its influence in elections at all levels.

Institutionally, the RNC was well positioned to pursue this goal. Unlike the DNC, the Republicans had been engaged in party-building activities for more than a decade and had well-established candidate recruitment, campaign services, and political outreach operations (Conway 1983). They also had a more secure financial base. In 1990, the RNC raised over $68 million in federal funds alone, as opposed to only $14 million for the Democrats. During the first six months of 1991, the RNC raised over $23 million (in both federal and nonfederal funds), compared to slightly more than $5 million for the DNC. This financial base, when combined with the RNC's larger staff and greater technological capabilities, suggested that the Republicans had achieved a level of organizational development that would allow the party to play a major role in national and state legislative elections.

Despite their success in presidential elections throughout the 1980s, the Republicans had been plagued by continuing Democratic majorities in Congress and most state legislatures. In an effort to reverse this trend, the party emphasized the importance of "down-ticket" programs; that is, party programs designed to assist state and local candidates. These programs, which included voter registration and mobilization efforts similar to those being developed by the Democrats, encompassed a wide array of activities, all of which were designed to increase Republican voting strength at all levels of government.

The RNC therefore devoted significant resources to activities designed to strengthen the party in nonpresidential elections. For example, the RNC considered the redistricting process to be an important vehicle for improving Republican prospects in 1992 and beyond. Party officials, however, could not rely on state legislative committees to protect Republican interests, since the majority of state legislatures were controlled by Democrats. The RNC leaders also considered the opportunity to gain seats through this process to be so important that the task could not be left to some other organ, as the Democrats had done.[4] The party therefore spent substantial amounts, primarily from soft money accounts, on redistricting battles in selected states. In 1991 and 1992, the RNC spent over $2.2 million in at least twelve states on redistricting efforts.[5] In most cases, according to Federal Election Commission (FEC) reports, the RNC sent soft money funds to data analysis and computer graphics firms to research and design various redistricting models. In other instances, the RNC simply transferred funds to ad hoc committees organized for the purpose of coordinating redistricting efforts, such as the Massachusetts Redistricting Task Force. The national party thus provided the funds needed for what has become a highly sophisticated, technologically advanced process. It thereby provided valuable assistance to state parties and state legislative committees, most of which would not have been able to finance such services on their own.

Many political observers expected that the RNC would also exploit the favorable political environment of 1991 to prepare for the presidential race. By getting an early start on fundraising and strategic planning, the party organization could help lock up Bush's renomination and provide him with a substantial head start in the election. The party did begin to plan a strategy along these lines. In late summer and early fall, members of the RNC staff began to develop an aggressive financial plan based on a series of fundraising events designed to raise millions of dollars before the election year. The plan, however, was never implemented because the party had problems securing commitments from the White House for scheduling the president's appearance at these events.[6] This experience exemplified one of the major problems the RNC faced throughout the 1992 cycle—fragmented party leadership.

As the party in control of the White House, the Republicans had to operate within a more complicated organizational context than the Democrats. Because the president is the de facto leader, although not the titular head, of the party, the party in power has to coordinate its activities with the White House (Davis 1992). This situation can benefit the party since it provides the organization with access to the government and the perquisites that accompany the Oval Office. But it also limits the national party organization's efficacy, since policy is largely dictated by the White House and political operations are split between the White House, political staff and the party apparatus, which can produce internal tensions and lack of coordination (Barnes 1989a).

This coordination problem might have been resolved if Lee Atwater, Bush's handpicked chair, had not fallen ill. At the time of Atwater's selection, "it seemed likely that Bush would run his reelection out of the RNC, thus placing the party apparatus at the center of presidential politics to a degree unseen for years" (Ceasar and Busch 1993: 36-37; see also Barnes 1989a). After Atwater's death and the selection of Clayton Yeutter, a former CEO of the Chicago Mercantile Exchange and Secretary of Agriculture in the Bush administration, as his replacement, this plan was never fully put into effect. Instead, party decision making was further complicated as the election year approached, since the creation of Bush's campaign committee established yet another organization with responsibility for electoral and political activities. This organizational disarray continued into the election year. In February 1992, Yeutter, who was criticized for being an ineffective party manager, was replaced with Rich Bond, a former deputy chair of the RNC and Bush's 1988 deputy campaign chair.

Despite these obstacles, the RNC did take some steps during the primaries to assist President Bush. First, the RNC and some state party organizations undertook "a concerted effort" to keep David Duke, the former Ku Klux Klan leader, off Republican primary ballots (Smith 1991). Duke, who declared his candidacy for the Republican nomination on December 4, 1991, hoped to enter twenty-eight primaries, but his ballot access efforts were opposed by Republican officials in a number of states, which often forced his campaign to pursue nonparty-related means to make the ballot, such as court challenges and ballot petitions (Smith 1991; Cook 1991). In some states, such as Georgia and Florida, where the party controlled the ballot access process, the party successfully kept him off (Cook 1992). The chief objective of these efforts was not to deny Duke the nomination (no party leaders thought he had a realistic chance of beating the president), but to ensure that he and his followers would not be represented at the national convention, where they might gain the sort of media exposure that would link Duke to the Republican Party (Smith 1991).

The national party organization was less successful in stifling the insurgent candidacy of former Nixon speechwriter and conservative television commentator Pat Buchanan. Buchanan entered the race in December on a platform designed to mobilize conservative activists. He attacked Bush for violating his tax pledge and advanced a policy agenda based on trade protectionism, immigration restrictions, and foreign policy isolationism. Buchanan's candidacy thus highlighted conservative dissatisfaction with Bush and asked right-wing activists to abandon the president for the sake of ideology. Buchanan's challenge also demonstrated the limits of party influence in nomination contests. Even with the Republicans' renewed institutional strength and party-oriented delegate selection rules, any individual with resources and adequate levels of personal support can enter a bid for the nomination. What is most interesting about the Buchanan challenge is that the national party leadership did not take a hands-off approach toward the race or even present a public image of neutrality. Instead, the party leadership actively sought to discourage this challenge. Buchanan charged that the party hierarchy was treating him like Duke, noting that he was denied access to party contributor lists, denied opposition research on Democrats, and given no assistance in his efforts to qualify for the ballot in certain states (Cook 1991: 3736). Chairman Bond did little to disavow this perception; in fact, in a nationally televised interview, he claimed that one purpose of Buchanan's campaign was to "basically highjack David Duke's message on race and religious tolerance and put a jacket and tie on it and try to clean it up" (Bond quoted in Jehl 1992). This and other statements from Bond calling for Buchanan to end his campaign and support the president led Buchanan, at one point, to call for Bond's resignation and to urge his supporters to withhold contributions to the RNC until Bond was removed (Jehl 1992; Dionne and Devroy 1992; *The Washington Post* 1992). Bond remained, but so did Buchanan, who had no chance at gaining the nomination yet stayed in the race in hopes of having some influence on the party platform and the convention.

The Conventions

Although the national party organizations have the formal responsibility for the presidential nominating conventions, in practice the nominee's campaign operation exercises the greatest influence over these quadrennial spectacles. The party committees oversee site selection and logistics, and are technically responsible for enacting the nomination, passing a party platform, and managing the convention program. But in recent decades these activities have been overshadowed by the convention's role as a public relations vehicle for promoting the presidential ticket, as well as general election themes and strategies (Davis 1983; Shafer 1988; Smith and Nimmo 1991). The orchestration of the convention has therefore become a crucial concern to presidential candidates. Consequently, campaign operatives and political consultants have usurped many of the functions formerly carried out by party officials. The party leadership still participates in these functions, but they are usually relegated to the role of assisting in the implementation of candidate strategies and providing less visible media services for the party's nonpresidential candidates (Herrnson 1994: 59). One of the functions the party leaders do perform is to help broker relations between competing candidates or between the nominees and various groups within the party. This often takes the form of assisting campaign staff in the development of platform concessions or convention speaking opportunities that can be used to satisfy reticent groups or former opponents. A party chair's effectiveness in fulfilling this role, however, depends on a number of factors, especially the chair's internal party political relationships and ability to influence convention decision making. The varying levels of success the party chair may achieve are suggested by the experiences of the party leaders in 1992.

Given his actions prior to the convention, it is not surprising that Ron Brown actively sought to ensure the event's success and produce a united party for the fall campaign. He supported the position that only those who had endorsed Clinton would be allowed to speak, and he served as Clinton's liaison to Reverend Jackson in the period prior to the convention (Ayres 1992). Brown also relied on his personal relationship with Cuomo, perhaps the party's most prominent liberal spokesman, to encourage him to deliver the speech nominating Clinton (Germond and Witcover 1993: 344-45).

Brown further helped to guarantee a unified party and convention by using his authority over the platform committee to ensure that the platform would reflect the positions of the party's nominee, Bill Clinton, which were essentially the positions staked out by the DLC. The DNC chair has the potential to influence platform deliberations because he holds significant authority with respect to the composition of the platform committee. Under party rules, most of the 161 committee members are selected at the state level, but the chair appoints the cochairs of the committee, the vice chairs, and twenty-five party leaders and elected officials who serve as committee members (Maisel 1994). In addition, the DNC head is responsible for selecting the membership of the Drafting Committee, which in practice is the most influential group in the platform-writing process because it develops the draft that becomes the working document for committee deliberations.

In 1992, Brown selected the Drafting Committee with two goals in mind: to assure the domination of Clinton supporters so that the platform would reflect the positions Clinton would run on in the fall, and to include representatives of groups considered critical to a winning coalition in the general election (see chapter 17 in this volume). As L. Sandy Maisel (1994) has noted in his study of the 1992 process:

> Chairman Brown named New Mexico Congressman Bill Richardson as chair of the Drafting Committee early in the process, but he did not name the other members until early June, well after the nomination of Bill Clinton was assured. The appointment of Drafting Committee members reflected Brown's desire that the convention be run in such a way as to enhance the nominee's chances in November. Thus, Brown permitted the Clinton staff to dictate roughly half of the members of the committee. He in turn used the remaining committee slots to guarantee representation by those groups, important to the party, that he did not want to slight (1994: 676).

The document produced by this group met Brown's expectations; it reflected the central themes and issues that formed the basis of Clinton's candidacy. Although the draft did go through some changes when considered by the full committee, this body was clearly controlled by the Clinton forces and few substantive changes were made (Maisel 1994). In the spirit of party unity, the committee, with the Clinton campaign's support, even approved four minority planks put forth by the Tsongas camp for full convention consideration. These planks, however, were not a source of major controversy, and eventually the Tsongas forces withdrew all but one of the proposals.

Since DNC rules mandate the proportional allocation of convention committee positions based on each candidate's vote share in caucuses and primaries, Clinton supporters would have formed the majority even without Brown's assistance. However, Brown's actions minimized the potential for internal party divisions surrounding the platform deliberations and thus guarded against the showcasing of intraparty squabbles at the convention. Brown's effectiveness was also in large part a function of the fact that he was working to assist the nominee, who already had control of the convention. Moreover, he benefited from a general sense of pragmatism that permeated the party by the time of the convention. After enduring so many presidential losses, potential critics of the platform, particularly party liberals, were in no mood to weaken the party by engaging in a divisive platform debate. Although Jerry Brown was still contesting the nomination at the convention, the delegates were not interested in a fight, and the Democrats enjoyed their most unified convention of the postreform era.

In sharp contrast to the Democrats, the Republicans faced serious internal party divisions in advance of their convention. Buchanan's challenge had served to heighten conservatives' dissatisfaction with Bush's economic policy, and the Christian Right had been active throughout the primaries to guarantee that they would have a voice in convention proceedings (Oldfield 1992). These activists succeeded in gaining representation on convention committees in part because RNC rules are less candidate-oriented than the Democratic guidelines. Although the RNC chair is responsible for selecting the chair and cochairs of the platform committee (which is technically called the Committee on Resolutions), the 107 members of the committee are appointed by state party organizations in a manner largely determined by the individual states. Moreover, while Bond appointed the chair and cochairs, these selections were "in fact dictated by the president's reelection committee" (Maisel 1994: 681).

The selection of Senator Don Nickles of Oklahoma to chair the Republican platform deliberations represented an effort by the Bush-Quayle committee to provide the conservative wing of the party with a candidate with whom it could be comfortable. This selection also reflected the GOP's broader convention strategy. In June, campaign officials developed a plan designed to use the convention as a vehicle for reassuring the conservative wing of the party about Bush's candidacy in order to form a conservative coalition they felt would be the key to victory in a prospective three-way presidential race with Clinton and Perot (Wines 1992; Duffy and Goodgame 1992: 272). To mobilize this constituency, Bush strategists returned to the theme of "cultural warfare" that had worked well in previous elections

(Dionne 1991; Baer et al. 1992). By emphasizing "traditional family values," the Republicans hoped to assuage the right wing, especially Buchanan and his supporters (Goldman and Matthews 1992: 68-69), and to distinguish Bush from Clinton, while at the same time elevating the concerns of the plurality of the electorate who did not trust Clinton and had an unfavorable view of his personal life (Kelly 1992).

This focus on family values fueled a debate within the party over the campaign's message. Some party leaders, including Buchanan, Vice President Quayle, and officials of Christian Right organizations, accepted this approach, arguing that the party should position the Democrats as out of touch with average Americans due to their advocacy of such issues as abortion and gay rights. Others, including Representative Vin Weber of Minnesota, argued that "values issues" had to be linked to an economic agenda (Baer et al. 1992). Bush and the RNC leadership appeared uncertain about the direction the campaign should take. Thus, in the weeks leading up to the convention, the party leadership failed to set a clear course. During this period the Republicans also displayed other signs of dissension, including forcing Bush to reject the advice of some party leaders "to drop Quayle from the ticket, to fire his economic team as a sign that he would now address the economy, and even to step aside and let another candidate carry the Republican banner" (Quirk and Dalager 1993: 69; see also Goldman and Mathews 1992: 65-69).

The issues debate might not have been so prominent if the Republican platform committee had been as submissive to the wishes of the party chair and nominee as their Democratic counterparts. But the Republicans were not so fortunate. Since it became clear early on that Bush would win the party's nomination, issue activists devoted their attention to being selected as delegates and convention committee members. This was especially true of members of the Christian Coalition, who wanted a party platform that reflected their preferences on such core issues as abortion, gay rights, and religion. As a result, the platform committee included a significant number of conservative activists. In fact, according to one estimate, 20 of the 107 members selected at the state level were members of the Christian Coalition (Oldfield 1992). The rules and dynamics of the Republican nomination process thus allowed the sorts of "issues amateurs" who are normally associated with the Democratic party, to exert an influence on the Republican proceedings. This phenomenon was also observed by Maisel, who concluded that "in an ironic twist, issue activists whose prime concern was not with winning the election but rather for specific policies came to play a key role in a Republican convention because of lack of candidate competition, the exact opposite circumstance under which issue purists gained prominence in the Democratic party" (1994: 682).

Accordingly, the party platform became a focal point of party and media attention in the weeks prior to the convention. Conservatives upset with Bush's economic policy, led by Weber and Congressman Robert Walker of

Pennsylvania, pushed for a return to Reagan-era economic principles and, at one point, adopted proposed platform language stating that Bush had made a mistake in agreeing to the 1990 budget compromise, which included a major tax increase. Christian Right activists, hoping to protect the antiabortion language of past platforms, defeated a weak effort to change the party's position and went on to add provisions on a host of preferred policies, including a paragraph lauding the two-parent family, new passages on home schooling and pornography, and a specific reference to the country's "Judeo-Christian tradition." The committee also adopted a number of antigay and lesbian provisions, apparently with little input from the Bush campaign (Oldfield 1992: 27-28). In the end, the party produced a document the president could stand by, but not before Bush campaign officials had entered into some relatively public arm-twisting, including the need for Charles Black, a Bush consultant, to convince an economic subcommittee to reconvene and eliminate the reference to Bush's tax "mistake" (Maisel 1994: 689).

Bond also did his part to unite the conservative coalition at this time. He launched a bitter attack against Hillary Clinton in a speech before the RNC, and joined Quayle in an attack on the news media (Germond and Witcover 1993: 408). He thus assisted in the overall implementation of the Republican "cultural warfare" strategy. Ultimately, the Republican right was appeased by the platform that emerged, as well as by the attention given to the values issues by the speakers, primarily conservatives, selected to address the convention. But this party cohesion was achieved at a significant cost: the Republican convention left a distinct impression on the public of a party that had gone too far to the right. According to polls taken after the event, a majority of the electorate felt that the president had spent more time attacking the Democrats than explaining what he would do; they disapproved of the emphasis placed on homosexual issues; and 76 percent felt that the criticism of Hillary Clinton had gone too far (Frankovic 1993). Or, as Mary Matalin, a former RNC official and top Bush campaign adviser, frankly observed, "We were in a deep, deep hole after the convention" (Wines 1992).

The General Election

Both national party committees played a significant role in the general election campaign. Although the presidential campaigns were managed by the respective candidate organizations, and the parties' activities were limited by the provisions of federal campaign finance law, the RNC and DNC still mounted extensive political operations designed to assist their presidential nominees, as well as other federal and nonfederal candidates running under their party's banner. Both party organizations provided their candidates with the kinds of campaign services and assistance that had become commonplace in the 1980s. For example, they established communications outreach programs for distributing daily messages to media outlets and partisan opinion leaders; they made their media facilities available to candidates to develop television advertisements and videotaped messages; they made coordinated expenditures on behalf of their federal candidates; and they made direct campaign contributions to selected federal and nonfederal candidates. In addition, they conducted a range of programs designed to improve voter turnout and party support.

Major party candidates who accept public funding for their general election campaigns are prohibited from accepting private contributions from other sources, including political parties. Federal law does, however, allow party committees to raise and spend funds on party building and other generic activities, such as voter registration drives and mobilization programs, which are designed to benefit all party candidates and thus indirectly benefit the presidential nominee. Because these programs, which are known as "joint activities," help both federal and nonfederal candidates, they may be financed through a combination of federally limited and nonlimited funding. The latter type of funding is popularly known as "soft money," since it is not subject to the more stringent limits of federal law. In 1992, both parties relied heavily on soft money to influence the outcome of the elections.

While the RNC has been conducting extensive soft money efforts for some time, the DNC has usually been hampered by its failure to match Republican fundraising efforts. In 1992, however, the Democrats effectively competed with the Republicans due to the fundraising generated by the favorable political circumstances following their national convention. Relying on a fundraising effort managed by Rahm Emmanuel, who had served as Clinton's chief fundraiser during the prenomination campaign, the Democrats capitalized on Clinton's popularity and on promising electoral prospects to raise about $20.1 million in nonfederal funds from July 1 to election day, as compared to an estimated $12.8 million for the Republicans. This success allowed the Democrats to narrow the resource gap that had developed over the first eighteen months of the election cycle, during which the Republicans had surpassed the Democrats by a margin of about $11 million.[7]

The DNC's financial success in the months after the convention was a crucial factor in the 1992 race because it allowed the party to implement the electoral strategy it had been developing since 1988. The cornerstone of this strategy was the coordinated campaign operation, which served as the main vehicle for registering and mobilizing Democratic voters. The DNC targeting plan and coordinated campaign program were implemented in almost every state, with heavy concentration on states the DNC political operation had identified as essential to a presidential victory. The program encouraged the state party organization, with DNC support, to serve as a coordinating agent for various federal and state and local campaigns, and to carry out a joint program of voter identification and turnout on behalf of all participating Democratic candidates. The party and campaign organizations worked together to conduct extensive phone bank and canvassing operations to identify and mobilize the Democratic vote, usually in shared headquarters, relying on computerized voter lists and targeting information developed by the party.

To finance these efforts, the DNC transferred approximately $9.5 million in soft money funds to forty-seven states, much of which was used to develop voter files, conduct registration drives, and cover overhead expenses. The DNC also spent at least $1.9 million on telephone bank equipment that was sent to thirty-four state parties. The Democrats thus conducted an extensive party-based voter identification effort similar to those carried out by the RNC in past elections. The RNC also sponsored registration and mobilization efforts in 1992, as it continued to provide the services that have become almost a standard part of the party's operations in national election campaigns. The RNC transferred approximately $5.4 million in soft money funds to forty-two states, and provided at least twenty-five state party organizations with telephone bank equipment, at a cost of over $1.5 million.

The RNC and DNC also spent significant sums from their soft money accounts to assist party campaign organizations and candidates. The RNC emphasized direct contributions to party committees and candidates. The party transferred funds to state legislative campaign committees, as well as state party committees, in at least fifteen states. The RNC also contributed a total of $1.2 million in nonfederal funds to candidates seeking office at the state level, including about $800,000 to candidates in twenty-three states during the general election period. These efforts were conducted as part of the RNC's "down-ticket" programs to help build Republican support in state legislatures and capitols around the country, and thus reverse the pattern of recent elections in which the party wins the presidential race but fails to capture a majority of the nation's statehouses.

The Democrats spent none of their soft money during the 1992 general election on direct contributions to candidates. The contributions that were reported were actually "in-kind" contributions of polling information. The DNC hired the firm of Stanley Greenberg, Clinton's campaign pollster, and five other Washington-based polling organizations to conduct surveys in thirty-one states. In twenty-seven of these states, all of which were targeted by the coordinated campaign operation, polls were conducted at least two or three times during the course of the campaign. The results were shared with the state party committees, the presidential campaign, and other candidates in an effort to help them target their appeals and voter canvassing efforts. Soft money thus allowed the Democrats to provide a valuable resource, statewide polling data, to state parties and candidates.

The RNC also did some polling, although apparently on a more modest scale. The Republicans reported spending some $220,000 on polls and surveys in thirty-nine states that were shared with state parties and candidates. This DNC and RNC activity benefited affiliated party committees and candidates in a number of ways. It provided high-quality survey research to a substantial number of committees and candidates. Such information helps promote effective communication with voters and enhances the ability to target resources more efficiently. In addition, in most cases, this service facilitated access to information that the recipient committee might not have been able to afford on its own, or at least it helped reduce the cost incurred by the recipient for polling services, since it helped defray the amount the candidate had to spend on polling services. This is especially true with respect to the presidential campaign, in that the party polling would allow the campaign to assess its support in targeted states without having to conduct polls of its own on a regular basis in each state.

The national party organizations also invested heavily in generic advertising, especially television advertising, that encouraged the electorate to "Vote Democratic" or "Vote Republican." Both DNC and RNC used a combination of federal and nonfederal monies to pay for the production and broadcast of ads. Overall, the Democrats spent about $14.2 million on advertising and the Republicans spent about $10 million (Frisby 1992). The Republicans basically followed the strategy employed in the past few elections, in which they spent substantial amounts of soft money on generic advertising. The scope of the DNC's efforts, however, vastly exceeded those of the past. While the party did broadcast some ads in 1988, the total amount spent was only about $1 million (Labaton 1992). The resources available to the party in 1992 allowed it to dramatically increase this aspect of its electoral program.

Generic advertising allows the national committees to participate meaningfully in elections and build support for party candidates at all levels. This form of communication can be especially beneficial to the party's presidential ticket, particularly when the ads are designed to reinforce the nominee's message, as they were in 1992. The Democrats, for example, used soft money to finance ads that did not mention Bill Clinton directly (to do so would violate federal contribution laws) but did emphasize the economic message that was the foundation of Clinton's campaign. These ads also helped the presidential campaign to decide where to allocate its resources. During the last week of the campaign, for instance, the Clinton campaign was running tight on money and thus decided to buy a half-hour of national television time as opposed to additional broadcast time in the highly competitive state of Texas. The Democrats, however, did not leave Texas unattended; instead, the DNC broadcast generic ads in the state to spread the party's message. The Republicans adopted a similar strategy. The Bush campaign, facing substantial resource demands because the president was trailing Clinton in a majority of the states, relied on party advertising to strengthen its support in traditional Republican strongholds and in crucial battleground states like Texas and Florida (Frisby 1992).

Conclusion

The 1992 presidential election highlights the organizational revitalization of the RNC and DNC that has been widely noted in recent years. Although the presidential selection process remains a largely candidate-centered system in which the candidate's campaign committees play the leading role, both parties were active participants at each stage of the process. Most importantly, each national party organization provided its presidential ticket with substantial electoral assistance in the general election through party spending designed to benefit the ticket indirectly, either by building support for the party or by identifying and mobilizing partisan·supporters.

The major change from past elections is that the Democrats were better prepared to compete with the Republicans as a result of the particular dynamics of the 1992 contest. As Paul Herrnson and David Menefee-Libey (1990) have noted, the organizational development of party organizations is associated with two conditions: a perceived crisis that opens a window of opportunity for change and a political entrepreneur who takes advantage of this opportunity. Both of these conditions existed for the Democrats in 1992. When Ron Brown assumed the leadership of the DNC, the Democrats were demoralized, and emerging factions threatened to divide the party. Brown seized the opportunity created by the Democrats' string of defeats in national elections to establish clear electoral goals for the party. By focusing attention on common electoral goals rather than potentially divisive ideological concerns, Brown was able to minimize intraparty tensions and restructure the national party organization to fulfill his objectives. He then pursued a course of action designed to promote party unity and ensure a meaningful party role in the conduct of the 1992 presidential campaign.

Interestingly, Brown was able to achieve his objectives in part by relying on the limited authority the DNC chair is granted under party rules. Although the rules are generally considered to have undermined the role of the party leadership in the presidential selection process, Brown used his position to broker relations between members of the DNC and the DLC, and to try to moderate the tone of the nomination contest. He also used his authority to influence the platform and convention proceedings in a way that helped unify the party behind Clinton's candidacy. His success, however, was in large part due to the personal relations he enjoyed with key party members such as Cuomo and Jackson, his willingness to implement the Clinton strategy, and the lack of major opposition from issues activists within the party.

In contrast, the Republicans enjoyed few of the conditions that led to the Democrats' success. After the death of Lee Atwater, the party organization lacked strong leadership. In order to strengthen the organization, the White House supported the appointment of a new chair during the election year. The new leader, Rich Bond, was confronted by divisions among party moderates and conservatives over economic policy and social issues, which rose to the forefront as a result of the nomination bid by Pat Buchanan and the heightened attention to party policy that developed in the absence of a serious challenge to President Bush. In addition, the party rules allowed issues activists to gain access to the platform-writing process, which forced an internal party debate that culminated in a convention that failed to attract wide support among the electorate.

Whether the party organizations will continue to play a prominent role in future presidential elections remains to be seen. The 1992 experience produced no major change in the factors that encourage candidate-centered elections. Rather it was shaped more by the particular circumstances that accompanied the election than by any institutional changes in the national party organizations. The role of the party organizations in the future, as in the past, is likely to depend on the entrepreneurship of the party leaders, the opportunities for influence available to the party committees, and the particular dynamics of the race. It will also depend on any actions the Congress may take with respect to campaign finance reform, since reform may alter the provisions for soft money financing that were crucial to the financing of party electoral activity in 1992. Whatever the future holds, the 1992 experience clearly shows that national party organizations can play an important role in presidential elections and can have a substantial influence on electoral outcomes.

Notes

1. See Cotter and Bibby 1980; Conway 1983; Schlesinger 1985; Kayden and Mahe 1985; Huckshorn, Gibson, Cotter, and Bibby 1986; Herrnson 1988; Sabato 1988, Frantzich 1989.

2. The author thanks Erik Belenky for his assistance with the research for this chapter and acknowledges the support of the Colby College Social Science Grants Committee.

3. After Michael Dukakis's 1988 defeat in the presidential election, many DNC members expressed dissatisfaction with the campaign staff members from the Northeast who had been sent to manage their states in the general election. Senator Tom Harkin of Iowa, one of the candidates for the 1992 Democratic presidential nomination, thus sought to appeal to these party leaders in September 1991 when he declared at a meeting of the DNC: "If I'm your nominee, you will not see hordes of young Iowans coming into your state to tell you how to run your state" (Toner 1991c).

4. Because of their limited fundraising success from 1989 to 1991, the DNC could not commit sizeable sums to redistricting battles. Most of the funding on the Democratic side was generated through an independent group, Impact 2000, which was established by major Democratic fundraisers and labor groups to finance redistricting efforts.

5. These states included Illinois, Virginia, California, Massachusetts, New Mexico, Maryland, New Hampshire, Oregon, Ohio, Georgia, North Carolina, and Arkansas. Figures are based on amounts disclosed in reports filed at the Federal Election Commission.

6. Remarks delivered by Margaret Alexander at the Citizens' Research Foundation Presidential Finance Officers conference, Washington, D.C., 1992.

7. Unless otherwise noted, the figures reported here and throughout the rest of this section are based on the FEC disclosure reports for nonfederal accounts filed by the DNC and RNC for the 1991–92 election cycle.

6

Party Strategy and Campaign Activities in the 1992 Congressional Elections

Paul S. Herrnson

There was an old woman who lived in a shoe,
She had so many children she didn't know what to do,
She gave them some broth without any bread;
She whipped them all soundly and put them to bed.
—from *The Annotated Mother Goose*
William S. Baring-Gould and Ceil Baring-Gould, eds.

The 1992 congressional elections posed many challenges and opportunities for political parties. The election cycle was characterized by a record number of congressional retirements, widespread public dissatisfaction with government, and an emphasis on "change" among politicians. Over a decade of organizational modernization enabled national party committees to amass the resources needed to play a significant role in these elections. However, allocating these resources would not be an easy task. Both parties fielded unusually large numbers of highly qualified challengers and open-seat candidates, and many House and Senate incumbents were extremely anxious about their prospects for reelection. The 1992 congressional elections presented party decision makers with an acute case of a familiar ailment. Like the old woman who lived in the shoe, the parties had a severe shortage of resources—in this case campaign money and services—and an abundance of deserving beneficiaries clamoring for them.

This chapter analyzes the strategies and activities of party organizations in the 1992 elections. Interviews with the staffs of the Democratic and Republican national, congressional, and senatorial campaign committees and the managers of over a dozen PACs provide insights into how the political parties selected candidates for support and into the kinds of assistance they distributed. Survey data collected from 362 major party congressional candidates and campaign managers, and personal interviews with a smaller group of campaigners, give insights into their perspectives on party campaign activities.[1] Campaign finance data furnished by the Federal Election Commission (FEC) are used to examine the parties' spending patterns.

The 1992 Elections

Some of elements of the political climate that surrounded the 1992 congressional elections were typical of recent election cycles. An incumbent president was gearing up for reelection, the nation was suffering from a weak economy, and Americans were taking pride in their country's most recent display of military force in the Middle East. Following the completion of the census and the reapportionment of House seats, state governments began redrawing congressional districts. George Bush was enjoying record levels of presidential popularity during the Gulf War; only after the war did his levels of support plummet (Frankovic 1993).

Civil rights continued to occupy a place on the political agenda, in both some familiar and some new forms. Racial and gender discrimination and violence were relevant issues in many campaigns due to the highly publicized studies of the unequal salaries and advancement prospects for women and blacks, the beating of black motorist Rodney King by four white police officers, and Anita Hill's testimony against Supreme Court nominee Clarence Thomas. Gay rights found its place on the agenda after the military's long-standing policy against homosexuals serving in the military became a salient issue. The Supreme Court's ruling in *Thornburg v. Gingles*, which declared that states could not draw election districts in ways that diluted minority representation, had a major impact on several House elections.

Perennial issues like health care and education also occupied a space on the political agenda. Moreover, as has been the case in most recent elections, voter dissatisfaction with the political establishment in Washington was high. The savings and loan crisis, government "gridlock," and congressional scandal left many voters frustrated and angry with their elected officials. Much of this hostility was directed toward Congress, and many incumbents were preparing to respond using a strategy that had served them well in the past—running for reelection to Congress by campaigning against the institution itself (Fenno 1975). Nevertheless, all of these issues took a back seat to the economy, which was on almost everyone's mind.

Although no one of the events or conditions that preceded the 1992 election was particularly unusual, as a collectivity these factors created some unique possibilities for congressional candidates, parties, PACs, and other politically active groups. Redistricting, scandal, declining job satisfaction, and a myriad of personal considerations led an unprecedented sixty-six House members to retire.[2] An additional nineteen members of the House lost their primary election races and another two died before the general election.[3] The result was record numbers of new, redrawn, and open House seats. The retirement of eight senators and the defeat of another, Senator Alan Dixon in the Illinois Democratic primary, also insured that many seats in the upper chamber would be competitive.[4]

The sheer number of open-seat contests—ninety-one for the House and nine for the Senate—gave politicians who had been waiting for the chance to run for Congress on a level playing the opportunity to do so. It also gave parties and interest groups the opportunity to try to replace some of their old foes in Congress with more sympathetic members. The political conditions that preceded the election ensured the appearance of many new faces in the 103d Congress.

The political climate affected virtually every aspect of the 1992 congressional elections. It affected who ran for office, the strategies they used, the resources at their disposal, and the decisions made by the over 104.4 million citizens who voted on election day (Federal Election Commission 1992). It also influenced the funding decisions of political parties, PACs, and wealthy campaign contributors. The climate created intense competition among congressional candidates both in their election districts and in the nation's capital. Candidates had to compete with opponents in their election districts for votes and with other congressional candidates, including their fellow partisans in Washington, D.C., for campaign resources.

Political Parties and Contemporary Congressional Elections

The roles that political parties play in congressional campaigns have been shaped by the same forces that fostered the development of the modern, candidate-centered election system (Sorauf 1980; Herrnson 1988). This system emphasizes campaign activities requiring technical expertise and in-depth research, which many candidates lack. Incumbents usually turn to political consultants, PACs, and interest groups for campaign assistance. Nonincumbents, particularly House challengers, have more difficulty assembling the money and expertise needed to wage a competitive bid for Congress.

Party committees in the nation's capital have developed into major repositories of campaign money, services, and political advice. The Democratic and Republican national committees focus most of their efforts on presidential elections, giving some attention to gubernatorial, statehouse, and a small number of mayoral elections. They also undertake considerable efforts to strengthen state and local party organizations. The national committees' involvement in House and Senate elections, however, is relatively limited. It usually involves conducting a few candidate training seminars, furnishing candidates with party manifestoes and "talking points," and cooperating with their congressional, senatorial, state, and local campaign committees in a coordinated effort to mobilize voters. Congressional candidates in search of money, election services, or assistance in running their campaigns rarely turn to their national committee for help.

The parties' congressional and senatorial campaign committees, sometimes referred to as the "hill committees,"[5] on the other hand, have developed into major centers of support for House and Senate candidates. The congressional campaign committees focus the vast majority of their efforts on House races, and the two senatorial campaign committees focus on Senate contests, though party committees at all levels cooperate with one another in a variety of areas. In 1992, the Democratic Congressional Campaign Committee (DCCC) amassed a budget in excess $12.8 million, while its rival, the National Republican Congressional Committee (NRCC) raised just under $34.4 million. The two senatorial committees—the Democratic Senatorial Campaign Committee (DSCC) and the National Republican Senatorial Committee (NRSC)—raised $25.4 million and $72.3 million, respectively.[6]

In addition to their members, who are selected by their colleagues in the House or Senate, the hill committees employ highly skilled political professionals. The DCCC and DSCC employed sixty-four and thirty-five full-time staff respectively, and their Republican counterparts had eighty-nine and 130 full-time employees during the 1992 election cycle. For the most part, the members function like boards of directors, setting priorities and giving staff the support they need to raise money and recruit candidates. The staffs oversee the committees' daily operations, are very influential in formulating their campaign strategies, and play a major role in implementing those strategies, particularly in selecting candidates for campaign assistance and providing it to them. The campaign committee staffs are divided along functional lines; different divisions are responsible for administration, fundraising, research, communications, and campaign activities. In 1992, both the DCCC and the NRCC added redistricting divisions to focus on the decennial redrawing of House districts. The NRCC also added an in-house polling operation to its political division.

Party Strategy, Decision Making, and Targeting

The hill committees have a common overriding goal of maximizing the number of seats their party holds in Congress (Jacobson 1985–86). They become heavily involved in some elections, giving selected candidates large campaign contributions and making substantial campaign expenditures on their behalf. Many of these candidates also receive assistance with aspects of campaigning requiring technical expertise, in-depth research, or connections with PACs, campaign consultants, and other groups that possess some of the resources needed to conduct a congressional campaign. Finally, the campaign committees participate along with other party committees in generic, party-focused election activities that are designed to help the entire ticket get elected.

The campaign committees focus most of their efforts on competitive House and Senate contests, but protecting incumbents is also a major priority. Pressures from nervous incumbents can skew the distribution of committee resources away from competitive challenger and open-seat candidates and toward members of Congress who hold relatively safe seats. The funds available to a committee and the aspirations of its chair and other members can also affect the way it distributes its resources (Herrnson 1989).

National political and economic conditions are additional factors that influence which candidates get campaign resources. When the president is popular and the economy is strong, the campaign committees of the president's party usually invest more resources in competitive challenger and open-seat races. Conversely, the out-party committees use more of their resources to support incumbents. When national conditions do not favor the president's party, the patterns are reversed: the in-party committees take a "protectionist" posture that favors incumbents, and the out-party committees go on the offensive, using more of their resources to help nonincumbents (Jacobson and Kernell 1983). The unpredictable nature of national political conditions, economic trends, and events that take place in states and congressional districts means that committee decision making and targeting are necessarily imperfect. As a result, some safe incumbents and uncompetitive nonincumbents inevitably receive committee assistance, while a number of competitive nonincumbents get little or no help.

The conditions surrounding the 1992 election cycle made strategic decision making and targeting very difficult, especially for the two House campaign committees.[7] Redistricting, a process that is always fraught with ambiguities, was complicated by the Supreme Court ruling in *Thornburg v. Gingles*. It caused many states to run behind schedule in redrawing the boundaries of their congressional districts, resulted in many redistricting plans being challenged in court, and delayed primary elections in several states.

Factors besides the huge number of redrawn or newly created seats complicated the committees' tasks. President Bush's popularity seesawed up and down, making it difficult for the committees to decide whether to pursue offensive or defensive strategies. The House banking and post office scandals, and the hostility that voters directed toward Congress, had a similar effect. Bounced checks, and other unrelated ethical lapses, resulted in a large group of incumbents, like Mary Rose Oakar (D-OH), Bill Goodling (R-PA), and Nick Mavroules (D-MA), finding themselves in jeopardy and gave numerous challengers an unexpected boost. The late retirements of some House members and the primary defeats of others further complicated the committees' efforts.

As a result of the uncertainty surrounding the 1992 elections, the NRCC and DCCC delayed drawing up their "watch" lists of "opportunity" (or competitive) races and had difficulty paring their lists down to size. The lists that the committees initially compiled were extensive. Each included roughly three hundred elections, more than three times the number listed in a normal election cycle. These lists were revised and shortened over the course of the election cycle, but going into the last week of the election both committees listed over 150 races as top priorities—more than three times the number they had included in the 1990 election.

Individual candidates are selected for placement on the committees' watch lists on the basis of several criteria. The competitiveness of the district and incumbency are the first two considerations. Candidates running in districts that were decided by close margins in the last election or competing in open seats are likely to be placed on a committee's watch list and targeted for campaign assistance. In 1992, House members running in incumbent vs. incumbent contests or who were in jeopardy for other reasons were also considered top priorities.

The strength of the candidate and the quality of his or her campaign organization are considerations for nonincumbents. Those who have had political experience, are well known, or who have celebrity status are also likely to be targeted. Challengers and open-seat contestants who have assembled professional campaign organizations are prime candidates for party support as well (Herrnson 1989). A professional campaign organization assures the committee that the resources they contribute will be properly utilized, especially if campaign committee officials are familiar with the consultants who have been hired.

A variety of idiosyncratic factors may also come into play when the committees select the candidates who will initially be given the most support. An incumbent who is accused of committing an ethical transgression, is perceived to be out of touch with people in the district, or is in trouble for some other reason is a likely candidate for extra committee help. These difficulties also often provoke a response by the other party's campaign committee, resulting in the incumbent's opponent also benefiting from extra party money and campaign services.

Although 1992 was proclaimed to be the "Year of the Woman," and party leaders worked aggressively to recruit women to run for Congress, campaign committee staff maintain that gender was not a criteria that was used to decide who would be given campaign assistance (Biersack and Herrnson 1994). Women were targeted only to the degree that their races were expected to be competitive.

Finally, ideology is not a stated criterion for targeting candidates. Campaign committee staffs explain that ideology is irrelevant in all their decisions, except to the degree that it can influence a particular candidate's competitiveness. An extreme right-wing Republican challenger running in very liberal Democratic district, for example, would be evaluated as uncompetitive not because of the candidate's political leanings, but because of being out of step with the district. As Deborah Flavin, director of political education at the NRCC, explains:

At the NRCC our only ideology is that you have a "big R" by your name. There is no litmus test on any issue. We ask candidates how they feel on "issue X" and "issue Y". Then, we help them articulate what they feel. We are here to help Republicans win.

The staffs of the Democratic committees voice similar sentiments.

The committees' lists of competitive elections are continuously revised throughout the election cycle. Campaign committee field coordinators who are assigned to monitor congressional races within designated regions advise their colleagues in Washington, D.C., about the latest developments in individual elections. As a result, some candidates drop in priority and are cut off from party help, while others gain more committee attention and support. The tremendous uncertainty surrounding the 1992 elections was expected to make targeting very difficult for party committees. Early in the election cycle both House campaign committees decided to distribute their resources broadly. As Tom Cole, executive director of the NRCC, stated in December 1991, "We are going hunting with a shotgun instead of a rifle this year." DCCC decision makers confirmed that they, too, would employ the "shotgun" approach.

Campaign Spending

Party spending in congressional elections is severely restricted by the limitations imposed by the Federal Election Campaign Act (FECA). National, congressional, and state party campaign committees can each give $5,000 per primary, runoff, and general election to a House candidate.[8] The parties' national and senatorial campaign committees can give a combined total of $17,500 to a Senate candidate. State committees can contribute an additional $5,000 to Senate candidates.

Parties can also spend larger sums of money on behalf of individual candidates. This spending, often referred to as "coordinated expenditures" because they can be made in direct coordination with a candidate's campaign, typically consists of campaign services that a hill committee or some other party organization gives to an individual candidate or purchases from a political consultant on the candidate's behalf. Coordinated expenditures frequently take the form of polls, radio advertisements, television commercials, fundraising events, direct-mail solicitations, or issue research. They differ from campaign contributions in that the party retains some control over them, giving it the ability to influence some aspects of how the campaign is run. Originally set at $10,000 each for a state and national committee, the limits for coordinated expenditures on behalf of House candidates are adjusted for inflation and reached $27,620 per committee in 1992.[9] The limits for coordinated expenditures in Senate elections vary by the size of a state's population and are also indexed to inflation. They ranged from $55,240 per committee in the smallest states to $1,227,322 in California. Although state and national party committees are each authorized to spend the same amount in coordinated expenditures, the committees often create "agency agreements" that allow the parties' congressional or senatorial campaign committee to take over a state party's share of the expenditure in situations when a state party committee does not have the funds to make them (Herrnson 1988, 1995).

Coordinated expenditures are the vehicle of choice for most party activity in congressional elections. Their higher limits, possibility for creating agency agreements, and the direct role they afford party committees in individual candidates' campaigns make coordinated expenditures an attractive avenue for party involvement. Not surprisingly, the campaign committees spend greater portions of their money on coordinated expenditures than on contributions (see table 6.1). Another reason for the attractiveness of coordinated expenditures is that they enable the parties to take advantage of economies of scale when purchasing and distributing campaign services. Because the parties purchase the services of political consultants in large quantities, they pay below-market rates, which enables them to provide candidates with services whose true market value exceed the FECA's coordinated expenditure limits.[10]

Table 6.1 National Party Spending in the 1992 Congressional Elections*

| | House | | Senate | |
	Contributions	Coordinated Expenditures	Contributions	Coordinated Expenditures
Democratic				
DNC	$0	$913,935	$0	$195,351
DCCC	818,846	4,132,292	18,682	2,606
DSCC	10,000	2,600	618,450	11,233,120
State and local	366,477	750,451	72,699	487,415
Total	$1,195,323	$5,799,278	$709,831	$11,918,492
Republican				
RNC	$778,503	$832,347	$9,000	$0
NRCC	686,916	5,166,647	3,500	0
NRSC	78,500	0 ,	614,814	16,485,039
State and local	626,057	86,8908	127,960	3,617,303
Total	$2,169,976	$6,867,902	$755,274	$20,102,342

*Figures include contributions and coordinated expenditures by the parties' national, congressional, and senatorial campaign committees for all major party candidates in two-party contests, except incumbent vs. incumbent House elections. They do not include soft money expenditures.
Source: Federal Election Commission.

Most party spending in congressional elections is done by the four hill committees. In 1992, the NRCC spent over $5.85 million in the campaigns of Republican House candidates, roughly $900,000 more than the DCCC. The RNC and NRSC spent an additional $1.7 million. Total Republican spending in House races reached $9.04 million, over $2 million more than that spent by the Democrats. Although the Democrats were out spent by their Republican counterparts, the spending gap between the two parties has closed considerably over the last six election cycles.[11] This is due both to a falloff in Republican receipts and improved Democratic fundraising.[12]

Democratic and Republican state and local party committees spent $1.1 million and $1.5 million, respectively, in the 1992 House elections. This accounts for only 16 percent of all party spending made directly in House campaigns. Although House campaigns are waged locally, national parties play a bigger financial role in them than do state and local parties.

National parties also out spent state and local parties in Senate elections. The NRSC was the more active of the senatorial campaign committees, out spending its rival by $6.3 million in 1992. The Republican committee also transferred almost $2 million more to state party committees than did the DSCC.[13] The two senatorial committees accounted for the lion's share of party spending in Senate elections.

As expected, the national parties distributed most of their campaign money to candidates in close elections (see table 6.2).[14] Turning first to the House, the Republicans' allocation patterns indicate that they pursued a fairly aggressive, offensive strategy. The NRCC, and other Washington-based Republican committees, directed 75 percent of their contributions and coordinated expenditures to challengers and open-seat candidates. The remaining money was committed to incumbents.

GOP money was fairly well targeted. Hopeful challengers (whose elections were decided by margins of 20 percent or less) and open-seat prospects (whose elections were decided by the same margin) got 34 percent and 26 percent of the party's funds. Incumbents in jeopardy (whose elections were decided by 20 percent or less of the vote) got 22 percent. The party gave only 5 percent of its funds to "shoo-ins" (incumbents whose contests were decided by margins greater than 20 percent), 10 percent to "likely losers" (challengers whose races were decided by margins greater than 20 percent), and 5 percent to open-seat candidates running in one-party districts (where the race was also decided by more than 20 percent of the vote).

The Democrats' allocation strategy is more difficult to discern from its spending patterns. This is partially due the impreciseness of DCCC targeting. Democratic House members, who outnumbered Republicans incumbents 267 to 167, received a total of 43 percent of the party's expenditures, with Democratic shoo-ins raking in a full 21 percent.[15] Democratic challengers received 36 percent of the party's money, and the party

Table 6.2 The Allocation of National Party Funds in the 1992 Congressional Elections

| | House | | Senate | |
	Democrats	Republicans	Democrats	Republicans
Incumbents				
In Jeopardy	22%	20%	18%	39%
	(72)*	(79)	(6)	(6)
Shoo-ins	21	5	5	8
	(121)	(41)	(8)	(6)
Challengers				
Hopefuls	16	34	42	19
	(41)	(72)	(6)	(6)
Likely losers	20	10	5	5
	(79)	(121)	(6)	(8)
Open seats				
Prospects	15	26	29	29
	(50)	(50)	(8)	(8)
One-party dist.	5	5	–	–
	(34)	(34)		
Total**	$5,479	$7,074	$10,907	$16,037
	(397)	(397)	(34)	(34)

* Number of races are in parenthesis.
** In thousands of dollars.
Source: Compiled from Federal Election Commission data.

allocated more money to challengers who were likely to lose than those who had better odds of winning. Democratic spending in open-seat contests was somewhat better targeted, but as has been the case in previous elections, the Democrats continue to spend substantial sums of money on incumbents who do not need it and on nonincumbents who are not likely to benefit from it (Jacobson 1985–86; Herrnson 1989).

It is relatively easy for the parties to target their money in Senate elections. DSCC and NRSC officials have to assess their candidates' prospects in only thirty-three to thirty-five races that take place within boarders that do not shift every ten years because of redistricting. The result is that virtually all of their money is spent in close elections. In 1992, the Democrats spent all but 10 percent of their money in competitive contests, favoring hopeful challengers and open-seat candidates over incumbents in jeopardy, shoo-ins, and likely losers.[16] The Republicans distributed all but 13 percent of their funds to candidates in close elections, but favored incumbents in jeopardy over hopeful challengers and open-seat contestants. Both parties perceived open-seat elections to be contests where some hard fought battles would take place. These spending patterns indicate that the Democrats took a highly aggressive posture, while the Republicans took the complementary defensive position.

From a candidate's point of view, the most important thing is the actual amount of party money in his or her campaign. Republican House candidates in close races benefited from greater national party spending in 1992 than did the Democrats they ran against. GOP committees in Washington spent an average of $34,000 on Republicans in jeopardy, about $12,000 more than the Democrats spent on the challengers who hoped to take away their seats (see table 6.3). These figures amount to 5 percent of the total spent in the campaign of a typical GOP House member in jeopardy and 11 percent of the funds spent on the average Democratic hopeful. Democratic national party organizations typically spent just $17,000 on their House members who were in close races, which amounts to $16,700 less than the GOP spent on the challengers who hoped to defeat them. These figures represent 2 percent and 10 percent of the money spent in these campaigns. The GOP also out spent the Democrats by better than two to one in competitive open-seat contests. Although Republican House candidates benefit from their party's greater wealth and superior targeting, hopeful challengers of both parties, who have the most difficulty in raising money, are the greatest beneficiaries of party spending.

In 1992, Republican senators in jeopardy benefited from the most national party spending, an average of almost $285,000 more than was spent on the Democratic hopefuls who hoped to take away their jobs. These figures represent 16 percent and 15 percent of these candidates' respective budgets. Republican hopefuls benefited from approximately $508,000 national in party spending, accounting for roughly 21 percent of the campaign spending in their races, and about one and one-half times as much money as the Democratic party spent on the incumbents whom these GOP candidates tried to unseat.

Both parties were important players in Senate open-seat contests, accounting for 11 percent of the money spent in Democratic campaigns and 17 percent in GOP bids for office. Bruce Herschensohn was the greatest beneficiary of national party money. The NRSC spent a total of $2,472,144 million in his race for California's open Senate seat, which comprised 24 percent of the funds spent directly in conjunction with his campaign.[17] The DSCC and DNC invested a total of $1,635,960 in the campaign of Congresswoman Barbara Boxer, the ultimate victor in the race.[18] This accounted for 14 percent of all the funds spent in conjunction with her campaign. Spending by Republican party committees in the nation's capital broke the $1 million mark in five 1992 Senate races, and Democratic national party spending exceeded it in three.[19]

Table 6.3 Average National Party Spending in Congressional Elections*

| | House | | Senate | |
	Democrats	Republicans	Democrats	Republicans
Incumbents				
In jeopardy	16,860	34,410	333,100	1,052,900
Shoo-ins	9,705	4,227	63,814	208,544
Challengers				
Hopefuls	21,888	33,565	767,910	507,816
Likely losers	13,563	5,906	98,255	91,712
Open seats				
Prospects	16,941	36,466	400,148	585,972
One-party dist.	8,093	11,379	—	—
All candidates	13,802	17,818	320,083	471,677

* Figures include contributions and coordinated expenditures by the parties' national, congressional, and senatorial campaign committees for major party candidates in two-party contested elections. They do not include soft money expenditures. The number of races is the same as in table 6.2.
Source: Compiled from Federal Election Commission data.

Campaign Services

The parties' congressional and senatorial campaign committees provide selected candidates with assistance in specialized campaign activities, such as campaign management, gauging public opinion, issue and opposition research, and campaign communications. They also provide transactional assistance, acting as brokers between candidates, PACs, individual contributors, and political consultants. The DCCC and NRCC typically become closely involved in the campaigns of candidates on their watch lists and have little involvement in others. Their Senate counterparts work with all of their candidates but are less involved in the details of running their campaigns. All four committees play important roles in congressional elections.

Campaign Management

Candidates and their campaign organizations can get help from their hill committees with hiring and training campaign staff, making strategic and tactical decisions, and other management-related activities. The committees maintain directories of campaign managers, fundraising specialists, media experts, pollsters, voter list vendors, and other political consultants that candidates and managers can use to hire staff and to purchase campaign services. Committee officials sometimes recommend particular consultants, especially to House challengers and open-seat candidates.[20]

The campaign committees also train candidates and managers in the latest campaign techniques. The DCCC and the NRCC hold training seminars to introduce campaigners to innovations in targeting, fundraising, and other election activities. Seminars for incumbents, which are held in the committees' headquarters, cover such topics as staying in touch with the district, getting the most political mileage out of congressionally franked mail, defending unpopular votes, and PAC fundraising. Seminars for challengers and open-seat candidates focus on more basic subjects, such as the "stump" speech, filing campaign finance reports with the FEC, and building coalitions. Even long-term members of the House and Senate find the seminars beneficial, if for no other reason than they remind them to do things they already know they ought to be doing (see, e.g., Anderson and Binstein 1993).   In 1992, both committees introduced a number of innovations in their management-related service programs, including the use of precinct-level election results, geodemographic data and polls to help campaigns plan their mailings, electronic media ads, voter mobilization drives, and candidate field trips. Over the course of the election cycle, the NRCC held training schools that were attended by 199 candidates and 76 spouses. The committee also cosponsored, with the RNC, a series of week-long intensive programs in campaign management, communications, and fundraising that were attended by 314 campaign staffers (National Republican Campaign Committee 1992). Although this activity pales next to the six- to twelve-week training programs the committee once conducted under the guise of the Republican Campaign Academy,[21] it is more extensive than the training sessions organized by the Democrats. According to DCCC national political director Rob Engel, the Democrats traditionally devote fewer resources to candidate and campaign manager training because they "have a very deep bench [of candidates and consultants], a much deeper bench than the Republicans."

The hill committees also serve as centers for strategic advice. Committee field representatives and staffs in Washington serve as important sources of tactical information. Because they follow congressional elections nationwide and can draw on experiences from a previous election cycles, the committees are among the few organizations that have the knowledge and institutional memory to advise candidates and their managers on how to deal with some of the dilemmas they encounter (Hershey 1984).

Gauging Public Opinion

Candidates can also receive significant assistance in gauging public opinion from national party committees. The DNC and RNC circulate the findings of nationwide polls in newsletters and memoranda they distribute to members of Congress, party activists, and congressional candidates. In 1992, the DNC undertook a major polling effort that included statewide polls designed to furnish information to the Clinton-Gore campaign, and to Democratic candidates for governor, state legislatures, the House, and the Senate. The RNC focused most of its attention on the presidential race.

The congressional and senatorial campaign committees conduct or commission hundreds of polls and targeting studies in a given election cycle. In 1992, the NRCC hired a director of survey research to conduct polls for 117 Republican candidates and to assist others in purchasing and interpreting surveys from private polling firms. The committee took benchmark polls for incumbents, challengers, and open-seat contestants, recruitment surveys for potential candidates, and tracking polls for a small group of candidates who were running neck and neck with their Democratic opponents at the end of the election. Many of these polls, which had a market value between $8,000 and $10,000, were given to candidates as in-kind contributions or coordinated expenditures of $1,800 to $3,500, using a depreciating option allowed by the FEC.[22] The committee also carried out two national surveys to measure the effects the check-bouncing scandal had on public opinion, to test some anti-Congress and anti-Democratic attack themes, and to examine public response to several defense-related issues.

The DCCC did not hire a director of survey research or conduct "in-house" polls for its candidates in 1992. It explored this possibility after the 1990 election cycle, but chose to continue to rely on private polling firms instead. As it had in the past, the committee gave selected candidates surveys that were purchased from prominent Democratic consultants as in-kind contributions or coordinated expenditures. It also cooperated with the Democratic national and senatorial campaign committees in taking statewide and national polls.

Selected candidates also receive precinct-level targeting studies from the hill committees. In 1992, the DSCC and DCCC used geodemographic data and election returns provided by the National Committee for an Effective Congress (NCEC), a leading liberal PAC, to help Democratic candidates design their voter mobilization strategies, guide their media purchases, and carry out other communications and field activities (Herrnson 1994b). Republican House candidates received similar assistance from the NRCC's redistricting and campaign divisions, and Republican Senate candidates got targeting help from the NRSC's campaign division.

Issue and Opposition Research

During the 1980s, party organizations became major centers for political research. The DNC and RNC extended their traditional research activities in several new directions, most of which are party-focused rather than candidate-directed. Members of Congress, governors, state legislators, and candidates and activists at all levels are routinely sent issue briefs and talking points on salient national issues.

Candidates for Congress also receive party-focused research materials from the senatorial and congressional campaign committees. The parties write issues booklets that discuss the economy, crime, drugs, health care, and other national concerns to help candidates formulate their positions and prepare for campaign debates. The booklets include footnoted facts, summaries of a party's major achievements, and criticisms of the opposing party's performance and programs. In 1992, the NRCC distributed its issues handbook to 350 Republican primary and general election challengers and open-seat candidates, and House Democrats distributed their issues handbook to all of their candidates, and to thousands of Democratic activists.[23]

More important than the issue booklets are the issue packages the hill committees provide to selected candidates. These include information drawn from major newspapers, the Associated Press wire service, the Lexis/Nexis electronic data base, and government publications. The packages present a detailed description of the district, hard facts about issues that are important to local voters, and talking points that help candidates discuss these issues in a thematic and interesting manner. Candidates can access additional information by dialing into the committees' electronic bulletin boards. Many candidates make extensive use of this information when developing their campaign themes and policy positions. Open-seat candidates and challengers, who have none of the congressional perks enjoyed by incumbents, use party research as a substitute for the studies that House members get from their staffs, the Congressional Research Service, or the General Accounting Office.

In 1992, the NRCC conducted opposition research on every Democratic member of the House. Highly detailed opposition research packages were assembled on the 120 most vulnerable Democratic House members (National Republican Congressional Committee 1992). The DCCC had a smaller task to perform since fewer Republicans occupied the House seats. Each hill committee also conducted opposition research on many of its own members of Congress so they could "inoculate" themselves against attacks they anticipated would be made by their opponents.

Campaign Communications

The hill committees also give selected candidates assistance with campaign communications. Both the DCCC and NRCC have state-of-the-art television and radio production facilities on their premises and can furnish candidates with technical and editorial assistance in producing their TV and radio ads. They also have satellite capabilities that enable candidates to beam their television communications back to their districts instantly and interact "live" with voters. This technology is extremely popular with incumbents from western states.

Each media center produces several "generic" or "doughnut" ads that they customize to meet the specific needs of individual candidates. One generic radio ad that was heard in connection with House campaigns across the country, was based on the television show "Lifestyles of the Rich and Famous" and portrayed incumbent Democrats as jet-setters who vacation around the world at taxpayers' expense. Originally developed during the 1990 election, this NRCC ad was also used by many Republican challengers in 1992.

House candidates and their consultants can use the congressional campaign committees' recording and editing suites to produce individualized radio and television commercials.[24] Committee production staff are available to give technical and editorial advice. In a small number of campaigns, the NRCC goes several steps further. A communications division staffer meets with the candidate, his or her pollster, campaign manager, and a party political operative to design a full-blown media campaign. The staffer develops advertising themes, writes television and radio scripts, and produces the ads. The staffer may help design flyers and other printed matter (Herrnson 1988).

In 1992, the NRCC produced 188 television advertisements for forty-five House candidates: twenty-three incumbents and twenty-two challenger or open-seat candidates. According to Peter Pessel, one of the committee's producers, two-thirds of the ads were specifically designed for individual candidates. The remainders were doughnut ads with visual inserts and voice-overs. The committee also produced radio ads for forty-five House members and forty-four nonincumbents. The DCCC provided a much larger crop of candidates with less personalized service. Just over 170 House members and seventy nonincumbents used the Democrats' Harriman Communications Center to record and edit their television commercials. Under twenty used the committee's facilities to record their radio advertisements, most preferring to tape their radio ads in their campaign headquarters and other sites.

By providing candidates with issues packages and communications assistance, the congressional and senatorial campaign committees have clearly contributed to the nationalization of American politics. Few congressional candidates needed to be told the economy was the major issue in 1992, but the hill committees helped them discuss this issue thematically and frame it in ways that were more meaningful to voters. The committees' opposition research also contributed to many campaigns, but in ways that many voters might not look upon favorably. Just as the hill committees assist candidates in putting a positive spin on some aspects of their campaigns, they help them put a negative spin on others, thereby contributing to the mudslinging that has become commonplace in congressional elections.

Fundraising

In addition to providing contributions, coordinated expenditures, and campaign services, the hill committees also help selected candidates raise money from individuals and PACs. To this end, the committees give the candidates strategic advice and fundraising assistance. They also expend tremendous amounts of time and other resources furnishing PACs and Washington insiders with information that they can use when formulating their contribution strategies and selecting individual candidates for support.

The hill committees help candidates raise money from individuals in a variety of ways. They help candidates design direct-mail fundraising letters and give them tips on how to organize fundraising committees and events. Sometimes the committees host the events or assist in setting them up. In 1992, the NRCC introduced an innovation in fundraising when it employed satellite technology to help candidates raise big contributions from wealthy individuals. The committee arranged for Secretary of Housing and Urban Development Jack Kemp, House Minority Whip Newt Gingrich, and other GOP leaders to address contributors at Republican fundraisers across the country from the party's national convention in Houston. The broadcast "appearances" of these dignitaries helped bring in large sums of money.

The committees also work to steer large contributions from wealthy individuals, PACs, or members of Congress to needy candidates. It is illegal for the parties to "earmark" checks they receive from individuals or PACs for specific candidates, but committee members and staff can suggest to contributors that they consider giving a contribution to one of the candidates on their watch list. The NRSC has led the way in pioneering new ways to broker money to congressional candidates, but all four hill committees have been innovative in brokering contributions to congressional candidates in competitive races. Some of the most successful recent innovations have been introduced by DCCC Chair Vic Fazio. In 1992, Fazio succeeded in getting his House Democratic colleagues to contribute money from their campaign chests and PACs to the DCCC and Democratic candidates in close contests. He raised over $600,000 from House Democrats to help retire the DCCC's 1990 election debt (Democratic Congressional Campaign Committee 1992). Following the death of Republican House member Sylvio Conte in February 1990, Fazio was able to convince over fifty Democratic House members to "pony up" large contributions to help Democrat John Olver beat Republican Steven Pierce in a special election held in Massachusetts' First District. Fazio and the DCCC also played a critical role in steering over $300,000 in contributions from Washington PACs, lobbyists, and other insiders to Olver's successful campaign (Democratic Congressional Campaign Committee 1992).

The campaign committees assist candidates in raising PAC money in two ways. First, they give candidates the knowledge and tools to raise PAC money. The committees help candidates design PAC kits they can use to introduce themselves to members of the PAC community.[25] Candidates can get lists of PACs that include each committee's address, a contact person, and a mailing label that can be used to send a solicitation. The lists also indicate how much cash each PAC has on hand so candidates will not waste their time soliciting committees that have no money or take "no" for an answer when a PAC manager "claims poverty" but still has funds.

The committees also tutor candidates on how to approach PACs for money. Kristine Wolfe, the NRCC's director of coalitions and PACs, explains that most nonincumbents need to be coached on how to fill out the questionnaires that many PACs use to learn about candidates' issue positions. According to Wolfe, giving an answer that is only marginally different from a PAC's stand on a core issue can cost a candidate a contribution. Moreover, answering a question in a misleading way can result in a candidate getting a reputation as a "chameleon" and can freeze up prospects for raising PAC money once the managers of different PACs confer with one another.

The hill committees also assist candidates with designing the grassroots part of their PAC fundraising strategies. They instruct candidates on how to win endorsements from state-level branches of federated PACs and how to build coalitions among local PAC donors. As Wolfe's assistant, Matt Niemeyer, explains, "It's difficult for the manager of a national PAC to say no to a request [for a contribution] when it comes from a PAC's state affiliate or local donors."

A second way the parties help candidates raise money from PACs is through the manipulation of the information environment in which PACs make their contribution decisions. This is one of the major activities of the campaign committees' PAC directors and other top party officials. A PAC director's major goals are to channel the flow of PAC money toward their party's most competitive congressional contenders and away from their opponents. This an especially difficult task to perform on behalf of House challengers and open-seat candidates because they are largely unknown to the PAC community and unable to use the powers of incumbency to leverage PAC money. Some junior House members also need to have attention called to their races. The campaign committees often enlist the support of party leaders, committee and subcommittee chairs, or ranking members to attend a candidate's fundraising event or call a PAC manager on a candidate's behalf. Former DCCC chair, Tony Coelho, was legendary for his ability to "fry the fat" out of PACs (Jackson 1988). All four hill committees make meeting rooms and telephones available to facilitate PAC fundraising.[26]

The hill committees use a variety of approaches to circulate information about House and Senate elections to PACs and other potential contributors. The committees' campaign expenditures are one form of information that can have a tremendous impact on the fundraising prospects of nonincumbents. Large party expenditures can help them raise money because they draw the attention of PACs, wealthy individuals, and political journalists who give contributions or write about congressional elections (Herrnson 1988). PAC receptions, often referred to as "meet and greets," serve similar purposes. They give candidates, especially nonincumbents, an opportunity to ask PAC managers for contributions. The hill committees routinely hold meet and greets in their headquarters buildings. In presidential election years, they are also held at the parties' national conventions.

The committees also mail watch lists and information packages that discuss individual candidates' electoral prospects and financial needs to supportive PACs. Other mailings provided details on candidates' races, including poll results, press clippings, endorsements, campaign highlights, and revelations about problems experienced by their opponents. These mailings commonly ranged from ten to twenty pages in length and are sent to approximately one thousand PACs. During the heat of the election season, the campaign committees' PAC directors sent out mailings on a weekly or biweekly basis.

In addition to mailings and meet and greets, the committees' PAC directors hold briefings to discuss their opportunity races and inform PAC managers about their candidates' progress. These briefings provide PAC managers with the opportunity to ask committee staffers questions about specific campaigns and afford PAC managers with an opportunity to discuss their contribution strategies with one another. PAC briefings are an important forum for networking among campaign finance elites.

PAC directors and party leaders spend a tremendous amount of time making telephone calls on behalf of their most competitive and financially needy candidates. Some of these calls are made to PAC managers who are recognized leaders of PAC networks. The DCCC and DSCC, for example, work closely with the NCEC and the AFL-CIO's Committee on Political Education (COPE), while their GOP counterparts works closely with the Business-Industry Political Action Committee (BIPAC). The committees encourage these "lead" PACs to endorse their top contestants and communicate their support to other PACs in their networks.

Finally, the hill committees send streams of communications to the editors of the *Cook Political Report*, the *Rothenberg Political Report*, and other political newsletters that are heavily subscribed to by PACs. These newsletters handicap congressional races and provide information on developments in campaigns located across the country. Party officials undertake tremendous efforts to keep the newsletter editors abreast of the latest developments in their candidates' campaigns, speaking with them several times a week. Charlie Cook and Stuart Rothenberg, who edit the newsletters that bear their names, confirm that hill committee officials are major sources of their political information.

By helping candidates understand how the PAC community works and furnishing PACs with information about candidates, the congressional and senatorial campaign committees have become important intermediaries in the fundraising process. They have entered into symbiotic relationships with some PACs that have enabled them to become brokers between candidates and PACs (Sabato 1984; Jackson 1988). The relationship is based largely on honest and reliable exchanges of information about the prospects of individual candidates. In some cases the information exchange is a bilateral. The NCEC, BIPAC, and other "lead" PACs have information that they share with the committees (see Biersack 1994). Campaign committee officials recognize that any attempt to mislead a PAC manager by providing inaccurate information could harm the committee's credibility, curtail its influence in the PAC community, and undercut its ability to help its candidates (Herrnson 1988).

Hill committee communications to PACs are somewhat controversial because they can have a major impact on the fundraising prospects of individual candidates. Candidates who receive their campaign committee's endorsement derive significant advantages in raising PAC money, while nonincumbents who do not receive endorsements usually collect significant funds from PACs. PAC managers have been known to justify refusing a contribution request because a nonincumbent was not included on a hill committee's watch list. The campaign committees' brokerage activities clearly play to the advantage of some candidates and harm the prospects of others.

The Impact of Party Services

When asked to discuss the importance of campaign assistance from local, state, and national party organizations, PACs, unions, and other groups in aspects of campaigning requiring professional expertise or in-depth research, candidates and campaign aides involved in the 1992 House elections rank their party's hill committee first. About one-third of all House candidates and managers consider their congressional campaign committee to be at least moderately helpful in campaign management. Roughly 40 percent gave similar assessments for hill committee assistance in gauging public opinion. Over half of all the House contestants report that committee issue research plays at least a moderately important role in their campaigns, with 20 percent describing it as very important and another 11 percent asserting that it is extremely important. More than 40 percent of the House candidates, mostly challengers, also rely heavily on their congressional campaign committee for opposition research. About 30 percent of all House campaigns receive significant DCCC or NRCC help in producing their campaign communications. Slightly more candidates and campaign aides find that hill committee to be moderately important to their fundraising efforts. However, House candidates report receiving greater fundraising assistance from PACs and other interest groups. The DCCC and NRCC are also rated lower than state and local party organizations and interest groups in grassroots activities, reflecting their lack of direct involvement in these aspects of campaigning.

Most Senate candidates and campaign managers give evaluations of hill committee assistance that are as favorable as those given by House candidates even though the DSCC and NRSC staff tend to be less involved than their House counterparts in formulating or implementing candidates' campaign strategies.[27] Instead, senatorial campaign committee staffs provide candidates with feedback, advice, campaign contributions, and election services purchased from political consultants. They also help candidates collect money from PACs and wealthy contributors. The senatorial campaign committees are rated above any other group in every area of campaigning except for providing information about voters, voter mobilization, and volunteer recruitment, where state and local party organizations and interest groups are ranked higher.

The evaluations of House and Senate candidates and campaign managers indicate that most hill committee help is given to candidates in close races, reflecting the parties' goal of winning as many seats in Congress as possible. As was the case with campaign spending, the NRCC distributes its campaign services more effectively than does its Democratic counterpart. Both senatorial campaign committees also concentrate their resources in close races. Hill committee assistance is more important to hopeful challengers and open-seat prospects than it is to incumbents in jeopardy, reflecting the fact that incumbents have problems in getting reelected, but they are rarely due to an inability to raise money, assemble a campaign organization, or communicate with voters.[28]

The hill committees also play bigger roles in the campaigns of Republican House and Senate candidates than in the campaigns of their Democratic opponents. The campaign evaluations, like the distribution of national party money, indicate that the NRCC and the NRSC outperformed the two Democratic hill committees in 1992. The gap between the committees has shrunk in recent years, but a Republican advantage persists.

Party Differences

There are major differences in the parties' performance in House elections. The Republicans spend more money, distribute more services, and target them better than the Democrats. For example, over 80 percent of all national party spending in House contests was done in close races, as opposed to only 54 percent of all national Democratic party spending. The spending differences in open-seat races are especially telling. The Democrats spent, on average, just under $17,000 to help House candidates for open seats in competitive districts and an average of $8,000 to help open-seat candidates in one-party districts. The Republicans, on the other hand, typically spent over $36,000 and $11,000 to help GOP candidates in these same contests.

The disparities in party targeting merit some explanation. First, Republican party organizations have traditionally taken a more businesslike approach to allocating campaign funds. The NRCC's decision-making process is more staff driven and less politicized than that of its Democratic counterpart (Herrnson 1989). The Democrats' control of the House, greater diversity, and the leadership aspirations of DCCC chairmen and members occasionally override the committee's stated goal of maximizing House seats. Second, the NRCC has always been one step ahead of the DCCC in gathering campaign information. The Republican committee was the first to have staff observing campaigns in the field. Its new polling division may have given it an advantage over the DCCC in targeting. Third, Rob Engel explains that House Democrats' heavy use of the DCCC's media center, which the committee counts as a contribution or coordinated expenditure, to some degree inflate the figures for party money spent in connection with shoo-in incumbent races. Finally, according to Engel, a difference in philosophy might also have been at work. His committee tried to "keep more races alive, for a longer period, before bailing out," which led Democratic funds to be distributed more broadly, and less effectively, than Republican money.

Conclusion

The 1992 elections provided political parties with the opportunity to contribute to the sea change that was expected to take place in the U.S. Congress. Democratic and Republican party committees located in the nation's capital were poised to play a role in this election, but were confronted with a barrage of requests for help from an unusually large number of highly talented candidates. Moreover, they had to select candidates for support under conditions of extreme uncertainty. The NRCC was able to cope with the demands of this unusual election cycle better than its Democratic counterpart. The parties' senatorial campaign committees had a less complex task to perform, and both committees targeted their resources extremely effectively. Nevertheless, all four hill committees, as well as many other party organizations, made important contributions during the 1992 congressional elections.

Notes

1. The material in this chapter is drawn from chapters 4 and 6 of Herrnson (1995). A detailed discussion of the survey and the data is presented there. I wish to thank Robert Biersack for assistance with the analysis of campaign finance data; Michael Gusmano, Robert Tennant, and Candace Kahn for assistance with data collection. Financial support for this research was provided by a grant from the Graduate Board and the Center for Political Leadership of the University of Maryland.

2. The previous modern (post-1946) record for House retirements was 49, set in 1978 (see Ornstein, Mann, Malbin 1992).

3. The previous modern (post-1946) record for House members defeated was 8, set in 1946 (see Ornstein, Mann, Malbin 1990).

4. The number of Senate retirements in 1992 has only been exceed twice since 1946: 9 senators retired prior to that election, and 10 retired prior to the 1978 election (see Ornstein, Mann, and Malbin 1992).

5. The term "hill committees," referring to the congressional and senatorial campaign committees, probably originates from the fact that they were originally located in congressional office space on Capitol Hill.

6. These figures include only "hard" dollars that can be spent directly in federal campaigns (see Federal Elections Commission 1993).

7. The information on committee strategy, decision making, and targeting in 1992 is drawn from personal interviews tat were conducted over the course of the election cycle. Interviews were held with several officials at the congressional campaign committees, including Rob Engel, National Political Director, DCCC, Eric Wilson, Deputy Director, DCCC, Marty Stone, Regional Field Coordinator, DCCC, Tom Cole, Executive Director, NRCC, Kris Wolfe, Director of PACs and Coalitions, NRCC, Matt Neimeyer, Deputy PAC Director, Kevin O'Donnell, Director of Survey Research, NRCC. On committee strategy and decision making in previous elections, see Jacobson and Kernell (1983) and Herrnson (1989).

8. These are each considered separate elections under the FECA. Party committees, however, usually only give contributions to general election candidates.

9. Coordinated expenditure limits for states with only one House member are $55,240.

10. Party committees can also give "in-kind" services in lieu of cash contributions; however, they are more likely to use the coordinated expenditure route.

11. In 1982, for example, the NRCC spent just under $7.5 million on House elections and the DCCC spent a total of $761,000 (Sorauf 1992).

12. An NRCC decision to transfer almost $1.9 million to 21 state party committees instead of forming agency agreements with those committees also contributed to the decline in NRCC money that was contributed to or spent on behalf of Republican House candidates. According to Tom Cole, the NRCC negotiated agreements to transfer the funds, much of it "soft" money that could not be spent directly on federal candidates, with the understanding that the state committees that receive the funds would spend an equal amount of "hard" money on their House candidates' campaigns. The transfers enabled the NRCC to use its "soft" money, which flows outside of the FECA's contributions and spending limits reporting requirements, to help its House candidates. The DCCC transferred about half as much money to Democratic state committees; most of the money it transferred was hard money that could have been spent legally on federal candidates. On soft money, see Drew (1983), Sorauf (1988). The information on party transfers is from FEC (1993b). The information on NRCC strategy is from a personal interview with Tom Cole on January 11, 1993.

13. The transfers include both hard and soft money.

14. The figures include spending by all three national party organizations because they are subject to a common limit and thus must in coordination with one another. Crossover expenditures, such as those made by the senatorial campaign committees in House campaigns, usually consist of polls that are shared among House and Senate candidates. Separating hill committee spending from all national party spending barely affects the figures in table 6.2. Similarly, the patterns for the distribution of all party money, including state and local committee expenditures, resemble those in the table.

15. Rep. Bernard Sanders, an Independent from Vermont, accounts for the 435th House seat.

16. The Senate candidates are grouped using the same vote margins as are House candidates. All of the open-seat Senate races are classified as competitive.

17. Herschensohn spent a total of $7,859,072, received $17,500 in contribution from the NRSC, $5,000 from the California Republican Party, and $1,000 from the Republican Club of Leisure World. He also benefited from an additional $2,454,644 in NRSC coordinated expenditures. These figures exclude party soft money expenditures and independent expenditures by PACs and other groups.

18. Boxer spend a total of $10,363,251, received $17,500 in contributions from the DSCC, $950 from the DNC, $5,000 from the Democratic State Central Committee of California, $1,258 from the Sacramento County Democratic Committee's United Campaign Committee. She also benefited from $16,735 in DNC coordinated expenditures, and $1,600,775 in DSCC coordinated expenditures, and $118,614 in Democratic State Central Committee coordinated expenditures.

19. In addition to the Herschensohn race, the Republicans spent over $1 million in campaigns waged by John Seymour, Alfonse D'Amato, Arlen Spector, and Paul Coverdell. The Democrats spent over $1 million on Boxer's, Dianne Feinstein's and Robert Abrams's campaigns.

20. In some cases, the congressional campaign committees require candidates to use the services of one of their preferred consultants as a precondition for committee support. Although these cases are rare, they can arouse the ire of both candidates and political consultants (Herrnson 1988; Frantzich 1989; Salmore and Salmore 1989).

21. The NRCC closed down its campaign academy because of the difficulty its graduates had in finding employment in nonelection years and because the costs of maintaining the academy became prohibitive. For more information on the academy (see Herrnson 1988: 57, 15, 156–57.)

22. The allocable costs of the polls vary by type, size, and when they were released to the candidates. FEC regulations specify that candidates must pay 100 percent of the costs if they receive the poll results within 15 days of when it was completed, 50 percent if they receive them between 16 and 60 days, and 5 percent if the results are received between 61 and 180 days. After 180 days, a poll can be given to a candidate free of charge.

23. The Democrats' issues handbook, *Taking Charge of America's Future*, was written and printed by the House Democratic Caucus with the assistance of staffers from the DCCC, DNC, the Democratic Leadership Conference, and the Clinton Campaign.

24. A small number of Senate candidates and other party dignitaries also use the committee's media equipment.

18. PAC kits typically include information about the candidate's personal background, political experience, campaign staff, support in the district, endorsements, issue positions, and campaign strategy.

19. Outside meeting rooms and telephones are necessary because it is illegal to solicit campaign money from the capitol complex.

20. It is difficult to make generalizations about Senate campaigns because of the small number of Senate elections that occur in one election cycle, the tremendous diversity in the size and composition of the states that form U.S. Senate districts, and a different one-third of all Senate seats are up for election every two years. The fact that only 28 (41%) of the Senate campaigns returned completed questionnaires is additional cause for concern. In order to improve the strength of the findings about Senate campaigns, the generalizations in this section are based on observations that span the 1984, 1986, and 1992 election cycles.

21. Incumbents rarely have difficulty raising money; and, as Gary C. Jacobson notes, their fundraising and spending are driven largely by their perception of the threat a challenger poses to their reelection (Jacobson 1980, 1992).

7

The Nationalization of Party Finance, 1992–94

Robert Biersack

Our general understanding of American political parties has evolved over the past twenty years as the parties have faced a changing electoral environment. The American electorate, as it has become more urbanized with more accessible information about politics, has moved away from simple partisan queues to guide its voting decisions (Wattenberg 1990). This change has been coupled with a shift toward candidate-centered politics in which individual candidates develop their own organization and message outside the direct control of the party.

Faced with an electoral world in which neither candidates nor voters were inexorably linked to parties, the Republican and Democratic National Committees and their state and local counterparts were forced to redefine their role in the democratic process and develop organizational forms consistent with their new place in the political world (Schlesinger 1965; Cotter et al. 1989).

The parties now primarily provide services to selected candidates. Rather than delivering votes on election day (although voter mobilization remains an important party activity), they deliver polls and issue research, along with financial support and campaign expertise, to candidates who choose to associate themselves with the party and successfully compete for nominations (Herrnson 1988).

Providing these services efficiently requires a level of stability and financial strength not common for parties in the days when precinct volunteers represented the basic "currency" of party activity. The parties' literature in recent years (Cotter et al. 1984; Jacobson 1986; Herrnson 1989) has documented the transformation of parties by tracking increasing financial strength and organizational capability and describing how those resources have been translated into specific campaign services. How those funds are raised and distributed among national, state, and local organizations is the focus of this chapter.

The shift from concentrating on voters to focusing on campaign services has altered relationships within the parties among the national and state and local organizations. Parties once described as stratarchical, guided by local organizations mobilizing voters (Schattschneider 1942), have been transformed into hierarchical organizations where large-scale fundraising capabilities have permitted the national committees to increase their influence over state and local counterparts (Cotter and Bibby 1980).

Describing the full organizational and financial condition of the parties has been difficult, however, because of the federal nature of the rules under which they raise and spend money. The wide variety of elective offices at different levels of government, along with the constitutional sovereignty of states in conducting those elections, complicates the process for participants and observers alike.

This chapter describes changes in one element of the federal structure that took place in 1991, and the impact of those changes on what parties do and what we know about them. Laws and regulations regarding the financing of politics must conform to the constitutional mandate of federalism. The rules that apply to candidates for the national legislature and the presidency are not the same as those in effect in state legislative or gubernatorial elections, and these differences affect what parties can do in support of different candidates, as well as what is readily known about their behavior.

In campaign finance jargon, money that would be permitted in elections for state or local office, but would not be permissible in federal elections is commonly described as "soft money." Some states, for example, permit corporations or labor unions to directly contribute to candidates for state and local office, while contributions to federal candidates from these sources are forbidden. (These organizations can create voluntary PACs to contribute in federal races, but the corporations or unions themselves are not allowed to participate.) Political parties that are active in all campaigns must find a way to meet the restrictions of both systems. In general, any money allowable under state or local rules that might have even an indirect effect on a federal race is soft money. Defining the boundary between federal and state or local activity is one of those details in which many devils can be found, and in 1991 that definition changed substantially.

As a result, a more complete picture of party activity at the national and state levels is now available from a single source. For the first time, the national parties were required to disclose all of their financial activity in one place. National party organizations have been heavily involved in financing politics at all levels as financial resources have gained more prominence in American politics. We can now document, in 1992 and 1994, the extent of their involvement in financing party and candidate activity at all levels, and a full accounting of this national party activity will be summarized here. One of the biggest concerns about the use of "soft money" is the assumption that it is actually raised and spent in conjunction with the presidential campaign.

That is, contributors to soft money accounts are thought to be making these big dollar contributions in order to influence the presidential election, and parties are assumed to place these funds in areas where they will have the most effect on the presidential race. A preliminary review of soft money spending patterns presented here suggests that the motives for spending these funds are more complex than this conventional wisdom suggests. The pattern that emerges from both the presidential campaign cycle in 1992 and the off-year elections of 1994 is not obviously dependent on presidential politics, though the relationship between federal and state or local campaigns remains murky.

While still incomplete, a fuller picture of state party activity is now available as well. The state parties are generally found to be financially sound and involved in a variety of activities directed toward candidates and voters. The extent to which states rely on national parties for funding and valuable services has also been disclosed completely for the first time. State parties are not completely dependent on their national counterparts for financial and other support, but the financial relationship between the national and state parties is clearly important in the development of the institutions at both levels.

The Regulatory System

Federal court rulings handed down in the late 1980s required the FEC to write new regulations that would identify a more specific standard for allocation among federal and nonfederal elections and insure that the allocation rules were being followed. (Prior to these rulings, the allocation of spending by parties between federal and nonfederal races was largely up to the discretion of the party itself.) The long and complex rule-making process that followed resulted in changes in the way party organizations could allocate their activities and also changed the disclosure requirements to permit more comprehensive reporting of financial activity for both national and state and local party organizations. The previous standard that any reasonable method could be used to allocate expenses was replaced with specific allocation procedures that have two basic elements.

First, administrative expenses of party organizations and the cost of generic activities that indirectly affect all candidates must now be allocated according to specific percentages for national party committees (at least 60 percent federal in nonelection years, 65 percent federal in election years) and according to the composition of the next general election ballot for state and local party organizations. Each type of race (president, U.S. Senate, U.S. House, governor, other statewide offices, state senate, state representative, local offices) receives one point, and the allocation ratio is the proportion of federal offices relative to total offices on the ballot. (During 1991 the commission amended the rule to add an additional nonfederal point for each state.) In the 1991–92 election cycle this ballot composition ratio ranged from a low of 25 percent federal in Delaware, Mississippi, Montana, Rhode Island, and West Virginia to a high of 75 percent federal in Maryland. During the 1993–94 election cycle, without a presidential campaign, the ratios ranged from 12 percent in Alabama and several other states to 40 percent in Mississippi (see table 7.3). State party organizations must raise at least enough funds under federal rules to pay the federal portion of their general overhead expenses.

Other types of activity continue to have flexible allocation methods. For example, fundraising costs may be paid on a "funds received" basis, where the cost of the fundraiser is allocated according to the proportion of funds actually received that would be allowable under federal restrictions. Thus if 20 percent of the funds received from a specific event met FECA requirements, 20 percent of the costs must be paid from federal funds. A similar rule is used for activities that are specifically exempt from contribution or expenditure limits by the 1979 amendments (yard signs, etc.) and for activities that directly support both federal and nonfederal candidates. These activities must be paid for according to a "funds expended" method where the federal share of the cost must be commensurate with the federal portion of the activity.

The second important change in the rules for party committees involved the method for paying bills and reporting activity to the FEC. National party organizations are now required to disclose all activity of all aspects of the organization, whether federal nonfederal or mixed. State and local party organizations are required to pay all bills for allocable activity from their federal account and report transfers received from nonfederal accounts to pay the non-federal portion of these expenses. This change effectively reversed the flow of funds and reporting. Where prior to this time only transfers out of federal funds for these purposes were disclosed, now the full value of the activity is reported with the nonfederal portion being transferred into the federal account. As a result, a more complete picture of party finance is available from a single source, and compliance with the new rules for allocating expenses can be assessed.

As a result of these reporting changes, information available at the FEC now accounts for all national party financial activity, and a significantly greater proportion of state party finance as well. The only aspect of state party activity that is not reported is activity that is specifically and exclusively devoted to state and local campaigns. Direct contributions to those nonfederal candidates, along with expenditures exclusively devoted to those races, remain the exclusive purview of state law and need not be disclosed at the federal level.

Party Finance in the New Regulatory Era

With these reporting requirements now on the books for two elections, a new picture of overall party finances emerges. Party committees at all levels reported receipts of about $680 million in 1991–92, and $598 million in 1994, up from about $300 million in 1990 and $375 million in 1988, the last presidential election cycle. Approximately 25 percent of all activity reported by the two major parties represents activity disclosed for the first time during the 1992 election cycle. Democratic national committees (including the DNC and the senatorial and congressional campaign committees) reported raising $37 million in nonfederal funds in 1992 and $47 million in 1994, while their counterparts at the state and local levels reported $35 million in 1992 and $43.2 million in 1994 as the nonfederal share of allocable expenses. Republicans at the national level (RNC, NRSC, and NRCC) raised $52 million in soft money in 1992, and increased that total to $59 million in 1994. State and local Republican committees increased the nonfederal share of their allocable activity from $29 million during 1992, to $40.7 million in 1994. The increase in state and local soft money is probably due to the rule that allows a greater share of overhead expenses to be paid with soft money when there is no presidential election.

While complete information about nonfederal activity of national parties is not available for earlier years, it has generally been assumed that this activity is very dependent on the existence of a presidential campaign. It is estimated that the two parties raised $40 to $50 million from these sources during the 1988 campaign (Alexander and Bauer 1991). In 1990, however, the combined total for both parties was reported to be about $25 million (Goldstein 1991). During 1993 and 1994, however, both national parties raised significantly more soft money than they had in the 1992 presidential cycle. Democratic national committees raised $46.9 million from sources that would not be permitted in federal campaigns, 27 percent more than in 1992, while Republican national organizations raised $59.4 million from these sources, 15 percent higher than their 1992 total. With full disclosure and consistent allocation rules, it now seems clear that the ability of the parties to raise soft money is not dependent on a presidential campaign.

New allocation rules may have had their greatest effect on state and local parties, which were required to use federal funds for a significant portion of their activities in the 1992 campaign. Democratic state and local committees raised $58 million in "hard" money acceptable under FECA restrictions during the 1992 cycle, up from $36 million in 1990. Republicans at the state and local level reported 1992 federal revenue of $64 million, compared with $39 million raised from these sources in 1990. While some of this increase may represent greater fundraising success in a highly competitive election year (including a presidential race), clearly at least part of this growth in federal funds at the state and local level is the result of mandated ballot composition ratios for federal and nonfederal funds described above. Patterns of fundraising over several cycles suggest that use of the ballot as a guide for allocating activity between federal and state/local races means these parties must raise more funds within FECA limits than the allocation methods previously used by state and local party organizations. During the 1994 election cycle, Democratic state and local parties raised $47.6 million in "hard" money. This decline might be expected, since the ballot in 1994 often had significantly fewer federal races, allowing for more "soft" money spending. Republican state and local parties, on the other hand, raised $75 million from federally allowable sources in 1993–94, even more than they had raised in the preceding presidential cycle.

Table 7.1 summarizes the receipts of the Democratic and Republican National Committees in 1991–92 and 1993–94. This represents a full accounting of all monies raised by these committees, including any nonfederal accounts. The tables show that during 1992 at least two-thirds of all funds raised by the national committees were raised within the restrictions and prohibitions of the FECA. The Democratic National Committee increased its dependence on "soft" money in 1994, with soft money representing half of DNC receipts. Both national committees relied more heavily on contributions from individual people that fell within the limit of $20,000 per person per year than any other source of funds, hard or soft. Moreover, the RNC raised more absolute dollars in both election cycles from individuals in increments of less than $200 each than it raised from all soft money sources combined. While Republican organizations have experienced difficulty with their direct mail fundraising operations in recent years (resulting in declining revenue in several cycles leading up to 1992), that program remains the most formidable part of their fundraising apparatus.

The DNC, by contrast, showed greater reliance on larger contributions and was more dependent on institutional support. It is noteworthy that the DNC received more financial support from corporations in its nonfederal accounts than it received from organized labor. This does not include direct campaign involvement by labor organizations, however, nor does it include union efforts to communicate with and mobilize their members.

The senatorial and congressional campaign committees of the two parties are similar to the DNC and RNC in terms of sources of funds. Republican committees (NRSC and NRCC) have substantial direct mail donor bases whose small contributions accounted for a large majority of the $72 million in "hard" dollars raised by the Senate committee and $34 million raised by the House committee. Democratic committees (DSCC and DCCC) were more dependent on larger contributions and support from PACs, and the federal totals raised were considerably less than their Republican counterparts—$25 million for the senatorial (DSCC) and $13 million for the House (DCCC).

The two senatorial committees diverged in terms of soft money, however, with the DSCC raising only $600,000 outside federal limits intended almost

Table 7.1 Major Party Fundraising and Spending, 1992 and 1994 (in millions of dollars)

	DNC		RNC	
	1991-92	1993-94	1991-92	1993-94
Funds Raised				
Total	$97.4	$83.1	$121.6	$133.5
Federal	65.8	41.8	84.4	87.4
Nonfederal	31.6	41.3	36.2	46.1
Sources				
Federal				
Individuals	54.9	34.9	79.0	79.7
PACs	3.0	2.0	.4	.4
Other	8.0	4.9	6.0	7.3
Nonfederal				
Individuals	15.5	20.5	20.0	30.5
Corporations	11.5	12.0	12.0	10.0
Others	4.6	8.8	4.2	5.6
Funds Spent				
Total	95.5	86.0	117.5	129.4
Federal	65.0	44.0	81.9	85.3
Nonfederal	30.5	42.0	35.6	44.1
Purposes				
Federal				
Contributions	0.0	0.1	.9	.5
Coordinated expend.	11.7	0.1	13.9	4.9
Transfer to states	6.5	2.8	1.1	5.5
Joint administrative	27.3	16.4	32.5	30.7
Joint fundraising	2.0	2.3	4.5	1.3
Operating expenses	14.6	13.7	27.0	33.7
Other	2.9	8.6	2.0	8.7
Nonfederal				
Contributions	0.0	.7	1.2	3.6
Transfer to states	9.5	10.9	5.3	7.6
Joint administrative	15.3	11.8	18.9	20.5
Joint fundraising	1.5	5.2	3.0	1.5
Building fund	2.9	.5	7.1	4.9
Other	1.3	12.9	.2	6.0

Source: Federal Election Commission.

exclusively for support of its building and facilities, while the NRSC raised about $9 million and transferred about $1.5 million to state party organizations. Totals raised by the nonfederal accounts of the two House campaign committees were similar—$6 million for the Republicans and $5 million for the Democrats. Here again, the Democratic Congressional

Campaign Committee used most of its soft money for administrative expenses and facilities, while its Republican counterpart also transferred $1.7 million to the states.

Table 7.1 also compares the spending of the two national committees. In each case funds raised and spent under the restrictions of the FECA are examined separately from those raised and spent outside federal law. They suggest that the two parties used somewhat different spending strategies during the campaign. The RNC spent a larger proportion of its funds on national overhead expenses, including purely federal operating expenses, fundraising, and building funds. They spent comparatively less in direct support of state and local party organizations. For example, while the DNC spent 10 percent of its federal dollars and 31 percent of its non-federal funds in 1992 in direct support of state parties, the corresponding percentages for the RNC were 1 percent in federal funds and 15 percent for nonfederal resources.

It is important to note here that both national committees made a large portion of their transfers to states in the form of in-kind services. For the DNC, many of the nonfederal transfers were actually regional polling results commissioned by the national committee and distributed to the states. The RNC spent most of the federal dollars it used in support of state parties on a voter mobilization phone bank that operated in the last days of the general election campaign. In many cases, these in-kind transfers can have considerably greater real value than the dollar value attributed to them because the national parties can often provide these services for considerably less than the private sector.

State Party Activity

Table 7.2 summarizes the expanded, but not complete reporting of financial activity of state party committees under the new reporting rules. It shows that these organizations have developed substantial financial resources. In only 20 percent of the states did the Democratic party organizations raise less than $500,000 during either election cycle. For Republicans, 28 percent of the states reported receipts under half a million dollars in 1992, and only 14 percent were under that level in 1994. By contrast, about 96 percent of all PACs that reported raising any money in 1991–92 raised less than $500,000.

The table also reveals little overall difference between the two parties in terms of financial capability at the state level. While there are significant differences on a state by state basis between the two parties, overall organizations at this level show a remarkably equal access to financial resources.

Improved disclosure of state party activity does not, however, mean complete disclosure at the Federal Election Commission. Any activity related

Table 7.2 State Party Disbursements Reported to the FEC, 1992 and 1994

State	DEMOCRATS			REPUBLICANS		
	1991-92	1993-94	% change 1992-94	1991-92	1993-94	% change 1992-94
Alabama	$1,104,129	$2,137,307	94	$813,960	$688,941	-15
Alaska	284,869	403,051	41	176,433	231,820	31
Arizona	822,909	1,190,203	45	1,154,509	1,521,442	32
Arkansas	2,164,880	1,006,099	-54	538,299	474,772	-12
California	12,192,839	11,427,433	-6	6,251,173	8,800,589	41
Colorado	2,090,427	1,663,849	-20	2,438,319	1,605,749	-34
Connecticut	1,074,158	1,574,422	47	1,051,007	594,732	-43
Delaware	518,964	573,561	11	1,150,403	770,871	-33
Florida	1,859,925	2,830,115	52	4,750,182	8,959,755	89
Georgia	4,492,793	3,305,864	-26	2,413,472	2,627,013	9
Hawaii	1,199,356	419,72-65	-65	302,979	627,036	107
Idaho	382,924	374,878	-2	1,107,779	1,078,820	-3
Illinois	2,857,360	1,045,484	-63	1,815,648	1,951,318	7
Indiana	2,647,955	2,661,827	1	2,143,796	3,455,163	61
Iowa	1,929,523	1,942,603	1	2,223,873	1,984,348	-11
Kansas	390,061	537,485	38	668,910	569,581	-15
Kentucky	1,526,498	902,049	-41	1,051,156	1,083,189	3
Louisiana	1,835,185	616,575	-66	338,759	368,135	9
Maine	583,346	1,194,097	105	49,549	369,994	647
Maryland	1,286,890	818,271	-36	773,296	871,519	13
Massachusetts	1,451,734	2,102,109	45	1,994,830	1,967,390	-1
Michigan	3,549,243	3,579,512	1	5,528,094	7,391,751	34
Minnesota	3,334,992	3,821,389	15	2,661,001	3,889,554	46
Mississippi	896,281	161,378	-82	104,707	706,283	575
Missouri	1,563,712	1,292,650	-17	1,959,781	1,547,165	-21

Montana	869,704	825,348	-5	431,425	585,804	36
Nebraska	487,504	834,525	71	996,567	1,226,398	23
Nevada	1,023,718	80,668	-92	278,933	520,187	86
New Hampshire	393,813	318,455	-19	387,573	504,689	30
New Jersey	3,586,538	2,029,057	-43	4,652,854	4,087,251	-12
New Mexico	807,692	1,116,777	38	524,736	749,153	43
New York	4,322,320	4,435,068	3	2,369,607	4,162,922	76
North Carolina	4,281,012	2,587,866	-40	1,959,998	1,077,521	-45
Ohio	3,676,770	3,139,054	-15	6,016,173	5,113,407	-15
Oklahoma	413,164	486,343	18	558,166	1,055,635	89
Oregon	1,015,521	750,490	-26	492,485	879,880	79
Pennsylvania	2,901,905	2,370,614	-18	3,455,392	4,087,100	18
Rhode Island	134,874	225,314	67	302,944	285,072	-6
South Carolina	456,798	483,779	6	539,481	589,679	9
South Dakota	864,024	521,273	-40	707,292	624,973	-12
Tennessee	1,109,940	2,409,129	117	1,380,925	2,026,569	47
Texas	4,233,267	4,115,800	-3	7,002,858	5,665,822	-19
Utah	559,785	763,758	35	756,632	755,352	0
Vermont	534,611	458,413	-14	438,556	491,402	12
Virginia	1,066,432	3,146,498	195	1,938,146	3,064,146	58
Washington	1,503,530	2,266,926	51	2,593,057	3,567,908	38
West Virginia	501,135	204,399	-59	194,477	127,359	-35
Wisconsin	1,742,400	1,563,537	-10	2,689,962	2,861,886	6
Wyoming	229,509	331,401	44	274,180	583,741	113
Total	89,598,154	83,644,624	-7	85,381,385	99,521,387	17

Note: Activity totally related to state and local races is not reported to the FEC.
Source: Federal Election Commission.

Table 7.3a National Party Financial Support of States (Democrat)

State	1991-92				1993-94			
	Federal % of Ballot	DNC Federal Transfers	DNC Soft Money Transfers	Total DNC Contributions to State/Local Parties	Federal % of Ballot	DNC Federal Transfers	DNC Soft Money Transfers	Total Contributions to State/Local Parties
Alabama	50	$16,766	$53,291	$70,057	12	$28,147	$318,250	$346,397
Alaska	50	2,750	8,000	10,750	20	12,022	15,000	27,022
Arizona	34	61,372	52,215	113,587	22	91,665	206,673	298,338
Arkansas	50	402,725	231,537	624,262	12	12,778	110,000	122,778
California	44	668,039	1,204,814	1,872,853	22	164,014	700,000	864,014
Colorado	33	111,909	88,261	200,170	12	27,252	182,000	209,252
Connecticut	43	92,000	135,222	227,222	22	7,455	135,000	142,455
Delaware	25	37,316	40,431	77,747	25	15,626	98,750	114,376
Florida	43	35,694	116,896	152,590	28	103,463	481,257	584,720
Georgia	33	404,671	648,497	1,053,168	12	29,212	241,859	271,071
Hawaii	43	17,518	30,000	47,518	29	5,156	16,000	21,156
Idaho	50	11,100	20,500	31,600	12	11,462	20,000	31,462
Illinois	50	230,608	463,132	693,740	12	50,762	75,000	125,765
Indiana	33	13,800	19,999	33,799	25	29,868	30,000	59,868
Iowa	43	120,745	172,262	293,007	13	163,194	349,614	511,808
Kansas	50	12,016	12,778	24,794	14	16,660	23,500	40,160
Kentucky	33	34,000	106,000	140,000	25	4,200	6,000	10,200
Louisiana	33	58,043	378,432	436,475	33	14,733	23,000	37,733
Maine	33	82,442	63,232	145,674	29	53,547	104,599	158,146
Maryland	50	89,023	74,300	163,323	22	66,300	0	66,300
Massachusetts	40	270,744	1,500	272,244	33	99,229	561,000	660,229
Michigan	29	431,073	330,627	761,700	25	174,169	838,967	1,1013,136
Minnesota	40	14,094	161,020	175,114	25	107,663	421,376	529,039
Mississippi	25	2,300	100,000	102,300	40	32,082	5,000	37,082
Missouri	30	191,084	337,464	528,548	29	30,439	56,770	87,209

State								
Montana	25	24,560	108,689	133,249	28	30,600	125,471	156,071
Nebraska	40	10,600	14,500	25,100	25	7,300	5,000	12,330
Nevada	43	14,683	36,101	50,784	22	10,069	20,000	30,069
New Hampshire	37	26,400	84,800	111,200	17	34,043	64,000	98,043
New Jersey	33	655,027	243,258	898,285	29	83,115	154,000	237,115
New Mexico	29	99,322	92,018	191,340	22	18,508	96,000	114,508
New York	37	243,037	612,125	855,162	22	50,439	1,664,896	1,715,335
North Carolina	30	167,897	596,300	764,197	20	28,965	92,200	121,165
North Dakota	37	9,350	54,150	63,500	33	15,718	51,500	67,218
Ohio	33	620,931	279,043	899,974	22	46,387	116,745	163,132
Oklahoma	37	15,263	0	15,253	13	45,281	1,742	47,023
Oregon	33	132,956	171,540	304,496	14	33,074	50,000	83,074
Pennsylvania	33	364,672	572,579	937,251	28	224,415	682,216	906,631
Rhode Island	25	40,140	10,000	50,140	25	29,170	0	29,170
South Carolina	43	30,288	52,276	82,554	14	25,371	10,000	35,371
South Dakota	37	10,100	43,103	53,203	13	4,313	20,000	24,313
Tennessee	37	194,223	260,961	455,134	33	97,396	310,703	408,099
Texas	29	445,786	1,035,766	1,481,552	22	136,324	771,706	908,030
Utah	33	5,800	8,000	13,800	33	10,764	35,000	45,764
Vermont	33	35,622	43,420	79,042	22	5,820	41,750	47,570
Virginia	40	2,306	25,812	28,118	25	79,404	481,642	561,046
Washington	33	93,137	82,492	175,629	33	121,879	238,486	360,365
West Virginia	25	117,793	0	117,793	29	5,959	0	5,959
Wisconsin	43	225,778	215,146	440,924	28	24,989	113,000	137,989
Wyoming	33	3,800	8,000	11,800	22	7,968	75,000	82,968
Total		7,001,303	9,500,489	16,501,792		2,527,402	10,240,672	12,768,074

Robert Biersack

Table 7.3b National Party Financial Support of States (Republican)

	1991-92				1993-94			
State	Federal % of Ballot	RNC Federal Transfers	RNC Soft Money Transfers	Total RNC Contributions to State/Local Parties	Federal % of Ballot	RNC Federal Transfers	RNC Soft Money Transfers	Total Contributions to State/Local Parties
Alabama	50	$5,596	$3,731	$59,327	12	$1,071	$516,428	$517,499
Alaska	50	21,450	13,550	35,000	20	22,500	52,500	75,000
Arizona	34	96,800	68,400	165,200	22	276,700	51,800	328,500
Arkansas	50	0	11,500	11,500	12	52,500	42,500	95,000
California	44	1,625	489,650	491,275	22	871,500	74,500	892,000
Colorado	33	50,650	74,401	125,051	12	5,000	135,000	140,000
Connecticut	43	18,500	0	18,500	22	394,000	0	394,000
Delaware	25	6,250	61,750	68,000	25	33,345	86,793	120,138
Florida	43	201,519	222,432	423,951	28	287,500	512,500	800,000
Georgia	33	179,181	292,860	472,041	12	1,625	338,375	340,000
Hawaii	43	0	0	0	29	100,500	431,500	532,000
Idaho	50	12,875	15,625	28,500	12	2,133	202,220	204,353
Illinois	50	53,334	175,785	229,119	12	0	87,500	87,500
Indiana	33	4,000	90,497	94,497	25	11,250	118,750	130,000
Iowa	43	69,231	136,921	206,152	13	32,655	243,090	275,745
Kansas	50	0	15,000	15,000	14	90,000	14,250	104,250
Kentucky	33	1,300	51,059	52,359	25	108,250	4,000	112,250
Louisiana	33	90,533	30,177	120,710	33	30,000	0	30,000
Maine	33	585	25,671	26,256	29	40,559	100,241	140,800
Maryland	50	19,000	0	19,000	22	135,416	0	135,416
Massachusetts	40	19,300	0	19,300	33	69,200	0	69,200
Michigan	29	306,758	307,325	614,083	25	790,945	63,000	853,945
Minnesota	40	12,939	10,850	23,789	25	139,589	437,500	577,089
Mississippi	25	12,000	8,500	20,500	40	20,000	7,000	27,000
Missouri	30	41,853	207,987	249,840	29	0	93,355	93,355

Montana	25	11,153	54,221	65,374	28	27,010	48,190	75,200
Nebraska	40	0	0	0	25	0	68,900	68,900
Nevada	43	750	49,366	50,116	22	19,700	145,300	165,000
New Hampshire	37	40,977	8,500	49,477	17	75,000	10,000	85,000
New Jersey	33	113,442	184,793	298,235	29	13,000	323,322	336,322
New Mexico	29	18,525	22,627	41,152	22	49,383	95,617	145,000
New York	37	13,000	0	13,000	22	485,550	1,069,450	1,555,000
North Carolina	30	42,479	325,452	367,931	20	15,571	30,928	46,499
North Dakota	37	61,775	253,775	315,550	33	16,254	0	16,254
Ohio	33	128,209	968,891	1,097,100	22	0	750,00	750,000
Oklahoma	37	10,875	69,903	80,778	13	97,684	135,000	232,684
Oregon	33	9,766	20,000	29,756	14	20,305	97,624	117,929
Pennsylvania	33	7,350	226,381	233,731	28	302,900	114,100	417,000
Rhode Island	25	0	14,000	14,000	25	94,125	10,000	104,125
South Carolina	43	0	239,500	239,500	14	125,092	4,265	129,357
South Dakota	37	0	25,178	25,178	13	9,000	21,000	30,000
Tennessee	33	89,066	22,522	111,588	33	124,000	291,000	415,000
Texas	29	51,369	184,377	235,746	22	70,500	216,500	287,000
Utah	33	0	0	0	33	8,650	41,050	49,700
Vermont	33	6,200	101,833	108,033	22	24,735	56,500	81,235
Virginia	40	115,325	9,000	124,325	25	25,000	91,000	116,000
Washington	33	5,275	256,725	262,000	33	128,350	55,650	184,000
West Virginia	25	4,000	0	4,000	29	0	0	0
Wisconsin	43	237,210	20,000	257,210	28	277,800	33,500	311,300
Wyoming	33	2,500	7,880	10,380	22	53,750	16,250	70,000
Total		2,224,525	5,398,595	7,623,120		5,525,597	7,337,958	12,863,545

exclusively to state and local elections remains completely within the purview of state law and is only disclosed if required by that state law. In some respects, the partial nature of the information about state parties included here makes their financial position more impressive than it first appears. Any purely state and local activity would only enhance the already strong financial performance of these organizations.

One state party organization (the New Jersey Republican Party) chose to disclose all of its financial activity in its federal reports. New Jersey is one of only two states that hold state elections in odd-numbered years, so it may represent an unusual case. In this instance, however, about 25 percent of the total funds spent during the cycle were devoted to direct support of state and local candidates ($1.2 million out of $4.6 million spent) in an election cycle with no gubernatorial campaign. Extrapolating from a single case is very problematic, but it seems likely that in many cases total state party activity would be at least 25 percent more than what is reported here. National party support represented about 11 percent of the total fundraising of the New Jersey Republican Party during 1991–92.

Party Integration

The regulations and reporting rules now in place permit a better examination of the financial relationships between national parties and their state components. Table 7.3 lists for each state the sum of all national party financial support for both the 1991–92 and 1993–94 cycles. The Democratic National Committee and its congressional campaign committees provided some monetary or in-kind support to every state Democratic organization, with amounts ranging from $10,750 in Alaska to nearly $1.9 million in California. The Republican national organizations provided financial assistance to all states except Hawaii and Nebraska, and provided nearly $1.1 million in funds and services to the Ohio Republican party alone.

Roughly two-thirds of the support given by national committees came from sources outside the limits and restrictions of the FECA, to be used for nonfederal elections. Some of these funds might have been used as part of the state soft money share of joint activity. They might also have been used for strictly state and local purposes, which would mean their ultimate use could not be isolated in state party filings at the FEC. The full scope of state party activity remains out of our reach here, and this limitation also affects our ability to fully specify the relationship between national parties and their state counterparts. We know the total amount that the national organizations have provided to the states, but we do not have a full picture of how much money the state parties generated on their own. As a result, our conclusions about the dependence of "subordinate" levels of party on national fundraising must be seen as cautious and preliminary.

How the national committees choose among the states when allocating scarce resources is no doubt a complex calculation. Clearly the size of the state and the complexity and competitiveness of elections are critical factors. In a presidential election cycle, it is also reasonable to assume that the nature of that campaign would shape national party priorities, as would the existence of a competitive gubernatorial race. Other factors might include the capacity of the state party to use funds or services to their best effect, and the relationship between state party leaders and the national committee. Finally, state campaign finance law may restrict the types of national party support that could be accepted and thereby affect the total amount of financial assistance provided.

A cursory examination of DNC transfers to state parties in table 7.3 suggests that, while the demands of the presidential campaign are plainly associated with the distribution of soft dollars, other factors are as work as well. There are states with large numbers of electoral votes in which the presidential margin was very close whose state committees received relatively little DNC soft money (Florida, Virginia, and Indiana, for example). On the other hand, some relatively small states received much more soft money (e.g., Louisiana). Deviations from a purely presidential strategy are also apparent when RNC soft transfers are examined. Here states like North Dakota, Washington, and South Carolina received far more soft money support from the national party than their place in the presidential campaign would suggest—faring better than big competitive states like Texas and New Jersey and Florida. The existence of competitive gubernatorial elections seems to have been important here, and factors like the role of state campaign finance law, which are not included in the table, may also be important.

Just as important as the dollar value of national party support at the state level is the proportion of total state activity provided in this way. While new reporting requirements imposed in the 1992 election cycle disclose more of the activity of each state party in one place, a complete examination of this question is still dependent upon information available only at the state level.

Conclusion

This chapter has described the context within which state and national parties raise and spend the "mother's milk of politics." As such it represents a starting point for further more careful consideration of the role of finance in the development of parties at all levels. The information provided here reinforces findings of other studies of party organization by demonstrating once again that parties at the state level are, for the most part, large and complex financial organizations. How (or in fact whether) these resources are translated into meaningful political activity is an important question beyond the scope of this effort.

We have also begun to probe the financial relationships among different levels of party, finding some states that appear quite dependent on their national counterparts and others that seem more inclined or more able to go it alone financially. How these financial ties affect other aspects of intraparty relationships is another area of inquiry that the information presented here can only partially inform.

8

How We Are Doing: Party Leaders Evaluate Performance of the 1994 Elections

Andrew M. Appleton
Daniel S. Ward

The 1994 elections produced a dramatic change in the American political landscape. The capture of both the U.S. Senate and House of Representatives by the Republican Party for the first time in forty years came as something of a shock to many seasoned observers. The breadth and depth of the victory was even more remarkable as Republicans won governorships and state legislature seats in all regions. These results prompted commentators to issue dire predictions of the impending disintegration of the Democratic Party and parallel rosy forecasts of Republican ascendancy. Although some of the immediacy of the results has now receded, most observers would agree that the 1994 elections have had a profound impact upon both major parties.

There is a common theme embedded in this commentary, namely, that electoral outcomes, particularly dramatic ones, have an impact upon party organizations themselves. This perspective corresponds to the adaptive view of party organization that has received much attention by scholars in the last fifteen years. At the general theoretical level, such a view has been articulated in its most comprehensive form by Panebianco (1988), Schlesinger (1991), and Harmel and Janda (1994). In the American context, this approach is reflected in the work of the Party Transformation Study (Cotter et al. 1989; Harmel and Janda 1982; and Gitelson, Conway, and Feigert 1994).

However, these scholars do not see party adaptation occurring in the same way. For example, some argue that there is just one standard for assessing electoral success, and that is victory (Schlesinger 1991), while others see a more complex picture, which may include a better than expected performance or simply improvement at the polls (Strom 1990). In addition, some scholars understand party change as forward looking, adapting organizational practices to fit anticipated outcomes (Schlesinger 1991), while others stress that change follows electoral outcomes (Harmel and Janda 1994; Panebianco 1988). Another point of difference concerns the type of outcomes that produce adaptation. Some scholars argue that adaptation is likely only in the case of "catastrophic failure," that is, when parties fall far short of previous levels of performance (Harmel and Janda 1994; Panebianco 1988). Another possibility is that parties adapt to unexpectedly positive performances (Appleton and Ward 1994b).

One of the challenges to understanding party adaptation is to discover the mechanism by which electoral outcomes, however conceived, are linked to organizational change. While repeated observation may yield a statistically compelling association between electoral results and party adaptation, fundamental question still remains: what is the causal mechanism by which the election results are translated into organizational change?

In our view, party leadership is important to answering this question. After all, leaders play a key role in organizational adaptation, and their views, practices and expectations influence the interpretation of events and structure the resulting change. From this point of view, a number of basic questions come to mind. First, how do party leaders define electoral success? What tools do they use to develop their expectations? Which factors do they regard as important in elections and what role do they assign to their own organizations? Second, how well do leaders predict elections? How do prior expectations relate to their evaluation of their party's performance at the polls? And what other factors influence these evaluations? Finally, how are performance evaluations related to organizational change? Here we offer a preliminary exploration of these issues for state party leaders and the 1994 elections.

Data and Methods

This chapter is based on a two-part survey of Democratic and Republican state party leaders surrounding the 1994 elections. The first part was mailed in mid-September of 1994 and a follow-up was sent out three weeks later. The questionnaire was addressed to the chair of each state party; the chairs were asked to pass it on to the executive director if he or she preferred not to participate. This approach yielded a return rate of 54 percent (23 Democratic and 31 Republican responses), which is quite reasonable given the proximity of the survey to a major election.

The second part was conducted early in 1995, with an initial mailing sent the first week in February and a follow-up two weeks later, addressed to the same sample. This survey yielded a response rate of 46 percent. A total of twenty-six parties responded to both the pre- and postelection surveys. In some cases, the same individual did not respond to both the pre- and postelection survey, so the over-time data must be viewed with some caution.

The preelection survey included five-point Likert scale items on criteria for electoral success or failure, the tools used to establish electoral expectations, the role of the state party versus other organizations in various kinds of races, and the roles played by state and national parties in the campaign. We also asked respondents to predict the outcome of the upcoming elections in their states. In the postelection survey, we asked the party leaders to evaluate their parties' electoral performance, account for the sources of that performance, and speculate on the impact of the outcomes on organizational changes, also using five-point Likert scales.

Data Analysis

What Constitutes Success?

In order for a party to evaluate its performance, it must establish standards for success or failure. The most obvious of these is winning elections, and one that is reinforced by the dominance of single-member districts and plurality voting. But other standards are possible, including doing better than expected or improving at the polls, even if short of victory. For example, Republican Party organizations in the South during the 1960s were not likely to have measured their success by victories alone. "Making progress" by doing better than before or by achieving a relatively high percentage of the vote could satisfy. Similarly, winning a single important race in the context of opposition party dominance might be a reasonable goal as well.

With this question in mind, we asked party leaders to indicate the relative importance of several factors for measuring their success in the impending elections: "winning races," "doing better than in the previous election," "maximizing your party's share of the vote," and "winning a specific race." Table 8.1 shows the results broken down by party; the entries indicate the mean scores on five-point scales ranging from 1 (not at all important) to 5 (very important).

Table 8.1 Performance Evaluation Criteria

	Party	
	Democrats	Republicans
Winning races	4.70*	4.86
Winning a particular race	4.53	4.19
Maximizing vote share	4.18	4.04
Doing better than before	3.45	3.68

Note: N = 54 for tables 8.1 to 8.6; N = 46 for tables 8.7 to 8.10. Where questions were not relevant to all states, actual numbers of responses were lower.
* 5 = very important

Interestingly, respondents to both parties ranked these criteria the same. These results suggest that leaders shared a perception of a highly competitive environment, where winning races was far more important than doing better or simply maximizing votes. Among the respondents who rated winning a particular race as important, the vast majority chose the governor's race as the key indicator of success for that election, a result that fits with the historic connection between state party organizations and the governor's office (Cotter et al. 1989: 93).

However, there is some variation in these standards of success. In table 8.2, we take the average for each respondent across the "win" and "win a particular race" categories (labeled "win") and the "do better" and "vote share" categories (labeled "do better"). Here we can see that southern respondents rate relative success significantly higher than other regions. This appears to reflect lingering modes of evaluation by the once minority Republicans. Thus, while victory is the principal standard for electoral performance, relative measures of success are not unimportant.

The Tools of Performance Evaluation

How do party leaders arrive at electoral expectations, be it for victory or some relative measure of success? We asked respondents to rate the importance of a number of sources of information for determining their preelection expectations, using the same five-point scales as above (i.e., where 5 means "very important"). These sources include traditional means of information gathering, such as past experience, canvassing, local intelligence, and news reports, and more modern means, such as three kinds of polls (polls conducted by the party itself, by private polling firms, and by the media), and national party intelligence. Table 8.3 provides the mean responses, broken down by party and by traditional versus modern techniques.

Table 8.2 Regional Variation on Evaluation Criteria

	Win	Do Better
Northeast	4.81*	3.58
South	4.79	4.32
Midwest	4.54	3.50
West	4.41	3.88

* 5 = very important

Table 8.3 Tools for Performance Evaluation

	Democrats	Republicans
Traditional Techniques		
Past Experience	4.41*	4.03
Canvassing	3.73	3.52
Local Intelligence	3.48	3.42
News Reports	3.09	3.03
Average	3.68	3.50
Modern Techniques		
Private poll	3.18	3.73
Media poll	2.96	2.97
National Intelligence	2.90	2.89
Own poll	2.78	2.54
Average	2.96	3.03

* 5 = very important

Once again, the Democrats and Republicans rank the items the same, with just one exception: Republicans put private polls in second place whereas Democrats put them in fourth (this difference is not, however, statistically significant). Both parties tend to favor traditional techniques over modern ones, with past experience providing parties with their most reliable information, followed by canvasing and "reports from the field." There is some evidence that personal experience may affect these patterns information: longer-serving leaders relied more on past experience and also ranked private polls higher.[1] Along these lines, few of the state parties conducted their own polls and national party information is among the least important.

Which Organizations Matter?

Do state party leaders believe their organizations matter in elections? If not, standards of success and tools of performance evaluation are simply academic exercises. We asked respondents to rank the importance of four kinds of political organizations in determining the outcome of gubernatorial, congressional, and state legislative races in their states. Table 8.4 reports the mean responses, using the same five-point scales as before (i.e., where 5 means "very important").

Table 8.4 Organizational Impact on Election Outcomes

Organization	Governor's Race		Congressional Races		State Legislative Races	
	Dem	Rep	Dem	Rep	Dem	Rep
Candidate campaign	4.94*	4.92	4.78	4.90	4.74	4.75
State party	4.28	4.27	3.87	3.65	4.17	4.63
National party	2.83	2.96	3.74	4.00	1.61	2.48
Independent organizations	2.28	2.63	2.77	2.62	2.41	2.63

* 5 = very important

Once again, there is considerable consistency between the two parties. Candidates' campaign organizations are considered to be most important in all three types of races, and generally by a wide margin. The state party is second ranked, with the exception of Republican congressional races, where national party organization were more influential. Finally, independent organizations (such as the League of Women Voters, etc.) are considered least important in all but state legislative races for Democrats, where the national party also was of little relevance. Thus, state party leaders clearly view their own organizations as a central player in elections across the board. But they also recognize their own limitations in comparison to the candidates themselves. To be sure, candidate-centered politics is powerfully reflected in these data.

What Role for the State Party?

If state parties are perceived to matter in elections, then what role do they play? We asked the respondents to rate the importance of the state and national party organizations in a list of campaign activities, applying the same five-point scale as before. Table 8.5 reports the mean responses. Here there are some important differences between the Republicans and the Democrats. Although both rank candidate support and canvassing as the two most important activities, they diverge after that point. Democrats place considerably more weight on producing print materials, and Republicans rate their role in TV and radio advertising significantly higher.

Responses on the national parties' role in state campaigns are revealing and generally support the results from table 8.4, where the national parties were shown to be of minimal importance. Democratic state leaders fail to rate a single activity at the midpoint (3) or higher, while Republicans rate polling at the midpoint and candidate support a bit higher. Three important differences appear for Republicans and Democrats on national party evalu-

Table 8.5 Party Role in the Election Campaign

| | State Party | | National Party | |
	Dems	Reps	Dems	Reps
Candidate support	4.30 (1)*	4.29 (1)	2.48 (4)	3.29 (1)
Canvassing	4.30 (1)	4.03 (2)	1.86 (8)	2.46 (7)
Print material	4.22 (3)	3.61 (5)	1.87 (7)	1.89 (8)
Media	3.74 (4)	3.87 (3)	2.48 (4)	2.86 (4)
Issue research	3.52 (5)	3.39 (7)	2.91 (1)	2.97 (3)
Opposition research	3.43 (6)	3.68 (4)	2.78 (2)	2.86 (4)
Polling	3.30 (7)	3.16 (8)	2.09 (6)	3.00 (2)
TV/Radio advertising	2.74 (8)	3.42 (6)	2.57 (3)	2.62 (6)

* 5 = very important; ranking of responses in parentheses

ations: canvassing, polling, and candidate support. In each case, the Republicans rank the role of the national party higher than Democrats. These results reflect the relative success of the Republicans' national organizations in providing assistance to the state parties and candidates at the state level.

Predicting Election Outcomes

How well did state party leaders predict the outcomes of the 1994 elections in their states? We asked the respondents their expectations regarding the results of the five kinds of races: U.S. House of Representatives, U.S. Senate, governor, state lower and state upper houses of the state legislature (not all states had each kind of race in 1994). Table 8.6 reports the mean gap between outcomes and expectations in all five types of races, for the whole sample and broken down by party. The entries represent the absolute value of the mean difference between prediction and outcome. In the case of gubernatorial and U.S. Senate races, predictions were for the percentage of the vote; for U.S. House and state legislative races, the respondents predicted the net change in the party's delegation.

Democrats predicted less well than Republicans in all types of races. This may be a reflection of the unusual outcome of the 1994 elections, but it should be noted that our measure captures underestimation as well as overestimation. On average, party leaders were off by nearly eight percentage points on governor's races, with Democrats performing slightly worse than Republicans (though the difference is not statistically significant). In U.S. Senate races, the Democrats scored considerably worse than Republicans, and in this case the difference in means test is significant at the .05 level. For the

Table 8.6 Expectations and Performance in the 1994 Elections

	Mean Gap*	Std Dev
Governor (percentage points)		
Both parties	7.74	5.25
Democrats	9.08	6.72
Republicans	7.00	4.25
U.S. Senate (percentage points)		
Both parties	3.84	7.18
Democrats	8.40	7.82
Republicans	1.31	5.52
U.S. House (seat change)		
Both parties	1.38	1.33
Democrats	1.75	1.59
Republicans	1.11	1.05
State Legislature		
Lower House (seat change)		
Both parties	1.64	9.37
Democrats	7.06	9.62
Republicans	2.04	7.30
State Legislature		
Upper House (seat change)		
Both parties	1.18	4.03
Democrats	3.80	4.33
Republicans	0.52	2.76

* absolute value of gap between prediction and outcome

U.S. House, and state legislative seats, Democrats again performed worse than Republicans (significant at the .10 level for the U.S. House, at .05 for the state legislature).

Another consistent pattern was that of overestimation: party leaders anticipated better outcomes than they achieved. This may reflect general optimism among party leaders or an unwillingness to predict defeat publicly. The exception was Republican predictions for state legislative election outcomes, which were better than expected. There is little doubt that this finding is a result of the unexpectedly strong performance of Republicans at the state level in 1994. Even the overly optimistic chairs did not foresee the extent of the Republican sweep that was to come.

Postelection Performance Evaluations

The postelection survey queried leaders about their party's performance in the 1994 election, also for gubernatorial, U.S. Senate, U.S. House, and state legislative races. The questions were worded to take expectations into account: "How well did your party perform in the 1994 U.S. House elections in your state, compared to your prior expectation?" Responses were recorded on a five-point scale ranging from 1 ("much worse than expected") to 5 ("much better than expected"), and were then collapsed into three categories, "worse" (responded 1 or 2), "same" (responded 3), and "better" (responded 4 or 5). Table 8.7 breaks down these results for each kind of office, first by the actual election results (gain, lose, no change) and then by preelection predictions (accurate or underestimated party performance, and overestimated performance.)

Table 8.7 Determinants of Performance Evaluation

| | Evaluation Score | | | | |
| | Change in Seats | | | Prediction | |
	Gain	Lose	No Change	Under/Even	Over
U.S. House Races					
worse	0	8	3	1	6
same	4	2	9	1	8
better	11	2	5	8	2
U.S. Senate Races					
worse	0	2	3	0	3
same	0	0	9	1	6
better	4	0	9	3	2
Governors Races					
worse	0	3	7	0	6
same	2	0	6	3	2
better	4	1	9	5	3
State Legislative Races					
worse	0	12	0	0	7
same	3	7	0	1	3
better	16	0	0	7	2

Note: Table contains actual number of responses in each category.

As might be expected, these data reveal that postelection evaluations are strongly associated with electoral success—even when the question is framed in terms of expectations. Not a single respondent whose party gained seats thought they had done worse than expected. On the other hand, three respondents who reported losses (two in U.S. House and one gubernatorial race) claimed to have done better than expected. In addition, a fair number of leaders whose parties gained or lost seats claimed to have performed roughly as expected. These patterns parallel our previous findings on winning versus doing better as a standard of success: while victory is a key factor, postelection performance evaluations are also a function of relative expectations.

Determinants of Party Performance

What factors determined the outcome of the 1994 elections? We asked respondents to evaluate the significance of both the national and state party political contexts, the quality of their own candidate and the opposition, media campaign coverage, campaign issues, their own candidates' financial resources, and those of the opposition. Table 8.8 reports the mean score on each item for the four types of races, broken down by party and performance evaluation score.

A. National versus State Political Context. It is not a surprise to find that national politics was rated more important in U.S. House and Senate races than in gubernatorial and state legislative elections, and that the reverse is true for state offices. In addition, Democratic respondents consider national politics to be more important than Republican respondents in all but U.S. Senate races, where the scores were even. Conversely, Republicans rated state politics higher than Democrats in each type of race. Clearly, state Democrats considered the national political context to be a determining factor in their poor showing in 1994. This pattern held even at the level of state legislative races, where Democratic respondents viewed national politics as more important. Second, with the exception of governors' races, parties that fared worse than expected tended to blame national politics. On the flip side, those parties faring better than expected gave greater weight to state politics in all but U.S. House races, where the scores were even. It appears that parties that performed poorly were eager to place the blame as far away from their own doorstep as possible, while those doing better saw the explanation as being closer to home.

B. Quality of Candidates. The quality of a party's own candidates was considered a more significant factor than the quality of the opposition's candidate. One exception was found among Democratic respondents in gubernatorial races, where the quality of the opposition was rated more significant. Among parties performing better than expected, the quality of one's own candidates was rated first or second. Parties performing worse

Table 8.8 Party Performance Score by Party and Performance Evaluation

	Political Context		Candidates				Finance	
	National	State	Own	Rival	Media	Issues	Own	Rival
U.S. House Races								
Dems	3.87*	3.48	3.70	3.35	3.61	3.43	3.87	4.00
Reps	3.82	3.77	4.41	3.91	2.95	3.95	4.09	3.68
Performance Evaluation								
worse	4.42	2.92	3.17	2.67	3.75	3.75	3.42	3.75
same	3.40	3.93	4.13	3.87	3.07	3.33	3.93	3.87
better	3.83	3.83	4.56	4.06	3.17	3.94	4.39	3.89
All	3.84	3.62	4.04	3.62	3.29	3.69	3.98	3.84
U.S. Senate Races								
Dems	3.77	3.23	3.62	3.62	3.85	3.38	4.08	3.92
Reps	3.77	3.38	4.62	4.42	3.54	3.54	3.92	3.85
Performance Evaluation								
worse	4.75	2.50	3.25	3.00	.375	3.75	3.50	3.50
same	3.70	3.20	4.10	4.22	3.40	3.10	3.70	4.00
better	3.50	3.67	4.42	4.17	3.92	3.67	4.42	3.92
All	3.77	3.31	4.12	4.00	3.69	3.46	4.00	3.88
Governors' Races								
Dems	3.00	3.56	3.75	4.00	3.88	3.88	4.19	4.19
Reps	2.94	4.12	4.24	3.82	3.35	3.76	4.12	4.00
Performance Evaluation								
worse	2.91	3.36	3.36	3.73	3.82	3.55	3.91	4.27
same	3.00	4.38	3.75	3.63	3.63	4.00	4.00	3.75
better	3.00	3.93	4.64	4.21	3.43	3.93	4.43	4.14
All	2.97	3.85	4.00	3.91	3.61	3.82	4.15	4.09
State Legislative Races								
Dems	3.43	3.14	3.62	3.10	3.05	3.05	3.62	3.76
Reps	3.00	4.53	4.16	3.79	2.68	3.89	3.79	3.42
Performance Evaluation								
worse	3.54	3.31	3.31	3.25	3.31	3.15	3.15	3.38
same	3.30	3.50	3.90	3.20	2.60	3.00	4.20	4.30
better	2.94	4.35	4.29	3.71	2.71	3.94	3.82	3.35
All	3.23	3.80	3.88	3.44	2.88	3.45	3.70	3.60

* 5 = very important

than expected tended to rate the impact of their own candidates as very low. This result was statistically significant at the .01 level. And there appears to be a general unwillingness to credit the opposition, even though such credit would serve to inoculate party leaders against blame. The quality of the opponent was rated most important by parties that performed better than expected, indicating that some success is attributable to poor opposition. Thus, a party's own candidates were an asset instead of a liability.

C. The Role of Media and Campaign Issues. What impact did campaign issues and media coverage play in determining the performance of state political parties? According to our respondents, relatively little. Across all types of races, media coverage is considered more important in statewide races than in the legislative elections. Democrats rated media as more important than Republicans in all races, while parties performing worse than expected tend to rate media as more significant than those that did better. Taken together, these results suggest that media were more subject to blame than credit—not a surprise to any political observer. Republicans and better performing parties were more likely to consider campaign issues to be significant than their counterparts among Democrats and poor performers. As a result, we can conclude that issues were viewed as a positive factor among satisfied party leaders, though not necessarily as an impairment for dissatisfied leaders.

D. Party Finances. Among all respondents, their own candidates' finances were considered more important than the opposition's finances across election types. However, some interesting patterns emerge. First, Democrats rate the opposition's finances to be more significant in all elections. In fact, in three of the four election types, Democrats rate opposition finances to be more or as important as their own. Multivariate analyses of variance confirmed this finding, significant at the .05 level, for U.S. House and state legislative races. Clearly, Democrats view themselves as relatively underfinanced. Across the performance evaluation categories, the impact of money is apparent. In all four types of races, parties faring poorly viewed the opposition's finances to be equally or more important than their own. For the parties performing better than expected, the opposite is true, and by a wide margin. This result is confirmed at the .05 level. Apparently, in the view of party leaders, money matters in all types of political races, helping winners and hurting losers.

Performance Evaluation and Organizational Change

The postelection survey was administered only a relatively short time after the 1994 elections. Nonetheless, two-thirds of the respondents reported having already held an official evaluation of the party's performance, such as state central committee meetings, retreats, analyses of election returns, conferences and questionnaires; most of the remaining respondents planned such an evaluation. To assess what organizational changes might result from the election results, we queried party leaders about the likelihood of party building efforts, using a five-point scale ranging from 1 ("not at all likely") to 5 ("very likely"). Most respondents considered party building to be quite likely, with a mean response of 4.24, though Democrats (4.46) considered such efforts more likely than Republicans (4.00). Table 8.9 gives the overall mean party building score[2] for each office and level of performance evaluation, and parallel data for each party.

Clearly, party building was more likely for poor performers than for strong performers, providing some support for the hypothesis that parties change in response to electoral downturns. There is one important exception, however: better performers in gubernatorial elections viewed party building as most likely. This finding may also reflect the connection between governors and state party organizations.

If party building was to take place, what activities were most likely to be changed? We asked respondents how likely changes were in each of the following categories: candidate recruitment, get-out-the-vote drives, fundraising, polling, office size, staff size, provision of candidate services, and party leadership. We used the same five-point scale as above (i.e., 5 means "very likely"). Table 8.10 reports the mean responses for all respondents, and then broken down by party and levels of performance evaluation.

Overall, improvements in fundraising received the highest rating and changes in structural aspects of party organization (office, staff, polling, leadership) received the least attention, with electoral functions (candidate services, recruitment, GOTV) falling between. The Democrats forecast more change across the board over Republicans by large margins, and there was

Table 8.9 Performance Evaluation and Likelihood of Party Building

Mean Build	Evaluation Score		
	Worse	Same	Better
Overall	4.50*	4.47	3.89
U.S. House	4.55	4.27	3.94
U.S. Senate	4.58	4.27	4.00
Governor	4.44	4.20	4.59
State Legislative	4.38	4.60	3.94

Note: For the Democrats, 10 parties are categorized as "worse" on the overall evaluation score, 8 as "same," and 6 as "better." For the Republicans, these figures are 0, 9, and 13 respectively.

Table 8.10 Types of Party Building Changes by Party and Performance Evaluation

	Recruit	GOTV	Fundrais.	Polling	Office	Staff	Cand Serv.	Leader.
Dems	3.75*	3.79	4.25	3.36	2.75	2.96	4.00	3.35
Reps	3.38	3.05	3.82	3.05	2.36	2.36	3.73	3.27
Performance Evaluation								
worse	4.30	3.80	4.50	3.67	3.10	3.20	3.90	3.40
same	3.76	3.47	3.94	3.00	2.35	2.59	4.06	3.47
better	3.00	3.22	3.89	3.16	2.47	2.47	3.68	3.11
All	3.50	3.37	4.04	3.20	2.57	2.67	3.87	3.31

* 5 = very likely

a particularly large gap in GOTV. Among the poorest performing parties, candidate recruitment emerges substantially above the mean, though otherwise the differences across the categories are fairly consistent, with parties that were most disappointed most likely to forecast change.

Conclusion

Our analysis of the manner in which state party leaders both approached and evaluated the 1994 midterm elections has revealed intriguing findings. Party leaders expect to win elections, although relative expectations of success were sometimes important. Of great interest was the manner in which state party leaders built expectations, with traditional party organizational techniques ranked higher than their more modern counterparts. State party leaders held their own organizations to be central players in the electoral process, although they recognize the candidate-centered nature of campaigns. Our data also show that the national party was seen as an important part of the congressional electoral landscape, particularly among Republicans. State parties were active in campaigns, providing services such as candidate support and voter canvassing. There is an impressive correspondence between the reported relative weight of activities between the two parties. Party leaders did not, however, predict elections particularly well.

On the outcome side, we find that while winning was important to performance evaluations, leaders also took into account prior expectations. In forming post hoc cognitive maps of electoral performance, state party leaders viewed candidate quality as being determinant, and, interestingly, media coverage as less important. Universally, campaign finance was seen as vital to understanding performance, with Democrats seeing themselves as relatively underfinanced in the electoral market.

Lastly, we can report that leaders view organizational change as being linked to electoral performance: the more poorly a party fared in comparison to its expectations, the more change was anticipated. Not surprisingly, the dimensions of change were closely linked to the activities rated as important to outcomes, with financing ranking number one. Partisan differences were once again evident, with Democrats being more likely to anticipate change, paralleling their poor performance in the 1994 elections. However, there is some evidence that party leaders also respond to unanticipated victories with plans for change.

This chapter is only the beginning of a potentially fruitful line of inquiry. Nonetheless, we are confident that our results show the link between electoral outcomes and party change to be both complex and quantifiable. The data that we have generated indicate that the Democratic Party may be engaged in a process of quite substantial change at the state party level; but Republican state party leadership also see postelection adaptation as likely. To the question, How are we doing? party leaders seem to be fairly uniform in their response, "Quite well, but more can be done."

Notes

1.   These conclusions are based on simple bivariate correlations between the rankings of each item and an experience index created from responses to a number of questions about the leader's political history. The index is at a maximum of 6 from a respondent who is party chair, has served in that position in the party previously, was active in a party in another state, and has held public office (i.e., the respondent receives a score of one for each item). The correlation is positive and significant for the two items noted in the text.

2.   In order to explore the relationship between performance evaluation and party building, we created an overall evaluation score averaging the performance evaluations of each kind of race (i.e., U.S. House, U.S. Senate, governor, state legislative), and recoded the result into "worse" (1.0–2.5), "same" (2.51 to 3.5), and "better" (3.51 to 5.0).

9

The Republican Victories in 1994:
A View from the Grassroots

John C. Green

The 1994 midterm elections were a great and largely unexpected triumph for Republicans. Journalists and pundits struggled to find words adequate to describe the outcome, labeling it an "earthquake," "tsunami," "tidal wave" and "revolution," but "no superlative or metaphor seemed large enough to encompass the results" (Balz and Brownstein 1996: 55). Political scientists were only modestly less surprised and effusive. Ladd (1995: 1) proclaimed 1994 to be "entirely clear and unequivocal . . . a major off-year victory"; Jacobson (1996: 1) called it "extraordinary"; and Burnham (1995: 363) described it as "very probably the most consequential off-year election in (exactly) one hundred years." Talk of "realignment" and a "new era" came from all quarters.

Unlike popular commentators, however, scholars were quick to put 1994 in a broader context. The Republican gains were large but not necessarily permanent, the results were caused as much by long-standing trends as new departures, and the outcomes were generated through the basic operation of American politics rather a fundamental alteration. In part, scholarly caution revolved around the role of the Republican Party itself in the outcome. Some analysts stressed the underlying forces at work in the campaign (Ladd 1995), while others pointed to the unusual efforts of GOP leaders and organizations (Burnham 1995; Jacobson 1996).

This chapter reports the perspectives of grassroots Republican officials in four key states in 1994, and these mirror the mixed assessments of scholars. On the one hand, these respondents identified Republican candidates and opposition to "big government" as the most important factors in the election itself. But on the other hand, party unity and the activities of Republican committees, including the Contract with America, best explained their assessments of the party's performance in each state. These patterns reveal both the depth and the fragility of the Republican victory in 1994.

An Unusually Partisan Election

Just how big was the Republican victory in 1994? At the federal level, the GOP took control of both houses of Congress for the first time in forty-two years by winning a net of fifty-two seats in the House and eight in the Senate. This success extended to the state level as well, with the gain of eleven governors and another thirty major statewide offices, giving the GOP control of a majority of governorships and most state constitutional offices. The victory extended to a net of 469 state legislative seats, generating control of fifty state legislative chambers and eighteen legislatures, the largest number in forty years. And the Republicans enjoyed a similar level of success for local offices, particularly in the South. Not a single incumbent Republican was defeated for federal or statewide office, and perhaps only a handful for lower offices, while dozens of Democratic incumbents lost up and down the ticket.

As much as anything else, it was this highly partisan nature of the outcome which made the 1994 election so unusual, especially when compared to other Republican midterm gains, such as in 1966 and 1978. Of course, important features of contemporary politics militate against this kind of partisanship in elections (Beck and Sorauf 1992: chap 16). First, contemporary campaigns are candidate-centered, and individual candidates routinely operate with little regard to their party. Second, many critical issues generate sharper divisions within rather than between the parties, undermining a consistent message. Candidate-centered politics and cross-cutting issues are encouraged by a host of other actors, from interest groups and social movements to the news media. Finally, divided government, resulting in part from constitutional arrangements but also from candidates and issues, makes it difficult to hold one party responsible for government performance.

How did the Republicans overcome these factors in 1994? Writing about GOP congressional gains, Jacobson offers a concise description:

> In 1994, the Republicans won the House by fielding (modestly) superior candidates who were on the right of the issues that were important to voters in House elections and by persuading voters to blame a unified Democratic government for government's failures. (1995: 2)

No doubt the GOP benefited from some good fortune in each of these areas. A variety of factors, ranging from scandals to retirements and redistricting, produced a larger than usual number of open seats and unpopular Democratic incumbents, making it easier to recruit high quality Republican candidates. Major changes in the economy and social life focused public dissatisfaction on the role of government, giving the "antigovernment" party an excellent opportunity. In addition, Democratic-control institutions, including the White House and the Congress, had performed poorly on a number of high profile issues, setting themselves up for blame. Indeed, the GOP made its biggest gains precisely where these factors were most prominent, for example, in open seats with high-quality candidates and in conservative areas where President Clinton was particularly unpopular (Jacobson 1996).

The Republican Party was, however, unusually active in 1994, both terms of the scale and variety of its programs. First, the GOP leadership continued its vigorous, decade-long effort to recruit good candidates at all levels (Pitney and Connelly 1996). The work of a reinvigorated National Republican Congressional Committee and Newt Gingrich's GOPAC is but the best documented part of these efforts (Balz and Brownstein 1996). As a result, the GOP fielded a slightly larger number of experienced candidates than in the past (Jacobson 1996). In addition, their large pool of inexperienced candidates appear to have been more adept and better organized than their previous counterparts (Maisel et al. 1996). Recruitment was aided by three factors for which the party organizations can take credit: a unified message, a united coalition, and an unusual level of campaign resources.

Unlike most midterm contests, the Republican leaders developed a unified antigovernment message that permeated the campaign. The "Contract with America" offered by the Republican congressional leadership (see chapter 19 in this volume) was the most prominent part of this effort, but similar "contracts" were offered by twenty-five state Republican parties (Little 1996). Beyond these documents themselves, key elements of the Contract were promoted by other state parties and by candidates who did not formally endorse the documents themselves. Although the direct impact on voters was probably very small, the Contract had a strong, positive effect on Republican candidates, invigorating and nationalizing their campaigns (Burnham 1995; Jacobson 1996). This unified message both reflected and encouraged a united party coalition, linking together increasingly diverse Republican constituencies (Balz and Brownstein 1996). For example, groups with libertarian biases, such as taxpayers groups and gun owners, worked closely with groups dedicated to morals regulation, such as the Christian Right and pro-life activists. The business community was unusually united in its support of the Republican effort.

A solid candidate corps, a unified message, and a united coalition allowed the Republicans to acquire an unusual level of campaign resources (Jacobson 1996). For example, the Republican National Committee (RNC) raised some $133 million in hard and soft money in 1994—10 percent more than in the 1992 presidential campaign (see chapter 7 in this volume). These funds allowed the RNC to contribute $20 million directly to candidates and state parties in addition to its usual range of high quality services. Again, the congressional Republicans have been studied most fully: incumbents were persuaded to contribute heavily to the party's coffers and then helped challengers raise funds (Balz and Brownstein 1996). Similar efforts occurred at the congressional, state, and local levels.

What effect did these activities have on the election outcome and on the overall performance of the GOP? While the answer is far from clear, we can offer a unique perspective on the question: the views of Republican officials at the grassroots. To date, scholars have focused primarily on the perceptions of national party leaders and candidates in assessing election outcomes, and the perception of local party officials have been less frequently investigated.

Data and Methods

This chapter is based on surveys of 1994 Republican state convention delegates in four states. Random samples of one thousand delegates to the conventions in Washington state, Texas, and Minnesota were surveyed in early 1995, with the following return rates (excluding undeliverable mail): Washington, 60.0 percent (506 usable returns), Texas, 59.6 percent (507 usable returns), and Minnesota, 59.5 percent (511 usable returns). A random sample of one thousand delegates to the 1995 Florida "Presidency III" convention were surveyed in early 1996, with a return rate of 45 percent (404 usable returns). The same survey instrument was used in all four states, which included a host of items assessing the 1994 Republican electoral performance in the state, the degree of Republican unity, and the impact of prominent issues and organizations on the outcome.

These states ran the gamut of election outcomes in 1994 (Barone and Ujifusa 1995). Washington state was certainly a Republican success story. The GOP gained six House seats, ousting five Democratic incumbents, including Speaker Thomas Foley, and gaining control of the lower chamber of the state legislature. The Republicans had nearly as good a year in Texas, where they captured the governorship, two congressional, several statewide and a number of legislative seats. Florida was less positive. Although the Republicans gained three congressional seats and took control of the state Senate, they narrowly lost the governorship and a number of other close races. The Republicans narrowly avoided an electoral disaster in Minnesota. The party's state convention endorsed a religious conservative, Allen Quist, over the sitting Republican governor, Arne Carlson. Although Carlson was eventually reelected, the GOP just maintained its hold on other federal and state offices. All four states experienced a similar high level of party effort, including state-level versions of the Contract with America or similar themes by statewide candidates.

Assessing the 1994 Election

Table 9.1 reports on GOP delegates' assessments of the 1994 election in their states, reporting first the percentage of the most positive responses and then the mean score (all items were five-point Likert scales). The table begins with general queries about the overall GOP performance and the degree of party unity. The results generally follow the election returns. Better than one-half of the Washington state delegates reported an "excellent" performance and one-quarter claimed their state party was "solidly united." Texas and Florida reported lower numbers, while Minnesota came in last, with just one-tenth of the delegates offering an excellent assessment and almost none claiming the party was united. It is noteworthy that even in a very successful year, these delegates were far from satisfied with their party's performance.

The rest of table 9.1 reports assessments of the impact of various organizations and issues on the 1994 elections. These data reveal the usual suspects in contemporary campaigns. In terms of organizations, Republican candidates rated first or second in all four states, followed by prominent social movements and interest groups, including the Christian Right, prolife, term limits, gun control, business, and taxpayers groups. Note that local and state Republican organizations fared about as well as the interest groups, but substantially behind the candidates, an interesting finding, given than to some degree these respondents are evaluating themselves. The national GOP ranked almost last, beating out Ross Perot's 1992 backers (see chapter 14 in this volume). Candidate-centered politics is clearly evident in these findings, but on the other hand, candidates did not dominate the process completely.

A similar pattern holds for assessments of the impact of issues. In all four states, opposition to "big government" ranked first, followed closely by "disgust with politics as usual," and then by welfare programs and President Clinton's popularity. These issues were closely related, of course, and linked to the Contract with America and its state variants. However, the Contract itself received many fewer mentions, ranking a distant fifth in Washington and Florida, and sixth in Texas and Minnesota. Social issues, including abortion, gun control, and affirmative action, and local economic conditions, appear at the end of the list. The similar patterns of responses across states reveals the degree to which issues were nationalized in 1994.

Thus, these grassroots Republican officials saw the 1994 election turning on the strength of their party's candidates and potency of antigovernment messages, supplemented by allied interests, party activities, and a number of secondary issues. These patterns change very little when controls are instituted for a other variables, such length of service in the party, professional or amateur style, issue positions, or membership in party factions. For example, controlling for association with the Christian Right does not alter the relative importance of these assessments. These patterns certainly support cautious interpretations of the 1994 election offered by scholars.

Table 9.1 GOP Performance and Contributing Factors in the 1994 Elections; State Convention Delegates

N of Cases	Washington (506)		Texas (507)		Florida (404)		Minnesota (511)	
	%	Mean	%	Mean	%	Mean	%	Mean
State Republicans								
Successful*	54	1.62	39	1.73	22	1.93	10	2.65
United**	25	2.07	15	2.31	19	2.19	1	3.52
Organizations*								
GOP candidates	59	1.52	48	1.76	50	1.65	46	1.78
Christian right	35	2.16	51	1.81	27	2.38	33	2.18
Local party	30	2.31	26	2.44	26	2.45	17	2.67
Prolife groups	27	2.42	40	2.05	17	2.64	33	2.11
Term limiters	25	2.31	24	2.31	16	2.75	14	2.68
State party	24	2.44	23	2.56	26	2.34	12	2.94
Pro gun groups	23	2.37	24	2.39	12	2.91	16	2.68
Business groups	22	2.28	18	2.52	16	2.50	14	2.59
Taxpayer groups	21	2.48	11	2.82	17	2.58	5	3.04
National party	10	3.02	12	2.97	9	2.95	11	3.13
Perot backers	3	3.64	2	3.89	9	3.12	2	3.71
Issues*								
Big government	78	1.28	65	1.47	58	1.60	49	1.73
Disgust politics	71	1.43	64	1.58	52	1.78	40	2.00
Welfare	44	1.88	45	1.85	43	1.89	33	2.06
Pres. Clinton	44	2.12	57	1.90	31	2.48	30	2.47
Contract America	34	2.10	34	2.10	34	2.09	23	2.49
Abortion	33	2.34	45	1.99	20	2.57	35	2.20
Gun control	30	2.39	30	2.26	12	3.05	16	2.80
Economy	23	2.51	19	2.60	24	2.27	14	2.67
Affirm action	11	3.21	17	2.90	11	3.07	6	3.68

* Percent "excellent" GOP performance; 1 = "excellent", 5 = "poor"
** Percent GOP "solidly united"; 1 = "solidly united", 5 = "badly divided"
*** Percent "a great deal" of impact; 1 = "a great deal" , 5 = "none"

The Republican Party's Performance

How are these factors related to the delegates assessments of the GOP's own performance in 1994? Table 9.2 reports correlations between the dele-gates' performance assessments and their perception of party unity, organizations, and issues. Not surprisingly, the strongest correlate of perceived Republican performance in each state was the degree party unity; delegates who felt the party was united were more likely to report it did well the campaign. These correlations set a bench mark against which to judge the remaining items (first column under each state).

The next strongest correlates of perceived Republican performance are organizational, however: the state and local GOP committees. Indeed, the coefficients for the state committees are not that far behind party unity (reflecting perhaps the state-level character of these delegates). Republican candidates and the national committee compete for third place. With rare exception, the remaining groups show much weaker links to the GOP's performance. A similar situation holds of issues. The Contract with America ranks first or second in all four states, and is only bested by opposition to big government, one of its key themes. Few of the other issues show associations of comparable size. Note, however, that none of the issue coefficients exceed those of the party organizations. Similar patterns obtain for party unity (the second column under each state).

Thus, the delegates' assessments of Republican performance are most associated with the party itself: the degree of unity and the activities of party organizations, including the Contract with America, aided and abetted by candidates, other issues, and allied interests. At first blush, these findings appear to contradict those in table 9.1, namely that party organizations were not particularly important. But these findings are, in fact, quite consistent. Each set of data report different things: the first concerns the election itself, and the second, performance of the Republican leaders and organizations in the campaign. The most prominent factors in the election, GOP candidates and opposition to big government, were seen by some delegates as a positive factor and by other as negative factor in party performance. Even in a good Republican year, many Republican candidates performed poorly and not all issues helped win races. In fact, many important groups and issues were judged divisive, detracting from the party's overall effect. The Christian Right is a case in point. Although quite active in all of these states, and an important ingredient in many Republican victories, the Christian Right was a detriment in other races and viewed with alarm by Republican moderates (cf. Rozell and Wilcox 1995).

These patterns hold up in multivariate analysis. In all four states, party unity is the most important of these variables in explaining Republican Party performance, followed by the party organizations, GOP candidates, and a combined measure of antigovernment issues, of which the Contract with America was a part.[1] At least from the perspective of these delegates, the activities of the party itself made an independent contribution in 1994. Such perceptions may have an affect on future developments in party organizations themselves (see chapter 8 in this volume).

Table 9.2 Correlates of GOP Performance and Unity in 1994; State Convention Delegates

N of Cases	Washington (506)		Texas (507)		Florida (404)		Minnesota (511)	
	Perf	Unty	Perf	Unty	Perf	Unty	Perf	Unty
Party Unity**	.51	—	.37	—	.51	—	.46	—
Organizations								
State party	.35*	.33*	.29*	.29*	.46*	.48*	.43*	.38*
Local party	.29*	.31*	.12*	.15*	.33*	.33*	.29*	.26*
GOP candidates	.27*	.23*	.16*	.21*	.20*	.20*	.29*	.29*
National party	.25*	.28*	.17*	.24*	.23*	.29*	.26*	.22*
Business groups	.12*	.19*	.02	.10*	.16*	.22*	.12*	.14*
Term limiters	.10*	.08	.00	.15*	.27*	.11*	.19*	.21*
Christian Right	.02	.00	.00	.12*	.09	.02	.12*	.05
Taxpayer groups	.01	.00	.01	.06	.24*	.24*	.19*	.16*
Pro gun groups	-.02	.09	-.07	.14*	.13*	.10*	.03	.08
Pro life groups	-.08	-.11	-.02	.14*	.09	.10*	.08	.06
Perot backers	.01	-.09	.01	-.02	-.01	-.12*	.01	-.03
Issues								
Contract America	.21*	.23*	.12*	.14*	.21*	.14*	.19*	.26*
Big government	.06	.13*	.16*	.02	.21*	.15*	.21*	.14*
Welfare	.00	.13*	.12*	.08	.18*	.12*	.15*	.10*
Disgust politics	-.02	.05	.03	.03	.04	.13*	.19*	.09
Affirm action	-.01	.03	.02	.03	.14*	.11*	.13*	.14*
Pres. Clinton	.03	.03	.01	.04	.04	.10*	.13*	.13*
Abortion	-.12*	-.08	.00	.09	.13*	.06	.08	.13*
Economy	-.04	-.03	.04	.00	-.02	.02	.09	.07
Gun control	-.01	.11*	.02	.11*	.08	.02	.01	.01

Key: Perf=Overall Republican performance at the polls; Unty=Overall Republican unity.
* significant at .05 level or better
** r between assessment of GOP success, unity, and other factors.

Conclusion

Of course, from one perspective, the association of party activities with party performance is hardly surprising, and neither are the links between candidates, issues, and electoral outcomes. But it is the divergence of parties and elections that complicates the assessment of 1994 and structures the broader literature on American democracy. Much of the doctrine of party responsibility rests on the notion that party can and should dominate the electoral process. Indeed, for many it is this lack of party control over the electoral process that allows for candidate-centered campaigns, crosscutting issues, interest group interference, and divided government (Aldrich 1995: chap 9). In many respects, 1994 was just the sort of election envisioned by the doctrine of responsible parties (Beck and Sorauf 1992: 433–38); it is gratifying to note that the activities of party leaders and organizations may have contributed to these unusual results.

However, one must be careful not to overstate the impact of party in 1994. As the delegate reports themselves suggest, candidates, issues, and interest groups played a major role in the election, a source of continuity that is likely to survive the recent change in party effort. In 1994, an unusual confluence of political forces disciplined candidates, heightened ideology, and coalesced interests, making it possible for Republican leaders, from the national capitol to the county seat, to maximize the party's gains. Even under such circumstances, the parties purchase had its limits. All this suggests an old point that is often overlooked, namely, the instrumental character of party organizations (Sartori 1976: 25–30). More than anything else, the Republicans needed a collective effort to achieve an improbable victory in 1994, and ironically, it was that pragmatism that helped produced an unusually partisan campaign.

Recognizing the instrumental character of the Republican effort in 1994 also suggests that there may be long-term consequences. The GOP has finally translated thirty years of strength at the presidential level into victories at the congressional, state, and local levels (Ladd 1995). But all these gains just add up to parity with the Democrats, suggesting a period of highly competitive elections. Under such circumstances, instrumental parties will be particularly valuable (Schlesinger 1991). Perhaps they will be responsible as well.

Notes

1.   A discussion of the full model is beyond the scope of this chapter, but it included measures of the strength of statewide candidates and controlled for election results as well the party and issues measures discussed in the text. Overall, the models were quite robust, explaining about one-half of the variance.

10

Local Political Parties and Legislative Races in 1992 and 1994

John Frendries
Alan R. Gitelson
Gregory Flemming
Anne Layzell

Shortly before Speaker Tip O'Neill's retirement from the House of Representatives in 1986, he reminded a group of constituents of the one law of politics that had governed his overall perspective of the American political system: "All politics are local." This often-repeated quote has been used over and over again by textbook authors to remind students that the nexus of the political system is located at the local level, where politics and government have such a significant impact on public policy.

Ironically, the locus of most contemporary scholarly research and journalistic attention on party organization has focused elsewhere—at the national and state levels. This pattern is at once understandable, valuable, and problematic. It is understandable in that national and state politics are both more dramatic and more accessible to scholars and national columnists. It is valuable in that much has been learned about the new and changing nature of party organizations at the national and state levels;[1] those changes and the subsequent debate on the nature of party transformation over the past thirty years are reflected in several of the chapters in this volume. However, it is also problematic because the past three decades have been marked by a dearth of scholarship on local party organizations in their manifold roles of organization building, fundraising, recruitment, getting-out-the-vote, campaign coordination, and patronage, particularly in subcongressional races. Here we seek to address this limitation in the extant literature, focusing on the electoral role of contemporary local parties in state legislative races.

Local Political Parties and the Electoral Process

To observe that there has been limited research on local political parties is not to suggest that there has been no research in this area (see, for example, Crotty 1986; Margolis and Green 1992). Indeed, one type of local party organization, the urban machine, has been described as "the most written about, the best recorded, and the most romanticized in U.S. political history" (Crotty 1991a: 1155). However, research on political machines has little relevance for an understanding of contemporary local parties. Other research on local parties extended beyond the study of machine politics.[2] The collective scholarship of Cutright and Rossi (1958), Katz and Eldersveld (1961), Wolfinger (1963), Cutright (1963, 1964), and Crotty (1971), seeking to identify the electoral consequences of county, municipal, and precinct-level party activity, found moderate relationships between party activity and electoral outcomes. However, prior to 1980 almost all research on party organizations below the state level were case studies with little generalizability. In addition, with the exception of Crotty's 1971 article, all of the work documented party activity from the 1950s and early 1960s, a period that predated much of the perceived decline in local and other party organizations. As we have noted elsewhere (Frendreis and Gitelson 1993), with popular and scholarly accounts advancing the thesis of party decline, the stage was set for the contemporary period of research into the structure and activity of local parties.

The 1980s marked an important new generation of research on local party organizations beginning with the Party Transformation Study (PTS), the most systematic and broad-based research study generated in this century to examine state and local party structures (Cotter, Gibson, Bibby, and Huckshorn 1984; Gibson, Cotter, Bibby, and Huckshorn 1985). The PTS focused on the measurement and analysis of party organizations' roles and functions. In effect, Cotter and his colleagues asked the classic question of whether parties matter. They argued that local party organizations, in reacting to a changing political environment, maintain a fairly high level of programmatic activity and that their conclusions "[did] not support the thesis of party decline" that was common in other accounts (1984: 57).

Three significant conclusions about local party organizations stemmed from this work. First, despite the evolving and changing roles and functions of party organizations over the past three decades, local party organizations continued to be an integral and essential actor in the political process. This finding directly disputed the decline of party thesis. The second conclusion directly challenged Eldersveld's theory of "stratarchy," asserting that the party organizations at the national, state, and local levels were far more integrated than Eldersveld's model suggests. This view was also supported by the later work of Gibson, Frendreis, and Vertz (1989).[3] A third conclusion was that the strength of party organizations was independent of the strength of the party-in-the-electorate and the party-in-government.

Frendreis, Gibson, and Vertz, drawing on a subsequent survey of the PTS county organizations, found further evidence that local county party organizations were involved in electorally pertinent activities, "including candidate recruitment, joint planning with candidate organizations, and various independent campaign activities" (1990: 225). These authors surmised that county party organizations are dynamic and autonomous political institutions and that party organizations do have an impact on electoral politics.

Some of the conclusions of this work have not gone unchallenged. In a 1986 study examining local party organizations in twenty-five New Jersey communities in Middlesex County, Lawson, Pomper, and Moakley (1986) took issue with Cotter and his colleagues regarding the prevalence of party organizational stratarchies and the legitimacy of Eldersveld's (1964) party decision-making model. A separate analysis of the New Jersey setting by Pomper (1990) also questioned the electoral relevance of local party activity. The work of Lawson and her colleagues, however, does seem to confirm the findings of the other studies that local party leaders "seek and get electoral linkage with the political process" and that those leaders are "active and they direct their activism into electoral campaigns" (Lawson et al. 1986: 367).

Overall, then, the literature is mixed in its view of local party organizations. Although possessing a storied machine past, it is evident that the role of local parties has diminished over time. However, the most recent studies that have focused on local party organizational attributes describe organizations that are vital—and, in fact, are becoming stronger, not weaker. This paradox of organizations which are becoming structurally more developed, but functionally less effective, demands further investigation.

While many scholars are dubious that the parties are electorally irrelevant, there is relatively little empirical evidence that directly addresses the electoral role of local parties in the age of candidate-centered campaigning. Like studies of local party leaders, surveys of candidates reveal a modest role for local parties. Two candidate-based studies focusing on congressional races contribute to our understanding of the role of party organizations in the electoral process. Paul Herrnson's research (1986; 1988; 1993) makes it clear that party organizations, while not inconsequential, have less impact on the campaign process than a candidate's own organization, PACs, and campaign consultants. This general conclusion is important, although it masks significant variation regarding specific campaign functions. While party organizations play a less important role in activities like fundraising, at the same time they play a relatively significant role in volunteer recruitment and get-out-the-vote efforts (Herrnson 1986). A later study by Kazee and Thornberry (1990), focusing on the recruitment of congressional candidates, replicated the Herrnson findings, noting a moderate role for party organizations in this phase of the electoral process. Studies of party leaders suggest, however, that the overall role of local parties is greater for more local races at the county or state legislative district level (see Frendreis et al. 1990; Pomper 1990).

We have argued elsewhere that there are three reasons why studies of local parties should focus on lower level offices.[4] First, local party leaders themselves believe their organizations are most pertinent and effective with regard to lower-level offices. Second, lower-level offices, including state legislative and county offices, are accountable for public policy that is substantively important and collectively represents billions of dollars in annual revenues and expenditures. Third, what transpires at the local level is relevant for electoral and partisan politics at higher levels. For example, the underdevelopment of the Republican Party in many parts of the South may be more a function of party activity and partisan politics at the local level than it is of national and statewide politics (Frendreis et al. 1990: 231-32).

Local Party Organizations and the 1992 and 1994 Elections

This chapter focuses on the structural attributes and electoral roles of local party organizations. While our core analysis centers on our survey conducted of county party chairs in eight states in the 1992 and 1994 elections, we also briefly report, from that same survey, on analysis appearing elsewhere (Frendreis, Gitelson, Fleming, and Layzell 1993) addressing the perspective of those people actually contesting elections—state legislative candidates—and their perceptions of the role of party organizations in the campaign process.

In 1992, and again in 1994, we surveyed all Democratic and Republican county party leaders and all Democratic and Republican general election candidates for the upper and lower state legislative houses in eight states: Arizona, Colorado, Florida, Illinois, Missouri, South Carolina, Washington, and Wisconsin. These eight states were selected in order to provide representative coverage with respect to regions and the degree of party strength and competitiveness within each state (based on data reported in Cotter et al. 1984).

Two separate survey instruments were developed, one for chairs and one for candidates, but, where possible, the two sets of subjects were asked identical questions. In order to maintain comparability with previous research, our questions for candidates were modeled on those previously asked of congressional candidates (see Herrnson 1988), while our party chair survey was modeled on the PTS surveys Gibson et al. 1989 and Cotter et al. 1984).[5] In 1992, a total of 1,657 candidates for state legislative office and 1,016 county party leaders were surveyed. Approximately 60 percent of all candidates and 65 percent of all chairs responded to the survey. Similar numbers of chairs and candidates were surveyed in 1994. Responses were relatively evenly distributed between Democrats and Republicans and, among candidates, between those who won and those who lost election.

Our findings are organized in order to focus on three specific questions regarding the electoral roles of local parties:

1. What are the structural attributes and resources of contemporary local party organizations?
2. In what electoral activities do local parties actually engage?
3. What roles do local party leaders see their organizations playing in the 1992 and 1994 elections?

In addition to these three questions, we briefly address two issues regarding the electoral roles of local parties as perceived by state legislative candidates:

1. What roles do candidates see party organizations playing in the 1992 and 1994 elections?
2. To what extent are the assessments of the parties' roles congruent between candidates and party leaders?

The Structural Strength of Local Party Organizations

In both 1992 and 1994, local party organizations continue to display the structural attributes noted in previous research. As a baseline for comparison, we have included in table 10.1 comparable percentages reported in Gibson et al. (1985) for the 1979–80 PTS nationwide survey.[6] It is clear that in terms of these indicators of structural strength, local parties have not weakened over the last decade and, if anything, they have become slightly stronger. This finding is significant, since there is some indication that the structural strength of local parties has greater electoral consequences than their activity level in a given election cycle (Frendreis et al. 1990). Our findings here of continued structural strength parallel those reported by Gibson et al. (1989) for major county organizations for the 1980–84 period. Most differences over time are slight; the largest increases are seen when county committees meet at least bimonthly during election periods, when the party chair devotes more time to party business during nonelection periods and when the county organization has a telephone listing. There are several significant differences between the parties; the largest include the probability that Republicans are more likely than Democrats to have formal budget procedures, paid full-time and part-time staff, year-round offices, and a telephone listing.

This pattern of steady or slightly increasing structural strength should not mask the fact that these organizations remain essentially volunteer operations. Parties report high levels of development in areas requiring little or no expenditures—having officers, holding meetings, and having bylaws. In areas

Table 10.1 Structural Attributes of Local Party Organizations, 1980, 1992, and 1994

	Percent Republicans 1980	Percent Democrats 1980	Percent Republicans 1992	Percent Democrats 1992	Percent Republicans 1994	Percent Democrats 1994
Has complete set of officers	81	90	92	94	97	94
Chair works at least 6 hrs. per week (election period)	78	77	82	79	82	78
County committee meets at least bimonthly (election period)	57	59	57	75	72	72
Has constitution, rules, or bylaws	68	68	77	71	80	79
Has formal annual budget	31	20	34	23	39	22
Chair works at least 6 hrs. per week (nonelection period)	26	24	40	34	35	34
County committee meets at least bimonthly (nonelection period)	49	53	58	56	63	60
Has some paid, full-time staff	4	3	4	2	6	3
Has some paid, part-time staff	6	5	8	4	8	4
Chair receives salary	1	2	1	1	2	2
Has year-round office	14	12	21	12	23	15
Has telephone listing	16	11	27	21	30	22
Has campaign headquarters	60	55	59	57	56	56
Maximum N	1,872	1,984	330	352	376	351

Source: 1980 data reported in Gibson et al. 1985; 1992 and 1994 surveys by authors.

requiring the accumulation and outlay of cash—paid staff, formal budgeting, and maintenance of a year-round office—most local party organizations remain relatively underdeveloped. But, this lack of development does not represent a weakened state from a previous level of high structural strength. Taken as a whole, our findings support the early conclusions of the PTS regarding the structural strength of local party organizations in the United States.

The Local Party Chairs' View: The Electoral Role of Local Parties

Our survey of county party chairs found that local party organizations were active in various spheres of electoral politics during 1992 and 1994.[7] The range of electoral operations covered everything from involvement in candidate recruitment to direct participation in campaign activities and responsibility for differing phases of individual candidates' campaigns. The prevailing opinion of county chairs was that their organizations were reasonably effective and productive as electoral actors.

Table 10.2 summarizes the percentages of Democratic and Republican chairs reporting that their party organization engaged in a variety of direct campaign activities during the 1992 and 1994 elections. An examination of the table reveals two patterns. First, as with structural strength, between the 1980 baseline year and 1994 there is no pattern of decline in campaign activity. In fact, with relatively few exceptions, the 1992 and 1994 party organizations were both a bit more active than the 1980 organizations. While there are declines in the organizations' reported activity in a few areas, such as voter registration and the buying of radio/TV time and billboard space, there are also significant increases in other activities for both the Democratic and Republican Party organizations, including distribution of posters and lawn signs, distribution of campaign literature, arranging fundraising events, and organizing campaign events. This finding that party organizations are at least as active in 1992 and 1994 as they were in 1980 also replicates the longitudinal findings of Gibson et al. (1989) for the shorter 1980–84 period.

A second pattern in table 10.2 is that neither the Republican nor Democratic Party has a distinct advantage with regard to direct campaign activities. Overall, in 1992, the average Republican organization engaged in 9.0 of the 17 activities measured, while the average Democratic organization engaged in 9.4 activities. In 1994, the average Republican and Democratic organizations engaged in 9.6 and 9.0 activities respectively. However, these differences, as well as the pairwise comparison between parties, are not statistically significant. But there were some Republican-Democratic differences that are statistically significant. During the 1992 election, Republican organizations were more likely to contribute money to candidates, while Democratic organizations were more apt to conduct registration drives,

Table 10.2 Campaign Activity Levels of Local Party Organizations, 1980, 1992, and 1994

Direct Campaign Activity	Percent Republicans 1980	Percent Democrats 1980	Percent Republicans 1992	Percent Democrats 1992	Percent Republicans 1994	Percent Democrats 1994
Distributes campaign literature	79	79	88	90	88	88
Arranges fundraising events	68	71	74	76	77	74
Organizes campaign events	65	68	77	81	81	78
Contributes money to candidates	70	62	75	67	79	68
Organizes telephone campaigns	65	61	58	62	64	57
Buys newspaper ads for party and candidates	62	62	60	65	68	62
Distributes posters or lawn signs	62	59	90	89	90	87
Coordinates county-level campaigns	56	57	57	59	58	60
Prepares press releases for party and candidates	55	55	62	65	65	61
Sends mailings to voters	59	47	58	51	61	56
Conducts registration drives	45	56	39	50	39	39
Organizes door-to-door canvassing	48	49	52	55	59	56
Buys radio/TV time for party and candidates	33	33	24	31	25	26
Utilizes public opinion surveys	16	11	15	15	20	12
Purchases billboard space	13	10	9	7	10	5
Coordinates PAC activity	n/a	n/a	4	10	7	8
Conducts get-out-the-vote effort	n/a	n/a	60	70	71	66

"Very" or "somewhat" involved in candidate recruitment:						
For city and local offices	45	44	48	42	52	44
For county offices	71	69	94	87	92	97
For state legislative offices	75	74	86	81	87	78
For congressional offices	64	62	69	64	72	65
Makes formal or informal preprimary endorsements	28	32	31	27	31	31
Maximum N	1,872	1,984	330	352	373	347

Source: 1980 data reported in Gibson et al. 1985; 1992 and 1994 surveys by authors.

buy radio/TV time, coordinate PAC activity, and conduct get-out-the-vote efforts. During the 1994 election cycle, this process was somewhat altered between the two parties with Republican organizations more likely to contribute money to candidates in addition to utilizing public opinion polls and purchasing bill board space. In 1994, the Democrats had no statistical advantages over the Republicans regarding direct campaign activities.

In addition to our findings regarding these direct campaign activities, party chairs also reported their organizations as actively involved in the campaigns of individual candidates. As the data in table 10.2 indicate, for both the 1992 and 1994 elections, over one-quarter of each party related that their organization made formal or informal preprimary endorsements of candidates. An even larger percentage for those elections were involved in the broader process of candidate recruitment, with well over three-quarters of the chairs in each party reporting involvement in the recruitment of county and state legislative candidates. In all cases the percentages are higher for Republican organizations. The Republican-Democratic differences are statistically significant for all organizations for county and state legislative offices, but pairwise only for county offices. About two-thirds of the chairs report involvement in the recruitment of congressional candidates. The recruitment data reconfirm earlier results indicating that local chairs discern their role to be greater for lower-level partisan races than for higher-level races such as for Congress. Overall, these data represent an increase over the 1980 baseline and, in fact, exceed the comparable 1984 figures for major local party organizations reported by Gibson et al. (1989: table 1).

The party chairs were also asked to assess the importance of their own county organization in various aspects of candidates' campaigns. Our findings, presented in table 10.3, generated three conclusions. First, county chairs overwhelmingly see their organizations as predominately local actors. For each of the five campaign areas examined, there is a monotonic decline in chairs' evaluations of their organization's importance as the scope of the race increases. An analogous pattern holds for their assessment of their organizations' overall effect on electoral outcomes: chairs feel that the local party organizations are more effective for local offices and less effective for higher offices. Second, there is relatively strong similarity of viewpoint between Republican and Democratic chairs. This similarity of perspective across party lines suggests that the parties have not cultivated different strategies at local levels. Third, while the chairs feel their organizations are of moderate importance to candidates' campaigns, they see their organizations as most important in such nuts-and-bolts areas as recruiting campaign volunteers, organizing campaign events, and get-out-the-vote efforts—each of which is a grassroots activity emphasizing ties to local voters.

Table 10.3   Chairs' Evaluations of the Importance of Their County Organization in Various Aspects of Candidates' Campaigns*

| | Republicans | | Democrats | |
	1992	1994	1992	1994
Campaign Management and Strategy				
County candidates	3.21	3.31	3.05	3.04
State legislative candidates	2.67	2.65	2.62	2.43
Congressional candidates	2.15	2.12	2.17	1.89
Gubernatorial candidates	1.93	2.05	1.97	1.87
Presidential candidate	1.68	n/a	1.84	n/a
Fundraising				
County candidates	3.21	3.30	3.11	3.19
State legislative candidates	2.81	3.01	2.74	2.73
Congressional candidates	2.37	2.47	2.43	2.30
Gubernatorial candidates	2.39	2.53	2.37	2.35
Presidential candidate	1.96	n/a	2.08	n/a
Recruiting Volunteers				
County candidates	3.73	3.59	3.61	3.50
State legislative candidates	3.59	3.55	3.51	3.29
Congressional candidates	3.33	3.22	3.23	3.05
Gubernatorial candidates	3.34	3.30	3.25	3.05
The presidential candidate	3.16	n/a	3.20	n/a
Organizing Campaign Events				
County candidates	3.59	3.62	3.56	3.40
State legislative candidates	3.27	3.33	3.32	3.04
Congressional candidates	2.94	2.96	2.98	2.74
Gubernatorial candidates	2.78	2.90	2.73	2.66
Presidential candidate	2.36	n/a	2.46	n/a
Get-Out-The-Vote				
County candidates	3.32	3.49	3.44	3.47
State legislative candidates	3.23	3.41	3.39	3.31
Congressional candidates	3.13	3.31	3.36	3.19
Gubernatorial candidates	3.15	3.32	3.31	3.21
Presidential candidate	3.10	n/a	3.29	n/a
Maximum N	330	375	352	344

* Table entries are mean scores, measured on the following scale: 1=not important; 2=slightly important; 3=moderately important; 4=very important; 5=extremely important.
Source: Survey by authors.

The Candidates' View: The Electoral Role of Local Parties

Thus far we have reported on the structural attributes and the electoral role of local party organizations as seen by county party chairs. But how do candidates see the involvement of county parties? Our survey of state legislative candidates reveals a very similar view of county parties, with a few expected differences. (These data are more fully presented in Frendreis et al. 1993.)

First, as with research on congressional races (Herrnson 1988), we found that family and friends were the most important factor in influencing a potential state legislative candidate's decision to run for office. However, local party organizations were the second most important factor affecting their recruitment. Second, our data show that state legislative candidates regard local party organizations as being of greatest benefit with regard to grassroots activities like voter registration, organizing campaign events, recruiting volunteers, and get-out-the-vote efforts. Third, local party organizations are regarded as less important in campaign management and the development of campaign strategy. Apparently it is in this area that candidate-centered campaigning has taken over most fully.

Overall, the evaluations by state legislative candidates in 1992 and 1994 suggest that candidate-centered campaigning is developing as much at this level as it is at higher levels of electoral politics. Candidates do not rely exclusively on local party organizations to facilitate and promote their races for office. At the same time, however, there is agreement between candidates and party chairs as to which aspects of a campaign local party organizations have the most and least to offer. While there are substantial gaps between the absolute ratings the chairs and candidates give to the county party organizations, there is basic agreement on the relative importance of parties to the different aspects of campaigning. Local organizations are perceived by party chairs and state legislative candidates as most important in reaching out to the grassroots—recruiting volunteers and getting voters to the polls—while least important to the creation and maintenance of the campaign infrastructure—fundraising and campaign management.

Local Political Parties and the Democratic Process

Contemporary debate over the status of party organizations has spanned the past four decades, beginning with the report of the American Political Science Association Committee on Political Parties (1950) calling for a "responsible party" system. This debate has engendered considerable concern over the state of parties in the post-World War II era. Indeed, a decade ago, a team of prominent political party scholars observed that "[t]he last twenty years have not been kind to American political parties" (Gibson et al. 1985:

139). In fact, few American political institutions have seen their collapse (Broder 1971; Sundquist 1982; Crotty 1984; Wattenberg 1990, 1991), and alternately, their revitalization (Schlesinger 1985; Kayden and Mahe 1985; Pomper 1981; Price 1984; Gitelson, Conway, and Feigert 1984), reported so often in scholarly publications, textbooks, and the popular press. Unquestionably, the past four decades have been marked by a volatile and changing party system.

We have argued here that any definitive evaluation of the tangible roles of local party organizations is hampered by the limited amount of contemporary research on their status. Further research may reveal the propensity for the continuing evolution of American parties; for simplicity we identify three possibilities (Frendreis and Gitelson 1993). First, American parties may be emerging into "responsible parties" (American Political Science Association Committee on Political Parties 1950). Although our research and PTS found an increase in organizational strength among local party organizations coupled with signs of a growing vertical integration of national, state, and local organizations, there is little evidence of movement toward the responsible party model.

A second prospect is what might be called the "disintegrating" model in which parties continue to lose influence with candidates and voters. Some research suggests that this is the case, particularly research on the hold parties exercise over the long-term loyalties of voters (e.g., Wattenberg 1990). Further support for this thesis is found in the evolving move from party-run to candidate-centered campaigns for major offices including presidential, gubernatorial, and congressional races. However, without further research, it is premature to assume the wholesale extension of this phenomenon to more local races.

We have chosen to label a third possibility the "adaptive brokerage" model (see chapter 23 in this volume). In this view, local parties (as well as national and state parties) have adapted to changes in the electoral environment, developing new roles, particularly that of bringing together candidates, consultants, and contributors. The specific role of political parties varies according to the electoral context. Where a party has been historically weak, the local party organization—aided by state and national organizations—may play a broader role in recruitment and direct electioneering. In more competitive areas and for higher visibility races, where candidate self-selection is the norm, adaptive brokerage parties would deliver resources to candidates—money, volunteers, newly registered voters—while the candidates themselves would be expected to deliver the votes. This view of parties as adaptive organizations was the view of the PTS researchers and seems to reflect the intuitions (and hopes) of many other party scholars (e.g., Gitelson, Conway, and Feigert 1984).

Essentially, the key unanswered research question is whether local parties are closer to the disintegrating model or the adaptive brokerage model.

Democratic theory is not impartial with regard to these two possibilities, however. While adaptive brokerage parties may be less than perfect vehicles for the organization of political debate and the development of public policy, the most likely alternative—electorally irrelevant parties—are wholly inadequate to the requirements of American politics. The need to better understand the evolving form and functions of local and other parties is more than a scholarly imperative; it is a practical necessity.

Notes

1. Key 1956; Cotter and Hennessy 1964; Huckshorn 1976; Conway 1983; Schlesinger 1985; Epstein 1986; Bibby 1986; Herrnson 1990; Paddock 1990; and Bibby 1990.

2. Both this research and the work on political machines is reviewed more extensively in Frendreis and Gitelson (1993) and Frendreis et al. (1993).

3. This difference in findings may be due to the time differences in the two studies, but by the 1980s, while party structure in the United States was not, strictly speaking, hierarchical, it was increasingly organizationally integrated.

4. For a fuller examination of this thesis, see Frendreis and Gitelson (1993) and Frendreis et al. (1993).

5. Copies of the complete questionnaires are available from the authors.

6. We are employing the earlier PTS data as a baseline because both data sets are based on surveys of the universe of country organizations, whereas the 1984 survey of county organizations by Gibson et al. (1989) over sampled major party organizations. Comparisons over time in this and other tables must be tentative, since such comparisons are between the 8 states surveyed in 1992 versus all 50 states surveyed by the PTS researchers. We note, however, that the 8 states surveyed in 1992 were selected in such a way as to be a representative grouping of states with regard to local party strength.

7. The results reported in this section are developed more fully in Frendreis et al. (1993) and Frendreis and Gitelson (1995).

11

Where's the Party?
A Second Look at Party Structure in New York State

Daniel M. Shea
Anne Hildreth

Beginning with the Party Transformation Study (Cotter et al. 1984), a new of generation of scholars has shed a different light on the party decline thesis (Bibby 1987, 1990; Kayden and Mahe 1985; Gibson, Frendreis, and Verts 1989; Frendreis and Gitelson 1993; Pomper 1990; Kazee and Thornberry 1990; Gitelson et al. 1994; Beck and Haynes 1994). The point of agreement is that party organizations have become revitalized. While the context in which parties operate has been dramatically altered (Kayden and Mahe 1985; Schlesinger 1985, 1991) and the functions of the parties may be changing (Arterton 1982; Frantzich 1989; Herrnson 1986, 1988), party organizations, at the very least, have become stronger. Although these studies do not profess to directly challenge the party decline perspective, they have certainly complicated the debate.

Adding still more complexity has been the emergence of state-level legislative campaign committees (LCCs), modeled after the four national congressional committees—well reviewed by Herrnson (1986, 1988, 1994), Dwyre (1994), and others. LCCs are now found in forty states and in many they are major players in state legislative campaigns. Most scholars theoretically merge these new structures with traditional party units, generally the state party committees (Dwyre and Stonecash 1992; Gierzynski and Breaux 1991, 1994; Simon-Rosenthal 1993). The inclination to do so is understandable; in many states they comprise a significant resource base from which party candidates and legislative leaders benefit (Gierzynski 1992; Redfield and Van Der Slik 1992; Salmore and Salmore 1989; Jewell and Olson 1988; Johnson 1987; Giles and Pritchard 1985; Loftus 1985). Gierzynski and Breaux, for example, find little difficulty combining LCC money with state and local party coffers to assess the role of "parties" in legislative campaign finance (1995: 177).

Using a case study of New York, we examine several issues regarding the nexus between LCCs and traditional party organizations. First, we review work that joins state level LCCs with party organizations, work that makes the "integration assumption." Next, we develop a contrasting set of criteria for assessing this linkage, one that depends more heavily on the views of traditional party leaders, which we then investigate with interview data from county and state party officials.

In the end, this research makes two contributions to our understanding of LCCs. First, we show that the attitudes of traditional party leaders are as important as objective legal or financial measures in assessing the integration of LCCs and traditional party organizations. Second, rival conceptions of party organizations, especially electoral versus responsible models, are crucial to the assessments as empirical factors. The contrast between these different interpretations of LCCs suggest that the evaluation of this new player depends critically on the choice of party model; one that stresses electoral functions or one that views party from a more responsible vantage.

LCCs in New York State

The integration of LCCs and traditional party units makes sense if one were to take a literal, "strict constructionist" view of party organization. Prior to the late 1970s, few state legislative caucuses (or legislative leaders) had established centralized campaign units—notable exceptions being in Illinois, Wisconsin, Ohio, California, and New York. During the past decade they flourished and today are found throughout the nation. In roughly forty percent of the states holding these units there is some form of legal or structural tie between the state central committee and the LCCs (Shea 1995). New York State is no different. Here legislative campaign committees were created during the mid-1970s as appendages of their respective state party committee.

Within the bylaws of the Republican State Committee both an "Assembly Campaign Committee" and a "Senate Campaign Committee" are listed within a group of "other" committees. These units are to act "coterminous with the State Committee and to function as an integral part thereof" (Rules of the New York Republican State Committee 1993: 3). As for the Democrats, the LCCs are listed in the bylaws along with eight additional committees. The party leader in each house of the legislature is given control of his/her respective LCC, and has the power to appoint a treasurer and other members. As in the Republican bylaws, the relationship between these units and other elements of the state party, or between one another, is left unstated (Rules of the Democratic Party of the State of New York 1994: sec. 6).

With minor exceptions (primarily the Senate Democrats), the amount of money gathered by each unit has grown appreciably since 1984. For example, the Democratic Assembly Campaign Committee raised roughly $1.5 million in 1984 and $2.8 million in 1994. The Republicans in the Senate went from $750,000 in 1984, to over $3.3 million a decade later (New York State Board of Elections Financial Disclosure Data, 1984–1995). Dwyre and Stonecash (1992: 336) demonstrate that the percentage of candidate spending coming from these units has also steadily grown. The Senate Republicans, for example, contributed 34 percent of all candidate expenditures in 1984. In 1988 that figure had risen to 53 percent. Each of the other committees parallels this trend. By combining committees of the same party, we see that LCC coffers are now larger than each of the state party committee budgets.

Disclosure information too suggests that each of the LCCs uses a vast portion of its resources on a limited number of close state legislative races. In the 1992 general election, the Democratic Assembly Campaign Committee (DACC) vested most of its money on twenty-three races out of 150 with three candidates receiving over $100,000. The Republican Assembly Campaign Committee (RACC) was slightly more focused, targeting approximately seventeen races. Two of these races received over $150,000; both were unsuccessful challengers. The Senate Democrats limited most of their involvement to twelve races out of sixty-one. Senate Republicans used their money in as slightly broader fashion, infusing seventeen campaigns with resources (New York State Board of Election, 1993).

Drawing a sharp focus on disclosure data in New York State, Dwyre and Stonecash are straightforward in their rationale for joining LCC resources with state party committees budgets. They note:

> Cotter et al. (1984) may have seriously misrepresented the health of state parties by limiting their focus primarily to the traditional state party organizations. It is necessary to examine *all* party organizations in a state to assess the condition of the state party. (1993: 340; emphasis in the original)

From this perspective they find "party" committees in the Empire State doing well, much better than previously assumed. By combining LCC resources (particularly those of the majority party) with the state committee revenues, overall budgets appear to double. It is no wonder the party organizations appear to be thriving!

Although this type of conceptual integration between traditional party committees and LCCs is common, other scholars are beginning to question its wisdom. Some time ago Jewell and Olson suggested that LCCs in New York "are legal subdivisions of the state party committees but in practice they are about as autonomous as possible" (1988: 222). Sorauf, speaking of state LCCs more generally, suggests they "serve only the agendas and priorities of the legislative partisans" (1992: 120). If this were found to be the case—that LCCs neither work with traditional party units nor hold the same goals—what would be the justification for linking them together? Such a union may well rest on a restricted, primarily electoral, view of party.

We believe that to gauge integration solely on the basis of legal and financial linkages is excessively narrow, overlooking broader elements of traditional party structure and function. American political parties have been important community-based organizations, linking average citizens to their government. They help coalitions and give voters a choice—both in candidates and in policies—even in noncompetitive areas. They often encourage participation, mediate conflict, and empower the economically disadvantaged. They support a range of candidates under the party banner, oversee elections, and provide an outlet for the fulfillment of perceived civic duty. Before one links LCCs with parties it would seem necessary first to gauge the extent to which they either perform or aid traditional parties in the performance of these broader functions. Most would agree that American parties are not exemplary illustrations of "responsible" organizations. But few would suggest they engage only in short-term campaign activities. Our assessment of the union between LCCs and party necessarily requires a broader set of criteria.

The first, and most basic, test of the integration assumption concerns the extent to which traditional party leaders are aware of LCCs. Are county party committee chairs, for example, abreast of the LCC's activities within their own state? A necessary precursor to the conceptual combination of LCCs with party organizations would be a rudimentary understanding on the part of traditional leadership of what these units are, what they do, and what they seek to accomplish.

A second issue relates to the interdependence of the two bodies as they pursue goals. Do the LCCs work with party organizations on projects or in assisting candidates? Do they share facilities, staff, and equipment? Again, to accept the coupling of LCCs with traditional party units we would expect a modest level of project interdependence. Finally, the perceptions of party leaders regarding LCCs must be examined—what they do and who they benefit. Formal linkages aside, to what degree are these new political actors integrated into the informal network of traditional party leadership? Before we tie LCCs with state party committees on objective grounds, the subjective views of party leaders need to be understood.

We can make these assessments using the results of a survey of traditional party leaders in New York. Seventy-eight county party chairs were interviewed by telephone in the spring of 1991, forty-two Republican and thirty-six Democratic county party chairs for 63 percent of the overall population. Four separate attempts were made to contact each chair; grounds for omission appear random. In addition, leaders of both state party committees were interviewed in person during April of 1991.

Findings at the County Party Level

Exposure to LCCs

Exposure to LCCs should serve as a precondition to other forms of linkage. Levels of exposure will also have a strong bearing on attitudes and perceptions toward these new units. If the county party leader has had limited contact with these organizations—if they reside in a county that is either noncompetitive or where an incumbent runs unopposed—their view of LCCs will be different, perhaps more optimistic, than those who have had frequent contact.

Table 11.1 shows that roughly one-half of the chairs in the sample report campaign-related interactions with these new units. We divide the sample into three groups, depending on the respondent's level of exposure to either the assembly or senate LCCs of their party. "High exposure" notes the portion of chairs who reported at least one of the LCCs was involved in a campaign in their county; "moderate exposure" denotes chairs who have had other workings, contacts, or communications with at least one of the LCCs; and "no exposure" indicates the portion of chairs who have had no workings or communications with them.

The number of both Democrats and Republicans in the no exposure category is revealing. Although LCCs have been around since the 1970s, are key players in state legislative elections, have budgets that now surpass each of the state committee's, and are structurally linked to the state committees, a sizeable portion of county party chairs has had no interaction with them whatsoever. In fact, a large number of chairs seemed utterly unaware of these new units. As one upstate Republican noted, "I've never had any workings

Table 11.1 Level of Respondent's Interaction with LCCs, Controlled by Party*

	Democrats	Republicans	Total	N
High	49%	56%	52%	(39)
Moderate	25%	29%	29%	(24)
No exposure	26%	15%	19%	(15)

* Respondents were asked if either a Senate or Assembly LCC had been involved in a campaign in their county while they were chair. The high group denotes those in the affirmative. Those that said "no" were asked a follow up about other contact with LCCs. The moderate group are those with "other" contacts or workings, and the no exposure group reported no contact at all.

with either one . . . I couldn't begin to tell you what they do." This is particularly telling with regard to the Republican Party—in which each county chair serves on the state party's executive committee.

To examine whether this lack of contact was a function of some quality of the chairs in the no exposure group, controls were introduced for the frequency of contacts with the state committee, attitudes regarding the state committee, and tenure of the chair. None of these seemed to distinguish this group. In other words, county chairs with little contact with the LCCs are not isolated, disgruntled, or new.

The more likely explanation may lie in a closer look at the function of LCCs. Their principal activity is electoral; legislative campaign committees tend to target resources on close races. While it may seem reasonable to expect more systematic understanding of LCC activities across party leadership, no doubt strategic decisions limit their exposure in noncompetitive areas. In contrast, if LCCs are party units and if the legal/structural arrangements are more than superficial, one might expect each of the county chairs—key "cogs" of the traditional party structure (Eldersveld: 1982)—to have a basic understanding of LCC activities. We might also expect a minimal level of communication.

LCC/Party Cooperation

A second step in understanding the connection between LCCs and party committees is to move beyond exposure to cooperation on activities. These activities can be divided into two broad areas: institutional support, such as fundraising projects, and candidate-directed, such as running a telephone bank.

There appear to be few coordinated activities with regard to institutional support. Asked whether county committees "worked with [the LCC] to raise money," only 8 percent of the chairs answered in the affirmative. Moreover, just 11 percent said their committee "pooled resources with [the LCC] to fund projects." Candidate-directed interactions were also limited. Regarding strategic cooperation, respondents were asked "how often during the campaign [they] or other members of the county committee, talked with staff members of the LCC." Forty-four percent said communications were less than "a few times per month"; 22 percent said about once per week, and 19 percent said they talked on a daily basis. The party leaders were also asked to use a seven-point scale to measure "how much they think [the LCC] listened to the county committee's input during the campaign (1 being the lowest and 7 the highest)." The mode response was 3, with 65 percent noting 4 or less. Regarding yet another query, only 16 percent of the chairs stated the county committee worked with the LCC to develop a strategic plan for the campaign.

The chairs' responses to the types of activities conducted by the LCCs and the county committees suggests a picture of very segregated tasks. While 82 percent of the chairs mentioned the LCCs were primarily responsible for activities requiring strategic choices—such as targeting mailings, media development, and issue formation—only 19 percent suggested the county committees were also involved in such activities. Over three-fourths said the participation of the county committee was restricted to nonstrategic, traditional grassroots projects, such as door-to-door canvasing, stamping envelopes, and making telephone calls.

Finally, moving beyond strategic services to direct candidate services, the degree of interdependence was somewhat higher; 34 percent stated their committee "worked together with [the LCC] on projects for candidates during campaigns." But there is considerable variance on this point. While several chairs noted their committee's interactions with the LCCs centered exclusively on one or two short-term projects, such as "looking up telephone numbers for a poll," others stated they worked together on several on-going activities.

It makes sense that interactions between the county committees and LCCs would be greater for direct services than for strategic interactions. Legislative campaign committees are, after all, state-level units. A neat division of labor might be that the thematic oversight of the campaigns be will be left to the LCCs, while traditional party units are called upon to conduct labor intensive activities. Local party organizations may not find this problematic given that many of these activities buttress their broader party-building interests. This notion is echoed by Frendreis et al. (1994) in their examination of local party activities more generally.

But so far these findings reflect a very constrained notion of interdependence. Interdependence implies reciprocity, not simply one group aiding another. Moreover, cooperation along a very narrow range of activities does not imply organizational interdependence. For example, many party organizations rely upon labor unions for the use of their offices during campaign periods (telephone lines, conference rooms, and so forth). Union members may even assist on certain projects. Nevertheless, because the cooperation is limited in scope and duration, and is unidirectional, we could not conclude the two are interdependent.

Although county party committees may occasionally assist the LCCs, it appears far less common to find the LCCs helping the county committees. Table 11.2 notes the findings for two questions regarding LCC assistance to local party committees. Asked if the chair believed the LCC would "help on a local party project . . . such as putting together a voter registration drive," only 8 percent said it would be "very likely" and 19 percent "somewhat likely." Conversely, 28 percent believed it would be "somewhat unlikely," and 45 percent "very unlikely." Responses concerning financial help for a similar project were even more pessimistic: a full 76 percent noted it would be "very unlikely" that their committees would receive financial aid on a voter registration drive. Taken together, these data suggest a very superficial level

Table 11.2 Perceived Likelihood of Assistance From LCCs, Controlled by Party*

	Very Likely		Somewhat Likely		Somewhat Unlikely		Very Unlikely	
	D	R	D	R	D	R	D	R
Project help, like GOTV?	7%	10%	15%	30%	32%	25%	56%	5%
Financial help for local party activity?	—	—	—	5%	6%	19%	88%	67%

* N=38 (17 Democrat, 21 Republican);   Unsure = 6% Democrats and 10% Republicans. Probability using chi-square is .28 and .42, respectively.

of integration. As Cotter and his colleagues point out, "When one level of the [party] organization consistently exploits another for its own purposes, such an asymmetrical relationship cannot be considered interdependent" (1984: 72).

Overall Perceptions of LCCs

One final angle at understanding the relationship between LCCs and traditional party organizations is by taking a more direct approach. How do state and local party leaders evaluate LCCs? Do they combine these new organizations with their own?

Two questions were used to assess the perceived relationship between the state party organization and the LCCs. The first concerned their overall involvement in the campaigns. That is, did the activities of the LCCs "represent the wishes of the state party organization, state party leaders, or were they acting as independent units?" Table 11.3 notes the results, controlled by party. Few chairs perceive LCC actions as controlled either by the state party committee or state party leaders. For the Democrats, this seems consistent with the delegation of LCC control to legislative leaders in their bylaws. There are no such distinctions in the Republican rules, making this finding somewhat surprising. Table 11.4 reports the results of two direct questions tapping chairs' perceptions of the place of LCCs in the party structure. The first was an open-ended query: "In your own words, please tell me how you see legislative campaign committees fitting into the state party organization." Responses were coded into four groups: closely aligned, moderately aligned, moderately independent, and clearly independent. With regard to LCC objectives, chairs were asked whether they believed the new units were "only geared towards winning elections" or are "also concerned about other party activities." There appears to be support for our conjecture

Table 11.3 Respondent's Perception of Whose Wishes LCCs' Actions Represent, by Party*

	% Democrats	% Republicans	Total	N
State party organization	12	11	11	(4)
State party leaders	6	11	8	(3)
Independent units	82	78	81	(29)

Tau = .17

* This was a close-ended query: "Thinking back upon the legislative committee's overall involvement in the race, would you say their actions represented the wishes of the state party organization, state party leaders, or were they acting as independent units?"

Table 11.4 Respondent's Perceptions of LCC Fit in State Party Structure and LCC Objectives, by Level of Exposure and Party*

	Level of Exposure					
	High			Moderate		
	% Dem	% Rep	Total	% Dem	% Rep	Total
LCC Place in LCC Structure						
Closely aligned	7	0	3	13	6	8
Moderately aligned	0	11	6	25	18	22
Moderately independent	20	11	15	25	38	33
Independent	73	78	76	37	37	38
(N)	(15)	(19)	(34)	(8)	(16)	(24)

Tau = .20

Perceived Objectives of LCCs						
Only winning elections	82	47	63	78	43	56
Also party activities	6	33	21	22	19	20
Both equally	12	20	16	0	31	20
(N)	(17)	(21)	(38)	(9)	(15)	(24)

Tau = .19

* For the top portion of the Table, chairs were asked: "In your own words, please tell me how you see legislative campaign committees fitting into the state party organizations." In the second part, the questions was: "A number of county chairs have felt legislative campaign organizations are only geared toward winning elections, and in general do not care about party activities. While others have said that although they concentrate on state legislative elections, they are concerned about party activities. Which is closest your impression?" Choices were alternated each time.

that exposure to LCCs has a strong bearing on perceptions, with respondents in the moderate exposure group more likely to view LCCs as "closely aligned" or "moderately aligned" than the high exposure group. And county committee chairs who have worked closely with LCCs are much more likely to see the objectives of the LCC narrowly defined, as are those in the moderate group.

These results suggest that county chairs hesitate to merge the state party organization and legislative campaign committees. Although Republican chairs see a greater degree of harmony/coordination, overall they view LCCs as autonomous, beyond the reach of the state party organization. What is more, other control variables such as length of tenure, size of the county committee, and attitudes toward the state committee appear to have little effect on this perception.

The finding— that LCCs are viewed as geared toward winning elections, and conduct their activities accordingly—challenges prior academic conjecture. Dwyre and Stonecash note, "These legislative committees engage in general party promotion (e.g. Republican and Democratic fund-raising, voter registration, pro-party media, etc.) . . . [they] take care of general party concerns in which individual legislators would not be inclined to invest" (1992, 333). And Gierzynski notes, "[LCCs] appear to be very similar to the typical political party organization" (1992: 58). While the data does not altogether refute such claims, it does suggest that if LCCs carry out these functions, very few county chairs are aware of it.

Findings at the State Level

Of course, county chairs represent a geographically based unit of party organization that may be becoming less relevant in an age of media-driven elections. The evidence reported above may reflect standard organizational resistance to change. To supplement this view from the electoral trenches with a broader perspective on how LCCs fit into the party structure, we turn to interview data from the top leadership in each party.

The Republicans

It was immediately apparent during the interview with William Powers, chair of the New York State GOP, that the Republican LCCs were perceived as distinct organizations, certainly not coupled with the state central committee. In fact, a persistent theme during the interview was Powers's desire to merge the components into unified action.

Asked to give his description of LCC's place in his party's organization, Powers noted that, since the mid-1980s, each component had moved in separate directions. The senate Republicans had used their hefty resources to secure their frail majority, while Republican Assembly Campaign Committee

(RACC) seemed to have little reason to use its finite capital on the ailing state committee. As he saw it, one of his foremost tasks during the years ahead would be to "remind legislative leaders that the state committee is the heart of the party organization." In order for Republicans at all levels to be successful, there must be coherence and cooperation at the state level. "Many of the candidates for the Senate and Assembly begin their careers running for lower-level offices. [LCC leaders] should see these people as part of their 'farm team' and work with them from the beginning."

Here Powers appeared reluctant to rely on his authority over LCCs as state party chair. As noted above, according to party bylaws, each of the LCCs falls under the jurisdiction of the central party committee. His reasoning, nevertheless, was presented as pragmatic: each of the units would simply be better off working together. Perhaps he chose this vantage point because of an unwillingness to ruffle feathers or expose the weakness of the state committee. Another possibility is that LCC autonomy is now a strong norm.

This is not to say that Powers saw no recourse against LCC autonomy. The State Committee did possess, he believed, a very potent tool at its disposal—control of party nominations. Asked how he might compel the LCCs to work with the State Committee, Powers responded, "We control party nominations and it's that simple. Who do they think will carry petitions if we don't? They need us, so they've got to work with us." Unlike many states, New York's party nomination process requires extensive petition gathering, a time-and resource-consuming enterprise. As such, this logic represents a significant, although not unsurmountable, threat.

Beyond strategic cooperation, Powers was asked how often, and on what types of activities, the legislative committees and the state party interacted. The greatest area of cooperation appeared to be fundraising. Along running their own separate events, the three units did work together on a large fundraising gala each year. As for other institutional support activities—such as broad-based media programs, voter registration drives, and grassroots training programs, Powers conceded neither of the legislative units were likely to provide more than cursory assistance.

Interactions on candidate-specific activities were also scarce; few joint projects were conducted. To Powers this was somewhat disturbing when, during the final weeks of the 1990 gubernatorial campaign, the Republican State Committee ran out of money. Although they realized the race was lost, they were worried about being surpassed by the Conservative candidate, Herb London. Such an outcome would have had profound consequences for the Republican organization. Party ballot positions for all elections in New York State are fixed by the previous gubernatorial election returns, and a third place finish would have meant a shift from second to third slot. In New York, as in many states, control of board of election offices (county and state level) is divided between the two parties with the highest vote-getting gubernatorial candidates. This change alone could mean the loss of thousands of patronage positions. Finally, the embarrassment of coming in third place would have seriously jeopardized lower-level candidates for years to come, as well as hamstring future state-level fundraising. Calls for assistance to the LCCs were, nevertheless, unheeded.

The Democrats

When asked to describe how LCCs fit with the Democratic State Committee, William Cunningham, then political director, characterized it as distant. "There is no question," he noted, "each of the units operates independently of one another." Unlike Powers, he saw this relationship as generally a good thing. "By each LCC focusing on their own races, expertise and resources are available for gubernatorial campaigns and other races."

Cunningham did suggest, however, that state committee coffers may have been hurt by the LCCs. "Campaign contributions are, more or less, limited. Many would-be party contributors are now giving directly to [the LCCs]—primarily the Speaker's organization." Like the Republicans, there appeared to be little project interdependence. Both of the Democratic LCCs occasionally used state committee telephones during the final stages of campaigns and during special elections. There is also some coordination on get-out-the-vote drives in certain districts, as well as cooperation on legal matters such as postage and disclosure regulations. Nevertheless, neither of the LCCs regularly seeks advice from, or works with, the State Committee. Both the LCCs have headquarters separate from the State Committee and the direction of assistance, what little there is, nearly always in one direction— from the state committee to the LCCs. This was true for both financial interactions and candidate activities. Finally, according to Cunningham it was almost inconceivable that either of the LCCs would help a nonstate legislative candidate.

Controlling the governor's mansion is certainly a core concern of the Democratic State Committee. This organization was criticized during the 1986 and 1990 elections for concentrating its resources on the gubernatorial campaign and neglecting state-legislative elections, even though its candidate, Mario Cuomo, faced little real opposition. This was seen as particularly troublesome in 1990 when many believed the Senate was within their grasp (only three seats separated the parties) while Cuomo was certain of victory.

It is tempting to speculate that the neat division between the state committee and each of the LCCs best suits their needs. The Democratic Assembly Campaign Committee has become the electoral arm of the Speaker (now the most powerful Democrat in Albany), who is free to use its resources as he sees fit. The State Committee, on the other hand, might be used as a gubernatorial campaign organization. Neither unit would wish to have the other control its resources and dictate its activities. Many of Cunningham's comments echoed this notion.

The only player "out in the cold" is the Senate Democrats. From a traditional party perspective this might appear somewhat surprising. The division between the parties in the Senate is relatively narrow, while the other house is easily controlled by the Democrats. Why not pool resources in an effort also to control the Senate? Does it not take control of both houses of the legislature to control the policy agenda? This line of reasoning, nevertheless, assumes the LCCs and traditional party organization share identical goals.

Discussion

Interviews with state and county party leaders suggest that although party bylaws place LCCs within the party framework, practice and norms have reinforced their distinctiveness. Legislative campaign committees are rapidly expanding in New York State, both organizationally and in services provided to candidates, yet a significant portion of party leaders in the state have had little contact with them. This is certainly surprising considering that county organizations are often believed to be the core of the state party structure in New York, as elsewhere.

Interactions between county committees and LCCs during campaigns are limited to, at most, a few short-term grassroots projects. Considerable resources were extolled by the LCCs in 1994 on a small number of targeted races, and while commentators may conclude the "party committees" in these districts must be thriving, our study suggests that traditional party organizations may not have been involved, to any large degree, in these campaigns.

Several of the county chairs expressed resentment over the division of labor on campaigns "We felt shut-out," noted one chair, "[t]hey come here from Albany and do things that might work in New York City, but not here. . . . They never listen to what we have to say. If you ask me, that's why we lost [the] race." Other comments were similar. "We never know what kind of crap is going to hit the [voter's] mailboxes next." Also, "I'd get calls from people—and for that matter the media—and they'd ask me about what the campaign was doing. To tell the truth, I really didn't know what was going on. . . . It made me look stupid."

From a responsible party perspective the limited quality of LCC-party integration is disquieting. Throughout much of American history, local parties have played an important, if not central, role in the electoral process. Their withdrawal from the strategic hub of state legislative campaigns and relegation to only labor-intensive projects may hold long-term implications. An important organizational incentive behind local party activity is a perceived meaningful role in elections.

Findings here are illustrative of a centralization in campaign communications. The pattern in New York has been that legislative campaign committees target districts based upon their competitiveness, infuse these races with resources and depart after election day. Studies which merge LCCs with party and report an aggregate view of their activities obscure the selective nature of LCC attention.

In addition to their narrow geographic focus, these new units do not maintain, nor are they concerned with, community ties and other nonelectoral functions historically fulfilled by traditional parties. Would LCCs be concerned with filling out a party ticket simply in order to offer voters a choice? More likely, LCCs calculate each move based on electoral utility: notions of party tickets are abandoned, and targeted voters are reached by the most cost-efficient means available, often by electronic media and direct mail. The connection between the electorate and the party at the local level is severed. Candidate support is assessed on mass appeal rather than party loyalty or policy positions, thereby feeding the atomization of legislatures. Thus, the impact of the loss of direct intermediaries may be of no little importance. To the extent that LCCs supplant traditional geographic parties these "stronger party organizations" may jeopardize the quality of the political process more generally.

At the very least, then, it appears reasonable to label LCCs "party-like" from an election-centered perspective. By distributing resources to close races rather than reelection campaigns and by providing a host of campaign services, they may well be "very similar to typical political party organizations" (Gierzynski 1992: 58). But *even* from this restricted theoretical framework LCCs may not correspond well with "party." Downs (1957) speaks of a united pursuit of controlling government—not merely a single branch of the legislature. Urban party machines seek to dominate city hall, not simply a wing of the city council. It may, therefore, be unsettling for rational-efficient theorists (much less responsible party advocates) to tag these units party organizations.[1]

Several of the features in New York State's party system and state government more generally help explain the election-oriented nature of these new units, and their emerging relationship with traditional party committees. For rank-and-file members, the professionalization of the state legislature has meant increased pay, perks, prestige, and tenure. The number and quality of staff at each legislator's disposal and in-house support services have also added merit to their jobs. In turn, most state legislator's now see their posts as "occupations" and will use all of the resources at their disposal to hold on to them. Institutional changes have also caused important reverberations for legislative leaders. The shifting locus of power for external forces (the executive) to their body has meant the ability to contest policy and budget decisions, and to allocate resources. In many ways legislative leaders now stand on equal footing with the executive—a novel relationship, to be sure.

For both rank-and-file members and legislative leaders, then, legislative professionalization has placed an intense emphasis on elections. For members, reelections have become the dictate of a new profession. For leaders, electoral success has come to signify a means to control an entire branch of government. Elections have thus shifted from an external berth— that is, the concern of party organizations, interest groups, and individual candidates—to an institutional imperative. Compounding this new dynamic is the volatility of electorates. Instead of bringing campaign nuclei into the traditional party organization, as speculated by Schlesinger (1985: 991), the need to win elections and the uncertainty of outcomes have led to the emergence of largely autonomous legislative campaign committees.

Notes

1. It is true that, in the past, many state party committees have neglected state legislative campaigns in their pursuit to control the governor's mansion and that most of the state's patronage can be gained by attaining that one goal. Are these state committees also less "party like?" Two points can be raised in retort. First, even when it appears that state committees are narrowly fixed on gubernatorial campaigns, broad activities/concerns are undertaken. For a party to win a gubernatorial election it must mobilize its core constituencies and this helps the entire party ticket, including state legislative candidates. There are voter registration drives, platforms, get-out-the-vote efforts, joint press appearances, notions of tickets, and so on. There is always some concern for the long range interests of the party, no matter how focused the state committee appears to be. And the state committee would never dream of "running down" other members of the ticket simply to win the gubernatorial election. Second, if a state party committee were to focus *all* of its efforts on the gubernatorial election, at the peril of other members on the ticket, they would quickly be criticized for being candidate-centered instead of a "party" organization. This censure would come from party activists, journalists, and academics alike.

12

Responsible Political Parties and the Decentering of American Metropolitan Areas

Michael Margolis
David Resnick

The highest achievements of man are language and wind-swift thought, and city-dwelling habits.—Sophocles, *Antigone,* circa 441 B.C.

The lights are much brighter there,
You can forget all your troubles, forget all your cares
So go downtown.—Tony Hatch, "Downtown," 1965.

I came here from Oregon in April, 1982. I have been downtown about six times in 11 years. I live in Springdale. I have ready access to Forest Fair Mall, Tri-County Mall, Northgate Mall, various supermarkets etc. There are numerous movie houses in the area, a library, post office, parks, pools, etc. If I never see downtown Cincinnati again, I will have lost nothing. (Letter to the Editor, *Cincinnati Enquirer,* August 17, 1993.)

Much of the recent literature on American political parties at the local level has focused upon their "revitalization" and "transformation." Researchers have suggested that local parties have increased their organizational efficiency and professionalism (Cotter et al. 1984: chap. 1; Schlesinger 1991: chaps. 1, 7; see also Frendreis et al. in this volume). As such, they have measured the extent to which parties register new voters, recruit candidates for local office, consult with and coordinate the efforts of local candidates' campaign organizations, raise money, distribute literature, and otherwise publicize candidates' qualifications, campaign activities, and policy positions. Contrary to popular and scholarly perceptions of decline, several important studies have produced evidence of revitalized party activity at the local level (cf. Frendreis and Gitelson 1993). In addition, even though local parties continue to act independently, the Democratic and Republican party organizations have become more integrated across levels of government. As the national and state party organizations have acquired professional staff and permanent headquarters, they have increased their capacity to provide research and polling services, technical assistance, training for candidates and campaign managers, and cash transfers in support of local electoral campaigns, especially for Congress and the state legislatures (Cotter et al. 1984: chap. 4; Cutler 1993; Gibson and Scarrow 1993; Herrnson, this volume; Pitney 1993; Sturrock et al. 1994).

How local political parties interact with office holders and community organizations in addressing the problems of governing metropolitan areas, however, has received less attention. The lack of attention stems in part from the financial and logistical difficulties of collecting data on the thousands of local party organizations that operate under diverse state laws. Study is further complicated by the formal nonpartisanship of about half the municipalities, not to mention the governing bodies of many special districts (Margolis 1993: 33; Herson and Boland 1990: chaps. 7, 12; Ross and Levine 1996: chaps. 10–11).

Furthermore, there is a disjunction between the governmental units for which local parties run candidates and the scope of the problems that affect metropolitan areas. The borders of these problems do not correspond to electoral or jurisdictional boundaries of cities, townships, counties, or in some cases, even states (Dahl 1967; Rusk 1993). This disjunction creates problems for political analysis. Just as the boundaries within a metropolitan area tend to narrow the perspectives that public officials, party leaders, community activists, and the mass media bring to metropolitan problems, so they tend to limit the purview that political scientists bring to the problems they choose to study. Political institutions often place constraints over how political actors perceive problems and solutions. When political scientists focus on political actors too closely, they are liable to accept the actors' own understanding of the real and the possible. This leads them to underestimate the influence that institutions have on the actors' day-to-day political behavior (cf. March and Olsen 1984: 743–47).[1]

This chapter looks into how local political parties operate in metropolitan areas (MAs).[2] Our concerns go beyond the parties' ability to recruit and run candidates for local elective office. In particular, we ask how, if at all, local party leaders have altered their strategies and behaviors to adjust to the relative (and sometimes absolute) shrinkage of the population and resources of central cities (and counties) even as population and resources of MAs have grown. The party organization may hold a virtual monopoly on partisan elective offices by maintaining the loyalty and support of the party-in-the-electorate; but it is another matter for that party to work with candidates and elected officials toward solutions to the problems of declining central cities surrounded by burgeoning suburban municipalities, villages, and townships. The latter role calls for party organizations to link the party-in-government to the party-in-the-electorate (cf. Price 1984: chap. 4).

We find that local party organizations have been reluctant to recognize the new urban circumstances, however, and slow to adjust their operations to accommodate them. More broadly, we conclude that local parties are not alone. Other political, civic, and market institutions have also been reluctant to address metropolitan problems. This gives rise to calls for public authorities to surrender their resources and power to nonpartisan, quasi-governmental entities designed to take on these issues. For example, we discuss below the operation of Downtown Cincinnati Incorporated (DCI), a recently established independent management corporation that is working to transform downtown Cincinnati to resemble a suburban shopping mall.

In the next section we review the nature of the changes in the central cities and how these have affected urban lifestyles. We then discuss the role that theorists have argued "responsible parties" should play in democratic politics. This is followed by an examination of how well local parties and other organizations fulfill this role. In this section we present data on Hamilton County, the central county of the Cincinnati Consolidated Metropolitan Statistical Area (CMSA). Finally, we present our tentative conclusions and suggestions for further research.

The Decentered American City

Once upon a time, before the authors of this chapter became political scientists, the downtowns of America's great cities held a special wonder. They boasted ornate first-run movie houses, great legitimate theaters, concert halls, museums, churches, cathedrals, libraries, the biggest and best hotels, skyscrapers, restaurants, night clubs, department stores, specialty retailers, even stadiums, coliseums, and arenas. Built mostly along rivers or natural harbors, they were centers of transportation and commerce, the areas at which the highways and railroads converged. As late as the 1950s, respectable folks still "dressed up" before "going downtown."

The cities themselves still had the flavor of self-contained economic units. Many of the factories, markets, and warehouses that served the cities lay within their boundaries. Most of the businesses were still locally owned, and even the larger corporate enterprises usually had their home offices near their factories. The cities also served as the principal local markets for the farms in the surrounding areas.

Since mid-century, MAs of the United States have undergone a process of "decentering." The typical decentered MA no longer consists of a central city hub surrounded by a wheel of suburbs connected by spokes of railways and highways. The new MA may even lack a dominant urban center, and its geographic borders are not at all obvious to the casual observer. It consists of interspersed residential, recreational, industrial, and commercial zones that not only sprawl across traditional governmental units like cities or counties, but often extend across state lines. These dispersed elements are connected by grids of highways and are served by scattered shopping malls (Peirce 1993).

As the MAs have grown, the central cities' populations have declined, not only relative to the total population of their MAs, but often in absolute numbers. Disproportionate numbers of middle- and upper-class urban dwellers have moved outside the central cities' limits, and the relative (and in many cases absolute) affluence of the central cities has declined. Industries have moved their plants to cheaper tracts outside the cities' boundaries, and the cities' tax bases have shrunk.

Meanwhile, crime in central cities has increased relative to population. The cities have also become burdened with problems of air and water pollution, public transportation, public education, and poor housing stock. Providing adequate street and bridge maintenance, public sanitation, trash collection, solid waste disposal, police, fire, emergency medical services, public parking, and traffic control present further problems.

The central cities now have disproportionately nonwhite and poor populations, while most of the surrounding suburbs remain disproportionately white and affluent. A generation of suburbanites has no familiarity with the life of the old downtown. For most Americans under forty, the city center is at best a place to which they or some friends or acquaintances must commute to work. Fortunately, when they function properly, the superhighways (and in some cities, systems of rapid transit) can safely whisk suburbanites back and forth between their homes and downtown without requiring their paying much attention to the deteriorating city neighborhoods through which they pass.[3]

Far from being cultural wastelands, suburban communities have developed their own theater groups, night clubs, movie complexes, restaurants, and even symphony orchestras. The shopping centers, easily reached by automobile, provide clusters of services, including community meeting rooms. And in contrast to downtown, parking is usually free.

Kenwood Towne Centre is an example from the Cincinnati area. The "Towne Centre" is a shopping mall composed of specialty shops, restaurants, three department store "anchors," and a movie complex, but it serves as a reference point, art gallery, social center, and tourist attraction. Realtors advertise developments as located in Kenwood; people refer to themselves as living in Kenwood; Montgomery and Kenwood Roads even have signs telling drivers they are entering Kenwood. The energy of the old city center—restaurants, office complexes, hospitals—radiates along the highway grids near Towne Centre.

But governmentally, Kenwood Towne Centre is the center of a town that does not exist. It has no mayor. Its "citizens" elect no representatives. An anonymous corporation controls what businesses are established in the Towne Centre, what types of public messages are tolerated, what art is displayed, how many seats are provided in common areas, even what the temperature will be. The corporation employs a private security force to maintain law and order. Formally, the Towne Centre and the immediately surrounding households and businesses fall under the jurisdiction of four elected officials of Sycamore Township—a three-person board of trustees and a clerk. Notwithstanding their location in Sycamore Township, the Towne Centre and the surrounding complex draw people from various cities and townships throughout the Cincinnati area, including residents of the city of Cincinnati proper. More generally:

> Families create their own "cities" out of the destinations they can reach (usually by car) in a reasonable length of time. Indeed, distance in the new cities is generally measured in terms of time rather than blocks or miles. . . . *The pattern formed by these destinations represents "the city" for that particular family or individual.* The more varied one's destinations, the richer and more diverse is one's personal "city." The new city is a city *a la carte.* (Fishman 1992: 19)

As the decentered American city stretches across local governmental (and sometimes state) jurisdictions, developing and implementing public policies that address its problems becomes more complex. Officials or governmental bodies elected at the county level or below are disinclined to take responsibility for area-wide problems, such as public transportation, environmental pollution, economic development, low-cost housing, or crime. Indeed, most, elected officials we interviewed (see below) emphasized their efforts to do the best job governing their particular bailiwick, not taking on metro-wide problems. Even though certain metropolitan problems affect their localities, officials suggested that their constituents hold them responsible only for those problems for which they have formal legal authority.[4]

Those who want the public authorities to attack these problems face a dilemma. Either they must call for state or federal government to impose policies that intervene in local affairs, or they must call for local authorities to surrender powers to special districts or quasi-public commissions usually not elected by the public and not scrutinized by their representatives. Responsible political party organizations, at least in theory, offer one potential solution to this dilemma.

Parties and Metropolitan Politics in a Democracy

Political scientists who favor a "responsible parties" model of governance have argued that of all the major organizations that participate in American politics, political parties are "critical to achieving democratic accountability and responsiveness, to relating citizens to their broader political community, and to developing a capacity for cooperation and for addressing hard problems within and between the organs of government" (Price 1984: 116; American Political Science Association Committee on Political Parties 1950). Only the parties are expected by law to have one or more of their representatives—either elected or appointed—placed in every electoral precinct in the nation. Only the parties are so permeable that citizens can gain the rights and privileges of membership simply by declaring their desire to join. Only the parties have elected members who exercise public authority in nearly every locality and at all levels of government. Just as American political parties counteract the separation of executive, legislative, judicial, and state versus federal powers, so too they can overcome the separation of powers and jurisdictions within MAs.

In its strong form, the responsible party model calls upon party organizations to recruit candidates, conduct election campaigns, and develop principles, platforms, or programs that their candidates pledge to support. Once elected, public officials have a duty to implement these programs to the extent practicable. They must communicate and consult with party leaders, and they must work with other elected officials, especially members of their own party, to develop the appropriate public policies to implement these programs.

In its weak form, the responsible parties model calls for parties to register voters, raise funds, recruit candidates, and conduct electoral campaigns, but not for them to generate party platforms to which their candidates are pledged. Candidates need only declare their agreement with general party principles. Between elections, parties facilitate communication between elected officials and interest groups, and among officials at different levels of government. The formation and implementation of public policy, however, depends upon the demands of various interests among the electorate and the ideas and abilities of elected officials. As a rule, the party as an organization is indifferent to the content of these policies (cf. Frendreis and Gitelson 1993; Schlesinger 1991: chap. 6).

Responsible parties are the ordinary citizens' best hope for exerting control over decision-making elites. Without responsible parties, theorists suggest, elections tend to degenerate into exercises in demagoguery. Once elected, most officials lack the connections to forge the coalitions necessary to carry out their campaign promises. The policy process tends to be dominated by well-organized, and often well-endowed, interest groups with their own particular agenda. Public policy leadership, if any, tends to fall to officials like presidents, governors, and mayors, who have privileged access to the mass media (cf. Bachrach 1967; Ginsberg 1986; Lowi 1979).

Democracy generally begins at the local level. Here citizens can organize parties or interest groups to press their demands and to elect representatives who will satisfy them. The scale of government is small, and politics is more understandable and less intimidating. Moreover, the cost of political participation is usually not exorbitant. Guided by parties or local interest groups, citizens can engage in a rich exchange of ideas, facilitated by new communication technologies (Abramson et al. 1988; Fisher, Margolis, and Resnick 1996).

The responsible parties model, however, is not the only model for effective democratic politics at the local level. In response to the corruption of a few powerful turn-of-the-century party "machines," the reform movement developed a nonpartisan model. Local government should concern itself with "efficient, businesslike" delivery of services, not with matters of partisan politics. For municipalities nonpartisan politics is often facilitated by a council-manager form of government. In this form of government, an "honest, representative" nonpartisan council determines basic policy "that would work for the general interest of the city," and the city manager determines the best way to implement that policy (Charter Research Institute 1991: 5).[5] For townships in Ohio this ideal can be realized through a limited government headed by four elected officials: a single administrative clerk and a nonpartisan board of three trustees with no legislative powers beyond those delegated by the state.[6] "There is no Democratic way to pick up garbage. There is no Republican way to pave a street: only an honest and efficient way—so went one of the original Charter rallying cries still pertinent today" (Charter Committee 1988: 7).

There is a limit to the ability of a council-manager government to carry on its policies in a businesslike manner. A city government, unlike a business, cannot follow its customers when they move to the suburbs. The nonpartisan model can work as long as the city maintains a "great, orderly, prosperous, middle-class backbone." Unfortunately for Cincinnati and other declining central cities, this backbone has shifted to the suburbs (Pyle 1993: 25–26).

Partisan politics may be coming back into vogue because of the need for stronger leadership. As the central cities' resources have diminished, cities with strong mayors have been able to garner more federal and state dollars through grants than those with council-manager governments. They also have been able to lure more private investment back into the city center (Herson and Boland 1990: chaps. 14–15; Cole 1974; *Cincinnati Enquirer* 1993).[7] There is a trend among central cities to change from council-manager to strong, and often partisan, mayoral or chief executive forms of government. For example, St. Petersburg, Florida, has abandoned its city manager. Toledo elected its first strong mayor in 1993, and Metro Miami-Dade County strengthened the powers of the county executive in its two-tiered metro system, beginning January 1996. Dallas and Sacramento are contemplating similar changes.

Despite its seventy-year tradition of weak mayors and professional city management, Cincinnati's leadership now seems bent on revising the city charter to grant more power to the mayor. Nevertheless, the first attempt at revision failed. A charter reform plan calling for direct election of a strong mayor by plurality vote with no primary and no runoff was rejected by a surprising 64 to 36 percent in a referendum in August 1995, notwithstanding heavy financing by the Cincinnati Business Committee (CBC). Initiated by the CBC and endorsed by the Hamilton County Republican Committee, the plan would have separated the mayor from council and would have given the mayor the power to veto council legislation and to hire and fire the city manager. Opponents of the plan, which included the Charterites, the Democrats, the current mayor, the NAACP, and the Baptist Ministers Conference, characterized it as effectively eliminating the professional city manager and increasing the odds of electing a Republican mayor if the Democrats could not agree upon on a single black or white candidate.

After the referendum's defeat, however, Mayor Roxanne Qualls and her reform group, the Cincinnatians for Constructive Change, established a broad-based Forum for Charter Reform. Seeking support for an alternative plan that would strengthen the mayor but preserve the power of city council and the independence of the city manager, the Forum hired a mediator from the Center for Resolution of Disputes to bring together representatives of all interested parties, including the CBC and the Republicans. The Forum, now composed of representatives from twenty-one organizations, seeks agreement on a plan to be presented to the voters in November 1996.[8]

Nevertheless, no one contends that central cities can solve their major problems simply by reforming their charters. Regardless of their formal powers, strong mayors will still be leading central cities without the resources to solve their problems on their own. The leadership of villages, townships, smaller cities, and counties must become convinced that their communities have an important stake in the fate of the central cities. Otherwise, the cities are bound to decline further as high-paying jobs and capital continue to flow toward the suburbs (Herson and Boland 1990: 442–45).

Two other mechanisms have been proposed to bring city and suburbs together: nonpartisan quasi-governmental commissions that plan and implement public policies and special metropolitan authorities that provide or regulate particular services. Nonpartisan commissions, a time-honored tradition in Cincinnati, usually arise in MAs with council-manager cities. Metropolitan authorities develop when several neighboring communities have been individually burdened by common problems, such as sewage, waste disposal, pollution, public education, transportation, or safety. As we shall see in the next section, both city and suburban public and party leaders see the greatest potential for fostering greater cooperation between central city and suburban governments in these regional councils.[9]

Responsible Parties in the Decentered Metropolitan Area

If local party organizations operated in accordance with the responsible parties model, we would expect parties to play a significant role in addressing the problems of the decentered MA. The model calls for parties to raise funds, recruit candidates, assist in their electoral campaigns, maintain communication with officials between elections, and impose some form of party discipline. In addition, if the strong form of the responsible parties model applied, we would expect that parties would develop platforms or policy positions to deal with local and metropolitan problems, that agreement with these party positions would be a precondition for party endorsement, and that elected officials would consult regularly with party leaders to implement them.

In most cases, metropolitan problems such as traffic flow, sewage, air pollution, water purification, and crime control impinge upon life in the municipalities, villages, and townships outside the central cities. We would expect that other organizations, public officeholders, or civic-minded individuals would address metropolitan problems, even if local party organizations did not. As we suggested above, however, most of these groups and individuals have no responsibility to the general public. Only elected officeholders are directly responsible to constituent publics, and only those commissions or intergovernmental bodies appointed by elected officials have clear responsibility to the public's representatives. Actions of civic-minded individuals, independent commissions, or other organizations—even those appointed by public administrators—are at least two steps removed from review by the electorate.

If success for local party organizations were simply winning office and fostering policies that preserved their electoral and organizational advantages, we could declare local party organizations healthy and flourishing. Paradoxically, we could make this judgment even if their actions were largely irrelevant to solving the pressing problems of the MAs in which they operated. Indeed, we believe this sort of reasoning accounts for the judgment of researchers who present evidence that local parties have increased their resources since the 1950s and conclude that "the level of party organizational activity is in general far higher today than it was in the past, and, as a result, the effectiveness of parties is most likely increasing rather significantly" (Gibson and Scarrow 1993: 240).

Our concerns, however, extend beyond short- and long-term electoral effectiveness. We are interested in determining the extent to which local party organizations deal with metropolitan political problems. To this end we have reviewed the judgments of party scholars about the political activities of local party organizations; we have examined recent studies of how political and civic organizations and actors have addressed the problems of decentered MAs; and finally, we have conducted our own investigation of the role of local political party organizations in addressing the problems of the Cincinnati CMSA. To anticipate our findings: we uncovered few instances of party organizations playing a responsible role in metropolitan governance. Our interviews with Hamilton County party leaders and public officials revealed not only the political parties' low level of involvement in addressing metropolitan problems, but a low interest—and among some officials, a low comprehension—regarding any responsible role party organizations could or should take in addressing these problems.

Even though party scholars have debated the proper policy roles that American political parties should play at various levels of government, limited resources have forced most researchers to focus on higher levels of government.[10] Most research, in fact, concerns the organization and behavior of national party committees. Relatively less is known about the policy efforts of most state party organizations. A general pattern of increased professionalism and electoral effectiveness of state party committees, however, has led researchers to suggest that state parties are playing a stronger policy role than in the past. This is particularly true with regard to candidate recruitment where state parties are increasingly moving into the roles that satisfy the weak model of responsible party governance (Gibson and Scarrow 1993: 244).

Political scientists have done much less research on the policy roles of local party organizations than they have on the roles of national and state organizations. We know that local parties can no longer provide sufficient material incentives, such as local jobs and patronage, to gain mass electoral support. However, we have little evidence that they have successfully substituted ideological or policy (purposive) incentives. What evidence there is suggests that personal loyalty to candidates provides a more common motivation for party workers than does loyalty to party policies (Keefe 1994: 26-30; Margolis and Owen 1985). Moreover, despite increased party professionalism at the state and national levels and increased electoral activity at the local levels, candidate-centered rather than party-centered campaigns remain the norm at all levels of government (Crotty 1986; Salmore and Salmore 1989: 255-56).

Local party organizations do not seem to be directly involved in addressing metropolitan problems. The *Cincinnati Enquirer's* extensive report on "saving" the downtowns of seven midwestern cities suggests that local political parties have made little, if any, impact on public policies aimed at revitalizing the city centers. Although the *Enquirer's* reporters conducted interviews with public officials, business and civic leaders, and ordinary citizens, they spoke to no one in his or her capacity as a party official. In fact, the political parties received only two significant mentions in some twenty-two full pages of newsprint.[11]

Nonetheless, researchers may have failed to find local party organizations playing significant policy roles simply because they have not looked very hard. Most studies of local parties, after all, have focused on how well parties have performed electoral tasks. Other studies of urban politics have tended to focus on how officeholders, local elites, and interest groups—not political parties—have addressed the problems of central cities.

Our study makes a deliberate effort to look at the policy role of local political parties. In addition to monitoring local politics, we conducted interviews with party leaders, public officeholders, and political observers in the Cincinnati CMSA. The interviews, conducted in the summer of 1993 and the winter of 1996, were designed specifically to assess both the roles parties currently play in developing policy for the CMSA and the roles that party leaders and public officials wanted them to play.[12]

On the surface, the Hamilton County Democratic and Republican party organizations look stronger than average. Each has a permanent headquarters staffed by full- or part-time professionals. Each has auxiliary clubs or affiliated organizations. Each endorses candidates for local office, raises and disburses campaign funds, does mailings, and makes phone calls on behalf of party candidates.[13] Moreover, the city of Cincinnati itself has a third party, the Charter Committee, that also maintains a permanent headquarters with a professional staff, endorses candidates for city council, and carries out other tasks similar to those performed by the Democratic and Republican party organizations.[14] Electorally, these parties are remarkably successful. Nearly every elected officeholder in the county is affiliated with one of them, even though election for Cincinnati City Council, township trustees, and some municipal councils are officially nonpartisan.

When we scratch beneath the surface, however, a less flattering organizational picture emerges. While each of the parties has a role in endorsing candidates, party officials readily admit that most candidates are in fact self-starters. There is little, if any, active candidate recruitment. The party endorsements go mainly to incumbents and to those self starters whom party officials judge to be most electable (cf. Maisel et al. 1990: 150–52 and chapter 23 in this volume). Even after endorsement, candidates remain mostly on their own. The party endorsement confers a bona fides that helps candidates garner coverage in the local news media; it also facilitates access to lists of individuals who have contributed to the campaigns of previously endorsed candidates. The parties do little, however, to develop issues or strategies for the campaign; nor do they normally distribute substantial funds to support particular candidates.[15] By and large, candidates must develop their own personal organizations. In fact, officeholders report that many precinct leaders—mostly Democrats—cannot even be relied upon to pass out party slate cards on election day. For the primary election of March 19, 1996, for instance, the Democratic County Committee had candidates for only 415 of 1,061 precinct executive slots. And even the better organized Republicans could muster only 727 candidates. Even though the respective county committees will try later to fill these positions by appointment, many will remain vacant. The inability to elect or appoint so many of the parties' neighborhood officers hardly suggests strong grassroots organization.

The city of Cincinnati has lost approximately 138,000 people since 1970. Its 362,000 residents now comprise less than 40 percent of the county's population, and barely one-quarter of those living in the CMSA. Nonetheless, the county parties do little tracking of where their voters have moved. Each of the county party subunits—township, village, and municipal party committees—essentially runs its own electoral operation. Both county parties concentrate the lion's share of their efforts on winning offices in the city of Cincinnati and countywide. If anything, the parties still devote more attention to city than to county politics and elections.

Neither the party leaders nor the officeholders whom we interviewed indicated they had made significant adjustments to their electoral strategies or their policies to accommodate metropolitan problems. County party leaders lamented the flight of the middle class from the city to suburbs together with the attendant loss of revenues, stable neighborhoods, and potential for political and civic leadership. Nevertheless, they had nothing more to suggest concerning how the parties or government could cope with these problems beyond setting up (another) independent commission to study them.

Party leaders and public officials showed a remarkable tendency not only to focus almost exclusively on problems within their own particular bailiwick, but also on problems related to their own formal responsibilities. Democratic and Republican party leaders saw their organizations as primarily in a struggle to control the Cincinnati city council, the county board of commissioners, and the independent county offices. The executive director of the Charter Committee emphasized that Charter had to reinvigorate its city organization before it could concern itself with metropolitan problems. County officials claimed they did not have power to do much for the subunits of government, particularly the city of Cincinnati. Township and municipal officials outside the central city expressed concern about the problems of public safety, parking, and shopping downtown, but pointed out that they could not do much about them. Their constituents were more concerned with maintaining local roads and providing good local schools, police, and fire protection. Air and water pollution were problems, but they did not view them as their responsibility nor, as they saw it, did their constituents. Public transportation was a problem only if a local municipality lacked access to a line for those who needed to commute to the central city.[16]

Except for federally mandated contact through the Regional (Ohio-Kentucky-Indiana called OKI) Council of Governments, interviewees reported little or no contact with their counterparts in other counties in the CMSA. Indeed, Mayor Roxanne Qualls, long-serving Cincinnati Council representative to the OKI and its current chair, indicated that many elected officials still don't know who their counterparts are in counties across the state borders. Although the federal government now requires that OKI certify that all new local initiatives accord with regional plans for public transportation and pollution control (Ross and Levine 1996: 375), the idea of metropolitan government remains an anathema. Interviewees generally saw metropolitan government (or "unigov") as the intrusion of big government into local matters.[17]

The parties have no long-term strategies regarding policy. When we asked party leaders what they would do differently if they had all the money and staff they could use, they answered that they would continue to do what they do now, only more effectively. They would hire more staff, conduct surveys of voters, spend more money to advertise candidates, improve party headquarters, and the like. None expressed any plans to win over electors by promoting ideas or programs. Party officials listed the fight over the CBC charter reform plan as the only policy question on which the Democratic and the Republican county committees have taken the lead in opposition to one another since 1993. Early in 1996 the Democratic County Committee faced disagreement among its leaders regarding a March 19 referendum to increase the county sales tax to provide public finds to build new stadiums for the Cincinnati Reds and Cincinnati Bengals. After helping to negotiate some concessions from the Republican County Commissioners to cushion the tax's regressive impact, the committee delayed taking a position opposing the tax until barely four weeks before voters went to the polls. (See chapter 4 in this volume, on Democrats and Republicans functioning jointly as majority parties.)[18]

In sum, although the local parties remain electorally successful, neither their leaders nor their public officeholders envision them fulfilling the active policy role called for by the strong model of party responsibility. In fact, the party leaders generally are not interested in policy at all. Nor do the parties fully satisfy the criteria of the weak model of responsibility. They don't raise much money, they do little active recruitment of candidates, they rarely attempt to enforce party discipline, and even these rare attempts usually fail.

Conclusion

Political scientists are worried about the changes in the American political system that might make the political parties irrelevant. There has been a significant amount of research on local parties focused on the question of decline and possible revitalization, but most of that research has been centered on the political party as an electoral organization. There is relatively little research on other aspects of local party behavior that might erode the significance of party in American politics. Political scientists have argued that the electoral role is the key role of political parties. If they do not perform that role successfully, they are much less likely to perform other roles successfully, such as political socialization, facilitation of mass political participation, leadership recruitment, agenda setting, policy development, and the like.

Yet even if the electoral role of local political parties is a necessary condition for them to remain significant players in the nonelectoral aspects of American politics, it is not a sufficient one. Party organization and electoral influence may be on the road to recovery, and yet the role of parties may still be in a relative decline. Local parties in Cincinnati define their role very narrowly and show little interest in broadening their understanding of what they could do. Parties are simply trying to survive and make a good showing in the next election.

Political parties have the potential to unify our fragmented political system by uniting both citizens and officeholders across jurisdictions, thereby making local politics less parochial. Yet it is not sufficient to assume that if they have a continuing place in the electoral arena they will automatically fulfill the functions that political theorists have assigned them. At the local level we have a myriad of local jurisdictions. Parties must have both the will and the opportunity to play other roles (cf. Beck and Sorauf 1993: 16; Price 1984: 116).

It has become a cliche to say that all politics is local. Whatever weight such a generalization carries at the national level, it certainly carries much more at the local level. The problems in a small town may actually be regional problems, but local politics is local. The problem of parochialism cuts across the question of whether or not we have responsible political parties. Even if local parties conformed to the responsible party model, providing party principles and programs, controlling the process of nomination and imposing party discipline upon elected officials, they would not necessarily have any impact on the problems of fragmentation and parochialism. In theory, the party label, principles, and organization are not constrained by the legal boundaries and powers that comprise local jurisdictions. In reality, the practice of local politics is full of self-imposed constraints.

Because political parties have been narrowly defined as electoral organizations, the logic of responsible parties has been turned inside out. Responsible parties are supposed to elect candidates in order to achieve public policy goals. Elections are the means; policies and programs are the ends. But for local parties in Hamilton County, electoral victory is the goal, and policies and programs are but one of the less important means of achieving this goal.

According to Beck and Sorauf, the entire argument for responsible political parties "rests on replacing individual or group responsibility for governing with responsibility of the political party" (Beck and Sorauf 1993: 452). Yet, for the most part, the local political parties in our study prefer to shun responsibility. They prefer leaving political responsibility to public officeholders and others. While the party will render candidates assistance, often rather minimal, during electoral campaigns, once they are elected, the officeholders become the visible standard-bearers of political responsibility. Between elections the party fades into the background.

Even this picture of individual political responsibility is too optimistic. Individual standard-bearers often prefer to hand the standard to someone else, anyone else, who seems capable of handling the tough issues. The tendency of local political parties to shun responsibility for governing is something they share with local officeholders. Elected officials try to maintain that whatever is wrong is not their problem, and even if it is their problem, they can't be expected to solve it. Is there too much crime in the central city? Neither the suburban nor the county politicians have jurisdiction. And how can the voters expect the city officials alone to control the out-of-state drug traffic coming up I-75? Is traffic snarled? Are the sewers backing up? Is much of the housing dilapidated? These are problems that require the resources of state or federal authorities, the efforts of civic associations, or the investment of private corporations. Local politicians are constantly searching for nonpolitical solutions that relieve them of responsibility for making tough decisions. The seeming inability of local political parties to respond creatively to the changing urban environment is symptomatic of a general loss of faith in the ability of government to solve political problems.

Arguably one of the greatest problems for the city of Cincinnati is the ongoing decline of the central business district. Class "A" office rents have fallen by 25 percent since 1990, and retail sales figures have dropped significantly. There has been an overall loss of professional jobs in the downtown since 1990 as well as the loss of approximately three thousand federal jobs in the same period. Downtown hotels have gone bankrupt, and the city suffers from an undersized convention center. Downtown housing growth has been slow, and to top it all, the two major professional sports teams, the Cincinnati Bengals and the Cincinnati Reds, have threatened to leave town unless they get new stadiums (Downtown Cincinnati Inc. 1995).

The most recent attempt to revitalize the downtown has been the establishment of Downtown Cincinnati, Inc. (DCI), a private nonprofit organization that in the words of a *Cincinnati Enquirer* editorial, will "do for downtown what management companies do for malls" (1993). It is hoped that this new entity will effectively perform many functions that local government neglects or performs very poorly. In 1994, its first year of operation, DCI engaged in a well-publicized grassroots campaign to solicit ideas from ordinary citizens about what a revitalized Cincinnati would look like. More than four thousand area residents participated in the development of *Vision 2020*, a document containing the guiding principles for DCI in the coming years.

Since the creation of *Vision 2020*, DCI has developed detailed programs to implement the vision. These entail activities such as planning capital projects, recruiting retailers, providing a clean and safe downtown environment, and improving transportation, marketing, and public relations. These schemes require cooperation with organized business interests such as the Cincinnati Business Committee and the Chamber of Commerce, as well as community groups, OKI, and various government agencies in the city of Cincinnati and Hamilton County.

DCI is proud of its outreach and its attempt to involve all segments of the community in its revitalization effort. Or, to put it more precisely, its attempt to involve all segments of the community except the political parties. David Phillips, the chief executive officer of DCI, made it very clear to us that DCI is nonpartisan. Though it often has to deal with politicians, DCI does not have any official connection with any of the three local parties. Political parties are not involved at all in the creation or implementation of its projects. *Vision 2020* seems to us a vision of a revitalized city without the nasty odor of politics. Indeed, the DCI does not even conceptualize the problems facing downtown as political problems: solutions to the city problems will bypass the existing electoral process. The way out of the spiraling decline of the core city is not to back the candidates or platforms of one of the established political parties. Politics and the political system are essentially irrelevant.

Cincinnati is one of the few remaining core cities in MAs that still operate under the council-manager form of government, but DCI's proposed solutions do not even draw upon old-fashioned reform ideology. *Vision 2020* does not blame partisanship for thwarting and corrupting the political process. Nor does it envision a more competent city manager. Increasing the powers of city government, reorganizing its bureaucracy, eliminating political bottlenecks and the like are not options that DCI contemplates as necessary for executing the new plan for reviving downtown Cincinnati. Privatized government simply has to build a consensus and have the political system turn over power and money.

Thus, the solution to the decline of Cincinnati is to treat the center city like a shopping mall. The core city must be made more like the suburbs and treated as simply another shopping node. It must be adapted to the lifestyle and assumptions of suburban retail shoppers, to the citizens of the suburbs accustomed to their own ways of interacting with city services. As the city itself struggles to adapt to this new reality, what role does the local political party organization have in this major process of urban transformation? Seemingly, little or none.

Researchers have heralded the news that the reported terminal decline of local political parties has been greatly exaggerated. They claim to have found a revitalized and transformed party organization. Yet from the perspective of those who look for responsible parties to play a dynamic role in the process of governing, such optimism seems unwarranted. Local parties may not be declining as electoral organizations, but instead of confronting the new realities of decentered metropolitan areas, they are conducting business as usual.

We end on a rather pessimistic note. Though much of the data for our study come from the Cincinnati region and further research in other metropolitan areas will be necessary to confirm our findings, we still feel confident about our overall conclusions. The old central core city has undergone a profound transformation, but local political parties have not responded. Despite our hopes to the contrary, we find no evidence that they intend to respond in the future.[19]

Notes

1. For example, the *Cincinnati Enquirer* distributed three separate fall election guides in the Sunday paper of October 24, 1993. Readers received the guide for Hamilton County (Cincinnati and suburbs), the guide for Clermont, Butler, and Warren Counties (Southwestern Ohio), or the guide for Boone, Campbell, and Kenton counties (northern Kentucky). No special section covered Dearborn counties, Indiana, Gallatin, Grant, and Pendleton counties, Kentucky, or Brown County, Ohio. In short, the *Enquirer* prepared no comprehensive (or summary) guide for the metropolitan area for which it is the principal newspaper.

2. A metropolitan area (MA) consists of a central city with a minimum population of 50,000 or an urbanized area of 100,000 or more people (75,000 in New England) as defined by the Bureau of the Census. Geographically, an MA consists of one or more central counties, but it may also include adjacent counties with strong economic or social ties to the center. For statistical purposes an MA is designated either as a metropolitan statistical area (MSA) or as a primary metropolitan statistical area (PMSA) of a larger consolidated metropolitan statistical area (CMSA). CMSAs consist of MAs over 1,000,000 people that have one or more large central cities. CMSAs may contain smaller PMSAs. The key requirements for determining the boundaries of an MA are that the outlying counties (or cities in New England) have specified social and economic relationships to the central counties as measured by levels of commuting, population density, urban population, and population growth (U.S. Department of Commerce 1992). Ordinarily, no governmental unit to which citizens elect representatives corresponds to the boundaries of the MA.

3. Actually, more people commute from suburb to suburb than from suburb to central city. The suburbs contain more offices, and they also have more retail sales than do central cities. (See Fishman 1992: 12–17.)

4. There is also some evidence that voters do not hold local government responsible for problems like layoffs and unemployment. (See Margolis, Burtt, and McLaughlin 1986: 22.)

5. The Charter Research Institute is an organ of the Charter Committee. The Charter Committee (Charterites) is a good government organization that endorses candidates for city council and is effectvely a third party, participating in Cincinnati politics along with the Democrats and Republicans. The philosophy behind Cincinnati's Home Rule Charter remains as baldly "good government" as it was in 1924 when the voters adopted the council-manager form chapioned by the Naitonal Municipal League. " . . . council should hire a City Manager with a thorough knoledge of municipal services and proven skills as a professional administrator. This system was also inaugurated to depoliticize the city administration, and the Manager is responsible for running departments and programs without political bias. Council hammers out those political decisions that are part of the legislative process in a democracy, while the Manager is free to deal with the nuts and bolts of a large municipal adminstration" (Charter Research Institute 1991: 5). See also Seasongood (1954).

6. See Dorsey (1993: 59) for a paean to township goverments of "limited pwer, decisions by peers, [and] administration by consensus."

7. Of the six midwestern cities the *Enquirer* team compared with Cincinnati, the four with the most vibrant downtowns—Cleveland, Columbus, Indianapolis and Louisville—have strong mayors, while the two with the most depressed centers—Dayton and Toledo—had city managers.

8. The Forum includes representatives from the Republicans, Democrats, Charter Committee, CBC, Chamber of Commerce, Women's City Club, Women's Political Club, League of Women Voters, NAACP, AFL-CIO, Southern Christian Leadership Conference, Coalition of Baptist Ministers, National Committee of Negro Women, Urban Appalachian Coalition, Jewish Federation, The Charter Review Committee (previous review commission), Stonewall Cincinnati, Procter and Gamble, and the Coalition of Neighborhood Councils.

9. In recent years the federal government has begun to require that local communities conform to regional plans for clean air and water and public transportation. Metropolitan planning organizations, often regional councils of government composed of representatives from local governments, have been given greater control of the distribution of federal largess throughout the MAs (Rusk 1993: 112; OKI 1993; Ross and Levine 1996: chap. 11). We skip a discussion of the pros and cons of metropolitan government simply because consolidated metropolitan government is not a viable possibility at this time. Only three major consolidations have occurred in metropolitan areas over 250,000 since 1907: Indianapolis, Indiana (1969); Jacksonville, Florida (1967) and Nashville, Tennessee (1962) (Herson and Boland 1990: 260ff).

10. Schlesinger (1991 chap. 1), for example, argues that policy concerns detract from the parties' main mission: electing candidates to office. Gibson et al. (1989), on the other hand, argue that ideology can help rather than hinder electoral success. On the difficulty of doing comparative studies of local party organizations, see Margolis (1993).

11. In both instances, the state party organization, rather than the local party, played a critical role. The first involved the Republican business leaders of Cleveland seeking Governor James Rhodes's blessing for his lieutenant governor, George Voinovich, to return to the city and run for mayor against the politically unpalatable (and increasingly unpopular) Democratic incumbent, Dennis Kucinich. The second involved Louisville Democrats petitioning the Democratically controlled state legislature to authorize a referendum to allow their mayor to serve three consecutive four-year terms instead of being limited to only one term. In each case, we have at best an instance of the state or local party organization acting in accordance with the precepts of the weak model of party responsibility to recruit or retain a strong candidate. A consolidated copy of the full series can be obtained from the *Enquirer*.

12. Interviews were conducted by the authors in person or by telephone using a directed list of questions, but not a formal interview protocol. They lasted between 30 and 120 minutes. See note 19 for a list of interviewees.

13. The Republican Party is far better organized. It has a bigger budget, larger staff, more active committees, and more active affiliated organizations.

14. The Charter Committee is technically not a party. Ohio law requires that organizations maintain a statewide presence in order to qualify as official parties. (See Sturrock et al. 1994.)

15. Neither of the major parties develops a platform or principles to which candidates are asked to adhere. Rarely do the parties repudiate one of their own, regardless of his or her performance. When the Republicans did refuse to endorse incumbent Guy Guckenberger for Council in 1989, he ran successfully as an independent Republican. The party subsequently relented and appointed him to a vacancy on the County Board of Commissioners. He became commission president in 1994. The Democrats were happy to endorse Tyrone Yates in 1993, even though he was first appointed and then subsequently elected to council as a Charterite. The Republicans have been similarly happy to accept Democratic turncoats, such as Kenneth Blackwell and James Cissell. The Charter Committee's principles preclude their imposing any more guidance on candidates than the general admonition to campaign and to govern "for the good of the whole city" as opposed to any particular neighborhood or special interest (See Miller 1993).

16. Even here the view of transportation is rather parochial. County commission chairman, John Dowlin, complained that even the OKI metropolitan transportation plan assumes everyone wants to travel downtown. "I don't see enough cross-town transportation. There are as many jobs in Blue Ash as there are in downtown Cincinnati" (Calhoun 1993).

17. Qualls' elevation from council member to mayor in January 1994 signaled a new emphasis on regional concerns. Her "State of the City Address" (January 6, 1994) called for regional cooperation to solve the city's problems. Among other things, she proposed formation of a Cincinnati/northern Kentucky port authority to tackle big-ticket projects like financing a new stadium and expanding regional convention facilities. This regional focus was her own

initiative. The Hamilton County Democratic Party had taken no official position on these issues.

18. Mayor Qualls and Charterite Bobbie Sterne ended up voting with three Republican members of council to endorse the tax increase. The four other Democrats on council voted against endorsing the proposal. On February 19, 1996, the Democratic Party executive committee, dominated by labor interests, voted against endorsement. The major sticking point was no labor agreement guaranteeing 100 percent union contractors. Even though the Aronoff Center for the Arts and the projected Fountain Square West construction lacked such an agreement, approximately 80 percent of the jobs were (or were expected to be) union. The percentage varied by trade, however, running from nearly 100 percent for the steel workers to as low as 20 percent for the painters.

19. Interviews: **Tim Burke**, Chairman, Hamilton County Democratic Party, August 1993–present; face to face, August 19, 1993; telephone, February 2, 1996. **Loi Conway,** Executive Director of Charter Committee; face to face, August 3, 1993. **Robert Dorsey,** Chairman, Anderson Township Board of Trustees, Republican; face to face, August 19, 1993. **John Dowlin,** President, Hamilton County Board of Commissioners 1992-93, Republican, former mayor, city of Sharonville; face to face, August 23, 1993. **Aaron Herzig,** Executive Director, Hamilton County Democratic Committee; telephone: short interviews January and February 1996. **Gregory Jarvis**, City Manager, Covington, Kentucky; face to face, October 7, 1993. **David Krings,** Administrator of Hamilton County; telephone, February 1, 1996. **Jerry H. Lawson,** convener and mediator, Forum for Charter Reform; professional mediator, Center for Resolution of Disputes; telephone, February 5, 1996. **Thomas Luken,** former mayor of Cincinnati, former member of Congress, Chairman, Hamilton County Democratic Party, 1991–93; City Councilman, 1992–93; face to face, August 25, 1993. Also short interview by telephone in July. **Zane Miller,** former ward chairman, Cincinnati Democratic Committee, Campaign Manager for Southwestern Ohio, Eugene McCarthy for President, 1968, Professor of History and Codirector, Center for Neighborhood and Community Studies, University of Cincinnati; face to face, August 12, 1993. **Marilyn Ormsbee,** Executive Director, Charter Committee; telephone, January 26, 1996. **David Phillips,** Executive Director, DCI; telephone, February 1, 1996. **Roxanne Qualls,** member, Cincinnati City Council, Democrat, Council Representative to OKI Regional Council of Governments, 1993–94; chair 1992; Mayor, 1994-present; telephone, August 27, 1993; face to face, February 13, 1996. **Brewster Rhoads**, Democratic party campaign consultant and manager, Member, Hamilton County Democratic Executive and Steering Committees; face to face, October 11, 1993. **Dusty Rhodes**, Hamilton County Auditor, Democrat; face to face, August 27, 1993. **Eugene Ruehlmann,** Chairman, Hamilton County Republican Committee, Former Mayor of Cincinnati; face to face, August 16, 1993; telephone, February 1, 1996. **Bobbie Sterne,** member of Cincinnati City Council, Charterite, former mayor; face to face, January 19, 1996. **Greg Vehr,** Executive Director, Hamilton County Republican Committee; face to face, August 16, 1993. **Brandon Wiers**, former mayor of City of Forest Park, member, Commission on County Government Reform, member of Forest Park Democratic Committee; served on commission as representative of Charter Committee of Cincinnati; face to face, August 17, 1993. **Tyrone Yates**, member, Cincinnati City Council, Democrat, elected as Charterite for 1992–93 term, Vice Mayor, 1994-present; Adjunct Associate Professor of Political Science, University of Cincinnati; short interviews; face to face and by telephone, July 1993 and January 1996.

13

Change Comes to Youngstown:
Local Political Parties as Instruments of Power

William C. Binning
Melanie J. Blumberg
John C. Green

On May 3, 1994, Mahoning County, Ohio, witnessed an election that was in some respects typical of contemporary politics: a young "outsider" candidate defeated an aged "insider" in the Democratic primary. The challenger campaigned for "change," stressing honesty, reform, and leadership. In contrast, the incumbent ran on his long record, vigorously defending patronage, politics as usual, and accumulated power. These characters could have come from central casting.

The election was, however, strikingly atypical in other respects. The contest was not for public office but for the chair of a county Democratic central committee, and was actually 409 precinct races. Operating under the banner of "Mahoning Democrats for Change," the challenger's slate won two-thirds of these races, ousting a sixteen-year "boss." In effect, Mahoning County traversed a century of history in a single night, replacing a classic "machine" with an equally classic caucus of "reformers." There were more wonders still. The challengers orchestrated a modern, candidate-centered campaign, were led by the most promising local office holders, and ran on a platform stressing programmatic goals. The characters in this drama could indeed have come from central casting—but from several different movies.

This case runs counter to the expectations of most party scholars. Local parties are generally regarded as being in decline, largely replaced by candidates, interest groups, and the news media. But in at least one place, all these forces combined to revitalize a local party. Indeed, this case reveals much about what local parties have been and can be. Simply put, parties are instruments for amassing and deploying political power, and they can be adapted to the various circumstances facing politicians.

Models of Local Party

The experience of the Mahoning Democrats is strategically placed within the rich descriptive literature on American local parties, and each can help illuminate the other. A good place to begin is by noting the instrumental character of parties (Sartori 1976: 25–30): The politicians who form and re-form parties see them primarily as a means for solving basic problems in amassing and deploying power. Such basic problems include the organization of candidacies (choosing individuals to compete for office), the organization of campaigns (conducting appeals to voters), and the organization of policy (enacting government programs). Aldrich suggests that politicians form and re-form parties when four conditions are meet: (1) social change creates new political problems; (2) politicians see the need to insitutionalize solutions to these problems; (3) existing institutions cannot solve them; and (4) existing institutions are strong enough to thwart the development of solutions (Aldrich 1995: 284–85).

The literature has long recognized two idealized models of local party (Crotty 1986: 21), which might be labeled "party in control" and "party in service" (Aldrich 1995: chap. 9). Each model represents a different way that politicians solved the problems of amassing and deploying power. Party-in-control assumes that party leaders are in charge of key political resources, allowing them to "control" office and benefit seekers so as to enhance the party's influence over government personnel. Power is thus amassed within the party and deployed by its leaders. In contrast, the party-in-service assumes that party leaders occupy strategic positions in politics, allowing them to be of "service" to office and benefit seekers so as to enhance the party's influence over government policy. Thus while power is amassed outside the party organization (by office and benefit seekers), its deployment is coordinated by party leaders.

The urban machines of the late nineteenth century were a textbook case of party-in-control (Pomper 1992: chap. 5). They were formed to solve the problem of organizing campaigns, and they did so through a cadre of grassroots activists who contacted voters. The machine "bosses" marshaled these resources, which gave them "control" over the organization of candidacies and policy. Although admired for their effectiveness, the machines were criticized for corruption, internal autocracy, and a narrow view of government.

Reaction to the machines generated numerous reform efforts, of which the progressive movement of the early twentieth century is the best known (Pomper 1992: chap. 8). To the reformers, the most pressing problem was the organization of policy, and parties needed to be "re-formed" to seek good government. This meant reducing the "control" of party leaders. Indeed, some reformers were so thoroughly hostile to party-in-control they produced the opposite of the machine: "nonpartisan" local government (Crotty 1986: 6-7).

But others were guided by a service notion of party: party leaders were to help foster consistent party programs among office and benefit seekers. To this end, reformers advocated direct primaries and other forms of internal democracy. Although admired for their virtue, the reformers were criticized for their electoral ineffectiveness, elitism, and ideological fervor.

These distinctions can encompass three other pairs of party concepts. The machines were staffed by "professional" activists, motivated by material (spoils of office) and solidaristic (ethnic recognition) incentives, while the reformed parties were characterized by "amateur" or "purist" activists, motivated by purposive incentives (from honesty to ideology; Wilson 1962). In addition, the machines ran party-centered campaigns directed by party leaders in contrast to reformed parties, which coordinated candidate-centered campaigns directed by office seekers themselves (Salmore and Salmore 1989). Finally, the machines were given to pragmatic goals, stressing tangible government benefits, whereas reformed parties were characterized by programmatic goals, emphasizing ideological consistency (Orren 1982).

The case of the Mahoning County Democrats starkly reveals the shift from party-in-control to party-in-service, from an urban machine to a reformed party. As we shall see, something very much like Aldrich's conditions produced this sudden change. However, both the old and new parties were creatures of politicians, responding to the circumstances before them.[1]

The Youngstown Machine

From the mid-1930s to the mid-1970s, Mahoning County was dominated by a classic Democratic Party machine in the city of Youngstown, closely fitting the party-in-control model (Erie 1988; Mayhew 1986: 19-20). The machine grew out of the need to mobilize a fragmented and inactive electorate during the Great Depression. In fact, Mahoning County was a prototypical example of the New Deal coalition: attracted by flourishing steel mills, its population was heavily blue-collar, ethnic, and Catholic. In 1936, the area switched from its historic Republican roots to the Democratic Party of Roosevelt. This shift was symbolized by the defeat of a twelve-term GOP congressman by Michael Kirwan, who quickly became an important national Democratic leader, serving in Congress until his death in 1970. While many factors contributed to this change, it was quickly institutionalized in the Democratic Central Committee. The quintessential leader of this organization was Jack Sulligan, who rose through the ranks to become Democratic boss in 1949, a post he held until his death in 1975. Indeed, the passing of Kirwan and Sulligan, followed shortly by the closing of the steel mills in 1977, marked the end of an era.

The Youngstown machine was based explicitly on the notion of control. It was organized hierarchically, with the chair directing the organization through an executive committee made up of geographically defined ward and district leaders, each of whom directed the precinct leaders in his own area. This organization was highly professional in orientation, relying heavily on material incentives to motivate party activists, ranging from patronage to turkeys at Christmas. The machine regularly nominated candidates for most local offices, even participating behind the scenes in nonpartisan contests, such as school board elections.

Sulligan and his associates took a particular interest in controlling the organization of candidacies, adeptly using primary endorsements to minimize the effects of Progressive era reforms in Ohio election law. Sulligan made such decisions through the executive committee, but then required voice votes by the central committee to approve such decisions. Ambitious office holders recognized the need to "serve the party" and "wait one's turn" to receive the party's endorsement. Endorsed candidates were expected to pay "assessments," usually a percentage of their salary, to help defray campaign expenses, and to be "team players." Violating these rules would bring sure, swift, and long-term repercussions not only to the violator, but to friends and relatives as well.

These practices applied to outsiders as well. Statewide and presidential candidates carefully courted Sulligan, paying "assessments" and funneling campaign funds through the machine to get out the vote. Woe unto the office seeker who failed to cooperate with the machine! The local party could "sit out" the election, as apparently happened in the 1974 gubernatorial race. But such violations aside, the machine was fiercely partisan. For example, Sulligan aggressively backed the entire Democratic ticket in 1972, despite the unpopularity of the Democratic presidential nominee, George McGovern.

Great energy went into the organization of party-centered campaigns. Campaigning was a team sport. Endorsed candidates campaigned together and spoke on behalf of each other at neighborhood "house parties" and large citywide rallies, while the precinct leaders organized get-out-the-vote committees, voter registration drives, absentee ballot programs, door-to-door and telephone canvassing. Indeed, the machine was famous for its capacity to generate election day workers, and the role of precinct officials was quite explicit.

Ethnic and working-class appeals were the staple of such campaigns. On the first count, party leaders were careful to balance the ticket with the various ethnic groups in the Democratic coalition. For example, the Irish, Slavs, and Italians each received a place on the three-seat county commission. In addition, the ever-popular congressman Kirwan headed the ticket to "pull" the rest of the slate by generating high turnout. On the second count, the machine was closely allied with labor unions, so much so that it had to fight to maintain its autonomy from the industrial unions in the 1940s and 1950s.

But the machine did not owe its authority over activists and voters to any outside group or officeholder, but to its record of winning elections and dispensing the benefits that flowed from victory.

Once the elections were over, the machine was notoriously pragmatic on policy matters. Sulligan was primarily interested in patronage and other rewards to distribute to the party faithful. He personally checked the voting records of all public sector job applicants. He simultaneously chaired the county board of elections and the district staff of Congressman Kirwan, which put him at the center of government largess. Although supportive of core New Deal issues, party leaders were largely nonideological on local questions. With rare exception, the steel industry avoided party politics and the machine stayed out of economic development. However, business was routinely accommodated on specific matters such as zoning, tax assessments, city permits, and public services. Similar consideration was given to other interest groups, including, rumor has it, organized crime. Despite frequent accusations of corruption, most benefit seekers found it prudent to work with the machine.

Over the years, the Youngstown machine had its share of disputes, but they were settled internally. The experience of Don Hanni was typical. A long-time leader of a rebel faction within the party, he had little success against the Sulligan organization despite numerous attempts. However, three years after Sulligan's death, Hanni was able to wrest the party chairmanship away from Stephen "Bushel" Olenick, Sulligan's successor, in a classic insider battle. Hanni appealed to sitting precinct leaders by promising to make the central committee the governing body of the party, with all decisions by majority vote and secret ballot. Hanni prevailed in a close vote, 195 to 143.

The Hanni Era

Don Hanni served as party chair for sixteen years (1978–94), more than half as long as Sulligan, and his tenure was a period of great turmoil. He saw himself as a traditional boss in the mold of his hero, Mayor Daley of Chicago, and he preached the party-in-control model as well as any political scientist. He worked hard to maintain the machine's dominance in the organization of campaigns, and he managed to maintain an excellent get-out-the-vote effort. This meant rewarding loyalty with patronage. For example, a newspaper analysis found friends and family on the government payroll to the sum of $843,654 a year, with additional positions linked to Hanni allies (*The Vindicator* 1994a). Hanni defended such practices with vehemence, declaring: "I am a Jacksonian Democrat, and I believe to the victor goes the spoils . . ." (Niquette 1994a). Hanni also believed that the party organization should not be taken for granted by selfish candidates, claiming, "The only thing worse than a candidate is an officeholder." Using a combination of inducements and intimidation, he sought to impose discipline on office seekers. When such persuasions failed, Hanni could be a ferocious enemy; a favorite tactic was to employ "cutters" (ersatz candidates of the same ethnicity as a recalcitrant office seeker) to draw off votes in a primary. Faced with such obstacles, Hanni increasingly picked weak candidates whom he could control, a pattern that further undermined the machine.

Hanni supplemented traditional activities with a flamboyant public role, unlike the low profile of previous bosses. Known as the "bull moose" because of his large stature, confrontational style, and brash behavior, he enjoyed making outrageous statements, such as telling *60 Minutes* that all politicians in the Mahoning Valley took money from racketeers—including the local Democrats. This colorful rhetoric was accompanied by personal foibles— "whiskey and women" by his own account—which produced numerous well-publicized scrapes with the law (*Speed of Sound* 1994).

Hanni was particularly offensive to new groups in Mahoning County: affluent suburbanites with a financial stake in the region's image and reform-minded activists dedicated to "good government." These groups first found expression with the founding of the Citizens' League of Greater Youngstown in 1982, a classic group of progressive-style reformers. Originally concerned with organized crime, the Citizens' League quickly ran afoul of the machine and spent more than a decade fighting Hanni. A favorite tactic was to screen and endorse "qualified" candidates in opposition to the party. Such efforts were aided by the sympathics of the local news media, which is unusually concentrated in the area (three major network television affiliates, two popular radio call-in shows, a major daily newspaper, *The Vindicator,* several neighborhood papers, and other specialized publications).

These problems were paralleled by increased independence of local office seekers. In 1980, James Traficant, another party maverick with a colorful personal style, defeated the machine's candidate for sheriff. In 1982, Peter Economus, a antimachine candidate, prevailed for a Common Pleas judgeship. A more important loss came in the 1983 mayor's race, when the party's nominee, Patrick Ungaro, broke with the machine after an accusation of vote fraud by the machine. He never returned to the party fold, regularly winning reelection against serious opposition from the party. In 1984, Traficant once again defied Hanni, this time winning the congressional seat, which he has held ever since. And starting in 1986, Robert Hagan, a genuine New Deal Democrat, began beating a machine-endorsed candidate for state representative.

These problems sparked a series of intraparty revolts. The initial rebellion came in 1984, when Traficant, fresh from winning the congressional nomination, challenged Hanni for party chair. Although mostly a publicity stunt, which Hanni turned back handily 277 to 74, it revealed Hanni's weakness. Two years later, a pair of more serious challengers appeared: George Beelen, a history professor and member of the Citizens' League, and realtor Robert Bannon, an important suburban party leader and machine insider. Hanni turned these assaults aside 325 to 46 for Beelen and 35 for Bannon. Then, in 1988, another challenge was crushed 305 to 56 when Russell Saadey, a wealthy suburban developer and a close friend of Hanni's, spearheaded the attack. Discouraged by their inability to win with an "insider" strategy, the anti-Hanni forces did not field a challenge in 1990. Hanni took advantage of the lull to change the party rules in his benefit: he extended the chair's term to four years (newly allowed under state law) and abandoned the secret ballot for party business.

Yet another blow came in 1992, when two party-endorsed incumbent county commissioners were defeated by Frank Lordi and David Engler. Lordi was a typical party rebel, but Engler was something altogether different: a modern entrepreneurial candidate (Ehrenhalt 1991). Coming from a Republican background, Engler entered Democratic politics with an eye toward a political career. Always something of a Hanni antagonist, Engler had received the party endorsement for city council. He broke with the machine because it would not endorse him for county commissioner. Engler made no secret of his interest in higher office nor that the machine was in his way. For the first time Hanni faced an ambitious opponent with the resources of a major local office and personal incentives to displace him.

Democrats for Change

It is unclear exactly when the fifth and final revolt against Hanni actually began. David Engler admits he considered challenging Hanni soon after he was elected in 1992, and he had long agitated for "change" in the local party. He was also a member of the Democratic Leadership Council, whose message of "change" helped elect its former leader, Bill Clinton, to the White House. Certainly by the summer of 1993, Engler and his closest associates were seriously discussing a "change" in party leadership. This group included, among others, fellow commissioner Frank Lordi, and former law partner, Michael Morley. The discussions were wide ranging and involved consultation with Hanni's many enemies. A key strategic insight emerged from these conversations: Hanni could only be overthrown by electing new members to the central committee.

By early fall, Michael Morley had become the key actor in the challenge and was the presumptive candidate for party chair. Without his skill and dedication, the revolt could not have succeeded. Just as Hanni personified machine politics, Morley came to symbolize reform. He could describe party-in-service as well as any scholar. Slight, agreeable, and soft-spoken, Morley was a native of Youngstown who returned after law school, determined to make the area his home. He blamed local economic decline on machine politics and saw his career aspirations tied to improvements in both.

Something of a political novice, he apparently harbored few political ambitions beyond defeating Hanni.

The challengers then received an unexpected opportunity to further their cause. An article in Ohio's largest newspaper, *The Cleveland Plain Dealer*, depicted Youngstown as a dying area, complete with a corrupt machine and the last boss in Ohio (Luttner 1993). Engler responded with an opinion piece protesting the negative image, sounding what was to become the theme of the upcoming intraparty battle: "Some people never change. Some people change with the times. And some people change the times" (Engler 1993). Hanni quickly threw down the gauntlet: "If Mr. Engler feels that the Democratic Party is in such a deplorable state, why doesn't he run against me for chairman?" (Niquette 1993). Less than a week later, the challenge was in high gear.

The final revolt had three distinct phases: from early January to mid-February, 1994, the challengers recruited a slate of precinct candidates; from mid-February until late March, they organized their campaign themes and resources; and from late March to the May primary, they waged a public campaign on behalf of the reform slate. The sheer arithmetic of this effort is stunning, and may well have rivaled the best efforts of the machine at any point in its history. If nothing else, it reveals how much the challengers valued the local party.

Organizing Candidacies. On January 4, 1994, the reformers opened a "war room" in Morley's law offices, from which they directed their campaign. Symbolically, the campaign was launched from the suburbs, where the machine was weakest. The first order of business was recruiting a reform slate of precinct candidates. This effort involved extensive research on the existing central committee, complete with detailed maps, colored pins, and files. Based on this research, about thirty sitting members were asked to join the slate. The movement then recruited another 325 candidates, leaving only fifty-four mostly inner-city precinct uncontested. The Citizens' League, the anti-Hanni officeholders, and about one hundred community, business, and political leaders eventually participated in the recruitment (Niquette 1994b).

The movement leaders centralized the process of getting the slate on the ballot, training recruits to complete the necessary petitions, and then filing all the petitions together. In a move typical of insider politics, the board of elections—chaired by Hanni—declared approximately forty of the movement's petitions invalid. The challengers filed for forty write-in candidates (Niquette 1994c). During this period, the principal leaders were also involved in a number of other races against machine-backed candidates, including Engler's race for Democratic State central committee. The machine was caught off guard by the energy of the movement and the size of its slate. Meanwhile, it had plenty of trouble with its own slate. Due to past infighting, many of the sitting members of the central committee were recent appointees, and there were also a large number of vacancies. In addition, a survey of precinct candidates revealed that not all of the party's slate were strong Hanni supporters (Binning, Blumberg, and Green 1995).

Organizing Campaign Themes. Having successfully recruited a large enough slate to win control of the central committee, the challengers set about getting the slate elected. They adopted two issues: the first was that Hanni was bad and caused economic decline; the second was that the party should be reformed to aid in economic development. These themes were fully elaborated in the official platform of Democrats of Change. This document had a long preamble, tying Hanni's record to local economic decline and listing specific goals. Some were party reforms, such as a two-term limit for party chair and a prohibition of primary endorsements by the party. Others dealt with issues, for example, by creating "policy councils" on subjects such as economic development. Finally, the platform promised to demand reciprocity of state and national Democratic officials: the provision of economic benefits to the region in return for support at the polls. With the exception of the last plank, these matters were in the spirit of Progressive reform. The challengers proved to be very adept at attracting media attention, giving themselves a name, "Mahoning Democrats for Change," a catchy logo, and a steering committee of popular leaders, including Mayor Ungaro, Commissioner Lordi, and State Representative Hagan (Niquette 1994a).

Once these themes were articulated, the Change leaders turned to raising funds with which to conduct their campaign. The amount raised was quite impressive: Democrats for Change raised and spent some $160,000, more than twice the machine's funds of $67,000, and also more than was typically spent in countywide campaigns (e.g., Engler spent $67,000 in the 1992). Approximately three-quarters of this war chest came from the principal leaders (Morley, Engler, and Lordi) and development interests, many of whom did business with the country government and some who were prominent Republicans. The rest came from reformers and the precinct candidates. In contrast, Hanni's funds came from the party "regulars," unions, and business interests long allied with the party.

Organizing the Campaign. By the last week in March, the Change leaders had assembled formidable resources: a large slate of precinct candidates, popular issues, extensive publicity, and adequate funds. They then set about mobilizing voters. In some respects, their campaign was a modern, media driven operation, closely resembling a contemporary congressional campaign (Herrnson 1994: 74). In other respects, however, it resembled a party-centered campaign of the sort typically waged by the machine. It had a single slate of endorsed candidates running as a team on a common platform. The campaign employed a six-pronged strategy: (1) television and radio advertising, (2) telephone banks, (3) direct mail, (4) grassroots campaigning by precinct candidates, (5) print advertising, and (6) public appearances by Morley and other Change leaders.

The media campaign was clearly the linchpin of the effort, employing four high-quality television ads and two radio spots, attacking Hanni and linking Democrats for Change to economic renewal. A key aspect of the advertising was educating voters on how to vote for precinct candidates and how to identify Change candidates. On the first count, the ads said, "When you vote, the first thing on your mind should be the last thing on the ballot. In the bottom right corner, your neighborhood Mahoning Democrats for Change candidate is under the member of county Central Committee." On the second count, all of the advertising carried the instruction, "Tell us what street you live on; we'll tell you what precinct you're in, and who your candidate for Change is," followed by a telephone number.

All told, the reformers purchased 114 television spots and probably an equal number on radio, expending some $60,000 on media production and buys. These efforts were reinforced by other anti-Hanni primary candidates; most of these ads were produced by the same firm as the Change ads and totaled another 537 spots during the same time period. The media effort reinforced the second prong of the campaign, telephone banks. In order to handle the information requests, the reformers set up a "reverse" telephone bank with volunteers equipped with binders correlating street addresses with precincts and Change candidates: a caller's precinct number, polling location, and the name of the Change candidate could be provided quickly. Perhaps as many as nine thousand persons called the information number. The campaign also set up a conventional telephone bank that eventually called all of the registered Democratic and independent voters at least once.

The third prong of the attack was direct mail. The Change movement conducted four mailings: one to each Democratic and independent voter (signed by Morley, identifying the Change candidate); one to each voter signed by the Change candidate in their precinct; one to absentee voters; and a special mailing for write-in candidates. Support for the forty write-in candidates was quite extensive, including a special brochure with instructions on how to cast a write-in ballot, and pencils printed with the candidate's name that voters could take into the polls. The telephone and mail campaigns may have reached one hundred thousand potential voters.

The fourth prong was an extensive grassroots campaign. The Change leaders maintained frequent contact with the precinct candidates and held regular meetings to train them on door-to-door canvassing and to supply them with campaign materials. A study of turnout by precinct suggests that perhaps one-third of the reform slate canvassed their precincts heavily door-to-door and by telephone. Several hundred volunteers were mobilized to work the precincts on election day, covering about 85 percent of the polling places. In the waning days of the campaign, the campaign unleashed its fifth prong: a full-page ad in the major newspaper and half-page ads in neighborhood newspapers, which identified the entire reform slate by precinct.

Finally, Morley and other Change leaders campaigned in person and via the news media. Hanni and Morley had two debates, one on radio and one on television, that reinforced the differences in their styles. The greater Youngstown news media covered the campaign extensively, making it one of the top local news stories. The major newspaper, *The Vindicator* ran a three-part series on the battle for party control, including hard-hitting articles about the machine and its boss. Two days before the election, it broke a long-standing policy and endorsed the Change slate (*The Vindicator* 1994b).

Hanni's supporters had not been idle. Having filled their slate, machine operatives then prepared for a traditional grassroots campaign. But as the elections approached, insiders began to feel uneasy: The reformers appeared to be better organized than expected, and Hanni himself seemed to lack zeal for the fight. Hanni's closest allies urged a more extensive media campaign, but he was adamantly against it, insisting on the old style of politics. But eventually, the Change media onslaught evoked a response. First, the party leaders tried to mimic the Change movement by labeling their slate as "Democrats for a Difference." Second, the machine printed fifty thousand copies of a broadside entitled "Common Sense," and third, it aired a television ad featuring Hanni and former antagonist, Congressman Jim Traficant. Fourth, Hanni intensified his attacks on Morley, attempting to link him to wealth, suburbanites, and corruption. Finally, the machine intensified its grassroots effort, including a massive rally, door-to-door canvassing, and extensive mobilization on election day. Some of these efforts degenerated into intimidation by fearful patronage workers. Morley received death threats and had twenty-four hour police protection during the last six weeks of the campaign.

Despite a media poll showing Morley with a 52 to 17 percent advantage (Niquette 1994d; Ott 1994), most observers believed that the machine would hold enough city precincts to keep Hanni in power. However, the reform slate far exceeded expectations: a total of 275 reform candidates were elected, including twenty-five write-in candidates. Hanni himself was a casualty, losing his own race, which, along with another seventy-four losses in urban precincts, gave the Change slate two-thirds of the central committee seats. A parallel sweep of antimachine candidates in other races made the victory complete. Six weeks later, Michael Morley was elected party chair without opposition.

The Re-formed Party

Michael Morley assumed office with overwhelming public support and wasted no time in implementing the change he had promised. Although the new party is still evolving, the outlines of the party-in-service model is clearly visible, within the context of a local party organization in a one-party area. Unlike the machine, the epitome of party-in-control, the new party focuses on the organization of policy, with Morley providing a crucial "service" to his fellow politicians by spearheading economic development efforts. The new party also provides services to candidacies and campaigns, but like the Change campaign, these activities are largely organized outside of the party. As of this writing, most local observers give Morley high marks for revitalizing the local party and filling a vacuum in community leadership. His "service" approach to candidacies and campaigns has been more controversial (*The Vindicator* 1995).

The Organization of Policy. Much to the surprise of observers, Morley made good on the programmatic goals of the Change campaign. Taking advantage of his popularity, he redefined the role of party chair by becoming the key organizer of local policy making, particularly with regard to economic development, public spokesman in the community, and the chief advocate of the region with the state and national governments.

One of Morley's first activities was to bring together the local office holders to develop a joint approach to economic development. At the core of this gathering were key figures who had backed the Change campaign, including commissioners Engler and Lordi, Mayor Ungaro, state representative Hagan, and the newly elected antimachine candidates. But other officials were included as well: a majority of the Youngstown city council members as well as other county and suburban elected officials. Indeed, the only major Democratic political figure not participating was Congressman Traficant, who had backed Hanni. Together, these officials forged an alliance for economic development in the city and the county. This concordant quickly spread outward and upward to Democrats in neighboring counties, at the state level, and even to the Clinton administration. It eventually widened to the private sector, first to the development interests that helped finance the Change campaign, then to the leaders of civic institutions and the news media, and finally, if less completely, to labor unions and other groups traditionally allied with the party. In the end, this process even included the local Republican chair and the state Republican administration.

Such coordination quickly produced tangible results: the redevelopment of the central business district in Youngstown, the establishment of a cultural and fine arts district, new jobs in the private sector, and a free trade zone for the Youngstown-Warren Regional Airport (Niquette 1995a). Morley was the principal sponsor of these efforts, serving as agenda setter, consensus builder, and chief broker. He was so effective that he received official positions on a number of public and quasi-public boards. This activity may well extend to other topics in the future. The new party has developed the promised policy councils (now committees) on a variety of policy areas, such as crime, education, and community services. In addition, the new precinct leaders have been of 'service' to their neighborhoods as well, ranging from neighborhood block watch and clean-up projects to building a wheelchair ramp for a young woman in a city ward. They have also engaged in a host of community service projects, including a blood drive, a bike-a-thon to raise money for St. Jude's hospital, and a clothes drive for disadvantaged children. In some respects, these activities resemble the traditional "social services" of the machine, but also parallel a party building strategy advocated by Mike McCurry at the national level (Greider 1992: 266).

Partly because of this policy success, Morley has become a highly visible spokesperson in the community. His views are sought on a wide variety of issues, and his opinions are greatly respected. Morley has also become the chief advocate of the region to higher levels of government. This role also fulfills a Change campaign promise to extract greater resources from state and national Democratic officeholders. This expectation lead Morley into a series of tense encounters with the Clinton administration over federal jobs and grants. When the solicited benefits were slow to appear, Morley publicly criticized the White House and issued veiled threats of electoral repercussions in the 1994 and 1995 elections. Although results were eventually forthcoming, Morley's tactics produced a hostile reaction from a few local Democrats who believed that the local party chair should be a unquestioning defender of Democratic officeholders (Niquette 1995c). Morley had somewhat more success with state and congressional Democrats, gaining, for instance, a federal judgeship for Peter Economus, an early Change supporter, and with the state Republicans, who supplied funds for local development projects.

To a great extent, Morley has been able, like party bosses of old, to hold a position superior to that of elected officials. In this way, Morley has returned the Democratic Party chair to a position of influence it once had under Jack Sulligan. But he did it in a novel way, by making the local party into a forum for organizing policy. None of this would be possible, of course, without the support of Democratic officeholders, such as Commissioner Engler, or the alliance of suburbanites, developers, reformers, and journalists who backed the Change movement in the first place. To all these interests, the re-formed party offers an invaluable service: the possibility of tangible policy successes.

The Organization of Candidacies. Once in power, Morley immediately implemented the party reforms promised in the Change platform. Most of the changes were very popular, such as a two-term limit for the chair, but ending party endorsements in primaries proved very controversial. To the Citizens' League and the news media, the end of party endorsements was absolutely critical. Drawing on the Progressive tradition, they argued that rank-and-file Democrats would chose good candidates if the party stopped serving as a "selectorate" between candidates and voters—an ironic position, since both the Citizens' League and the news media routinely endorse primary candidates themselves. But other Change allies, schooled in the control model of party, opposed the nonendorsement policy, arguing that in a one-party area primaries are the real elections and the new party should screen for good candidates. Most party scholars would agree, of course (Schattschneider 1942).

Morley seems genuinely ambivalent about the no endorsement policy. Under heavy pressure from the reformers, he implemented the policy, arguing that would-be candidates should seek support from all party members and not just the backing of the chair. As Morley put it, "There are no deals to be made when you aren't endorsing." The party should be a neutral forum in which candidacies can organize effectively—a critical "service" that only the party can provide. Morley has made such services explicit, encouraging would-be candidates to seek support from precinct leaders, and offering all competitors a "level playing field." For example, in a hotly contested primary for municipal judge in 1995, Morley offered everyone access to the same resources: the names and addresses of precinct leaders, a calendar of events, voting statistics, precinct lists, and full access to party headquarters. Such resources would never have been made available to candidates under Hanni or Sulligan.

Unlike the machine, the reformed party is nonhierarchical. Gone is the chain of command from chair through ward and district leaders to precinct officials, and the party executive committee is a collection of advisers to Morley (including some who hold no other position in the party) instead of an instrument of control. The re-formed party is thus consciously a collection of "free agents" that cooperate with candidates as they see fit within the general framework of the party. One of the key functions of the chair is to maintain this framework, a function Morley takes very seriously. As in the Change campaign, Morley is in constant contact with the precinct officials (he held over ninety meetings in 1994), urging them to "get involved" in the party, campaigns, and other causes consistent with their own values and interests.

As with the Change campaign, the party literally "belongs" to the candidates who capture its label, and all party officials (and for that matter, outsider constituencies) are regarded as equals in the process. However, not all party officials actually carry equal weight. By virtue of his great popularity, Morley's support of a candidate is especially valuable and is sought avidly. Indeed, his personal backing of a candidate often has the force of an "official" endorsement. Because of Morley's deep-seated commitment to encouraging "good candidates" to run for office ("recruiting" is too strong a word given the informality of the process), he routinely confronts the limitations of the no-endorsement policy. It will be interesting to see if the new party will be able to maintain its autonomy in the midst of candidate-centered politics.

The Organization of Campaigns. The re-formed party displayed an even more radical departure with regard to campaign activities. On the one hand, Morley moved to expand party services, including a highly professional headquarters and a coordinated campaign among candidates, both reminiscent of Democratic Party efforts at the national level. But on the other hand, he directed much less attention to the direct mobilization of voters, the strong point of the machine.

Once in office, Morley created an attractive and businesslike party headquarters in a modern office building—a stark contrast to the machine era, when the headquarters was in Hanni's law office, a dilapidated building that also served as his residence. Indeed, local observers comment on the "Republican style" of the new party's operation. Morley hired a full-time director of operations and makes systematic use of a network of volunteers to provide extensive administrative support for party operations. Such activities included the organization and staffing of regular meetings, the publishing of a party newsletter, the distribution of mailing and precinct lists, assistance with candidate petitions and other activities of party officials, candidates, officeholders, and constituency groups. This kind of help was either not available or was tightly controlled under the old party.

In the 1994 general election, Morley ran a version of the "coordinate campaign" that had been used by state-level Democrats in 1992. The countywide Democratic candidates joined with the local and state party organizations to run a centralized slate and advertising effort, including a booth at the county fair. The candidates contributed according to their "ability to pay" and then held four meetings to plot strategy and determine how the funds were spent. Although the local party did not make any direct donations to its candidates, Morley appeared in the television commercials of several.

In contrast, remarkably little effort was directed to getting out the vote, a prime responsibility of local parties even in a candidate-centered era. For the first time in the history, the party did not pay "street money" on election day, and just $174 was spent on refreshments for poll workers. There was no systematic absentee ballot program or targeted door-to-door canvasing. Morley's final preelection communication to the central committee invited members to a Saturday morning meeting where campaign literature would be supplied "for anyone who would like literature to distribute in their neighborhoods prior to election day." Overall, the re-formed party spent $17,519 on the fall campaign, less than one-half of what the machine spent in 1990. The new party did sponsor a few social events during the general election campaign, but it never came close to matching the large rallies of the Hanni era. This low level of activity is all the more surprisingly when one recalls the scale and sophistication of the Change campaign just five months before.

The lack of grassroots effort can be explained in part by the weak statewide Democratic ticket in 1994 and the lack of strong Republican campaigns locally. As Morley put it, "I didn't feel I could ask people to work hard when it didn't matter." But these patterns also reveal the approach of the re-formed party to campaigns: it is the responsibility of individual candidates to persuade and mobilize voters, and the party plays a secondary service role. After all, Morley and the present party leadership did just that to gain control of the party with the Change campaign. Although the 1994 results were not particularly costly to the new party, the lack of grassroots attention could be damaging in the future. Mahoning County is a crucial source of Democratic votes in statewide and national contests, and Morley's influence will depend on how well he delivers the vote. It will be interesting to see if he puts forth more effort in the 1996 campaign.

Local Parties as Instruments of Power

What, then, is one to make of the Mahoning County Democrats? This case covers a century of local party development, from the Golden Age through the Progressive era into the future of service-oriented, programmatic parties. Despite their manifest differences, the old bosses—Sulligan and Hanni—and the new party leaders—Morley and his associates—share a common interest in amassing and deploying power. And as the circumstances changed, so did the form of the local party.

The Youngstown machine was built around the organization of campaigns in a fragmented and demobilized electorate. The traditional party-in-control solved this problem and gave party leaders great leverage over the organization of candidacies and policy. Like Hanni, political scientists may well have romanticized the capacity of the machine to control government for good ends, but Hanni never forgot the instrumental character of the party. In the final analysis, Hanni could and would not adapt fully to the political problems of a new era, particularly the organization of policy.

Progressive-style reformers and the news media were eagerly interested in solutions to these new problems. But just as the machine has been romanticized, reformers have been idealized as well. It is telling that they were unable to replace Hanni by themselves, and it was only when entrepreneurial office seekers got involved that a revolt against Hanni succeeded. The key difference is that Morley and his associates saw a positive role for the party. Indeed, the traditional and reformed parties differ not so much in their virtue but in the sources of power they tap and the uses to which it is put. Morley has re-formed the local party to solve the problems of organizing policy, and in the process has revitalized the organization, returning it to a position of prominence in the community.

The extraordinary campaign to replace Hanni reveals several things. First, in contemporary politics, extensive and sophisticated campaigns can be assembled without a traditional party organization. Indeed, given enough provocation, something very much like a traditional organization can be built in a short period of time and used with great effect. Thus, the organization of campaigns is no longer a pressing problem. Second, the party was judged to be valuable on its own right, so valuable, in fact, that the office seekers were willing to invest heavily in its capture. The party was valuable because it could be molded into an instrument to provide a wide range of services to politicians, services that could be found nowhere else. And third, local parties can be used to organize policy without controlling the organization of candidacies or campaigns.

To what extent will this case be replicated elsewhere? It may be that peculiar conditions of Mahoning County account for this situation. But if similar conditions are met in other locales, a similar revitalization of a local party could well occur.

Note

1. Unless otherwise noted, the information in this essay comes from personal interviews with Michael Morely, Don Hanni, and thirty-two other participants in the events discussed here; the authors wish to express their gratitude to all of them. For more details see, Binning, Blumberg, and Green 1995.

PART THREE

Independent Candidates and Minor Parties

14

Perot Activists in 1992-1994: Sources of Activism[1]

Randall W. Partin
Lori M. Weber
Ronald B. Rapoport
Walter J. Stone

In the spring of 1992, H. Ross Perot moved from being an interested citizen-billionaire being interviewed on *Larry King Live* to a potential presidential candidate virtually overnight. There is no doubt that Perot benefited from having deep pockets, but without a cadre of volunteer activists committed to overcoming the barriers to an independent campaign (Rosenstone, Behr, and Lazarus 1984), he could not have succeeded in getting his name on the ballot in all fifty states, let alone garner a substantial portion of the popular vote in the November general election. In many respects, the mobilization of thousands of grassroots activists in the spring and early summer of 1992 was the most remarkable feature of Perot's campaign. What caused these people to become active on behalf of H. Ross Perot during the 1992 campaign, and what are some of the possible consequences of that activism beyond the 1992 presidential election?

Sources of Third Party Activism

Explanations of political participation have long emphasized individual beliefs, attitudes, and resources (e.g., Verba and Nie 1972; Beck and Jennings 1982; Verba, Schlozman, Brady, and Nie 1993), although there is an equally long tradition emphasizing the importance of party mobilization (e.g., Katz and Eldersveld 1961; Crotty 1971; Kramer 1971; Beck 1974b). In their analysis of mobilization and political participation, Rosenstone and Hanson (1993) suggest that any complete explanation of participation must combine individual characteristics and resources with an understanding of mobilization effects. However, in the case of an independent candidacy like Ross Perot's in 1992, which individual attitudes and characteristics are likely to be important?   How are mobilization effects likely to be manifested in a nonpartisan campaign?

In this chapter we present an analysis of the sources of activism in the Perot movement by examining three broad classes of potential explanation.

1. *Individual demographic characteristics typically associated with political participation, such as income, education, and age.* These are usually treated as politically relevant resources enabling individuals to bear the costs associated with political involvement. Similarly, they may help account for participation because they place individuals in social contexts where they are more likely to be induced by others to participate (Huckfeldt and Sprague 1992).

2. *Attitudes toward the candidates and parties.* Whether from a social-psychological or from a rational-choice perspective, an individual's attitudes and preferences are relevant not only to vote choice, but to how involved they become in the campaigns. Exactly how these attitudes work in the context of a third-party campaign is not especially clear. However, Rosenstone, Behr, and Lazarus (1984) offer perhaps the most comprehensive theory of third-party support. They and others argue that roughly four groups of variables help account for support of third-party (and independent) candidates: (1) perceived failures of the major parties; (2) negative attitudes toward the major-party nominees; (3) generalized alienation from the political system; and (4) attraction to the independent candidate (cf. Mazmanian 1974; Canfield 1984; Smallwood 1983; Carlson 1981; Gillespie 1993). We will reduce these factors to a simple "push-pull" model of Perot support based on attitudes toward the candidates and parties: potential activists are "pushed" away from the major-party campaigns by their disaffection from the two political parties and/or their nominees; simultaneously, they are "pulled" toward the Perot presidential bid by their attraction to him, either because of ideological considerations or based on positive general evaluations of him.[2]

3. *Mobilization effects.* In previous work on activism in contemporary presidential nomination campaigns, we have found that political mobilization from these contests tends to "carry over" to the general election (Stone, Atkeson, and Rapoport 1992). We have also found that this political mobilization "spills over" to activism in lower-level campaigns (McCann, Partin, Rapoport, and Stone 1996) and perhaps even into party activity, such as officeholding, and interest group activity as well (Rapoport, Stone, Partin, and McCann 1992). We argue that the highly visible nature of the contemporary nomination process draws people into campaign activity on behalf of nomination contenders. Once mobilized, they become ripe for involvement in other partisan contests.

We take these previous findings to be broadly consistent with the sorts of mobilization effects Rosenstone and Hanson (1993: 174) discuss in describing the results of party appeals to potential activists. They suggest that such mobilization can affect perceptions of the stakes people have in political outcomes, thereby encouraging more involvement than otherwise would have occurred. These sorts of effects are easy to imagine at work in a party campaign where a formal apparatus exists to draw people into campaigns and other partisan arenas. Our research on nomination campaigns, however, leads us to ask whether similar kinds of mobilization effects may have been present in the Perot movement, deriving from either the major parties or the interest groups. Indeed, the attitudes, habits, and skills learned in one electoral arena may transfer quite readily to another. Thus, we expect to find mobilization from parties and interest groups into the Perot movement in 1992 and back into the parties in 1994.

Data Sources

Our principal analysis is of a national sample of individuals who called the Perot toll-free telephone number during the spring and early summer of 1992. This is a sample of potential Perot supporters because merely calling the Perot phone bank did not necessarily constitute active support for Perot's candidacy. At the time we sampled from the data base in August of 1992, it contained the names of about 450,000 people who had called throughout the spring and early summer. We mailed questionnaires to a sample of 1,901 just after Labor Day, and received usable responses from 1,321 for a response rate of 70 percent. As it happened, Perot reentered the campaign on October 1, when all but a handful of questionnaires had been returned. Immediately following the 1992 election, we mailed a follow-up questionnaire to all respondents to the first wave. We received 937 responses to the postelection wave, for a response rate of 71 percent among respondents to the first wave, and just under 50 percent of the original sample. We extended our panel study of potential Perot activists by recontacting our original 1,992 respondents shortly after the 1994 elections. We received 775 usable responses in our 1994 wave—a response rate of 59 percent for those who responded to the 1992 preelection wave and 83 percent for those who responded to the 1992 postelection wave.

During the early fall 1992 wave of the survey, we asked respondents about their activity levels for Perot prior to his dropping out of the race and for the candidates for the major party presidential nominations. We also asked about 1988 campaign activity levels in national, state, and local races. In addition, we included questions on attitudes toward and perceptions of the candidates as well as respondent demography. In the postelection wave, we asked about general election campaign involvement for Perot, Bush, and Clinton, and in various subpresidential races. We also repeated a range of attitudinal and perceptual items. In both waves we asked questions about involvement in a variety of political and nonpolitical organizations. The 1994 wave asked similar items, plus information on activity in the 1994 campaign.

For purposes of describing our Perot sample, we make comparisons with the electorate by way of the National Election Study's (NES) 1992 and 1994 surveys. Unfortunately, because Perot dropped out of the campaign in July, the NES asked very few questions about Ross Perot. Therefore, only limited comparisons with the national electorate are possible. We also compare the Perot activists with samples of 1992 activists drawn after the election from Iowa Democratic and Republican caucus attenders and Democratic attenders in Virginia.[3] These comparisons will allow us to define the contours of our sample of potential Perot activists by placing them in a context. In addition, we can get a preliminary feel for the viability of the broad explanations of Perot involvement by making these comparisons.

Who Were the Perot Activists?

As demonstrated in table 14.1, our sample of potential Perot activists is relatively well off, highly educated, and white. In these ways it is different from the electorate as a whole, much as we would expect when comparing a relatively active population with the general public. Whereas no more than a quarter of the electorate falls into the greater than $50,000 annual income bracket, a plurality of the Perot sample (47.6 percent) is placed there. Similarly, only 23.5 percent of the national electorate achieved an education level of college graduate or postgraduate work, while just under half of the Perot sample reached this level of educational attainment. With respect to age, the Perot sample is slightly older than the national electorate. Finally, our sample of potential Perot activists is remarkably unrepresentative of the national electorate when it comes to sex and race—only 38 percent of our sample is female (compared with 53.4 percent of the national electorate) and 4.4 percent of our sample is nonwhite (compared with 15.3 percent of the national electorate).

The first two of these demographic characteristics (income and education) are comparable to activists in general, while the last shows considerably smaller minority representation than among our sample of Democratic caucus attenders, but close to the typical percentages among Republicans. In sum, although our sample of potential Perot activists appears to differ from the national electorate with respect to demographics such as income, education, sex, and race, it seems to be comparable to major-party activists in these respects.

Table 14.2 presents the partisan affiliation and ideological self-placement of the Perot sample alongside that of the national electorate and those of our samples of Republican and Democratic caucus attenders. Not surprisingly, Perot activists are predominantly independent in their partisan attachments, with over 20 percent claiming strict independence and an additional 40 percent describing themselves as independents "leaning" toward one of the

Table 14.1 Demographic Characteristics of the National Electorate, Potential Perot Volunteers, and Major Party Caucus Attenders in 1992

	% National Electorate	% Perot Activists	Caucus Attenders	
			% Democratic	% Republican
Income				
Less than $30,000	50.3	25.1	26.4	33.8
$30,000–$50,000	25.0	27.4	30.9	32.2
Greater than $50,000	24.5	47.6	42.6	34.1
Education				
High school grad or less	51.9	16.0	19.8	22.9
Some college	24.6	34.5	21.2	29.8
College grad or postgraduate	23.5	49.5	58.9	47.3
Age				
Under 30	19.6	8.5	6.6	8.1
30–50	43.4	42.2	42.6	38.3
50–60	12.1	18.2	18.1	19.2
Over 60	24.9	31.1	32.7	34.3
Female	33.4	37.8	50.1	40.6
Nonwhite	15.3	4.4	5.9	1.3
N	2487	1321	764	385

Source: 1992 National Election Study; survey by authors.

two major parties. In comparison, about 12 percent of the public and under 2 percent of caucus attenders are strict independents. Notice, too, that the potential Perot activist is slightly more Republican than Democratic; 23 percent identify with the former and 17 percent with the latter. In the electorate as a whole, Democrats hold a 36 percent to 25 percent advantage. Ideologically, the Perot sample is just right of center, with a bare plurality at the moderate position. The electorate as a whole is a bit more centrist, but also leans to the conservative side. On ideology, the Perot sample is far more representative of the public than party activists. As is typical of committed partisans, the Democratic caucus attenders are predominantly liberal, while Republican attenders are mostly conservative.

Table 14.3 presents activity levels for both the Perot and caucus attender samples in partisan campaigns in 1988 and in 1992 (comparable activity items

Table 14.2 Political Identification of the National Electorate, Potential Perot Volunteers, and Major Party Caucus Attenders in 1992

	% National Electorate	% Perot Sample	Caucus Attenders	
			% Democratic	% Republican
Partisanship				
Strong Democrat	18.1	7.2	64.0	0.0
Democrat, not so strong	17.6	9.5	18.6	0.3
Independent, leaning Dem	14.4	19.5	13.0	0.0
Strict Independent	11.7	21.2	1.8	1.5
Independent, leaning Rep	12.4	19.7	1.5	12.0
Republican, not so strong	14.2	13.0	1.1	22.2
Strong Republican	11.2	9.8	0.0	64.0
Ideology				
Extremely liberal	2.7	2.1	8.3	0.0
Liberal	11.5	11.2	39.7	1.5
Slightly liberal	13.4	13.5	22.9	2.9
Middle of the road	31.4	23.1	17.0	8.8
Slightly conservative	20.3	22.8	7.9	17.1
Conservative	17.2	22.8	4.0	56.9
Extremely conservative	3.5	4.6	0.2	12.7
N	2487	1321	647	344

Source: 1992 National Election Study; survey by authors.

are not available in the NES sample), as well as the percentages of each sample holding party office, and the degree of interest-group involvement. Overall, callers to Perot's toll-free telephone number were not political neophytes. With respect to the 1992 election year, our sample of potential Perot activists was remarkably involved in politics. Over 70 percent of the sample was active in some way for Ross Perot during the preconvention phase of the campaign.[4] Furthermore, over one-quarter of the sample participated in Democratic nomination campaigns, and slightly more than 15 percent were active in the Republican nomination race. These rates of activity are about the same as those observed among party activists: fully 84 percent of the Perot sample was active in a preconvention campaign for Perot or in one of the parties (not shown in table 14.3). In comparison, 86 percent of the Democrats and 77 percent of the Republicans were active in their respective party's nomination campaigns, with only scattered activity for Perot among party activists.

In the general election stage of the 1992 campaign, activism for the eventual standard-bearer fell across the three columns in table 14.3. Just under 62 percent of the Perot sample was active for the Perot-Stockdale ticket in the fall, while larger proportions of caucus attenders remained active after the convention for their respective nominees. With respect to the partisan subpresidential races, the Perot sample shows lower rates of involvement than the party activists. Still, about one in ten were active on behalf of Republican or Democratic candidates in either House or state and local races in 1992.

Table 14.3 Political Activities among Perot Activists and Major Party Caucus Attenders in 1992

	% Perot Activists	Caucus Attenders	
		% Democratic	% Republican
Activism in early 1992			
Democratic nomination	28.6	86.4	4.7
Republican nomination	15.3	0.5	77.1
H. Ross Perot campaign	70.9	4.5	7.8
General election activism, 1992			
Bush/Quayle	12.3	2.3	72.9
Clinton/Gore	21.7	75.9	4.2
Perot/Stockdale	61.8	5.9	5.7
Republican House race	9.1	1.4	42.2
Democratic House race	10.4	25.9	3.6
Republican state/local	10.5	1.4	43.8
Democratic state/local	12.9	35.5	2.1
General election activism, 1988			
Bush/Quayle	23.0	3.2	68.2
Dukakis/Bentsen	14.4	55.0	2.1
Republican House race	10.4	0.9	32.8
Democratic House race	10.4	25.5	1.0
Republican state/local	13.9	0.5	47.4
Democratic state/local	14.3	34.5	2.1
Party officeholding			
Democratic office	10.2	29.2	1.0
Republican office	7.8	0.3	31.4
Either Party office	16.2	29.3	32.2
Overall Levels of Group Activity			
Active in no groups	32.2	28.8	25.5
Active in one group	25.9	31.0	31.9
Active in two or more groups	41.9	40.1	42.6

Source: Surveys by authors.

Even looking at party office, these Perot advocates show a significant level of involvement. About one in six either have held or are currently holding party office for one of the major parties (about half as great as the percentage for the party caucus participants). Finally, although the Perot sample was less active in 1988 than partisan caucus participants, such is not the case when we turn to group activity. The percentage of our Perot sample that purports to be active in at least two groups (41.9 percent) is directly comparable to the corresponding percentages from our sample of Democratic and Republican caucus attenders. As table 14.3 shows, the potential Perot supporters' overall level of past group activity is almost precisely the same as for the two sets of caucus participants, if not slightly higher.

Even this cursory examination of the history of political involvement among Perot respondents suggests possible links between the traditional parties, interest groups, and the Perot movement. These links may be consistent with a mobilization hypothesis: those drawn to activity by parties and groups may, as Rosenstone and Hanson (1993) suggest, become socialized to campaign activity and sensitized to their stake in electoral outcomes. In 1992, Ross Perot may have been able to tap into partisan and interest group quarters for his volunteer supporters, although it is clear that he mobilized a large cohort of newcomers to campaign activity as well.

Explaining Activism for Perot

Our strategy of sampling from Perot callers to identify activist volunteers in the 1992 Perot movement was successful. A substantial majority of our respondents were involved for Perot in some way, many quite extensively. At the same time, however, about 30 percent of the sample was not involved in the preconvention stage of the campaign, and almost 40 percent opted not to do anything for Perot after he redeclared in October. Indeed, only about 54 percent of our respondents voted for the Dallas businessman (data not shown). We thus have substantial variation *within* our sample of potential Perot volunteers. This variation allows us to explain activism on behalf of Perot by comparing those who became active with those who did not.

In searching for the sources of activism on behalf of Perot, we begin by drawing upon the three explanations outlined above: individual demographic characteristics, attitudes toward the parties and candidates, and mobilization effects of prior political activity. Despite the importance assigned to demographic factors in the literature, none of the social characteristics discussed above had any appreciable effect on activism for Perot (data not shown). Differences across age cohorts are small and inconsistent, both in the preconvention and fall stages of the campaign. Similarly, there are no consistent differences across the measures of education and income—although there does seem to be a small effect of income on preconvention activity on behalf of Perot, with those with higher incomes being slightly more active. Gender and race likewise showed no significant differences. These sorts of characteristics therefore do not help explain activism *within a population predisposed toward activity for Perot*. We know from table 14.1 that income, education, and sex differences between the Perot sample and the general population exist, but these differences do not help explain activism within the population of callers (McCann, Partin, Rapoport, and Stone 1996).

In addition to these measures of politically relevant resources, the "push-pull" model of support leads us to consider a range of attitudinal and perceptual variables. Respondents attracted to Perot, or who perceived him as close to their own ideological preferences, should be more likely to become active on his behalf—hence the "pull" toward Perot. Table 14.4 presents the percentage performing one or more activities on behalf of Perot during the early and late phase of the campaign, respectively, by perceived proximity to Perot and by overall evaluation of Perot. In contrast to the demographic variables, these "pull" factors appear to have an effect. There is, for example, a monotonic effect of ideological proximity on activity. Likewise, overall affect toward Perot has an impact: those who gave positive evaluations were much more likely to be active for Perot in both phases of the campaign than were those who were neutral or negative. Finally, the percentage of the popular

Table 14.4 Evaluations of Ross Perot by Perot Activists

	% Active for Ross Perot	% Active for Perot/Stockdale
Proximity to Perot		
0 (closest)	84.1	74.8
1	79.7	68.8
2	65.3	61.5
3 (furthest)	58.3	41.3
Evaluations of Ross Perot		
Positive	86.1	75.1
Neutral	58.6	46.6
Negative	47.1	37.1
Predicted Vote for Perot		
31–100%	87.2	85.4
21–30%	76.3	72.1
11–20%	73.0	65.2
0–10%	65.2	48.4

Source: Survey by authors.

vote the respondent expected Perot to win—a measure of the "electability" of Perot—is positively related to the level of activism on Perot's behalf. The relationship is positive and monotonic for both early and late Perot activity. This "electability" effect shows that respondents in our sample may have been susceptible to a wasted vote argument. As the expected success of Perot varied, the amount of activism on his behalf differed as well.

The "push" side of the explanation received a great deal of attention in 1992, and Perot himself played to this topic by being critical of the two parties and their candidates. Table 14.5 presents the effects of several evaluative measures of the two parties, of Bush and Clinton, and measures of long-standing affiliation with the major parties. As expected, the more negatively respondents viewed either party, the more likely they were to become active on behalf of Perot. Nearly 75 percent of the respondents who viewed either party or either nominee negatively were active on behalf of Ross Perot in the preconvention period, while somewhat lower percentages of those who were positive toward the major-party candidates and parties were active for Perot. The absolute percentages drop with respect to fall activity, but the monotonic relationship between evaluations of the parties and candidates and activity for Perot remains.

However, there is reason to suspect that these findings do not adequately capture the "push" element in Perot activism. Respondents who affiliated with either major party may have viewed their own party/nominee favorably, and the opposite party/nominee negatively. This pattern could contribute to the relationships in table 14.5 without really capturing a generalized discontent toward *both* parties. To check this, we present activity levels for respondents who viewed either both parties or both candidates negatively. These results remove the partisan effect and demonstrate a true "push" element. About three-fourths of the respondents who viewed either both parties or both nominees negatively were active for Perot in the preconvention period, and between 79 and 84 percent of the same respondents were active in the fall. On both these party and candidate indicators, activity levels were higher than in any of the categories of evaluation of the candidates or parties individually. This is added evidence in favor of the "push" effects.

Table 14.5 also shows that stronger partisans were less likely to become involved for Perot than weak partisans and strict independents. This is consistent with findings in other recent independent races (Converse, Miller, Rusk, and Wolfe 1969; Abramson, Aldrich, and Rohde 1994) and with the push-pull model because independence is associated with disaffection from the parties. Notice, too, that the drop-off in activity between the preconvention and fall phases of Perot's campaign is greatest among strong partisans (about 16 percent) and smallest among strict independents (7 percent). Independents may have been more susceptible to the "push" away from the major parties, whereas partisans were more likely to return to their party's nominee in the fall. Finally, as presented in Table 14.6, Republican identifiers as a whole were more likely to become involved in the Perot movement than Democrats. This is due to the significantly more negative attitudes Republicans had toward Bush than Democrats had toward Clinton.

Table 14.5 Evaluations of the Major Parties and their Presidential Nominees by Perot Activists

	% Active for Ross Perot	% Active for Perot/Stockdale
Evaluations of the Republican Party		
Positive	54.9	47.6
Neutral	68.6	61.2
Negative	74.8	63.1
Evaluations of George Bush		
Positive	58.2	53.5
Neutral	68.3	63.3
Negative	75.4	62.7
Evaluations of the Democratic Party		
Positive	63.0	35.1
Neutral	70.6	53.3
Negative	73.6	69.0
Evaluations of Bill Clinton		
Positive	61.4	38.2
Neutral	72.8	63.0
Negative	74.4	69.5
Evaluations of both parties		
Negative	76.8	78.9
Evaluations of both nominees		
Negative	74.0	84.2
Strength of party identification		
Strong partisan	56.9	40.9
Weak partisan	68.9	60.7
Leaning independent	73.1	64.6
Strict independent	82.2	75.0
Partisanship		
Democrat	66.2	49.4
Republican	70.4	66.2

Source: Survey by authors.

In Table 14.6 we test the notion that past political activity stimulated involvement for Perot. This relationship is likely to be a good deal more complex than carryover effects from nomination to general election campaigns in the same party (Stone, Atkeson, and Rapoport 1992). Even nomination activists who supported a losing candidate are involved in a partisan contest that presumably unites all nomination activists in a common purpose. In the case of past partisan activity (which we have already seen is substantial), Perot activists must transfer their loyalties away from a party cause to an independent candidate. This is clearly a less straightforward effect. As a result, it is not surprising that our results are inconsistent. While early activism for Perot increased as the level of presidential activity in 1988 increased, there is no relationship for later Perot activity in the fall stage of the campaign. This may reflect the difficulty of transferring to an independent candidate among those with past commitment to a partisan campaign. A similar effect is found when comparing Perot activism with previous group activities. Prior group activism lead to monotonic increases in activism on behalf of Perot in the early stages of his campaign, but the same measure does not appear to produce a monotonic increase in activism on behalf of the Perot/Stockdale ticket in the fall.

In sum then, we find little support for the individual resources explanations for Perot activism. In contrast, the attitudinal explanations were supported by strong potential effects of an attraction or "pull" toward the Perot campaign and a similar "push" away from the major parties and their respective nominees. Finally, with regard to the mobilization explanations, we find weak evidence in support of a partisan mobilization effect, with those

Table 14.6 Past Political and Group Activity by Perot Activists

	% Active for Ross Perot	% Active for Perot/Stockdale
General Election Activity, 1988		
0	70.4	62.2
1	70.9	59.6
2	74.1	64.8
Past Group Activities		
0	66.7	52.1
1	72.7	62.4
2	76.7	72.6
3	80.5	67.7

Source: Surveys by authors.

active in past partisan campaigns becoming active on behalf of Perot in the early stages of the campaign and no comparable effects on activism for Perot's general election bid. We find a similar group mobilization effect, where prior group activism appears to lead to early activism on behalf of Perot.

Multivariate Analysis

In order to capture adequately the impact of these possible explanations for activism on behalf of Ross Perot, we must estimate a multivariate model. By doing so, we will be able to control for some of the combined effect or spuriousness of these explanations. For example, the effect of past partisan activity on early Perot activity may be attenuated by strength of partisanship (already shown to affect Perot activism)—those with the strongest ties to a major party are more likely to support Perot by their actions. Not coincidentally, they are also those most active in past partisan campaigns (who are also less likely to become active for Perot). This analysis employs the same variables as above, including demographic characteristics, the "push-pull" attitudinal factors, partisan identification, expectation of Perot's electability, and levels of past participation.[5]

We present three parallel models predicting activism on behalf of Perot in both the early and late stages of the campaign. The first model predicts the degree of involvement in the early stage of the Perot campaign. The second model predicts the degree of involvement in the general election stage of the campaign. Finally, we reestimate this second model including the possible mobilizing effects from the earlier stage of the campaign. The results of these analyses are presented in table 14.7. Not surprisingly, given the absence of bivariate effects, the demographic variables have little impact on Perot activism, with gender falling just short of statistical significance in both models of general election activism.

The indices of negative ratings of the candidates and parties show a modest, positive impact on level of Perot activism in the early stages of the 1992 campaign, with only the negativity toward the two major parties reaching a level of statistical significance—the more negative a respondent was toward both major parties, the more likely he or she was to become active on behalf of Ross Perot in the spring and summer of 1992. In explaining activism on behalf of the Perot/Stockdale ticket in the fall campaign, both measures of negativity (toward the parties and toward the major-party nominees) prove to have a significant effect. Finally, the strength of partisanship is strong and significant in the expected direction for all but the last of the three models presented in table 14.7. The more strongly a respondent identified with one of the major parties, the less likely he or she was to support Perot through campaign activism.

Table 14.7 Pre- and Postconvention Activism for Perot: OLS Regression Analysis

	Preconvention Activity	General Election Activity	General Election Activity
Demography			
Gender	0.000	0.184	0.123
Age	0.009	0.005	-0.012
Education	0.017	-0.322	-0.038
"Push" factors			
Negative ratings of candidates	0.061	0.125*	0.073*
Negative ratings of parties	0.073*	0.124*	0.071*
Strength of partisanship	0.140*	0.182*	0.082
"Pull" factors			
Evaluation of Perot	-0.379*	-0.431*	-0.142*
Proximity of Perot	-0.062	-0.065	-0.035
Participation effects			
1988 campaign activity	0.200*	0.160*	0.008
Past group activity	0.027	0.026	0.007
Preconvention Perot activity	—	—	0.651*
Partisanship	0.080	0.144*	0.064
Expected Perot vote	—	—	0.007
Adjusted R^2	0.137	0.213	0.553
N	841	622	586

*Significant at the .05 level or better; figures are unstandardized regression coefficients.
Source: Survey by authors.

In looking at the "pull" side of our model, evaluation of Perot has a consistently strong, significant effect on level of activism for Perot—in both the early and later stages of the presidential campaign. The negative sign is consistent with the coding of this measure, where a low score indicates positive evaluations of Perot (see table 14.4, above). In contrast, ideological proximity of Perot is not a statistically significant predictor of Perot activism in either stage of the 1992 campaign.

Previous campaign activism (measured here as recall of 1988 general election activism) demonstrates a significant, positive effect on activism on behalf of Perot in the early stages of the 1992 contest. For activism in the later stage of the 1992 campaign, this direct effect of prior political participation is only significant when preconvention Perot activism is not included in the model (column 2). In contrast, prior group activity, which showed modest effects on Perot activism in the bivariate tables (above), is neither strong nor statistically significant in any of the multivariate models presented here.

Finally, there are mixed results about the partisan bent of Perot activists. Republicans were more likely to become active for Perot, but that difference is not significant in the model explaining preconvention activism (column 1), and is only significant in explaining general election activism on behalf of Perot when the preconvention activity measure is not included in the model. In addition, we can see that potential Perot activists may have been influenced by their perceptions of how well he would do in the fall campaign. Independent of the various affective measures, the more popular votes they thought he would receive, the more involved in his fall campaign they became. This effect falls just short of the standard cut off for statistical significance.

The Perot Movement and 1994 Party Change

The 1994 congressional election was an historic one for the American political system. For the first time in forty years, the Republican Party gained control of both houses of Congress. This dramatic partisan shift followed on the heels of the 1992 election, which saw the highest level of support for an independent presidential candidate since 1912. Our Perot sample in 1992 may provide a bellwether indicator of what happened in the 1994 congressional elections. After all, 1994 was an election when virtually all Perot supporters were faced with an electoral choice involving only candidates representing the two major parties, with no significant independent effort to draw them away from the two major parties.[6] How did these activists respond to the partisan context of 1994, and how did their response foreshadow prospects for change in the party system?

Table 14.8 reports the partisan affiliation, ideological self-placement, and selected issue positions for our Perot activists in 1992 and 1994, as compared to the national electorate. As was the case in 1992, the Perot supporters are more independent than the national electorate in 1994, although the results suggest some movement toward greater identification with the two major parties. For example, in 1994 the proportion of strict independents in our sample dropped from just over 21 percent in 1992 to 13 percent. Furthermore, the Perot sample became more Republican in 1994, with more than a 10 percent increase in self-identified Republicans. With respect to ideological self-placement, our sample continued to be more conservative than the electorate as a whole in 1994. Furthermore, as was the case with partisanship, a shift to the right occurred in ideological self-placement from 1992 to 1994. The ranks of both liberals and moderates were depleted between 1992 and 1994, while the proportion of conservatives increased by about 8 percent.[7]

Table 14.8 Party Identification, Ideology, Issue Opinions and Reported House Vote of the National Electorate and Potential Perot Volunteers in 1992 and 1994

	% National Electorate		% Perot Sample	
	1992	1994	1992	1994
Partisanship				
Democrat	50.1	47.4	36.2	33.9
Strict Independent	11.7	10.1	21.2	13.4
Republican	37.8	42.5	42.5	52.7
Ideology				
Liberal	27.6	20.0	26.8	21.8
Middle of the road	31.4	34.1	23.1	19.7
Conservative	41.0	45.8	50.2	58.5
Term limits				
Favor	81.6	79.1	89.1	84.4
National health insurance				
Favor	64.8	48.4	72.0	43.3
Reported two-party House vote				
Democratic	59.3	46.6	52.9	38.0
Republican	40.7	53.4	47.1	62.0
Smallest N	1370	942	814	642

Source: 1992 and 1994 National Election Study surveys; Perot survey by authors.

There is also evidence of change on two issues salient to the politics of 1992 and 1994: term limits and national health insurance. Support for term limits may be taken as an indicator of commitment to an important part of Perot's reform agenda, and on this item we find slight decreases in support, although the overwhelming majority still is in favor. A dramatic change occurred in both the national electorate and among Perot activists in support for national health insurance. In 1992, more than 60 percent of the electorate favored some form of government-sponsored national health insurance. By 1994, however, only a minority took that position. In our Perot sample, the change was even more dramatic as support for national health insurance plummeted from over 70 percent to about 43 percent in just two years. The decline in support for national health insurance—a keystone of Bill Clinton's presidential campaign and early presidency—most clearly indicates a marked shift to the right among Perot activists.

In table 14.9, we take advantage of the panel design to explore the substantial shifts in favor of Republican and conservative identification in our sample. From the top part of the table, it is clear that Republican identification increased primarily among the substantial group of 1992 independent identifiers. Fully 50 percent of all independents from 1992 shifted to Republican identification by 1994. On the other hand, only about one in eight changed to identify as a Democrat. In addition, Republicans held almost all of their own identifiers while making inroads into the Democratic camp. The pattern of ideological change is slightly different, affected by a more significant shift of 1992 liberal identifiers to moderate and conservative identifications. Only two-thirds of 1992 liberals continued to identify themselves as such two years later (compared with 90 percent of conservatives). In addition, 40 percent of 1992 moderates had become conservative by 1994. Considering that our sample from 1992 was already more Republican and slightly more conservatives than the electorate as a whole, these changes are not inconsequential for both the short-term and long-term makeup of partisan politics in the United States.

Table 14.9   Partisanship and Ideology of Potential Perot Activists: 1992 by 1994 Attitudes

		Partisanship in 1992	
	Democrat	Independent	Republican
Partisanship in 1994			
Democrat	76.9%	13.5%	4.9%
Independent	10.8%	36.2%	4.9%
Republican	12.3%	50.4%	90.3%
	100.0%	100.1%	100.1%
N	(277)	(141)	(309)

		Ideology in 1992	
	Liberal	Moderate	Conservative
Ideology in 1994			
Liberal	67.2%	12.4%	2.8%
Moderate	17.5%	47.7%	7.7%
Conservative	15.3%	39.9%	89.5%
	100.0%	100.0%	100.0%
N	(177)	(153)	(352)

Source: Perot survey by authors

Table 14.10 Percentage Active for Democratic and Republican House Candidates of Potential Perot Volunteers in 1988, 1992, and 1994

	Democratic House Activism	Republican House Activism
1988	10.4	10.4
1992	10.4	9.1
1994	18.0	29.6
(N)	(774)	(774)

Source: Perot survey by authors.

Table 14.11 House Campaign Activism of Potential Perot Activists: 1992 by 1994 Activism

| | House Activism in 1992 | | |
	Dem House	Inactive	Rep House
House Activism in 1994			
Dem House	18.5%	14.3%	5.3%
Inactive	42.6%	58.6%	22.8%
Rep House	8.8%	27.1%	71.9%
	99.9%	100.0%	100.0%
(N)	(109)	(342)	(186)

Source: Perot survey by authors.

Did this Republican and conservative shift affect political behavior? Table 14.8 shows that the slim majority of Perot supporters voting for Democratic House candidates in 1992 became an overwhelming Republican advantage by 1994, as nearly two-thirds voted for GOP House candidates. Although this change is consistent with what we find in the National Elections Study, the shift in the Perot sample was more dramatic.[8]

Similarly, the 1994 wave of the Perot sample reveals a dramatic increase in active involvement in House campaigns, especially to the advantage of Republican candidates.[9] This increase was apparently more than just a migration back to the major parties, since the level of activism surpasses both that from 1992 and what respondents recalled from the 1988 election year.[10] Table 14.10 shows this increase in party activism. Republican activism in

House races almost tripled from 1988 and 1992 levels of House activism (when approximately 10 percent of our sample claimed to have been active). Although not as dramatic, activism on behalf of Democratic House candidates jumped nearly 75 percent from the levels reported in 1992 and from 1988. It is remarkable that these respondents, who are unique because of their attraction to a nonpartisan antiparty independent presidential contestant, increased their activity in partisan House campaigns so dramatically. We are still in the process of exploring the basis for this increase in partisan activity, but it is already clear that mobilization by the Perot campaign in 1992 had an impact on involvement in the 1994 House races, independent of previous partisan activity (Rapoport and Stone 1995).

Finally, table 14.11 indicates the continuity of partisan House activism in 1994 by active involvement in 1992 House races. Once again, we see a clear shift to the Republican Party among Perot supporters. Fully 72 percent of those active on behalf of GOP House candidates in 1992 remained active for the Republicans in 1994. By contrast, less than one-half of those active in Democratic House races in 1992 continued to be active for the Democratic House candidate in their district. Further, among those who were *not* active for a House candidate in 1992 (60 percent of the sample), more than 40 percent became active in 1994, and of those two-thirds were active for Republican House candidates. The apparent lack of defection among Republican activists in our sample, coupled with the higher rates of defection among Democratic activists and higher rates of mobilization for the GOP among those previously inactive, show that Perot supporters provided a significant boost to the Republican party in the 1994 elections.

Conclusions

This research suggests mixed conclusions about the sources of active participation in the 1992 Perot movement. In the analysis of the Perot sample itself, we find very little effect of the usual demographic predictors of political participation. However, this does not mean that the personal resources and other characteristics of Perot activists played no part in enabling their participation. We saw that our sample of potential Perot supporters differed from the general population in quite predictable ways in income, education, and other measures. These factors distinguished those who called the Perot number from the electorate as a whole more than they did the levels of activism among those who called (McCann, Partin, Rapoport, and Stone 1996).

We find significant effects of our attitudinal measures and preliminary support for both the "push" and the "pull" sides of our model. The more attracted activists were to Perot, and the more repulsed they were by the major parties and their nominees, the more engaged in the Perot campaign they were. Perot attacked "politics as usual" and our evidence shows that he was successful in attracting a constituency of the discontented.

From the perspective of understanding the long-term consequences of the Perot movement for major party change, the participation effects we uncovered are perhaps most suggestive. We found support for the idea that prior and major party involvement stimulated participation for Perot. This suggests that Perot activated volunteers who might have been available to the major parties had he not been on the scene. Thus, the Perot movement, while formally nonpartisan and even antiparty, may ultimately have its greatest impact by affecting party politics in the years following the 1992 presidential election. And, in fact, we have consistent evidence that the Perot movement was part of a dramatic shift toward the Republican party in 1994.

We are only beginning our pursuit of a full understanding of these changes, and a complete accounting may have to await further data from the 1996 elections.[11] One possibility is that the Perot sample is comprised of a group of activists who are more susceptible to the short-term forces surrounding an election campaign than the electorate. We know, for example, that the Perot callers were more independent than the public as a whole, and this relative lack of partisan grounding may make them more susceptible to swings in the fortunes of one party or the other. Thus, in 1992, while many voted for Perot and were active in his campaign, among those who backed Clinton or Bush, Clinton was the clear favorite. In 1994, without Perot heading the ballot and without a concerted national campaign on his behalf, the Perot activists may have been especially susceptible to electoral forces that benefited the Republican party. The visible leadership from Newt Gingrich and other Republican leaders and the failure of the Clinton administration to deliver, especially on its commitment for health-care reform, may have combined with a prevailing cynicism about congressional incumbent performance to help produce a shift toward the Republican Party. If this is the explanation, the "shift to the right" is not so much an enduring partisan or ideological change as an expression of discontent with the Democratic Party, which until 1994 had held the presidency and both houses of Congress. Presumably, this sort of discontent also played a part in motivating change in the public, but it is reasonable to suppose that these forces were more strongly at work among Perot activists.

We must also consider the possibility that Perot activists actually helped produce the changes we see in the electorate. There is increasing sensitivity in the literature to the role partisan activists may play in producing broader patterns of change in the electorate (e.g., Carmines and Stimson 1989; Stone 1993; Herrera 1995; McCann, Partin, Rapoport and Stone 1996), and there is every chance that the Perot activists occupy a central place in explaining the remarkable changes attending the 1994 election. There was a clear attempt by the Republicans to appeal to Perot supporters in 1994. The "Contract with America" resembles the "checklist for all Federal candidates" found in the

Appendix to *United We Stand* (Perot 1992: 117–18). Increased levels of Republican activism among Perot activists may have helped reshape impressions of the Republican Party, and legitimized its claims to outsider status. The result may well have been increased mobilization of voters against incumbent Democrats and the party in general. As a result, these activists may have helped turn the tide to the GOP for the first time in more than a generation. If that can be demonstrated, the impact of the Perot movement on major party politics in the U.S. would extend well beyond the relatively narrow confines of its already dramatic effects in 1992.

What direction these activists will take in the long run is difficult to predict. It is clear, however, that these citizens hold the potential for creating a long-term impact on the American political system—particularly for the two major parties.

Notes

1. We are grateful to the National Science Foundation for support of the 1992 and the 1994 waves of the Perot survey on which this study is based (SES-9211432; SBR-9410869). The Center for Political Studies at the University of Michigan provided the American National Election Studies surveys from 1992 and 1994. We appreciate the continued support of the Institute of Behavioral Science at the University of Colorado for providing an environment that fosters our collaboration. We also thank Patricia Jaramillo for valuable research assistance.

2. Elsewhere we have taken up the effects of more generalized alienation from the political system (Atkeson, McCann, Rapoport, and Stone 1994). We have also considered the importance of "strategic" factors in explaining activism in a three-way race, although that too deserves a more complete analysis than we can include here.

3. We certainly do not argue that our caucus states somehow represent the entire nation, but we have found that cross-state variations within party samples are fairly small, especially on most of the indicators of interest in this chapter (Abramowitz, McGlennon and Rapoport, 1983; Stone, Abramowitz, Rapoport 1989).

4. We asked the Perot sample about the following activities: collecting signatures for a ballot petition, attending meetings or rallies, trying to convince friends to vote for Perot, telephoning or door-to-door canvassing, organizing meetings or coffees, and holding a position in the campaign. Caucus attenders were asked a similar list, excluding collecting signatures. For purposes of table 14.3, we count as active respondents those who have engaged in any of the activities.

5. The measure of electability we employ is the respondent's estimate of the popular vote Perot would receive in the fall election. We asked the question in our September-wave survey, when Perot was not a candidate. The variable, therefore, should be considered an imperfect estimate of respondents' perceptions of Perot's chances once he redeclared his candidacy in October. Interestingly, the aggregate mean estimates by the sample of each candidate's popular vote in November were almost exactly correct: Perot 18 percent, Bush 39 percent, and Clinton 43 percent.

6. Less than 5 percent of the Perot sample voted for an independent or third party candidate for the U.S. House of Representatives in 1994.

7. We have explored and rejected the hypothesis that the changes we observe are attributable to attrition in the sample because of differential patterns of panel nonresponse. When panel mortality is controlled, our conclusions remain undisturbed.

8. Although it is close to the shift one finds among Perot voters in the national electorate. Note that the National Election Studies survey overstates the Democratic vote in 1994. The actual breakdown of the two-party vote in the two years was 1992, Democratic 52.8%, Republican 47.2%; 1994, Democratic 46.4%, Republican 53.7%.

9. Activities included in the index are canvassing by telephone or door to door, clerical and office work in the campaign, contributing money to the candidate, and trying to convince friends to support the candidate.

10. A similar increase in the *absolute* percentage active is evident among party activists according to our active minority sample that tracked caucus participants over the same period. The relative increase in the Perot sample. However, was about twice the increase among party activists.

11. We are continuing the Perot panel through 1996 with a nomination wave carried out in February, 1996, and a postelection survey to be conducted immediately after the November election.

15

Minor Parties and Candidates in Sub-Presidential Elections

Christian Collet
Jerrold Hansen

In recent years, there has been much discussion about the breakdown of the two-party hegemony and the possible emergence of a 'third' party in the United States. Polls have showed a growing dissatisfaction with the two-party system, and a growing interest in the idea of a third party, with anywhere from 50 to 63 percent in favor (depending on how the question is worded).[1]   A number of prominent political observers have argued for a third national party (Lowi 1994; Black and Black 1994), or even a multiparty system (Lind 1995), and the media have shown endless fascination with the presidential prospects of Ross Perot and even Ralph Nader. Indeed, it is hard to recall a time in recent memory when the idea of a formal alternative (or alternatives) to the Republicans and Democrats has been more widely discussed and seriously considered.

This wave of interest overshadows the lack of systematic knowledge about minor parties and their candidates. Aside from scattered case studies of individual parties and independent candidate organizations (Canfield 1984; Spitzer 1987; Hazlett 1992; Herbst 1994: chap. 5), most research has been either an historical survey (e.g., Hesseltine 1957; Nash 1959; Key 1964: chap.10; Haynes 1966; Gillespie 1993) or an analysis of mass voting behavior (Mazmanian 1974; Rosenstone, Behr, and Lazarus 1984). Only a little work has been conducted on minor party activists (Elden and Schweitzer 1971; Partin, Weber, Rapoport and Stone 1994; Green and Guth 1986), almost none on minor party candidates, and with a few exceptions (Key 1964: 273-78; Gargan 1975; Scarrow 1983; and Spitzer 1987), the literature has focused largely on the presidential level—ignoring state and local elections.

In this chapter, we take a step toward filling this void. After a short discussion on the importance of minor parties, we present findings from a nationwide survey of minor party candidates undertaken shortly after the 1994 elections. Our results reveal that minor parties arise from the failing of the two-party system, with most having had prior experience with one of the major parties (and sometimes both). General frustration with party politics was the primary reason they left the major parties, and, interestingly, only a few were strong adherents of their new parties. This organizational weakness extended to their resources and experience in politics, but in other respects, these candidates resembled their major party counterparts. On the basis of these findings, we predict a continuation of minor party activity, but largely in its traditional role as "spoilers" in the two-party system.

Why Minor Parties Are Important

Why should we care about minor parties and their candidates? After all, aren't they just a fringe group that, as Key once put it, sits "outside the system" (1964: 255) on the sidelines of the political field? Furthermore, why should we be concerned with minor parties at the subnational level, where the successes of their candidates are "as rare as they are captivating" (Beck and Sorauf 1992: 48)?

First, the activities of minor parties can tell us a great deal about the state of the major parties. Scholars see minor parties as a "barometer" of feelings toward the Republicans and Democrats (Rosenstone, Behr, and Lazarus 1984: 223). Throughout American history, the presence of minor parties has been predicated on the level of public discontent with the major parties or major party "failure." This point suggests that minor parties should be largely made up of disaffected major party activists. But what might cause such a secession? Realignment theory suggests that it is the rise of a salient issue and the inability of the major parties to adequately deal with it that prompts desertion (Sundquist 1981). Indeed, party history is filled with "defining moments" when major party coalitions splintered, and economic discontent was particularly prominent (Mazmanian 1974). By this logic, minor party candidates, especially at the state and local levels, may be "forerunners" (Burnham 1970: 30) to transformations of the party system.

Along these lines, understanding minor parties can expand our knowledge of the party organizations in American politics. Some scholars have emphasized minor parties as mobilizing agents for the discontented voters (e.g., Mazmanian 1974: 77–81). This raises the question of how candidates recruit supporters and develop commitment to their organizations. The literature has several suggestions on the first point, including an alternative ideology, a charismatic or prestigious leader, and the political ambition of would-be candidates (Rosenstone, Behr, and Lazarus 1984; Mazmanian 1974). But longer-term viability requires the development of loyalty to the party organization itself (Eldersveld 1964), a result that might well be expected among small groups of homogeneous activists bound by common discontents and goals.

Finally, understanding minor parties can add to our knowledge of political participation beyond the political mainstream. It is unlikely, for instance, that minor party candidates exhibit the degree of professionalism that characterizes mainstream candidates (Beck and Sorauf 1992: 130–132). Indeed, most such candidates are likely to be what Canon (1990) has termed "hopeless amateurs," with very strong purposive motivations, but modest political experiences, especially in running for office. However, minor party candidates are likely to share the high socioeconomic status and interest in politics of their major party counterparts (Verba and Nie 1971).

But perhaps the most compelling reason for studying minor parties is that they are becoming increasingly active in elections. As table 15.1 shows, the 1992 and 1994 election cycles have seen dramatic increases in the number of minor party candidates competing for gubernatorial, U.S. Senate, U.S. House, and state legislative seats. Perot may have inspired many such candidacies, but there were more than in previous elections with significant third party presidential candidates, with record highs occurring for midterm elections in 1994.

These data also suggest a new wrinkle since 1990: the proliferation of political parties. For most of the twenty-year period between 1968 and 1988, the number of parties represented in subnational elections has stayed fairly consistent—between twenty-eight and thirty-eight—in spite of fluctuations in the number of candidates running. By 1992, however, the number of different parties running candidates had virtually doubled, to sixty-nine. Even after a small decline in 1994 to fifty-one, there were still nearly twice as many parties represented on ballots across the nation as there were a quarter century prior. In some states, such as California, minor parties are becoming fixtures in the state party system, often having notable influence on selected statewide, congressional, and state legislative races.[2]

Table 15.1 shows another important trend as well: dramatic increases in the numbers of elections with three, four, and five or more candidates. Consider that in 1968 only thirty races featured four candidates; a mere eight races had five or more. By 1992, the numbers had jumped to seventy-five and fifty-eight, respectively. The increase is similar in midterm years. The major implication of this trend is the *cumulative* power of minor parties. Put simply, an election with a third party taking a small fraction of the vote may make only a small difference, but a fourth, a fifth, and perhaps even a sixth party candidate may accumulate to have a considerable impact. Gubernatorial races in Alaska, Connecticut, Hawaii, Maine, and New York in 1994 and U.S. Senate elections in California and Minnesota in 1994, as well as California (Seat B: Boxer-Herschensohn), Georgia, New Hampshire, New York, Pennsylvania in 1992, were all high-profile instances where the presence of multiple candidates on the ballot may have influenced the outcome. In the case of Maine's gubernatorial race in 1994, the independent candidate (Angus King) was able to win with 35 percent of the vote in a four candidate race.

Christian Collet and Jerrold Hansen

Table 15.1 Minor Parties and Candidacies in the United States: 1968–1994

Number	Presidential election years						
	1968	1972	1976	1980	1984	1988	1992
of parties[b]	28	31	33	38	34	33	69
of candidates[a]							
Governor	11	19	26	11	9	7	18
U.S. Senate	22	40	65	54	39	42	72
U.S. House	180	190	335	264	190	189	440
State Legislature	664	756	820	902	702	764	1195
of races with[c]							
3 candidates	122	106	129	128	134	99	141
4 candidates	30	45	58	48	26	36	75
5+ candidates	8	13	45	26	9	13	58

Number	Midterm election years						
	1970	1974	1978	1982	1986	1990	1994
of parties[b]	34	35	35	32	15	32	51
of candidates[a]							
Governor	48	63	58	59	34	44	79
U.S. Senator	47	41	47	48	30	18	49
U.S. House	175	244	162	290	151	161	252
State Legislature	863	810	627	1040	689	533	876
of races with[c]							
3 candidates	127	129	98	168	112	103	141
4 candidates	24	39	36	49	28	28	55
5+ candidates	12	29	28	30	11	11	32

[a] Independent candidates are included, but write-in candidates, cross-endorsees and nonpartisans are excluded.
[b] Defined as the number of different parties appearing on ballots in a given year.
[c] Measure combines candidacies for governor, U.S. Senate and House; state legislative races were excluded.
Sources: Governor, U.S. Senate and U.S. House: Congressional Quarterly Almanac and America Votes. State legislatures 1968-1988: State Legislative Election Returns in the United States 1968-1989 Computer File (Ann Arbor: ICPSR). State Legislatures 1990-1994: Secretaries of State for the individual states.

Given this growing presence of minor parties and candidates in American elections, we might well ask, Where do these candidates come from and what are they like? The literature offers a number of possible answers to these questions. First, if minor parties arise from major party failure, then we would expect most to have been once affiliated with one of the major parties, or perhaps both. And given the salience of issues to this disaffection, we would expect minor party activists to be drawn most fully from the ideologically proximate major party. For example, we would expect to find that most currently involved in left-wing parties to have left the Democrats, and right-wing parties to have left the Republicans; as for those involved in other parties, we would expect mixed results. Second, we would expect that most minor party activists abandoned a major party because of salient issues or ideological discontent. We would expect a significant number of have abandoned a major party in a "defining moment" related to issues, candidates, or events, particularly those related to the economy. Third, we would expect the partisanship of minor party candidates to be fervent and strong, given their role in advertising and promoting their party, and the costs of operating outside of conventional politics. Finally, we would expect minor party candidates to have less experience than mainstream candidates, but to resemble them sociologically.

Data and Method

This chapter is based on a mail survey of every minor party candidate that ran for governor, U.S. Senate, U.S. House, or state legislature in thirty-six states in the 1994 elections (1082 cases),[3] excluding candidates who were listed ambiguously on their state's ballot as "unaffiliated" or "independent" (274 cases).[4] The original sample included members of forty-five different parties. The survey was distributed in two waves: the first, to the western states, in January, 1995, and the second, to the remaining states, in May 1995. Overall, 584 usable questionnaires were received, resulting in a response rate of 55.7 percent (excluding undeliverable mail).

This cross-sectional sample favored the parties that fielded the most candidates in the 1994 elections. As a consequence, there are nearly twice as many Libertarian respondents (58 percent of our total sample) as respondents from other parties. We account for this difference by controlling for the types of parties, which we sorted into five basic categories—"old" left, "new" left, centrist, "old" right and "new" right. The categorization depended on two factors: (1) the mean ideological self-identification (using a standard seven-point scale); and (2) our own examination—through either personal interviews or bibliographic research—of the parties' platforms and ideologies. Our use of the terms "old" and "new" is inspired by Inglehart (1987) and Flanagan (1987), who distinguished "old" and "new" politics in western societies,[5] with the former based on the traditional liberal-conservative spectrum, and the latter based on efforts to transcend this spectrum.[6]

The "old" left category includes many of the established socialist parties (e.g., Peace and Freedom, Socialist Workers), while the "new" left category contains the Green and Natural Law parties. The Green parties focus on environmentalism, but also embrace a variety of social and economic concerns (Coleman 1994; Goodin 1992). The philosophical foundation of the Natural Law Party is a belief in transcendental meditation as a cure for social conflict. In contrast, the centrist parties in the study are mostly state-specific and based on parochial issues. They often revolve around a prominent figure in the state's politics (e.g., Lowell Weicker's A Connecticut Party, or Hawaii's Best Party, led by nativist gubernatorial candidate Frank Fasi) or deal with pressing state issues (e.g., Alaska Independent Party, a longtime advocate of state autonomy from the federal government). Because of the Libertarian Party's consistent opposition to government intervention, it was placed in a separate "new" right category. The remaining conservative parties, such as the U.S. Taxpayers and American Independent Parties, were put in an "old" right category. Unlike the Libertarians, the "old" right parties favor some kinds of government regulation, including restrictions on abortion and illegal immigration. A complete list of parties and their categorization is provided in the appendix.

Data Analysis

A good place to begin is with the partisan origins of minor party candidates, which is reported in table 15.2. Immediately we see confirmation of our expectations: nearly 80 percent were previously associated with one of the major parties, and 14 percent were members of both. The centrist and old right parties had the highest percentage with major party backgrounds; by contrast, the new politics parties had the largest percentage of newcomers to party politics. Also, as expected, most of the candidates came from the ideologically proximate major party. Most left party candidates were once Democrats (58 percent in old and 53 percent in new left parties), while most of the right parties had come from the Republicans (40 percent and 55 percent, respectively). The centrists were split almost equally, with a slight edge for ex-Democrats. Overall, only about one-quarter of the sample had no previous association with the major parties, either having been previously unaffiliated or associated with another minor party. Thus, relatively few of these candidates were truly from "outside the system." Instead, minor parties are made up of those who have once been a part of the two-party system and have rejected it.

Table 15.2 Previous Party Affiliations of Minor Party Candidates

	Total	"Old" Left	"New" Left	Centrist	"New" Right	"Old" Right
% Republican	37	5	11	36	40	55
	(208)	(2)	(6)	(9)	(133)	(58)
% Democratic	26	58	53	44	19	17
	(145)	(22)	(30)	(11)	(64)	(18)
% Both	14	13	14	8	15	12
	(78)	(5)	(8)	(2)	(50)	(13)
% Another minor party	5	11	4	8	3	6
	(25)	(4)	(2)	(2)	(11)	(6)
% No previous party affiliation	19	13	19	4	23	10
	(105)	(5)	(11)	(1)	(78)	(10)
(N)	(561)	(38)	(57)	(25)	(336)	(105)

Note: Columns may not total 100 percent due to rounding.

Why did these candidates reject the major parties? Table 15.3 reports the explanations for why these candidates left the major parties. As one can see, there are very few reports of specific "defining moments," whether they be issues, individuals, or events. The exceptions are the candidates from the old right parties, many of whom changed because of the abortion issue. A few new left candidates mentioned the environment, some centrists and new right candidates referred to taxes and the deficit, and some on the left mentioned the divisive events of the 1960s (such as the Vietnam War). Virtually no one mentioned an affinity for an individual leader, and economic reasons were even scarcer than issues, events, or individuals.

Instead, the most common explanations for rejecting the major parties were general complaints of major party "failure," such as the inadequacies of the "system," major party "statism," or that the Republicans and Democrats were "ineffective," "hypocritical," or "corrupt." In the case of old left parties, a common answer was that the Democrats "no longer represented me" or were too "elitist"—the implication being that the party has abandoned its traditional coalition of minorities and the working class. New and old right parties complained that the major parties had contributed too much to the growth of government and that the GOP had abandoned "principles,"

Table 15.3 Reasons for Leaving Major Parties by Minor Party Candidates

	% Total		% "Old" Left	% "New" Left	% Centrist	% "New" Right	% "Old" Right
Specific issues	6	(25)	0	2	5	3	18
Supported individual	0	(1)	0	0	5	0	0
Specific event	2	(7)	10	2	0	1	0
Economic reasons							
Personal/Pocketbook	1	(3)	0	0	5	1	0
National/Sociotropic	3	(12)	0	0	5	3	3
Ideological Issues							
Party became too statist	16	(70)	0	0	0	23	11
Party moved too far left/right	4	(16)	10	2	5	3	4
No difference between two parties	8	(34)	7	12	5	7	8
General Party Failure							
Party was ineffective, not dealing with important issues (unspecified)	9	(40)	7	20	14	8	7
Party no longer represented people like me/my group	7	(30)	20	10	9	5	4
Party abandoned its general principles, lost touch with its traditional roots (unspecified)	8	(34)	3	5	14	7	12
Party broke its promises, was inconsistent, lost trust in party	8	(35)	3	5	5	10	6
Party was corrupt	2	(7)	0	2	5	1	2
Disliked party leaders	5	(20)	7	2	5	5	3
Party was elitist	5	(23)	13	7	5	4	6
Personal reasons							
Preferred minor party	10	(42)	7	20	9	10	3
Wanted to promote my own political career, run for office	1	(2)	3	0	0	0	1
Country needs more alternatives	1	(2)	0	0	5	1	0
Had no say in politics, party	2	(33)	4	0	0	2	2
Miscellaneous other reasons	8	(33)	7	10	5	7	9
(N)		(444)	(30)	(42)	(23)	(259)	(90)

Note: Column totals may slightly exceed 100 percent due to rounding and a few economic reasons falling under the heading of specific issues (e.g. taxes, budget deficit) being counted in both categories. N in parenthesis.

becoming "inconsistent" and "hypocritical." Many of these candidates claimed, in Downsian fashion, that there was "no difference" between the major parties and that was why they opted for an alternative. Some in the new politics parties—especially the new left—claimed that they simply preferred a minor party, but very few mentioned personal ambition.

Thus, rather than being predicated on a specific "defining moment" in their political or personal lives, most candidates were motivated by general frustration with the major parties, sometimes rooted in ideology. It wasn't a short-term crisis, as realignment theory might suggest, but rather an accumulation of experience with the two-party system that led these individuals to reject it.

Have these candidates replaced their old partisanship with new loyalties? We can shed light on this question by looking first at reported presidential vote in 1992. If minor party candidates were strong partisans, we would expect them to overwhelmingly support their party's presidential candidate. However, as table 15.4 illustrates, only the new politics parties did so. The other party groups supported the major party candidates instead: 65 percent of the old left parties backed Bill Clinton, 62 percent of the old right backed George Bush, and 53 percent of the centrist parties, lacking a presidential candidate of their own, supported Ross Perot. Thus, there seem to be two kinds of minor partisans: the new minor parties, who showed a measure of loyalty to their own candidate, and the old minor and centrist parties, who had a pattern of independence rather than alternative partisanship.

Table 15.4 Respondents' Vote in 1992 Presidential Election

	Total	"Old" Left	"New" Left	Centrist	"New" Right	"Old" Right
% George Bush	17	0	3	18	6	62
	(55)	(0)	(1)	(3)	(12)	(39)
% Bill Clinton	11	65	25	29	6	0
	(36)	(11)	(9)	(6)	(11)	(0)
% Own party's candidate	56	24	58	0	77	10
	(184)	(4)	(21)	(0)	(153)	(6)
% Another minor party's candidate	3	12	3	0	2	5
	(9)	(2)	(1)	(0)	(3)	(3)
(N)	(331)	(17)	(36)	(17)	(198)	(63)

Note: Columns may exceed 100 percent due to rounding. Question asked only of second wave of survey recipients.

Table 15.5 examines this issue more fully with a series of questions on party loyalty and independence, using five-point Likert scales. Overall, some 52 percent of the sample agreed that they "always support all of the candidates on my party's ticket," and almost the same percentage said that they would support "the Republicans and Democrats if they stood for more of my party's positions." The left parties showed the highest levels of support for their own party, followed by the right parties, with the centrists coming in a distant last. Interestingly, new left and old right parties were the most willing to back ideologically compatible candidates from the major parties, followed closely by centrists. In contrast, the old left and new right parties were the least likely to express this qualified support for the major parties, although the figures are better than two-fifths in both cases. Even more telling are the low percentages that agreed with the statement, "It is better to be a firm party supporter than a political independent." The old left parties were the strongest here, at two-fifths, followed by the new right with one-fifth, and the other groups under one-fifth.

Table 15.5 Measures of Partisanship and Attitudes Toward Party's Minor Party Candidates (cells report percentage strongly agreeing or agreeing with the statements)

	Total	"Old" Left	"New" Left	Centrist	"New" Right	"Old" Right
I would vote for Republicans and Democrats if they stood for more of my party's positions.	53% (305)	43 (18)	63 (37)	58 (15)	48 (164)	64 (71)
I always support all of the candidates on my party's ticket.	52% (302)	61 (25)	61 (37)	16 (4)	54 (185)	45 (51)
It is better to be a firm party supporter than it is to be a political independent.	22% (125)	42 (17)	15 (9)	12 (3)	23 (68)	17 (30)
The truth is, we probably don't need political parties anymore.	21% (123)	10 (4)	20 (12)	35 (9)	20 (68)	26 (30)
It would be better if in all elections we put no party labels on the ballot.	30% (175)	15 (6)	23 (14)	52 (13)	29 (100)	38 (42)

In spite of their independence, though, none of the parties exhibited dissatisfaction with the concept of political parties themselves, as evidenced by the low, across-the-board disagreement with the statement, "The truth is, we probably don't need political parties anymore." On another indicator of the usefulness of parties—opposition to party labels on the ballot—the results were mixed. But with the exception of the centrists, the tendency was toward a positive view of party labels.

In sum, most of our sample liked the idea of political parties, but showed less support for, and loyalty to, their own party. Rather than exhibiting the kinds of strong partisanship we expected from small, homogeneous, and ideologically based groups, the sample largely exhibited political independence and a lingering connection to the major parties.

This lack of party loyalty may be related to the relatively short amount of time these individuals have been involved with their party, as well as their past contact with the major parties. As one might expect, given the recent upsurge in minor party candidacies, most candidates were relative newcomers to minor party politics, with about one-third having joined since 1991. Not surprisingly,
it is the old right and left parties that have the largest proportion of longtime members (14% and 22%, respectively, joined in 1970 or earlier), but even here most were recent joiners.

The degree of contact with the major parties also made a difference. Candidates having had no prior party affiliation were more likely than those with prior affiliation to support their own party's candidate for president (71% to 52%), to "always support the candidates on their party's ticket" (62% to 49%), and were less likely to support ideologically compatible Republicans or Democrats (42% to 55%). However, on the statement asking whether "it is better to be a firm party supporter than a political independent," the two groups showed no differences (21% to 21%), suggesting that the *value* of political independence is shared by minor party candidates, regardless of their prior affiliations.

Finally, what are these candidates like in terms of their experience and demographic background? To begin with, they tend to have considerable experience in politics as activists, but, as we expected, not a lot as politicians. Our sample reported having spent an average of 10.1 years "active in politics," but nearly half (46.7%) said that they were running for office for the first time. Furthermore, more than 50 percent of the candidates ran what we classified as "barely" or "somewhat active" campaigns, having taken part in few traditional electioneering activities.[7] Simply put, we found a considerable proportion of candidates who "stood," rather than "ran" for office. This is likely due to efforts by the organization to merely increase the visibility of the party and get its name recognized. As the chair of the Libertarian Party of Arizona explained to us after the 1994 elections, "One of the things we have to do . . . is [have] a lot of candidates on the ballot. . . . We had some serious candidates, but we got a lot of people to just put their name on the ballot so that a larger sector of the voting public would see Libertarian candidates."

However, in spite of their great diversity, only subtle social differences exist in the socioeconomic makeup of the five party groups (table 15.6). The new parties tended to be younger, on average, than those in the old or centrist parties. Center and right party candidates appear to be more affluent. All

Table 15.6 Social Characteristics of Minor Party Candidates

	% Total		% "Old" Left	% "New" Left	% Centrist	% "New" Right	% "Old' Right
Age							
18-34	18	(102)	13	13	15	22	9
35-54	61	(336)	47	77	42	62	58
55+	22	(122)	41	10	42	16	33
Race							
White	87	(479)	70	85	76	88	94
Nonwhite	13	(73)	31	16	24	13	16
Education							
H.S. or less	23	(131)	19	7	0	25	28
2-year college	15	(86)	10	13	25	15	16
B.A./B.S.	36	(205)	36	45	29	37	29
M.A./Ph.D.	26	(155)	36	28	46	23	28
Income							
<$19,999	15	(99)	10	22	12	14	14
$20,000-39,999	8	(44)	5	15	8	8	6
$40,000-59,999	23	(122)	29	19	20	23	21
$60,000-79,999	13	(69)	13	7	12	14	12
$80,000+	19	(106)	13	18	28	20	16
Sex							
Male	80	(439)	57	69	80	88	76
Marital Status							
Married	83	(481)	81	85	88	82	85
Yrs. in state							
<10	15	(90)	9	19	8	20	7
11-19	12	(99)	7	12	4	16	6
20-29	19	(108)	15	25	12	21	13
30+	48	(279)	66	35	65	40	71

Note: Some columns may not total 100 percent due to rounding. N in parentheses.

of the respondents were extremely well educated (62% of the total sample had a bachelor's degree or above), with the Libertarians and old right parties having the highest percentage of those in the lowest educational categories. These candidates were overwhelmingly white and male, with only the old left showing much gender or racial diversity. High proportions were married and long-term residents of their states.[8] Thus, rather than being radical students, impoverished proletarians, or social drifters, most of these candidates are middle to upper class and well connected to their communities, much like their major party counterparts. The small social differences are not as large and consistent as one might expect, given the enormous ideological distances that remain between these minor parties and the major ones.

Discussion

Our results provide yet another piece of evidence that the two-party system is in a weakened state: minor party candidacies are on the upsurge, and they are substantially composed of major party defectors. While it is tempting to think of minor parties as representing individuals excluded from mainstream politics, it is more accurate to think of them as alternative organizations for those who have participated in the two-party system and rejected it. Even more interesting is the primary reason for this rejection: general dissatisfaction with the party system itself. This finding suggests that the contemporary growth in minor party candidacies may be different than in the past, more the product of *long-term* frustration with the two-party system rather than *short-term* failure of the major parties to resolve particular issues. Such deeply rooted hostility towards the "system" may be very difficult for the major parties to handle.

But at this point, most of these minor parties are weak organizations; their candidates are loosely tied "hopeless amateurs." Relatively few of these candidates supported their party's presidential candidate in 1992, and even fewer said that they gave consistent support to the candidates on their party's ticket. Many felt that being firmly in support of one's party was less important than being politically independent. This pattern was particularly evident among centrist and old politics parties. Although this lack of commitment may reflect their short time in minor party politics and lingering attachment to one of the major parties, it suggests that few minor parties are yet ready to displace the major parties. As Eldersveld put it, loyalty is "a structural property crucial to the party's viability as a collaborative team" (1964: 415).

There are some exceptions, however: the new politics parties show more organizational potential. They are not only among the fastest growing and most active minor parties, but also among the strongest in levels of partisanship and commitment. Their membership is young and well educated; their ideologies, which transcend both liberalism and conservatism, have the ability to appeal to a broad spectrum of people, attracting both discontented Republicans and Democrats. Furthermore, in at least the cases of the Libertarians and Greens, their philosophies are well developed, consistent, and not reliant on fleeting issues that can be easily co-opted by the major parties. With institutionalization, these parties—or some descendant of them—may indeed prove to be important in the next party system. No doubt, though, the traditional conflict between moderation for the sake of success and the desire to maintain ideological purity will pose a serious problem, as well a host of other obstacles: majoritarian electoral system, lack of funds, and the resources and institutionalization of the two major parties.

Until some kind of electoral transformation occurs, however, minor parties will continue to play the role of spoiler, and serve as constant symbols of major party discontent. From a positive standpoint, though, minor parties and independent candidates are beginning to get the attention that they have long craved. They may be beginning, slowly, to establish the credibility that they will need to make a substantive impact on American politics in the future.

Notes

1. Since 1992, a variety of major polling organizations—Gallup, Harris, and Yankelovich among them—have asked respondents whether they agree, disagree, or have no opinion toward the statement, "We should have a third major political party in this country in addition to the Republicans and Democrats." The affirmative responses since June of 1992 have varied from 50 percent to 63 percent. In questions where respondents are instead asked to choose a three-party system from a list of possible alternatives—rather than merely agree or disagree with the idea of having a third party—the numbers are less consistent, ranging from 30 to 53 percent.

2. In 1968, California had two significant minor parties, both offshoots of the polarization that occurred during the Vietnam War—the American Independent Party and Peace and Freedom Party. As of this writing in January 1996, both the AIP and PFP had maintained their status, and four more parties had qualified: the Libertarian, Green, and Natural Law Party as well as Ross Perot's Reform Party. Collet (1993) estimates that as many as thirteen legislative and congressional races in California in 1990 and eighteen in 1992 may have been affected by the involvement of minor party candidates.

3. States include Alaska, Arizona, California, Colorado, Connecticut, Delaware, District of Columbia, Florida, Hawaii, Idaho, Illinois, Indiana, Iowa, Kansas, Kentucky, Maine, Massachusetts, Michigan, Minnesota, Mississippi, Missouri, Montana, Nevada, New Hampshire, New Jersey, New Mexico, New York, Oregon, Pennsylvania, Rhode Island, South Dakota, Texas, Utah, Vermont, Washington, Wyoming. The state of Alabama had no minor party candidates running. Candidate address lists were never received for Georgia, Louisiana, Tennessee, West Virginia, and Virginia. A few surveys in the first wave of mailings were sent to candidates in major local races in Hawaii (6), California (1) and Montana (1). In states where cross-endorsements were permitted (e.g., New York), we distributed questionnaires only to those candidates who ran on a minor party ticket without a major party endorsement.

4. Making this distinction was occasionally problematic, due to the large number of parties that have the word "independent" in their names (e.g., "American Independent," "Independent American") and the ambiguities in some official candidate listings. Furthermore, some states,

such as Ohio, rather than recognizing a party label, simply list all non-Republicans and Democrats as "independent." Some states seem to allow candidates to give themselves any personalized party label of their choosing (e.g., New Jersey), even though that person may be essentially running an independent candidacy and is not part of an officially recognized party. As a consequence, we may have inadvertently included a small number of individuals that were running independent candidacies. We, do however, believe that these cases were minimized by certain items on our questionnaire that filtered out those who had not formally broken their ties with the major parties.

5. In spite of the conceptual inspiration that we draw from the work of Flanagan, it should be noted, however, that our use of term "new" right differs greatly from his. In our framework, which is strictly American rather than comparative, "new" right is libertarian; in his, it is authoritarian. In the comparative work on alternative social movements, there has been a tendency to lump libertarian and ecology parties into the same categories (e.g., Kitschelt's (1990) "left-libertarian" parties), but we felt that there was no justification for doing so in the case of American minor parties. American Greens clearly grew out of the "left"—and see themselves as very liberal—while Libertarians, in large part, can draw their roots to the laissez-faire economic theories that are closer to the American right wing. Furthermore, most Libertarians have some ties—past or present—to the Republican Party, and, when willing to classify themselves ideologically, say they are "conservative." The Libertarians and Greens do have some similarities, but because of their very different backgrounds, and their occasional differences on the role of government, we felt that they ought to be placed in different categories.

6. An important distinction between today's minor party activity and that which occurred earlier in the quarter century is the changing order of "major" minor parties. In the early 1970s, the most powerful minor parties in subpresidential elections were parties of the left and right; in the case of the former, the Socialist Workers and U.S. Labor parties (SWP and USLP, respectively), in the case of the latter, the American Independent Party (AIP), the movement led by George Wallace. In the 1974 House elections, these three parties accounted for slightly over a third (33.4%) of the alternative candidates fielded. But by 1994, the USLP had disappeared, and the AIP and SWP, although still alive, accounted for a scant 3.6 percent of all candidates for the House. Since 1990, though, the most powerful minor parties in the United States have been neither left, nor right wing, but rather those embracing the "new" politics (Inglehart 1990: chap. 8): Libertarians, in large part, and in the most recent election, the Natural Law Party. In the 1994 House elections, over two in every five candidates (40.1%) were affiliated with one of these two parties. Another "new" politics party, the Green Party, has emerged as well, and when fielding candidates, has performed well in the western and northeastern states. But they have yet to develop a national network comparable to the Libertarians, and have tended to focus on races at the local level rather than those higher on the ballot.

7. We measured the activity level of a candidate's campaign by asking him or her to identify, from a list of items, all of the activities that were performed during the campaign. The items included walking precincts, phone solicitation, displaying signs, taking part in debates, along with ten others. Those who identified 0-2 items were categorized as "barely active"; those who identified 3-4 were "somewhat active." "Active" candidate identified 5-7 items, and "very active" candidates identified more than 8. In total, 27 percent were "barely active," 23 percent "somewhat active," 36 percent "active," and 13 percent "very active."

8. We also found that high percentages of candidates' spouses either support the candidates own party (51%) or call themselves independent (16%). This would give some indication that alternative party politics may be a family affair, which could influence future generations of voters and activists.

Appendix. Categorization of Minor Parties*

Party Type	Score**	Party	States	N
Old Left	1.0	DC Statehood	Washington, D.C.	1
	1.0	Gun Control	WA	1
	1.0	Liberty Union	VT	3
	1.0	Progressive	VT	2
	1.0	Tax the Rich	CT	1
	1.0	Democracy in Action	NJ	1
	1.5	Peace and Freedom	CA, AK	21
	2.0	Socialist	OR	1
	2.0	New Alliance	IN	1
	3.8	Liberal	NY	7
	NR	Socialist Workers	UT, WA	2
	NR	Worker's World	MI	1
			Total =	42
New Left	1.5	Grassroots	IA, MN, VT	5
	2.0	Green	AK, CA, HI, ME, MN, NM, NY	26
	3.8	Natural Law	CO, CT, IA, NJ, VT, WA	30
			Total =	61
Centrist	3.8	Independent Fusion	NY	7
	4.0	A Connecticut Party	CT	2
	4.0	Good Neighbor	PA	1
	4.0	The Right Choice	RI	1
	4.0	Independent	MN	1
	4.0	Taxpayers Against Excess	PA	1
	4.0	Concerns of the People	CO	1
	4.4	Best	HI	5
	4.5	Alaska Independent	AK	3
	4.7	Independent	ME	4
			Total =	26

Old Right

Mean Party Placement Score**	Party	States	
5.0	Cool Moose	RI	1
5.5	Independent	CT	4
5.8	American	OR, UT	9
5.8	Conservative	NY	13
6.0	United Independent	IL	1
6.0	Patriot	WA, PA	5
6.0	Constitutional	PA	1
6.2	Right to Life	NY	29
6.2	Independent	UT	5
6.2	Independent American	NV, UT	20
6.3	Concerned Citizens'	CT	3
6.9	American Independent	CA, AK	10
7.0	Keep America First	NJ	1
7.0	Taxpayers	KY, CO, WI	7
7.0	LaRouche	NJ	1
		Total =	110

* Four parties were not classified, and hence dropped, because of a lack of available information about their ideology and issue positions: People of Vermont (Vermont), Fed Up Party (New York), Federalist Party (Minnesota), Capitalist Party (New Jersey). Two parties, Worker's World and Socialist Workers, were classified as "old Left" based on knowledge of their ideology only, since their respondents gave no response (NR) to the item on party placement. Because it is based only on our sample of candidates, we do not intend this table to be an exhaustive list of minor parties or of the states where they are active.
** Mean Party Placement Score (1-7).

16

Balance Wheels:
Minor Party Activists in the Two-Party System

James L. Guth
John C. Green

Political observers are often as attentive to the regularities of American politics as to their exceptions. A good example is political parties: the electoral dominance of the major parties focuses attention on the two-party system, and yet, third parties are an endless source of fascination. Similarly, scholars see minor parties as both a sign of major party weakness and evidence of the strength of the two-party system (Rosenstone et al. 1984; Beck and Sorauf 1992: 53–54). Minor parties help contain political distress unresolved by the major parties within the bounds of electoral politics, and they can facilitate major party adaptation by bringing new ideas, issues, and personnel into the process (Sundquist 1983; Brown 1991). Such effects are often linked to coalition building in the short term and to partisan realignment in the long run (Burnham 1970; Beck 1979). Thus, minor parties act as "balance wheels" for the "main axle" of two-party competition that drives the party system.

Recognition of such a role for minor parties in the two-party system, however, begs the important question, Why would anyone play these parts with no real hope of victory at the polls? In fact, relatively little is known about these activists, despite the attention lavished on third-party candidates and voters (but see chapters 14 and 15 in this volume; Hazlitt 1992; Herbst 1994: chap. 4; Elden and Schweitzer 1971; and Canfield 1984). Here we present a description of the policy motives and partisan commitments of a range of minor party activists, revealing them to be a diverse lot. Indeed, these findings suggest that minor parties play several different roles in the two-party system. Some challenge the current partisan alignment, offering intellectual resources for major party renovation. Others help reinforce the present party alignment by pressing for the inclusion of new issues, and still others help reorganize the alignment by shifting personnel between and within the major parties.

Minor Party Activists in the Two-Party System

From the point of view of electoral success, the two-party character of American politics is strongly evident. But from any other perspective, the United States has something closer to a "multiparty" system. One need look no farther than the major parties themselves: the Republicans and Democrats are actually loose alliances of formal organizations, including at least three national-level, fifty sets of state-level, and thousands of local committees. And the membership of these committees is frequently determined by other kinds of "partisan" organizations, including ideological factions, interest groups, social movements, and candidate committees. Indeed, such informal partisan groups are often more potent than the formal party organizations themselves (Schlesinger 1991).

Of course, American constitutional arrangements provide incentives for these diverse organizations to coalesce around the formal structure of the major parties. On the one hand, like-minded people are encouraged to cooperate by the desire to win elections and influence public policy (Schlesinger 1991; Aldrich 1995), and on the other, independent action is constrained by shared partisan commitments, including affectual attachment to the major parties, patterns of previous co-operation, agreement with and trust in major party leadership (Green and Guth 1994). Sometimes the confluence of such motives and commitments blend all these groups into a cohesive whole; more often, these diverse groups meld only partially, and in some cases, fail to unite at all. Minor parties are commonly understood to result from severe cases of such failure, where activists' policy motivations are so strong and/or their partisan commitments so weak that they organize challenges to the major parties at the ballot box (Rosenstone et al. 1984).

Because the major parties can fail to coalesce in several ways, one can imagine different ideal types of minor parties, whose activists are characterized by special patterns of motivation and commitment.[1] One of the most common failures is at the level of principle: the major parties fail to articulate a distinct enough political philosophy. Ideological factions within the major parties are dedicated to avoiding this problem, often with meager results, creating an opportunity for minor parties based on more consistent principles (Orren 1982: 15–18; Beck and Sorauf 1992: 50). Such "principled" parties are motivated by a distinctive political philosophy and a corresponding commitment to the minor party itself (and thus an absence of commitment to the major parties). Such a mix of motivations and commitments generates the desire to influence the personnel of government on behalf of the party's agenda. Principled parties are thus highly "responsible" versions of the major parties, offering a forum for the expression of alternative ideologies.

A less comprehensive kind of failure concerns particular issues, where the values or interests of a constituency are not adequately addressed by the major parties. Interest groups and social movements routinely participate in party politics to prevent this problem, often with modest impact, creating an opportunity for minor parties protesting this lack of attention. Such "protest" parties are motivated by salient issues and strong partisan commitments. Such a mix of motivations and commitments generates the desire to pressure the major parties to address their concerns. Protest parties thus represent a limited issue version of the major parties, offering a vehicle for issue advocacy (Orren 1982: 18–20; Beck and Sorauf 1992: 52).

Perhaps the narrowest kind of failure concerns candidates, i.e., party nominees who lack broad enough appeal. There is no shortage of well-organized candidacies in major party politics seeking to resolve this problem, with frequent disappointments, creating an opportunity for minor parties based on a person that was passed over. Such "personalistic" parties are motivated by support for a particular politician, often a prestigious one, and weak partisan commitments. Such a mix of motives and commitments produces activities directed at electing the minor party's candidate, pushing the major parties to improve the quality of their own. Ross Perot's 1992 presidential campaign is the most recent example. Personalistic parties are thus highly "pragmatic" versions of the major parties, offering a mechanism for fostering alternative candidacies (Orren 1982: 10–13; Beck and Sorauf 1992: 53).

Of course, real minor parties often combine all the elements of these ideal types—principled parties offer candidates, protest parties express ideology, and personalistic parties stress issues. Nevertheless, minor parties closely resembling these ideal types are found in the United States, and are apparently becoming more common (see chap. 15 in this volume). For example, well-established principled parties are common, such as the Libertarian and Green Parties, but they are not particularly well known (Hazlitt 1992). Protest parties are even more numerous, but their narrower focus affords them even less attention; the Right to Life and Peace and Freedom parties are good examples (Gillespie 1993). Personalistic parties in the form of "third party" presidential candidates, such as Ross Perot, are the most prominent (Mazmanian 1974; Rosenstone et al. 1994; see chap. 14 in this volume). In the following analysis, we will compared activists from principled, protest, and personalistic minor parties to each other and their major party counterparts on policy motivations and partisans commitments.

Data and Methods

The following analysis is based on the results of a mail survey of a national random sample of contributors to party and political action committees conducted in 1982 and 1983. All told, we received 2,827 usable responses for a return rate of 52.3 percent (excluding mail returned as undeliverable; for further details see Green and Guth 1986). Due to the extensive minor party activity in 1980, the sample included a host of minor party committees; these respondents were bolstered by a raft of self-identified minor party activists found among donors to liberal and conservative PACs. Despite the limitations of these data, they offer a unique opportunity to investigate the motivations and commitments of a range of minor party activists.

To facilitate such comparisons, we placed the party activists into eight categories, ranging from principled to protest to personalistic parties divided roughly between the left and right sides of the political spectrum.

1. *Citizens Party*. This party was dedicated to environmentalism, and its standard-bearer in 1980, Barry Commoner, drew about one-quarter of one percent of the presidential vote. The Citizens Party is an example of a principled party on the political left, although as we shall see, some of its activists would not have agreed with this placement.

2. *Left Protest Parties*. This category is the combination of a variety of protest parties located on the left, including the Social Democratic, Progressive, Women's, Peace and Freedom, Liberal, and DC Statehood parties, among others. Some of these parties might well belong in the principled category, but the small number of cases requires their aggregation; as we shall see, there is some empirical support for this decision.

3. *John Anderson's National Unity Campaign*. Donors to John Anderson's 1980 independent presidential bid and subsequent donors to his National Unity PAC; a personalistic party.

4. *Democratic Party*. Donors to national Democratic party committees.

5. *Republican Party*. Donors to national Republican party committees.

6. *George Wallace's American Independent Party*. Donors to the American Independent and American Parties, the remnants of George Wallace's 1968 independent bid; another personalistic party.

7. *Right Protest Parties*. This category is the combination of a variety of protest party located generally on the right, including the Populist, Conservative, Constitutional, Prohibition, Right to Life, and Taxpayers parties, among others. As with their counterparts on the left, some of these parties might deserve principled designation.

8. *Libertarians*. This party is dedicated to a philosophy of minimum government, and it is probably the most extensive and best organized minor party in the country (Hazlitt 1992). Its 1980 standard bearer, Ed Clark, received about 1 percent of the presidential vote. We consider it a principled party on the right, but many Libertarians would challenge this assignment as well.

Although these categories display the data to best advantage, they are hardly the only way minor parties can be classified. For example, one could distinguish between minor parties based on older, materialist disputes, such as standard of living issues, and those based in newer, post-material cleavages, such as quality of life disputes (Inglehart 1987). The two principled parties we are able to isolate, the Citizens and Libertarian Parties, are expressions of this newer division, which, among other things, calls into question the traditional liberal-conservative spectrum. Indeed, if one thinks of this continuum as a circle, the Citizens and Libertarian Parties would match each other in many respects. In contrast, the protest and personalistic party categories by and large reflect variations on the older cleavages that still differentiate the major parties.

Motivations: Ideology and Issues

What kind of policy motivations characterize minor party activists? A good place to begin is by exploring evidence on the ideology of party activists, presented in table 16.1. Although our left/right assignment of parties is somewhat arbitrary, it reflects an empirical reality. Beginning in the middle of the table, note that one-half of the Democrats claimed to be liberal or very liberal, and more than four-fifths of the Republicans were conservative or very conservative. The Anderson and Left Protest party activists matched or exceeded the liberalism of the Democrats, while the Wallace and Right Protest activists resembled the Republicans. The two principled parties, however, showed significant deviations from the liberal-conservative alignment: almost one-third of the Citizens Party and nearly three-quarters of the Libertarians identified with "other" ideologies. The former used terms such as "radical," "environmentally conscious," and "holistic approach," and the latter uniformly labeled themselves "libertarian." Write-in comments and materials sent with the questionnaires revealed a distinctive philosophical basis for these parties. Nevertheless, the Citizens Party activists clearly belong somewhere on the political left, and the Libertarians fit on the right, albeit less well.

Table 16.1 also reports on issues most salient to these activists, here measured by asking, What is the most important problem facing the nation? Economic issues make up a plurality in every category, but they dominate for the Democrats and Republicans, followed by the Anderson and Wallace donors, and then the other categories. Overall, minor party activists have a broader agenda than their major party counterparts, paying much more attention to social and foreign policy. Part of this diversity comes from the protest party activists, who frequently mentioned their special issues; there is also greater diversity within the economic category for all the minor parties (data not shown). Note that the Citizens and Libertarian activists have a special concern for the political process, with roughly one-quarter mentioning such matters, including numerous complaints about the "two-party system."

Table 16.1 Party Activists: Ideology and Issue Salience

	Citz	Left Prot	Andr	Dems	Reps	Wall	Right Prot	Libt
Ideology:								
Very Liberal	49%	60%	19%	15%	0%	9%	2%	1%
Liberal	16	4	36	35	1	6	2	8
Moderate	2	6	33	33	10	9	4	6
Conservative	2	3	7	13	58	29	24	10
Very Conservative	0	0	2	2	30	44	55	4
Other	31	27	3	2	1	3	13	71
Salient issues:								
Economic	37%	35%	51%	71%	64%	44%	38%	42%
Social	25	31	22	7	17	28	25	14
Foreign Policy	16	29	21	17	13	18	25	18
Political Process	23	6	6	5	9	10	12	26
N	(53)	(98)	(315)	(334)	(281)	(103)	(98)	(82)

KEY: *Citz* = Citizens Party; *Left Prot* = Left Protest Parties; *Andr* = Anderson Movement; *Dems* = Democrats; *Reps* = Republicans; *Wall* = Wallace Movement; *Right Prot* = Right Protest Parties; *Libt* = Libertarian Party.
Source: Survey by authors.

How do ideology and agenda translate into specific policy positions? Table 16.2 reports the net liberal positions on a number of important issues (calculated by subtracting conservative responses from liberal ones; positive figures represent a liberal bias, negative figures a conservative one). Again beginning in the middle of the table, one can see the expected economic divisions between Democrats and Republicans: the former support, on balance, government intervention in the economy, while the latter strongly oppose it. Here the Anderson, Left Protest, and Citizens activists are markedly more liberal than the Democrats. On the other side of the spectrum, the Wallace and Right Protest activists are also quite conservative, although rarely as much as the GOP, and Libertarians are the strongest apostles of the free market.

A more complex pattern appears on social issues. Democrats and the left minor parties hold solidly liberal positions on these issues. However, Republicans, and particularly Libertarians, are more moderate or even liberal on issues such gay rights and abortion. The Wallace and Right Protest parties are markedly more conservative on these matters, but do not match the intensity of their counterparts on the left. Even more complexity appears on foreign policy. For example, while the major parties show the expected divi-

Table 16.2 Party Activists: Positions on Economic, Social, and Foreign Policy

	Citz	Left Prot	Andr	Dems	Reps	Wall	Right Prot	Libt
Economic issues*								
Regulation:								
Environmental	91%	79%	73%	24%	-23%	-24%	-26%	-27%
Business	86	63	38	10	-75	-70	-56	-85
Natl Health Ins.	75	69	54	49	-66	-69	-54	-85
Balanced Budget	67	40	49	33	-52	-49	-41	-59
Social issues								
Gay Rights	93%	86%	86%	56%	4%	-21%	-25%	96%
Affirm. Action	83	69	53	35	-16	-39	-39	-62
Abortion	83	72	83	67	32	-16	-28	83
Gun Control	76	82	74	38	-16	-54	-50	-77
Foreign policy								
Defense Spending	91%	85%	81%	39%	-46%	-46%	-41%	71%
Support Dictators	77	66	23	-17	-45	-24	-31	49
Trade Restrict.	22	42	9	47	42	48	42	-84
Foreign Aid	21	25	34	17	-43	-71	-57	-85
(N) (53)	(98)	(315)	(334)	(281)	(103)	(98)	(82)	

*Positive signs indicate net liberal positions; negative signs indicate net conservative positions on each issue.
KEY: *Citz* = Citizens Party; *Left Prot* = Left Protest Parties; *Andr* = Anderson Movement; *Dems* = Democrats; *Reps* = Republicans; *Wall* = Wallace Movement; *Right Prot* = Right Protest Parties; *Libt* = Libertarian Party
Source: Survey by authors

sions on cutting defense spending and supporting foreign aid, both Citizens and Libertarian activists strongly agree the defense budget should be cut, but strongly disagree on the provision of foreign assistance.

Not surprisingly, data from a standard battery of incentive questions reveal that all minor party activists score very high on purposive motivations, such a pursuing public policy, and low on solidary (social contacts) and material motivations (jobs, career advancement). However, major party activists also give priority to influencing policy, and although they are more concerned with solidary and material benefits, these motivations are not particularly important to them either. Anderson and Wallace donors do show somewhat greater interest in supporting "good candidates," and as one might expect, report great hostility toward the major party candidates in 1980 and 1968, respectively (data not shown).

In sum, minor party activists appear to have strong policy motives for challenging the two-party system. The principled parties have a distinctive ideology, which challenges the basis of the major party alignment; the protest parties are intense proponents of their respective sides of the ideological divide; and personalistic parties are more moderate backers of such an alignment, with a special concern for good candidates. All these activists had a broader agenda and were more purposive in orientation than their major party counterparts.

Commitments: Partisanship and Party Evaluation

If minor party activists have strong motivations to challenge the two-party system, what about their partisan commitments, which might constrain such a challenge? Table 16.3 begins to answer this question with data on self-identified partisanship. Once again it is worth beginning in the middle of the table: a majority of major party activists strongly identify with their parties. Democratic donors differ modestly in this regard because they include a significant group of weak Republicans. Anderson and Wallace activists are dominated by weak Democrats and Republicans, respectively, with a small number of weak identifiers from the other major party. Protest party activists also identify, on balance, with the proximate major party and actually contain more strong partisans than Anderson or Wallace donors. But note that a significant minority identifies with a minor party. This pattern reaches its height with Citizens and Libertarian activists, where one-half or more identify with their own party; for Libertarians, the proportion is overwhelming. Information from the incentive questions suggests that more than one-half of the self-identified "partisans" were strongly attached to their party.

What about political behavior? Table 16.3 lists the reported presidential vote choice of activists from 1960 to 1980 (excluding individuals not active in each year). As might be expected, there was only modest support for minor party candidates among the major party activists in any year, and substantially more among the minor parties. On the left, Anderson donors strongly supported their candidate in 1980, but reported only modest levels of minor party support prior to 1980. The Left Protest and Citizens parties also voted strongly for their own parties' candidates in 1980, but showed a trend in minor party voting dating from 1968. Over on the right, Libertarians have an even higher level of minor party support, with nearly 90 percent voting Libertarian in 1980. Wallace and Right Protest activists reveal a different, but not unexpected, pattern: minor party voting peaks with Wallace in 1968, and declines—slowly—after that, so that there was still substantial minor party voting in 1980.

Where did these minor party activists come from? Few minor party activists claimed to have been raised as members of their parties (never more

Table 16.3 Party Activists: Partisanship and Minor Party Voting

	Citz	Left Prot	Andr	Dems	Reps	Wall	Right Prot	Libt
Partisanship:								
Strong Democrat	6%	34%	17%	51%	0%	6%	4%	1%
Weak Democrat	28	35	45	24	1	6	7	3
Independent	8	8	15	3	2	10	10	1
Weak Republican	2	5	15	18	36	43	19	4
Strong Republican	6	2	6	2	61	30	38	3
Other	50	16	2	0	0	5	22	88
Minor party vote:								
1980	80	62	82	9	2	44	27	88
1976	30	44	7	3	1	51	32	61
1972	15	38	6	3	3	60	39	26
1968	15	23	4	3	5	75	40	4
1964	4	8	1	2	0	10	4	0
1960	0	9	0	0	1	5	2	0
(N)	(53)	(98)	(315)	(334)	(281)	(103)	(98)	(82)

* Includes only respondents active in each year.
KEY: *Citz* = Citizens Party; *Left Prot* = Left Protest Parties;
Andr = Anderson Movement; *Dems* = Democrats; *Reps* = Republicans;
Wall = Wallace Movement; *Right Prot* = Right Protest Parties;
Libt = Libertarian Party
Source: Survey by authors

than 5 percent), although often twice as many (and three times for the Libertarians) originally identified with something other than a major party. Indeed, multiple party switchers made up roughly one-fifth of all the minor party categories. The largest number, however, defected from the proximate major party. For example, 35 percent of the Citizens activists were raised as Democrats, and 46 percent of the Libertarians started as Republicans. The protest parties showed another pattern, with more than one-third reporting intensified identification with the proximate party. And for Anderson and Wallace supporters, change came from the opposite direction: more than one-third of the Anderson activists had once been Republicans or Independents, and more than two-fifths of Wallace donors had once been Democrats or Independents. All this change stands in sharp contrast to the major party donors, more than one-half of which were lifelong, standpat partisans (data not shown).

How do these party activists evaluate the major parties? Table 16.4 provides two assessments. First, respondents were asked which of major parties was "better" on sixteen issues. Their responses were summed and divided into three categories: substantially "agree" with the Democrats or Republicans (on eight of sixteen issues or more), and "no difference," (less than eight for either party). Not surprisingly, major party activists strongly agreed with their parties, and overall, minor party activists showed a strong preference for the proximate major party. The Left and Right Protest parties rival major party activists in this regard, while the Anderson and Wallace donors are somewhat lower. Note, however, that the "no difference" percentage increases as we move toward the Citizens and Libertarian activists.

Similar results obtain for trust in major party leaders. The Democrats and Republicans by and large trust their leaders (the Democrats somewhat less, but then they had just suffered a major defeat in 1980). Interestingly, minor party activists followed suit, with the protest parties showing the highest levels of trust in leaders of the proximate major party, and the Anderson and Wallace donors, somewhat less. Once again the Citizens and Libertarian activists are different, with more than one-half trusting neither party's leaders. Citizens donors did have a strong bias toward the Democrats, and the Libertarians a very weak one toward the GOP.

Table 16.4   Party Activists: Evaluations of the Major Parties

	Citz	Left Prot	Andr	Dems	Reps	Wall	Right Prot	Libt
Major party Issue stands:								
Agree Democrats	53%	67%	52%	63%	11%	13%	16%	18%
No Difference	40	25	31	24	25	31	22	62
Agree Republicans	7	8	17	13	64	56	62	20
Trust major Party leaders:								
Democrats	46	62	32	49	3	8	7	5
Neither	54	33	62	42	29	47	37	81
Republicans	0	5	6	9	68	45	56	14
(N)	(53)	(98)	(315)	(334)	(281)	(103)	(98)	(82)

KEY: *Citz* = Citizens Party; *Left Prot* = Left Protest Parties;
Andr = Anderson Movement; *Dems* = Democrats; *Reps* = Republicans;
Wall = Wallace Movement; *Right Prot* = Right Protest Parties;
Libt = Libertarian Party.
Source: Survey by authors.

So, there were systematic differences in the level and type of partisan commitments among minor party activists. The principled parties possessed the weakest attachment to the two-party system, and strong self-identification with their own party. These attitudes translated into strong support for their parties at the polls, and a lack of issue agreement and trust of major party leaders. In contrast, Left and Right Protest parties had strong identification with the proximate party, strong issue agreement, and substantial trust in its leaders—combined with electoral defection to minor party candidates. Finally, the Anderson and Wallace donors exhibited yet another pattern: weak identification with the proximate party, substantial agreement with it on issues, and considerable trust of its leaders, combined with strong electoral support for their respective candidates in 1980 and 1968.

Minor Party Activists and Major Party Alignments

How are minor party activists related to the social constituencies that characterize major party alignments? Table 16.5 addresses this question with data on the demographic traits of party activists. All of these activists have high socioeconomic status (Guth and Green 1986), but they do differ in important ways.

First, the class divisions associated with the major parties are evident. In occupation, Democrats have a bimodal distribution, with a large group of business managers and a slightly smaller group of professionals, many employed in the public sector. The proportion of professionals increases steadily as we move across the left categories, from the Anderson to the Left Protest and Citizens parties, with an accent on "new class" professionals, such as writers, social workers, and college professors (Green and Guth 1991). In contrast, the Republicans are dominated by managers and professionals linked to the business community, a pattern that holds for the Wallace and Right Protest parties, who add a larger number of small business owners and housewives. Libertarians are again an exception, looking more like minor parties in the left: their largest category is technical professionals, such as engineers and computer scientists. A very similar pattern holds for educational attainment. Many Democrats and the left minor party activists have advanced degrees and most are college graduates. The Republicans, Wallace, and Right Protest parties are much less educated, with many activists lacking college degrees.

Regional location and religion add a cultural dimension to these class divisions. The Democrats once again show a bimodal pattern: the largest group comes from the Northeast and a slightly smaller group, from the South. Anderson donors are found everywhere but in the South, while the Left Protest and Citizens parties are heavily northeastern, with a smaller western contingent. In contrast, Republican and the right minor activists are quite

Table 16.5 Party Activists: Demographic Characteristics

	Citz	Left Prot	Andr	Dems	Reps	Wall	Right Prot	Libt
Education								
Post graduate	63%	41%	62%	54%	37%	35%	31%	52%
College graduate	22	47	22	25	28	33	27	28
Some college	13	8	13	14	22	13	25	15
H. school/less	2	4	4	6	14	19	18	4
Occupation								
Professional	66	73	51	38	16	21	22	20
Technical	13	18	14	12	12	10	19	41
Managerial	15	4	19	42	55	41	32	30
Other	7	5	17	8	18	29	20	10
Region								
Northeast	51	69	36	41	21	28	27	29
Midwest	18	9	32	8	24	29	18	23
West	31	14	25	17	26	25	31	33
South	0	8	8	34	29	20	24	15
Religion								
Secular	40	33	25	15	8	16	9	55
Non-traditional	27	21	14	7	5	10	9	16
Jews	11	13	13	14	1	10	6	4
Catholic	9	15	9	17	13	6	17	4
Protestant								
Mainline	13	12	35	34	58	32	24	21
Evangelical	0	6	4	13	15	26	35	0
Age								
To 35 years	24	46	24	10	3	13	10	38
36 to 50 years	38	39	25	26	19	33	27	35
50 to 65 years	22	12	33	38	42	32	23	22
65 years or more	16	4	19	25	36	22	41	5
(N)	(53)	(98)	(315)	(334)	(281)	(103)	(98)	(82)

KEY: *Citz* = Citizens Party; *Left Prot* = Left Protest Parties;
Andr = Anderson Movement; *Dems* = Democrats; *Reps* = Republicans;
Wall = Wallace Movement; *Right Prot* = Right Protest Parties;
Libt = Libertarian Party.
Source: Survey by authors.

evenly distributed by region. Religious differences are sharper. The Democrats are quite diverse, including substantial numbers of mainline and evangelical Protestants, Catholics, Jews, and Seculars. The proportion of Seculars and liberal Protestants increases steadily as we move toward the Citizens Party. The Republicans include more Protestants, a pattern accentuated by the Wallace and Right Protest parties, But once again the Libertarians resemble the left minor parties, with more than one-half in the Secular category. Finally, there are some age differences among these activists. The major party activists are older, with a majority over fifty years of age; the Anderson and Wallace donors show modest variations on this pattern. The Left Protest activists are the youngest, while their right counterparts are the oldest; the Citizens and Libertarian activists are also younger, with a majority under the age of fifty. These activists are overwhelmingly white and male, with the exception of the Citizens and Wallace activists, who were better than two-fifths female (data not shown).

These patterns suggest that the minor party activists represent degrees of departure from the major party alignments (Phillips 1982). The dominant group among left minor parties are younger, well-educated professionals from the east and west coasts with less conventional religious affiliations. Such activists embody the "leading edge" of the Democratic coalition, the cosmopolitan "new class" (Green and Guth 1994). The Citizens Party represents this trend most fully and the Anderson donors the least. In contrast, most right minor party activists are older, less well educated business managers and small business owners from across the county with more conventional religious affiliations. Such activists represent the "leading edge" of the Republican coalition, social and economic traditionalists (Green and Guth 1994). Libertarians are once again an exception: an element of the cosmopolitan new class with a thorough-going hostility to government.

Conclusion

What, then, accounts for minor party activism? Simply put, various combinations of policy motivations and partisan commitments lead activists to organize challenges to the major parties at the polls. No doubt some such activists actually believe they can win elections, but their primary impact is indirect, through their impact on major party alignments. In this sense, minor parties act as balance wheels for the main axle of two-party competition when their counterparts within the major parties fail to work together effectively.

However, different kinds of balance wheels arise from the various ways in which the major parties fail to maintain their equilibrium. Principled parties reflect the failure of the major parties to articulate consistent principles—a problem endemic to large "constituent" parties. Such minor parties are highly responsible, complete with their own kind of partisanship, and challenge the current alignment hoping, perhaps, to supplant one of the major parties someday. In the interim they offer intellectual resources useful in major party renovation. The Libertarians have most fully established themselves in this role, which they continue to play; the Citizens Party was less successful, but paved the way for a host of "green" parties. The popularity of libertarian and environmental perspectives among major party activists surely owes something to the activities of these parties. Ironically, each of these tendencies reflects the often contradictory values of the "new class" as it works its way into the party system.

Protest parties arise from the failure of the major parties to attend to specific issues, an inevitable difficulty in large coalitional parties. However, strong commitments to the existing party system are key. These activists demand that their major party attend to more issues in a more consistent fashion, thus reinforcing existing alignments. Our protest categories are mixed bags, a few activist from a multitude of minor parties, some of which might qualify as principled parties. Nevertheless, these activists are best understood as extensions of the existing party system. Advocating issues and pressing them upon the major parties is an important role that frequently succeeds in changing party platforms. The Peace and Freedom and Right to Life parties are good examples in recent times, each representing new or newly mobilized social groups that want the party system to attend more consistently to their concerns.

Personalistic parties develop from failures regarding candidacies, a perennial source of tension in large governing parties. These efforts serve as half-way houses for disaffected partisans, fostering a movement from one major party as well as mobilizing newly alienated groups already within the orbit of a major party. In this fashion, they help reorganize existing party alignments. Here the key is weak partisan commitments. These activists accept the two-party system, but are unclear where they fit in. Our two examples, the Anderson and Wallace donors, illustrate these patterns. Of course, the Wallace insurgency occurred more than a decade before our survey, and these activists show a greater accommodation to the Republican ranks. The GOP's ability to absorb the Wallace movement eventually helped shift the balance of major party competition; likewise, absorption of the Anderson movement may have helped the Democrats in the 1990s (Phillips 1982). Ross Perot's 1992 candidacy is just the latest example of such reorganization of the major party coalitions, although it is too early to foretell the nature of its impact.

Note

1. The following discussion relies very heavily on Orren (1982), and to a lesser extent on Rosenstone et al. (1984), Gillespie (1993), and Beck and Sorauf (1992: 48-53). Following Orren, the major parties might be labeled as "pragmatic."

PART FOUR

Party Policy and Values

17

A Tale of Two Parties:
National Committee Policy Making, 1992 and 1994

Laura Berkowitz
Steve Lilienthal

There is consensus that American politics is in trouble, and many of the complaints focus on the failures of the system. Dissatisfaction with the economy, frustration with foreign policy, and disgust with government gridlock and the impasse over the budget all contribute to this disenchantment. The American electorate, characterized by declining efficacy and increased levels of alienation and apathy, regards political parties as having lost touch. Not only is the intensity of partisanship declining, but the percentage of the electorate who view themselves as "independent" is now over 40 percent. There is a growing perception that the current party system is incapable of responding to the challenges of the 1990s.

The parties themselves are aware of these difficulties and are recognizing that people want to be appraised of the specific policy directions. Bill Brock, a former Republican national chair, expressed the problem cogently: "Voters don't have the foggiest idea of what we stand for in terms of governance" (Cook 1993). Parties are mindful of the chord struck by Ross Perot's charge that they are not responsive to citizens' concerns. The electorate not only wants to know what the parties stand for, but also want to be included in creating those policies.

Both the Democratic and Republican national committees (DNC and RNC) have instituted new programs to facilitate party policy making and involve their own grassroots membership. These initiatives include meetings, publications, surveys, new organizations, television programs, and media events aimed at furthering dialogue about issues and party philosophy. The potential of these innovations to make the national committees into significant forces for formulating and articulating policy proposals is the focus of this chapter.

Information used for this analysis was developed from personal and telephone interviews.[1] The findings suggest a genuine commitment to enlarge the scope of party activities. There appears to be enthusiasm for the idea that involvement in "the business of ideas" is not only needed to reinvigorate the national parties, but also may be necessary for their survival. This represents a significant change in the focus of the national committees; it is widely believed that preoccupation with electoral activities seems no longer sufficient to meet the challenges of the last decade of the twentieth century.

Past Attempts at Party Policy Making

Policy considerations have always been a secondary concern for the national committees. Their involvement in issues is related to their electoral role and their function as a communication forum for state and national party leaders. The DNC and RNC have traditionally exerted some limited influence in candidate selection and recruitment. Also, their national convention responsibilities include constructing a party platform, which necessitates policy considerations. The in-party national committees have worked to promote the president's program, while out-party committees have employed a defensive strategy, often responding to presidential initiatives by simply criticizing his proposals.

There are several factors that restrict the policy-making role of the national committees. Their historic lack of a strong policy orientation, competition with others to speak for the parties, little political influence over party officeholders, and the coalition nature of the parties all serve as constraining influences (Hames 1994). In the past there have been proposals for the national organizations to become more involved in policy development. Perhaps the most noted was the 1950 report of the American Political Science Association Committee on Political Parties, *Toward a More Responsible Two-Party System*. The report warned there is a "chance that the electorate will turn its back upon the two parties unless they become more participatory and issue-oriented. Those who suggest that election should deal with personalities but not with programs suggest at the same time that party membership mean nothing at all" (1950: 28). The report urged "formulations of programs linking state and local issues to questions of national and international concern [that would] help overcome unduly narrow views of party" (1950: 67). The programs were supposed to "bubble up" from the grassroots level. Having the parties place more emphasis "upon policy and the interrelationship of problems at the various levels of government [would make] association with a party . . . interesting and attractive to many who hold aloof today" (1950: 67).

There have also been previous attempts by both parties to become more policy oriented. In 1956, the Democrats formed the Democratic Advisory

Council (DAC) to serve as a policy-making body between conventions (Roberts 1994). Nine years later the Republicans created the Republican Coordinating Committee (RCC) in response to the devastating Goldwater defeat (Bibby 1994). Both initiatives, although short-lived, did succeed in mobilizing party elites to produce consensus. Policy position papers were generated by both groups. The RCC was more successful at articulating coherent policy positions, but some planks of the DAC platforms were used by the congressional candidates and the Kennedy presidential campaign. However, both organizations labored under handicaps that limited their effectiveness. Both were nonparticipatory, elite-based organizations. The policy positions agreed upon at their meetings did not necessarily translate into broad party-wide consensus. A similar problem bedeviled policy groups established with the national committees, such as under RNC chair Bill Brock (Klinkner 1994) and DNC chair Charles Manatt (Menefee-Libey 1994).

One of the few attempts at broader based, participatory policy formation was the Democrat's abortive midpresidential conventions of 1974 and 1978. These meetings did not produce a strong consensus, and they were eventually disbanded. However, they are noteworthy in that they foreshadowed both parties' current efforts to include a wider range of participants in developing policy stands.

The potential for national committees to advance policy direction is much greater today than at any previous period. The parties recognize that there is a danger they may be viewed as mere vote-getting organizations at the very time the public hungers for meaningful choices and a belief that their choices will make a difference. The way campaigns are conducted has also contributed to the growing alienation of the electorate from the parties. Media driven, candidate-centered campaigns serve to minimize the voters' role, and the increased reliance on computerized voting lists, mass mailings, and phone banks combine to depersonalize the connection between the party organization and its members. Substantive policy alternatives have been reduced to subliminal imagery and pictorial allusion (Lowi 1992a). However, technology is now being utilized to bridge the gap with the electorate. Innovations such as satellite and cable television are heralded as ways to again involve partisans who found their role devalued by the rise of mass media and computer technology. The parties hope that these techniques can provide activists with an opportunity to help shape the party's message. They also expect these new technologies and their expanded policy orientation will attract new constituents. While both parties seem eager to embrace this new technology, differences in how each committee has chosen to apply technological innovations will also be reviewed. The eventual success of these recent outreach attempts is as yet unclear, as is their influence on the long-term prospects of both major parties.

Republicans: Leading the Pack Again

Policy Making

The Republican Party has made the strongest early commitment to better communicate coherent principles and policies to voters. RNC chair, Haley Barbour, recently noted that "the National Committee must take the lead in emphasizing the principles that unite . . . [We] need a strong party per se, and must resist allowing the party to become subservient to any candidate, officeholder, or faction" (1993b: 1).

Interviews with current and former RNC staff suggest that Barbour has played a very active role in issue promotion. He polled over eight hundred thousand party officials, elected officials, donors, and activists by mail for their input on issues ranging from the budget to social policies. Almost 140,000 questionnaires were returned, a response rate that reflects the respondents' intense interest in expressing their views. Responses repeatedly expressed frustration that the GOP had not solicited or advocated the views of its grassroots membership.

The chairman and the RNC apparatus have also concentrated their efforts on reaching out to Perot's supporters. Soon after assuming the chairman's office, Barbour urged GOP state chairs to establish a working dialogue with their states' Perot activists. In the summer of 1995 he addressed a meeting convened by Perot and argued the GOP was becoming more participatory and rejecting the politics-as-usual tactics that had alienated Perotistas. The GOP, he claimed, replaced the traditional out-party strategy of running against the White House in off-year elections by promoting the Contract with America. Pat Baker, a United We Stand Member, said, "Most of the stuff in the Contract with America was in the Perot platform in 1992" (Pendleton 1994: 3).

Barbour was a key supporter of the concept of the Contract, providing the use of RNC facilities to wage the campaign to publicize the document. RNC funds were also used to underwrite survey research and to purchase a $265,000 advertisement in *TV Guide*. Charles Greener, former communications director of the RNC, credits the Contract with not only heightening visibility of important issues such as the balanced budget amendment and term limits, but also establishing a framework for a governing agenda once the party assumed control of the House.

The chairman has also developed a close relationship with the party leaders of the House and Senate. During the years the GOP held the White House, decisions regarding legislative strategies emanated from the White House. The RNC attempted to step in as a broker between the House and Senate by setting up a division of congressional affairs and strategic planning. This new division works to coordinate legislative efforts with the party's House and Senate leadership and to politically assist legislation that would help to define the differences between the two parties. It combines efforts with the RNC's communications division to arrange satellite TV news interviews and radio talk show interviews for members of Congress on the issue battle of the moment. It also plays a liaison role with coalition groups representing activists and businesses.

Republican governors have achieved a higher profile on Capitol Hill due in part to Barbour's efforts to better link them to the congressional policy-making process. Paul Hatch, executive director of the Republican Governors Association, credits Barbour with having helped build the bond between the governors and Capital Hill. "In the past, the Republican governors came to Washington to plead for waivers for their state from the federal government. That was frustrating. Now, when they come, they speak with one voice."

Barbour has made it a point to reach out to conservative groups and to boost causes favored by economic conservatives. His relations with social conservatives are much more tenuous. Barbour has addressed the CPAC convention, an annual gathering of conservative activists. A representative from RNC regularly attends weekly meetings of conservative groups held by Americans for Tax Reform. They have addressed meetings sponsored by Coalition for America, which are attended by prominent conservative legislators and representatives of conservative groups. Conservative activist Grover Norquist credits Barbour with having worked to bridge gaps between warring factions without sacrificing principles. For instance, when Norquist wrote a column in *The American Spectator* describing how supporters and opponents of legalized abortion worked together to defeat the Freedom of Choice Act, the RNC chairman helped see that copies were distributed to party leaders.

The RNC has not only relied on the traditional news media to advance its position but has also initiated generic advertising campaigns to present the party's point of view during important legislative battles. There has been some criticism during the winter and early spring of 1996 that the RNC had not been as forceful as it could have been in countering the impact of advertising run by the Democrats and their allies during the budget battle (Balz 1995: A11). While the RNC spent $2.7 million on generic advertising in 1995, one party strategist told *The Washington Post*, "Clearly some people felt there should be more" (Kurtz 1996: A8).

Republicans have also established the National Policy Forum (NPF), a research and education foundation that started holding town meetings across the country to allow politicians, activists, and the public at large, not all of whom were Republicans, to discuss issues. In an April 1996 interview Barbour characterized the NPF as "an outlet for the average citizen, the grassroots activist, the rank-and-file voter to have their say on what they think government policy ought to be and why." Officially, it operates independently of the RNC, although both organizations share the same chair. According to

Mary Crawford, former NPF communications director, one rationale for legally disassociating the NPF from the RNC was to include independents and even disaffected Democrats in its events. Crawford characterized its meetings as "think tanks in reverse" because of their participatory nature. Reports that included the thinking gleaned from the meetings were distilled into a booklet called "Listening to America," which was distributed to GOP candidates, activists, and the news media.

The RNC and NPF also use the more traditional method of print to disseminate their message. The RNC publication, *Rising Tide,* claims a circulation over 550,000. Noted authors Gertrude Himmelfarb of the City University of New York, Michael Novak, and *U.S. News and World Report* senior editor Michael Barone have written articles for recent editions. April 1996 is the scheduled release date for Barbour's *Agenda for America,* which he describes as "a foundational document of Republican thought and principle." Over fourteen hundred members of the NPF's policy councils were asked to participate in the drafting process (*Ideas Matter* 1995: 4).

The NPF has reissued the journal *Commonsense,* which the Republican National Committee had published in the late 1970s and early 1980s. Articles deal with domestic and foreign policy topics and are geared toward fostering the discussion of ideas. It may not influence Republican policy making directly, but it is intended to present a forum for the consideration of issues. Circulation is approximately twenty thousand, and recipients include mayors, governors, members of Congress, heads of university political science departments, and think tanks. While the RNC has no prior editorial approval on its contents and it operates under a separate copyright from the previous journal, Barbour reads all submissions.

New Technologies

Just as the Republicans proved more adept at harnessing the power of television advertising in the 1950s, and computer technology, direct mail, and survey research in the 1960s and 1970s, they are once again leading the Democrats in the use of cable and satellite television to communicate with their membership. If the widespread use of television advertising and computers replaced the old-style political gathering and citizen participation in politics, the GOP's use of cable and satellite television are helping to bring them back.

The RNC leaders realize that they have only scratched the surface of the new technology. Barbour suggests, "We're just starting to use technology in the way a lot of businesses and industries have been using it" (Seib 1994). They utilize satellite technology for the *Rising Tide* television program. *Rising Tide* is hosted by Chairman Barbour, accepts calls from viewers, and is structured along the lines of a news magazine. It is broadcast weekly by cable, including superstation WWOR, to a potential audience of over fifty-five million homes.

A typical broadcast, which aired July 6, 1995, featured reports on research from Americans for Tax Reform and the Tax Foundation in Washington, and on the tax cut of Gov. Christine Todd Whitman (R-NJ). It also described the new welfare reform program of Gov. George Allen (R-Va) and featured a woman in Houston who delivers food to women in need without accepting government assistance. The same show featured former congressman Jack Kemp addressing the need for a simpler, lower tax system. An RNC advertisement promises, "Whether it's welfare reform in Wisconsin, reaching out to minorities in urban America, or a tough stand on crime in Virginia, *Rising Tide* keeps you plugged into Republican messages and ideas at the local level." [2] Former RNC communications director Chuck Greener notes that its weekly airing enables the program to present up-to-the-minute news about important legislative and political events of consequence to Republican activists. College Republicans, Young Republicans, and local Republican women's groups often plan their meetings around the broadcasts of *Rising Tide*.

State parties have also started to work in conjunction with the RNC to make use of the new satellite technology. Washington state's Republican Party used the RNC's television facilities to link up party activists attending precinct caucuses with Senate Minority Leader Bob Dole (R-Kans), Sen. Slade Gorton (R-Wash), and Rep. Jennifer Dunn (R-Wash). Both cable and satellites were used to carry "The 1994 Republican Community Forum," during which those in attendance submitted issues questionnaires.

RNC broadcast facilities are used not only to produce *Rising Tide* but to disseminate a daily fifteen minute newsfeed and is the staging ground for satellite news interviews by Republican members of Congress with the news media back home. The yearly average of six hundred interviews is expected to be surpassed in 1996. Over twelve hundred live interviews with GOP legislators had occurred over the last two years. As former communications director Greener explains: "Haley realized if we fought toe to toe with the White House for the Washington, D.C., media, then we'd lose. But if we put Kit Bond (R-Mo) on Saint Louis television via satellite and let the White House compete with Bond, we'd win." The RNC's broadcast operations are expected to develop a teleconferencing capability this year.

An ambitious monthly program called Republican Exchange Satellite Network (RESN) was launched in 1993 by former governor Lamar Alexander (R-Tenn). Originally, the program concentrated on satellite broadcasts that were built around meetings of Republican activists. The idea was to help encourage participation. As the show started being broadcast on cable, the emphasis was less on group participation. Kevin Phillips, former RESN spokesperson, explained, "Once it went on cable, there was less of an incentive to organize meetings. But more people were watching." Alexander discontinued the broadcasts upon declaring his candidacy for the GOP's 1996 presidential nomination. After Alexander abandoned his effort, National

Policy Forum started airing its own broadcasts of a program called *Listening to America: A Neighborhood Meeting*, only to discontinue it after a relatively brief run. The NPF does have a World Wide Web site that includes summaries of *Commonsense* and transcripts of "megaconferences." These megaconferences, held in 1995 and 1996, feature prominent experts and congressional leaders discussing issues ranging from telecommunications, the tax code, and competitiveness. The RNC also regularly faxes material to deliver its message. According to the 1995 RNC Chairman's Report, the RNC Monday Briefing is distributed via fax to over three thousand officeholders, party leaders, and opinion makers. When President Clinton had finished delivering his 1996 State of the Union address, RNC faxes challenging his statements were promptly sent to almost one thousand journalists, radio talk shows, and Republican officeholders. The RNC is now on the Internet with its Main Street home page, and the party relishes the attention the news media has devoted to its site.

Issues

The RNC is pushing a wide variety of issues: tenets of private enterprise, market economics, economic growth through low taxes, individual freedom and responsibility, free trade, reduced government regulation, peace through strength, public and personal security, opposition to drugs and crime, and a belief in traditional family values issues. RNC advertising campaigns highlight these issues. One TV advertisement called "Let's Be Clear" was used during the budget debate in late 1995, and it featured clips of President Clinton giving varying accounts of how long it would take to balance the budget. The most recent RNC advertising initiative, timed to coincide with tax day on April 15, featured a couple discovering they owed more in taxes than they expected. The president, the wife notes, vetoed tax credits for children.

The Republicans' Contract with America represented a departure from politics as usual, but its overall impact may be much less than Republican strategists had hoped. Its success soon became overshadowed by simmering issues such as balancing the budget and Medicare. Likewise, Barbour recently expressed doubts about the future role of the NPF. "If Dole wins, we'll be interested in how NPF goes forward." An approaching presidential election and concern over helping put forward a strong party message during legislative battles has already reduced the scale of an innovative outreach program spearheaded by Barbour. Many anticipate a further change when the general election campaign is in full swing. The relative influence wielded by the nominee and national chair in drafting the RNC 1996 platform is also a matter of speculation. There is reason for skepticism about how long the RNC chair will remain an important party spokesperson, particularly after Barbour planned retirement at the end of 1996.

Democrats: Following Clinton's Lead

Policy Making

While Democrats are also concerned about encouraging dialogue on issues, they are concentrating primarily on developing new means of communicating the priorities of the president to the party's grassroots. The DNC is combining its traditional role of building and financing the party's national political apparatus with generating support for Clinton's programs (Barnes 1993). According to Craig Smith, former DNC political director, the role of the party used to be solely focused on elections, yet both message development and lobbying are needed today to actively support the president's legislative agenda (Tisinger 1993). The DNC and the White House work in tandem on common goals and coordinated strategy. The national committee is concentrating on generating grassroots support, while the White House has focused its efforts primarily on Congress.

Clinton's election has afforded the DNC its first opportunity in twelve years to initiate policy and control the policy agenda. Anita Perez-Ferguson, former education director for the DNC, emphasized the significant difference in reacting to a Republican president's initiatives and following the lead of one's own president. The national health care campaign, launched by the DNC in the fall of 1993, was the first new employment of this approach: the marshaling of resources to mobilize the governing party around an issue-oriented agenda. The DNC health care campaign had its own offices and staff (Kosova 1994) as it organized telephone banks, blanketed editorial page editors with letters and op-ed pieces, and sponsored activities designed to attract the attention of the press (Tisinger 1993). Arranging for trained and fully briefed surrogate speakers to address local groups on health care was another new service of the national committee. Wilhelm hoped the health care campaign would inaugurate an "activist network" that would establish a "full- scale dialogue between people and their government, and people and their party." He envisioned a "citizens' lobby," created to reach Americans who feel disenfranchised by politics as usual. This citizens' lobby would fight the special interests in Washington on issues of concern to working families.

Grassroots mobilization efforts in 1993 and 1994 were augmented with a more conventional advertising blitz, including extensive radio and TV advertisements supporting the president's policy agenda. In 1994, the DNC announced it would spend $400,000 a week to portray health care reform as a middle-class issue (Priest 1994). One DNC strategist conceded, "There are 255 million people in this country. You can't reach them door to door. The fight is in the media, not in the precincts" (Balz 1994a). Aggressive grassroots initiatives did not meet early expectations, and the health care outreach was eventually removed from the control of the DNC and handed over to Senator Jay Rockefeller's health care reform project (Kosova 1994).

The failure of the health care reform campaign and the devastating losses in the 1994 elections forced a major shift in both personnel and strategy for the DNC. According to a DNC spokesperson, there is currently no plan for the creation of a citizens' lobby. However, this is not to say that the DNC has abandoned its efforts to broaden the scope of its outreach programs. For over a year "rapid response teams" have been providing services, including a speakers' bureau, printed materials, and prepared letters, to the editor to various grassroots groups. The DNC is also conducing extensive polling to help White House policy makers determine which issues are of paramount concern to voters.

Virtually all senior-level personnel had been replaced even prior to the 1994 election cycle (Balz 1994b). In 1995, Wilhelm was succeeded by the team of Sen. Christopher Dodd (CT), as general chair of the party, and Don Fowler as chairman of the DNC in charge of overseeing its day-to-day operation. The new leadership team is expected to support Wilhelm's efforts to involve the membership in policy; both Dodd and Fowler have an exceptional feel for grassroots opinions and a strong grasp on the internal dynamics of Democratic constituencies (Broder 1995).

Prior to 1992, the main focus of the national committee was regional communication and the election of more Democrats; efforts were organized around geographic and regional lines. These regional undertakings have been expanded to include a network of constituency groups whose sole focus is to build communication around common issues. The DNC sees the constituency division and the Division of Inter-Government Affairs, both of which were founded in 1992, as significant innovations.

The Division of Inter-Government Affairs has expanded the means by which Democratic officeholders on both the local and state level are given relevant information on policy, elections, and all aspects of the party activity. Sue Charlton, its executive director, sees it as a means for the national committee to facilitate regular two-way communication with local officeholders. For example, in January 1996 the DNC sponsored a conference of Democratic mayors, at which mayors voiced common concerns, including the need for a summer jobs program. Other elected state and local officials, including city councilmen and secretaries of state, also meet for ongoing discourse.

The constituency division is an outreach to specific groups of Democrats who share mutual interests. The Youth Division, Latino outreach, Asian-American group, women's group and individuals concerned with disability issues are examples of initiatives geared toward activating specific elements of the party. Instead of party elites determining policy for the party's various constituencies, it is hoped that these groups will contribute input to insure their particular concerns are addressed.

In 1996, the steering committee of the DNC's national coordinated campaign team added EMILY's List, a women's group, to its membership.

The interest of the two groups have been frequently complementary, but according to EMILY's List spokesperson Frank Wilkinson, "When Pat Buchanan was given prime time access to the stage at the 1992 Republican Convention, the Democrats got religion on women. . . . The party's policies—and now its politics—reflect the commitment of Democrats to women." He is gratified that Chairman Fowler recognizes the need for the DNC to address issues of importance to women including economic security, crime, education, health care and protecting a woman's right to choose. The DNC is providing a multi-million dollar commitment to EMILY's List women's vote campaign targeting these issues to mobilize Democratic-leaning women voters.

New Technologies

The health care outreach innovations are examples of how the Democrats also embraced technologies of the 1990s. The DNC conducted two video teleconferences with health care spokesperson Hillary Rodham Clinton. Using hookups with five different media sites, approximately five hundred community activists were afforded opportunities to direct questions to the First Lady. The DNC continues to use video teleconferences for direct two-way party communication.

During the 1992 campaign the DNC assisted the Wisconsin Democratic Party with two statewide issue forums with party activists via satellite. Undecided voters and those leaning toward supporting the Democratic ticket were also invited by phone and mail solicitation to watch the meetings. Regional sites included a sports bar and a college campus. Senator Bill Bradley (D-NJ), Gov. David Walters (D-Okla), and then DNC chair Ron Brown participated in the forums, which also featured local candidates. Guests answered phoned-in questions from the regional audiences.

Former state party executive director Jonathon Sender estimated that well over one thousand people attended both meetings. The impact of the meetings resonated well beyond the halls; television stations would pick up the broadcasts and use excerpts in their newscasts. The *Wisconsin State Journal* credited the "video town hall meetings with providing a chance for people who otherwise never think or talk about politics to do so. That's what an election year should be all about" (1992: 11A).

The DNC has also made use of satellite technology in more conventional terms, such as press conferences. One interesting event was conducted in mid-April 1994 when Americans were filing their tax returns. To demonstrate the limited impact that the tax program would have on middle-class taxes, former Chairman Wilhelm appeared at a large baseball stadium with only 1.2 percent of the seats filled—the exact number Democrats claimed would pay more under the Clinton tax increase. The event was beamed to television news stations across the country. Since 1993, the DNC has also conducted "satellite media tours" with cabinet secretaries to discuss issues of importance.

Its constituency outreach also utilizes this technology to facilitate communication with local groups.

Another important communication innovation of the DNC is the "morning briefs," communications that are sent to over two thousand individuals, including state party chairs, big city mayors, Democratic state officials, and grassroots activists, by fax at least three times a week. They have been tremendously successful at communicating current party positions and topics of interest. Recipients are encouraged to further disseminate the morning briefings. For example, the New York State Democratic Committee regularly distributes copies to its local party committees. It is estimated that the morning briefs have a circulation of over ten thousand. According to Jill Alper, in 1995 the morning briefs were expanded to "satellite blast backs" which are now sent to every Democratic precinct leader. The Democratic Forum home page of the Internet is another recent technological outreach to the grassroots.

The Democrats have made significant progress, but they have not approximated the RNC's programming on a regular basis. Sue Charlton concedes that while satellite press conferences and video teleconferences were routine under Wilhelm, they are now used only occasionally on an issue by issue basis. Former DNC press secretary Catherine Moore has voiced skepticism about the effectiveness of such programs. "What is the value of reaching people you are already reaching? I wonder if the Republicans are reaching the people that are already with them" (Lambrecht 1994: 4A). The widening gap in technological innovation has some Democrats worried. One strategist complained, "One could argue that the DNC, by not competing with the RNC, is falling further and further behind. . . . They're still making Yugos, and the RNC is making BMWs. If the Republicans get back the White House, how can the Democrats expect to compete?" (Kosova 1994: 25).

Issues

It is perhaps inevitable that the DNC has become less a vehicle to promote an issue agenda within the party and more a public relations shop for Clinton's 1996 reelection campaign. According to Jill Alper of the DNC, the economy, crime, Medicare, and Medicaid are high on the president's agenda, and therefore on the DNC's agenda. Sue Charlton agrees that the main priority of the DNC is to reelect the president, and this means mustering support for the president's initiatives and policy positions. Since September of 1995 the DNC has spent nearly $15 million on television ads to burnish the president's image, and it has budgeted an additional $10 million (Kurtz 1996). The ads focus primarily around the ongoing budget battle between Congress and the White House. They argue that Democrats want "access to health insurance for all, education, job training, and more police, but Republicans will stop at nothing to stop President Clinton" (Kondracke 1996). Recurring themes include the threat that Medicare and student loans will be cut by Republicans attempting to balance the budget (Seplow 1996). The DNC has also aired ads commending the president for his legislation banning assault weapons. "President Clinton is right. . . . This is not about politics. This is about saving lives" (Brownstein 1996).

Constraints on the Shift to Issues

While there is much enthusiasm about both parties' recent policy orientation and new mechanisms to communicate about issues, there are reasons for skepticism about the long-term impact of these initiatives. The national committees have little long-standing commitment to policy making. They are by nature very responsive to the state and local committees, which have picked their own officers, nominated their own candidates, developed their own policy stands, and raised and disbursed their own funds without regard for the national committees (Beck and Sorauf 1992). They have become a significant force in American politics by building internal cohesion and attaining financial and organizational resources. In fact, their "nuts and bolts" efforts have been directed toward providing services and funds to individual candidates and campaigns, not in the development of policy.

While the national committees have achieved some measure of autonomy, primarily through their fundraising success, they have no scheme for creating policy. The president and other office holders have always been the source of policy and dictated the agenda for the party in power. Kenneth Hill, Vice President of the National Policy Forum, explains, "The whole process of policy development over the last twelve years (when GOP presidents held the White House) was an assistant secretary sitting in a Washington office telling everybody what the policy was." The out-party has historically relied on congressional leaders to articulate its concerns. Thus, there is no guarantee that these longstanding tendencies will change with this new-found enthusiasm for policy pronouncements and discussion.

Some elected officials are concerned that promoting issue agendas could drain resources from other grassroots efforts (Kurtz 1996: A8). Many Democrats fear their own campaign needs will be shortchanged by the DNC as its resources are expended lobbying for the president and his programs. This is an ongoing concern. "That is important to us, but we also need a first-rate political operation up and running. We've got to turn our attention to reelecting Democrats" (Barnes 1993b: 2834).

In the 1994 election cycle, some Democratic leaders maintained the necessity for some candidates, particularly in the South where Clinton's popularity was low, to distance themselves from the White House (Balz 1994b). Congressional leaders are also careful to guard their own party leadership roles; party unity does not extend to automatically accepting DNC pronouncements with which they disagree. For example, at a 1994 Cleveland DNC meeting, chairman Wilhelm attacked the president's congressional Whitewater critics. His words were repudiated the following day by then Speaker of the House Thomas Foley. Foley suggested, on national television, that personal attacks on members of Congress make for bad politics (Grove 1994). Likewise, Senator Richard Bryan (D-Nev) publicly complained about not being consulted about a DNC run health care advertising campaign in his state (Balz 1994c).

Another fundamental problem with the national committees taking the lead in policy initiatives stems from the nature of the parties. Each is comprised of broad-based coalitions. Authoritative policy statements have often fragmented these coalitions. According to DNC political director Don Switzer, "There will always be disagreements on policy in our party. But our party learned its lessons in 1980 when we tore ourselves apart. . . . This is our president. We're not about to get into a suicide war and tear ourselves apart for 1996" (Lambro 1994). Much the same thing threatens the Republicans on social issues. Morton Blackwell, a member of the RNC from Virginia, expressed concern that the NPF's plan to air different policy positions might backfire and foster disagreements. It could encourage publicity about disputes within the party and portray "the image of a Republican Party badly divided and fighting itself on these issues" (Berke 1993). Thus, both parties are well aware of the potential booby traps associated with policy making.

Conclusion

In order for the national committees to aggressively advance policy initiatives, they must walk a fine line. The DNC and RNC must avoid stepping on the toes of congressional leaders, state and local organizations, constituencies within the party, and candidates who look to them for support. If they completely avoid controversy and decisiveness, their efforts may be reduced to meaningless platitudes and broad generalities. These may not offend anyone, but neither will they give anyone a clear sense of direction.

There are many indications that the national committees are sincere in their commitment to move toward a more "responsible" role than merely dispensing cash and technological services. American politicians are experts at running campaigns that emphasize their own merits rather than party programs. Perhaps the new initiatives will enhance the role of the national committees in attracting better, more qualified candidates. Individuals committed to the party's philosophical direction might be motivated to run for office due to the appeal of a coherent policy stand by the national committees.

The success of Perot in 1992 was a clear signal that the major parties should begin to develop programs which link them and the citizenry on issues and around broad philosophical principles. Ongoing participatory policy forums will not only improve communication, but also may result in a more thoughtful, coherent party platform that directly addresses the voters' concerns. The GOP's Contract with America and efforts by House Minority Leader Richard Gephardt to craft a similar document on his side for the 1996 elections are proof that the parties have worked to achieve the unrealized goals of the DAC and RCC, and it may be possible that such documents will become regular features of American politics. These policy stances would not be dictated from the top but would arise from the bottom up, the result of a grassroots consensus. While it is premature to evaluate the success of these endeavors, recent policy initiatives may well affect the role and the future prospects of both national parties. Technologies developed in this decade may facilitate this dialogue.

Both parties have defined their differences, but a good percentage of the electorate want them to *settle* their differences, which helped to account for the large following expressing interest in a race by Colin Powell in late 1995 when the parties appeared to have reached an stalemate over the budget. One question that must be grappled with in an increasingly segmented American society is whether parties driven by concerns of their grassroots followings may leave out huge blocs of voters who are less partisan. To some extent, that would help to explain the Perot phenomenon; both parties have sharply defined differences, and the center feels left out.

Of course, challenges from the left (Ralph Nader and the Greens) and the right (Libertarians and the Taxpayers Party) suggest the electorate is fragmenting in places other than the center. The profusion of these small but active parties perhaps indicates that the major parties may simultaneously need to cater more to the grassroots and take sharper stands in order to hold the most ideologically committed. While the parties will not draw a large share of the vote, they could play a significant role in determining the winners and losers.

The persistence of dissatisfaction with current politics and the magnitude of problems confronting the two parties is cause for optimism that the major parties cannot only reconnect with the sizeable number of disaffected Americans beyond their immediate support bases, but rechannel their energies. America's political parties are endowed with money and a newfound sense of purpose that can be communicated with sophisticated technology. They are also confronting many skeptical, sometimes hostile voters and thorny issues that must be addressed. The opening statement of *A Tale of Two Cities* describes the times they confront: "It was the epoch of belief, it was the epoch of incredulity."

Notes

1. Information for this article was obtained through several personal interviews: Jill Alper, April 1996; Curt Anderson, February 1996; Haley Barbour, April 1996; Sue Charlton, March 1996; Mary Crawford, March 1994; Don Fierce, April 1996; Charles Greener, March 1996; Ed Gillespie, February 1996; Paul Hatch, April 1996; Kenneth Hill, summer 1993; Bill Kristol, April 1994, April 1996; Adam Sohn, May 1994; Alice Travis, May 1994; Judith Van Rest, April 1994; Mike Ware, April 1996; Frank Wilkinson, March 1996.

2. RNC advertisement (March–April 1994).

18

The Platform Writing Process: Candidate-Centered Platforms in 1992

L. Sandy Maisel

One never knows what to make of party platforms. On the one hand, they are the most important documents that a political party produces. The platform tells you what the party stands for; it defines in explicit terms why partisans deserve to be elected. On the other hand, they are worthless pieces of paper. How many citizens can tell you what is in the parties' platforms? Who knows where the differences really lie? Who cares?

Political scientists express this same ambivalence. Those who favor responsible political parties see the platforms as central to the parties' mission; they give citizens reasons to support the parties' candidates. They lay the foundation for the policies that the parties will adopt if elected. Voters can measure party performance against party promises and hold future candidates accountable for past actions.[1] Gerald Pomper and Jeff Fishel have both demonstrated that platforms do matter, that the two major parties' platforms can be used to distinguish the parties and that, once elected, party officeholders enact significant portions of what was in their platforms.[2] In the broadest terms, you can tell what will happen after an election by examining what the platforms say before the election.

But others feel that reading platforms is not a rational way to determine how one should vote. Morris Fiorina and others claim that past performance is a much more rational way to judge how a candidate will act in office than is reliance on future promises.[3] And this approach has a certain intuitive appeal. After all, regardless of what the data on enactment of platform promises say, how many prospective voters really believe campaign promises and campaign rhetoric?

In 1992, even those who doubt the importance of platforms generally acknowledged that the differences between the Democratic and Republican party platforms were so broad that the electorate had to take notice. The Democratic party platform was moderate and pointedly inclusive; liberal rhetoric of the past gave way to pragmatic appeals to voters who had deserted the party in recent years. The Republican platform was more extreme than many believed wise for political purposes; the document seemed to go to great lengths to exclude those who disagreed with conservative doctrine, particularly on social issues. The journalists covering the campaign were nearly unanimous in their belief that the religious right wing had taken over the Republican Party—and that this image, so vividly displayed throughout the Republican National Convention in Houston, hurt President George Bush's reelection campaign.

Thus, whatever one's view of platforms generally—or of their utility in predicting future legislative and administrative actions—most agree that the platforms produced in 1992 had an impact on the presidential election. Furthermore, again regardless of the view one holds of the importance of platforms, we know very little about how they are produced. That which we do know concerns the process a the pre-1968 reform conventions and is often based on anecdotal knowledge.[4] This article aims to fill that gap in our knowledge. In examining how the 1992 platforms were produced, I hope to shed light on differences between Democrats and Republicans as they go about their party business. I further hope to show why the two platforms differed so greatly—and to such an important effect—in 1992.

In looking at how the two processes differed and at whether the Republicans could have avoided the political error many believed they made, this chapter will look at three separate aspects of the process. First, I will describe the formal process followed by each party in 1992; in many ways the formal process, which varies from election to election as well as from party to party, tells a great deal about the outcome. Each party's platform went through several drafts; the second section of this article will explore the differences among the drafts to determine how the various stages in the formal process influenced the eventual outcome. Obviously, if little changed at a stage in the process, that stage was not very important. On the other hand, if noteworthy changes occurred at one stage or another, the significance of that stage would follow logically. Third, I will attempt to come to some understanding of the influence of key individuals. Again, the platform is a finished product, but it started somewhere, was amended somewhat, and emerged eventually. If one can identify the stages in the process that were most significant, then one has a better opportunity to identify those whose influence was most profound at those stages. The article will conclude with discussion of the impact of the process—and of party rules—on the outcome and of how the post reform process, at least as seen in 1992, differs from the process as it existed prior to the reforms.

The Platform-Writing Process

Most analysts have noted that Republican and Democratic party rules differ philosophically.[5] The Republicans believe that local units should operate with relative autonomy. Thus, the national party rules impose few restrictions on state and local party organizations. The Democrats, on the other hand, view the role of the national party as more central to their mission and, therefore, impose more rules on the constituent units. These differences have been noted frequently when rules for choosing delegates to national conventions are under examination. They are just as relevant for the platform-writing process.

The Democrats

Appointment of the platform committee. Democratic National Committee chairman Ronald H. Brown appointed the cochairs of the Platform Committee for the Democratic National Convention relatively early in the political year, at a time at which the party nomination was still in doubt. Brown's goal was to organize the convention in such a way as to give the eventual nominee the best possible chance in the November election. Thus, he appointed cochairs who were party centrists, who shared his goal of building a platform around which all Democrats could unite.

So much for the best-laid plans. Brown's designers were Colorado governor Roy Romer and Ohio congresswoman Mary Rose Oakar from Cleveland. Romer and Oakar began planning the convention process, including calling a national platform in Cleveland in May to hear witnesses testify on proposed platform plans. Then the House bank scandal broke, and Congresswoman Oakar was marked as a frequent bank abuser. Quickly, but with little fanfare, she was replaced by her colleague in the House, Nancy Pelosi from California.

The Democrats also name vice chairs of the committee. Somewhat typically, the Democrats name a large number—ten in all—who are appointed for highly symbolic reasons. The 1992 vice chairs included a former governor, two mayors, one United States senator and a candidate for the Senate, and three United States representatives and a candidate for the House. Reflecting the diversity of the Democratic party, the group was half male and half female and included two African-Americans and one Hispanic-American.

In addition to the officers, by party rules the Democratic Platform Committee is comprised of 161 delegates appointed among the states and the territories according to population and Democratic strength, and twenty-five additional party leaders and elected officials (PLEOs). The PLEOs are appointed by the party chair to assure that certain groups important to the Democratic party feel that they have representation at the Platform Committee level. Thus, the PLEOs include representatives of the Democratic mayors and other elected officials, representatives of the Democratic state chairs, the congressional leadership, major party donors, as well as labor, African-Americans, and other groups the chair feels deserve recognition.

The representatives form the various states are chosen by the state delegations to the national convention in proportion to the delegate strength of the candidates for president. In small states, which are permitted only one or two delegates, this is not possible. In those cases, the apportionment among the presidential preferences is carried out among the three convention committees—Rules and Credentials, as well as Platform. Thus, from Maine in 1992, the Tsongas delegates had the state's delegate on the Platform Committee, the Clinton delegates on the Rules Committee, and the Brown delegates on the Credentials Committee. Some states had not selected convention delegates—and many state delegations had not had time to meet —before the national hearing was held in Cleveland on 18 May. Those states chose temporary delegates who attended that hearing and reported back to their states' permanent delegates when they were named. The role of delegates listed the 161 delegates from the states plus the additional 122 who were named as temporary delegates.

In some ways, this listing of all of the delegates is a reflection of their importance. Service on this committee is largely honorific. Members are given credentials to at least one session of the national convention, have their names published in the report of the committee, and sit in on various meetings. However, because they are elected to reflect specific presidential preferences, and because each of the presidential candidates monitored the proceedings closely and informed their representatives of how they wished them to vote, the committee members played minor roles as individuals. Much the same can be said of the PLEOs: the symbolic value of their appointments was greater than the actual value of any actions they took as individuals.

The Platform Committee rules specify that the national chairman will also appoint a Drafting Committee to prepare an initial draft of the party platform for full committee consideration. In earlier years, the Democrats worked through a series of subcommittees in a manner parallel to they described for the Republicans below. Under the current rules, the Drafting Committee prepares the document that the entire committee then works on. Chairman Brown named New Mexico Congressman Bill Richardson as chair of the Drafting Committee early in the process, but he did not name the other members until early June, well after the nomination of Bill Clinton was assured. The appointment of Drafting Committee members reflected Brown's desire that the convention be run in such a way as to enhance the nominee's chances in November. Thus, Brown permitted the Clinton staff to dictate roughly half of the members of the committee. He in turn used the remaining committee slots to guarantee representation by those groups, important to that party, that he did not want to slight.

The Drafting Committee included nine men and seven women; four African-Americans, two Hispanic-Americans, and one Asian American; a United States senator, four representatives in Congress, a secretary of state, two mayors, and a county supervisor; a Democratic National Committee (DNC) officer and a state chair; four labor leaders, a number of strong supporters of Israel, and one gay activist. Appointments were highly sought and bitterly battled over. In the end, Brown named a number of ex-officio members, in addition to the representatives from the presidential campaigns whose role is designated in the party rules, in order to keep peace within the party. Even then, the congressional party leaders were denied representation and many were disappointed.

The composition of the committee represented an important statement for the Democrats. The Drafting Committee, deemed to be most influential by those structuring the process, was comprised with two goals in mind: (1) assuring domination by the Clinton forces so that the platform would reflect the views on which the nominee wanted to run; and (2) including groups thought to be critical for the building of a winning Democratic coalition in the general election.

Information gathering. The hearing phase of the platform process is a public way to gather information. In essence, hearings allow those with a stake in the process to air their views. No one pretends that hearings have much to do with determining the content of the platform; they are part of the politics of platform writing, providing interested parties an opportunity to be heard. The Democrats held only one public hearing in 1992. The meeting held in Cleveland in mid-May was a marathon affair. Approximately one hundred committee members listened to testimony from early in the morning until after midnight. Witness after witness came before the committee, presented statements, and answered questions; most also filed written documents, as did hundreds of others.

The national hearing revealed a good deal about the platform process. The morning witnesses were divided into four panels dealing with opportunity, responsibility, community empowerment, and national security. That division, with minor rhetorical changes, remained intact throughout the process. The platform reflected themes presented in the Democratic Leadership Council's earlier statements of policy goals for the future, themes never substantially altered throughout the process. Among the key witnesses were Democratic Leadership council (DLC) leaders and staff, each of whom reiterated Clinton campaign goals.

In addition, the Cleveland hearing presented those outside of the Democratic mainstream an opportunity to be heard. Jesse Jackson was given prominent billing, as was Atlanta Mayor Maynard Jackson, representing the Rebuild America Coalition, and Pennsylvania Governor Robert Casey, the Democrat's leading antiabortion activist. But mostly this was the opportunity for witness after witness—from the Americans for Democratic Action to the Veterans of Foreign Wars, from the American Israel Public affairs Committee (AIPAC) to the Arab American Institute, from the American Petroleum Institute to the Sierra Club—to be heard. For many it seemed that the process of being heard defined having an impact. What Judith Parris concluded about this aspect of the process two decades ago remains true today: "There is virtual unanimity among politicians and among writers on politics that the platform hearings have been, in Walter Bagehot's terms, more formal than efficient."[6]

The staff draft. Before the Drafting Committee convened, the staff prepared a working paper to structure discussion. The organization of the Cleveland hearing and the comments of the platform committee leaders clearly indicated that this draft had been under consideration for some time. The key variable here was that Bill Clinton had been assured the party nomination and Brown was intent on solidifying the party under the nominee's leadership.

Clinton had been a leader of the Democratic Leadership Council, a group of moderate Democrats united in the belief that the party could regain the White House with a platform and a candidate not emphasizing the most liberal positions. The DLC had resented its policy initiatives at a number of different meetings, the most noteworthy being its own national meeting in New Orleans. The parallels between the working paper on the platform and DLC documents were striking.

Platform Committee documents do not list specific staff members by responsibility; however, nearly forty individuals were singled out for thanks. Among these were a number of policy analysts associated with the DLC and the Clinton campaign effort. Bruce Reed, the policy director for the DLC, and Will Marshall and Jeremy Rosner, president and vice president of the affiliated think tank, the Progressive Policy Institute, clearly played major roles in drafting platform language. So too did Sandy Berger, who later headed the Clinton foreign policy advisory staff. In addition, Congressman Richardson consulted closely with John Holum, a longtime Clinton friend and supporter in working out the final details of the draft. The staff draft was a team effort, but it was a Clinton team. Many individuals had input to specific section, but the overall control was evidently closely held. The long-term DLC strategy for Democrats regaining the White House was to be played out carefully.

One clear example of a group seeking and achieving influence was the American Israel Public Affairs Committee (AIPAC). That AIPAC testified in Cleveland is incidental to the overall effort the Israel lobby put into achieving a plank strongly supporting Israel. The effectiveness of this effort can be seen in pro-Israel appointments to the Drafting Committee, as PLEOs, and as members of the full committee, and in every draft of the platform. AIPAC worked just as hard and just as effectively on the Republican platform, standing as one of the few groups obviously successful in achieving its goal at both conventions.

The Drafting Committee. The Drafting Committee, under the leadership of Congressman Richardson, met in Sante Fe on June 12 and 13. The site was chosen not only to show off New Mexico's hospitality but also to keep away all but the most interested. The entire group at the Drafting Committee sessions, including members, staff, media, and those seeking to influence the draft, numbered around seventy; for a process of this nature, that was laboring in relative obscurity.

The procedures at the Drafting Committee sessions were unique. Bill Richardson led the committee through the entire draft, with members able to comment on each section. John Holum, serving as executive director of the Drafting Committee, took copious notes on each comment as the draft was discussed. However, no amendments were offered, much less voted upon. Various members of the committee voiced concerns and suggested changes or additions, but no attempt was made to draft platform language. At each point Richardson noted the opinion of the committee member and stated that he would take their views under advisement. Richardson was often seem looking toward the Clinton staff in attendance, particularly toward Harold Ickes, who was leading the Clinton team. Eventually a code developed through which committee members came to understand whether Richardson would take views under advisement and include them or take them under advisement never to be seen again. But all decisions were made informally. The Drafting Committee members, all experienced politicians, knew that they had to work behind the scenes to assure the success of their proposals.

Two other items of note occurred during these sessions. First, three staffs were much in evidence. The DNC staffers were running the meeting administratively; they were visible and seemed to be impressed with their own influence. The Clinton staff served as a link between the two, monitoring that the meeting went well and ensuring that their boss's views were taken into account at every stage. Governor Roy Romer and Congresswoman Nancy Pelosi also brought key staff people to this meeting. They worked closely with the chair of the committee to be certain that the draft that emerged would be acceptable to their bosses. Both of the cochairs were worried that the draft platform was too general and too inclusive, that defining issues were not stressed. The conflict between these views was one of the subthemes of the deliberation.

In addition, Paul Tsongas's representative to the Drafting Committee, Ted Van Dyke, pressed for specific accommodations to his candidate's view on economic matters. He was given a good deal of attention, but the response to his presentation made it clear that the entire committee—those appointed by Brown as well as those designated by the Clinton campaign—were Clinton advocates. If Tsongas were to receive any concessions, they would be granted by the Clinton forces for political reasons, not because of the influence of Tsongas supporters on the process. On the other hand, Jerry Brown's camp took a different track. Governor Brown himself addressed the group and then held a press conference attacking the platform; his representative on the Drafting Committee played virtually no role. The governor's actions all but guaranteed that no concessions would be granted toward his policy agenda.

Full committee deliberations. The full Platform Committee met in Washington two weeks after the Sante Fe meeting of the Drafting Committee.

In the two-week period Bill Richardson and John Holum took the views of the Drafting Committee members, as well as others with whom they consulted, into account as they produced the Drafting Committee's draft. The members of the Drafting Committee had scant chance to see and no chance to have formal input into the Holum draft after the group left Sante Fe. However, many members were consulted frequently on individual sections in which they had interest.

That the full committee was only given one day in which to work its will is indicative of the importance of that group. The full committee worked under rules that required seconding by fifteen members before an amendment to the draft could be considered. That the Clinton forces were clearly in charge was evident from the start. Each candidate's supporters caucused the night before the full committee meeting. The Clinton delegation constituted a clear majority; they were unified enough to be able to work their will on any amendments proposed. As each item came up, Jim Brady, a DLC leader and the chair of the Louisiana Democratic party, who was serving as Clinton's floor leader, rose and stated his campaign's view on the amendment. His side lost no votes on which they had an opinion, though on an expansion of the abortion language to the health care plank they were forced to go along against their initial inclination.

A number of delegates to the full committee complained that the process was a done deal. Brown delegates were able to win some concessions on environmental issues, but the issue amateurs, who believed that Governor Brown represented a new wave of politics that was inescapable, were swept under the Clinton breaker before they knew what hit them. Despite their pleas to the contrary, the Platform Committee is not a deliberative body, and the full committee meeting is not a time for one's views. In 1992 this meeting was clearly the final step in a process that had been carefully orchestrated well in advance.

Adoption of the platform. Minority reports to the Democratic platform can only be filed upon request from a requisite number of Platform Committee members. Neither the Tsongas nor the Brown delegation had enough committee members to force a minority report; the views of the two camps were so far apart that they could not work together.

The Clinton campaign was in no mood to compromise with Brown, who had shown no inclination to come in line with the winning nominee. However, they were willing to accept overtures from the Tsongas delegation in exchange for pledges of future support. Eventually the Clinton camp asked their delegates to sign petitions for four minority planks, with proposals to stimulate economic recovery, put forth by the Tsongas camp, so that some debate on the platform would enliven the convention, though eventually the Tsongas forces withdrew all save one of their proposals. For the most part, the presentation of the platform to the national convention was an opportunity to showcase party leaders and to discuss the candidate's views.

The platform as adopted by the Platform Committee was passed unamended by the full convention.

The Republicans

Appointment of the Platform Committee. The Republican Platform Committee, technically called the Committee on Resolutions, is comprised of a chair, two cochairs, four vice chairs, and 107 delegates chosen at state level (a man and a woman from each state, the District of Columbia, Puerto Rico, and one delegate [all male in 1992] each from American Samoa, Guam, and the Virgin Islands).

The officers of the committee are appointed by the Republican national chairman. When the party's incumbent president is running for reelection, as was the case in 1992, the appointment of the officers is in fact dictated by the president's reelection committee. The 1992 Committee on Resolutions was chaired by Senator Don Nickles from Oklahoma, who also served as chair of the Republican Policy Committee in the United States Senate; the cochairs were Governor John Ashcroft of Missouri and Florida Congressman Bill McCullum. The appointment of these committee leaders, among the most conservative Republicans holding each of the offices they held, signaled that the Bush-Quayle committee thought it important that the conservative wing of the party knew it had a candidate with whom it could be comfortable. The committee officers were appointed at a time when Pat Buchanan's candidacy was proving as irritant to President Bush's march toward renomination. The appointments served to undercut the claim that the president was not conservative enough for his party.

The vice chairs serve the same role for the Republicans as they do for the Democrats. These are largely honorific roles; however, the vice chairs are highly visible to those watching the proceedings, and thus their appointments are considered symbolic as well. Two of the four vice chairs for the 1992 Committee were women—Cheryl Lau, the secretary of state from Nevada, and Leanna Brown, a New Jersey State Senator; Lau is also Asian-American. A third vice chair Orange County, California, Supervisor Gaddi Vasquez, in addition to being an Hispanic-American, is also a former police officer. The fourth vice chair was Greg Lushutka, an Ohio mayor; presumably he represented the so called Reagan Democrats now in the Republican party, and like Brown, he was from a pivotal state. Lau and Vasquez played prominent roles throughout the platform-writing process and in the presentation of the platform to the convention, perhaps signaling more prominent roles for them in the years ahead.

In accordance with the rules of the Republican party, the members of the committee from the various states were appointed by the states as the individual states saw fit. Most of the appointments were prominent and experienced politicians in their states—two governors and former governor;

two United States senators and a candidate for the Senate; five U.S. representatives and a former representative; eleven state legislators; eight members of the Republican National Committee; and four state chairs. Most states appointed at least one very prominent individual, though sixteen were represented by somewhat lesser figures. Less well known representatives from the states tended to fall into three categories—those representing prominent figures, such as the chief of staff to Gov. George Voinovich of Ohio or the former chief legislative assistant to Sen. Jesse Helms from North Carolina; long time party activists or contributors, many of whom had served on this committee at past conventions; or pro-life activists.

A vast majority of the delegates favored Bush for renomination, though a small minority did caucus with the Buchanan representatives present at the committee deliberations. Because Bush had little competition for the nomination, a number of committed issue activists were appointed as Bush delegates, though their primary allegiance might well have been to causes, not the party nominee. The lack of a contest in the Republican party seems to have had the effect of allowing "issue amateurs" to enter the process in prominent roles because of the laxity of Republican rules on nominee control over delegates pledged to them. Thus, in an ironic twist, issue activists whose prime concern was not winning the election but rather for specific policies came to play a key role in a Republican convention because of lack of candidate competition, the exact opposite circumstances under which issue purists gained prominence in the Democratic party.[7]

Information gathering. Platform writing is a political process, and the decisions on how to hold hearings, as a step in that process, are political decisions. In most recent years the Democrats have held hearings around the country in order to appear inclusive, while the Republicans have viewed the platform writing process as "in house" and have held relatively few public sessions, most often at the convention site just before the committee convenes. In 1992, however, the Republicans took their show on the road, holding hearings in San Diego, Kansas City, Salt Lake City, and Washington D.C., in advance of the Houston committee gathering. The cities were carefully chosen—Washington, for national exposure, and three Republican strongholds. The most controversial hearing, at which the abortion plank was open for discussion, was held in Salt Lake City, an obviously wise choice by those who did not want bad publicity from popular protests in the host city.

The Republicans sought to make political capital from the openness of their process, contrasting their process with the Democrats, in which only one hearing was held. In fact, Chairman Don Nickles's opening remarks to the national convention on 17 August cited the field hearings around the country and claimed, "Unlike the democrats, more than one hundred people testified, hundreds more wrote us their suggestions. . . . [O]ur process was prolonged, often passionate and very public."[8]

The staff draft. As had been true of the Democrats' Drafting Committee, when the Republican Committee on Resolutions began its work in Houston the week before the National Convention was to convene, it too began with a draft platform, a working paper, prepared by staff. Who the staff was, where they came from, how they worked, and how they interacted with the presidential campaign were all somewhat mysterious. But there was nothing new about thus mystery. More than half a century ago, Edward Sait noted that the basis of work by the resolutions committee was "a draft which someone has brought in his pocket."[9] Even then commentators had only vague ideas as to the document's author.

Committee on Resolutions documents for 1992 list an executive director (William Martin) with an immediate staff of five, three staff members assigned to the chair and cochairs, an editorial staff of four, a legal counsel, and twenty-one staff members including six lawyers assigned to six substantive subcommittees. None of these staff have prominent names, but many are familiar to those who have worked with Republican party committees over the years. What was clear from interviewing a number of the staff members was that many people knew something about the process, but few seemed to have a clear picture of the entire enterprise. Certainly Martin's role was important, but mainly administrative. Martin and platform editor in chief, William Gribbin, played roles in drafting the original working paper, but they did not work alone.

Two important names appeared on no committee documents—Republican campaign strategist Charles Black and Washington attorney and former Bush Cabinet secretary, Jim Cicconi; they were more involved in writing the first draft than anyone else, writing some themselves, shopping out portions to others, caring for the tone as well as the content. Similarly the name Jim Pinkerton does not appear as a committee staffer, but he too had a key role, eventually crafting the preamble as well as monitoring the platform to assure it rang the right neoconservative bells.

The draft platform, the starting point for committee deliberations, was carefully crafted to make the right appeals. Cicconi was the Bush-Quayle committee's man on the scene, working with staff to assure that the platform said what they wanted; he reported to Black, who only intervened at crucial times. They worked to achieve a tone consistent with the rhetoric Pinkerton had been producing for the new right; they worked through Martin and Gribbin and the other staff to achieve their ends. When the committee convened in Houston, they were presented with a document of over seventy pages divided into six sections for subcommittee deliberations and amendments. The basis of a platform was in place.

Subcommittee meetings. The draft platform was presented to six subcommittees that met in Houston just before the full committee convened the week before the national convention. Committee on Resolutions members were appointed to subcommittees by the chairman of the full committee, again after careful planning by the operatives from the Bush-Quayle Committee.

Thus, it was not by happenstance that thirteen of the twenty-one members of the Subcommittee on Individual Rights, Good Homes, and Safe Streets were female. Nor was it by chance that this subcommittee, which dealt with the controversial abortion plank, was chaired by Mary Potter Summa, an assistant district attorney from Charlotte, North Carolina, the former chief legislative assistant to Jesse Helms and a woman who according to the biography provided by the committee staff was "currently expecting her second child." Thirteen of the members were strongly pro-life, while only two impressed pro-choice views; the strongest advocate for choice on the subcommittee, Vermont State Senator John Carroll, was absent from subcommittee deliberations.

Similarly, thirteen of the eighteen members of the Subcommittee of Family Values, Education, and Health Care, including the chair and vice chair, were female. By contrast, sixteen of the twenty-one members of the Subcommittee of the Economy, Trade, Jobs, and the Budget were male; a majority of their views favored most conservative economic positions.

The role of the subcommittees was to debate and amend the draft prepared by staff and to report a new draft to the full committee. The subcommittees were given two days to accomplish this task. Unlike the Democrats' Drafting Committee, the Republican subcommittees followed a formal parliamentary procedures. The process resembled a mark-up session in the Congress. The one noticeable difference was that subcommittee staff members left the room to assure that Jim Cicconi approved the new language.

Full committee deliberations. The full committee meeting followed immediately upon the heels of the subcommittee deliberations. Shown nationally on C-SPAN, the full Committee on Resolutions debated the entire platform section by section. Nickles opened the first session but had to return to Washington for important Senate business. Ashcroft and McCullum chaired most of the day's deliberations.

The procedure was rather straightforward. Amendments had to be submitted in writing. They were debated and voted on, generally by voice vote or by a show of hands. Only on the abortion amendments was a roll call vote required. Ashcroft and McCullum gave the committee members a good deal of leeway in debating proposals; when he returned to the chair, Nickles exerted considerably tighter control. His attempt to speed the process resulted in some disgruntled committee members but allowed the group to finish its work in time for the social events that were obviously an important part of the preconvention week.

Adoption of the platform. The final step is the process was adoption of the platform by the full convention. The Committee on Resolutions draft was presented to the full convention by the chair. In turn, each subcommittee's section was presented by that group's chair. Minority planks required support from twenty-seven members of the Committee on Resolutions or from a majority of the convention delegates from six states. Only sixteen committee members supported the pro-choice alternative on the roll call vote, so the logical path to a minority report was through the state delegations. Two pro-choice groups, the Republican for Choice and the National Republican Coalition for Choice, were active in gaining public attention throughout the platform writing week, strove to reach this goal, but they fell short. Press reports emphasized that the Bush-Quayle committee worked hard to deny the minority an opportunity to embarrass the campaign with open floor debate on national television. Thus, the platform was adopted by the full committee without substantive debate and without amendment.

Commentary: Comparing Rules and Influences

A few distinctions should be noted. The rules of the two parties led to differences in the platform-writing process. The members of the Platform Committee elected in the various states were the only ones involved in adopting the Republican platform. In the Democratic party, the Drafting Committee, a committee appointed by the chair of the party with substantial input from the winning camp in 1992, played a major role. Related to this difference is the fact that the Clinton delegates to the Democratic platform committee caucused as a group and saw it as their mission to stand united against the delegates favoring the other candidates, while the Bush delegates—the vast majority in the Republican process—were less united behind Bush (against Buchanan) for they were committed to their own individual policy agendas.

Second, staff influence was very important in both cases. Democratic Chairman Ron Brown successfully structured the process so that the winning nominee could use the platform as another opportunity to bring the party together under his leadership. The Bush-Quayle Committee staff was in control of the Republican process, but they were less focused on how they wanted to use the platform in a strategic sense. When the leaders were chosen and the draft written, the committee seemed concerned about the Buchanan candidacy and about cementing the party's right wing against a challenge from Ross Perot. At the time at which the platform was amended and adopted, Perot had dropped out and platform committee seemed unnecessarily bent of excluding moderates from the Republican camp. This perception carried over into the general way in which the Republican National Convention was run and the picture portrayed for the nation.

The Influence of the Participants

Each party's platform went through three public drafts. Staff produced one draft; that draft went respectively to the subcommittees of the Republican Committee on Resolutions and to the Drafting Committee of the Democratic Platform Committee. The second draft emerged from the Republican subcommittees and the Democratic Drafting Committee. The third draft emerged from the two full committees and in each case was adopted by the national convention without amendment.

Methodology

The means used for analyzing the various drafts was detailed content analysis. The unit of analysis for this study was the paragraph. Each party platform was divided into major sections—six for the Republican and four for the Democrats—and subsections within these major headings. Some subsections were quite long, others only a sentence of two. Longer subsections tended to be broken into paragraphs, each of which dealt with one specific idea. The normal unit of analysis for a platform is a plank, but planks on which the entire platform is built are largely rhetorical fictions. The paragraph is the unit that can be defined and defended most rigorously.

Each paragraph is each draft of the two platforms was analyzed against the parallel paragraph in the subsequent draft. The comparison was characterized on a six item scale: no change; minor stylistic changes (word order, verb tense, individual words); major stylistic changes (expansion of ideas, inclusion of political rhetoric but not alteration of the policy advocated); substantive changes (different policies advocated); deletion; or addition (which were characterized as major or minor in terms of the scope of the policy advocated).

Three separate researchers read and characterized each paragraph, analyzing changes. When differences and resolved them to our mutual satisfaction. Fewer than 5 percent of the total paragraphs analyzed were coded differently. In addition, a running tally was kept of changes in subheadings. These changes were all rhetorical, not substantive. Little significance could be attributed to them.

The Republicans

The first conclusion one draws from looking at the content analysis of the drafts of the Republican platform is that there were very few changes at all. Over half of the paragraphs in the staff draft emerged unchanged from the subcommittees; almost another third of the paragraphs underwent only stylistic changes, and nearly half of those were only minor stylistic changes. An example of a minor stylistic change would be substituting the word "tenet" for "principle" when "principle" had been used in the sentence before. A more major change would be one such as the following:

> Staff draft: The kind of future is not a matter of chance; it is a question of personal responsibility. Barbara Bush captured the importance of that stewardship when she said, "In order to grow, you must choose a cause to serve larger than yourself."

> Subcommittee draft: The kind of future is not a matter of chance; it is a question of personal responsibility. Barbara Bush captured the importance of that stewardship when she said, "At the end of your life you will never regret not having passed one more test, not winning one more verdict, or not closing one more deal. You will regret time not spent with a husband, a child, a friend, or a parent."

One could certainly conclude that even this major stylistic change was only a minor change in the nature of the platform, highlighting again how few changes of substance were in fact made.

Of the fifty-five paragraphs added to the platform, most would be considered minor. Frequently two or three paragraphs were added on the same subject, first laying out the general area to be discussed and then stating the specific proposal. An example of this is the following two-paragraph addition (the first deemed minor the second major on the subject of education):

> Recognizing what every parent knows, that our current educational system is not educating our children, President Bush is leading an education revolution. We applaud the President's bold vision to change radically our education system. Our parents want it, our communities want it, our States want it, and our children want it—but the Democrat leadership in the House and the Senate continue to thwart the will of the American people for radical change in the way we educate our children.

> The Republican strategy is based on sound principle—that parents have the right to choose the best school for their children; that schools should teach right from wrong; that schools should reinforce parental authority, not replace it; that we should increase flexibility from federal regulation; that we should explore a new generation of break-the-mold New American Schools; that standards and assessments should be raised, not reduced to a lowest common denominator; that communities should be empowered to find what works; that the pursuit of excellence in education is a fundamental goal; that good teachers should be rewarded for teaching well; that alternative certification can bring desperately needed new people into the teaching profession; and that America needs public, private, and parochial schools.

These paragraphs were quoted at length because they demonstrate the kinds of additions to the platform deemed minor and major. Essentially the first paragraph is a lead-in to the entire issue of choice in the schools and the ways in which the Republicans view their ideas as different from the Democrats.

A high percentage of the changes in the draft made by the subcommittees were changes wrought by the subcommittee of the Economy, Trade, Jobs, and the Budget. This subcommittee, which included among its members two members of Congress who had been critical of Bush's handling of the economy (Robert Walker of Pennsylvania and Vin Weber of Minnesota) and a number of other staunch economic conservatives, got away from the control of the Bush-Quayle forces. At one point the subcommittee adopted a paragraph saying that Bush had made a mistake in agreeing to the budget compromise that led to a tax increase. Charles Black decided that language would not be acceptable in a Republican platform and worked with the subcommittee leaders as well as Bush critics to find compromise language. Eventually the subcommittee, which had concluded its business, was called back into session to adopt the compromise and rid the draft of direct criticism of the president. Thus, many of the changes, including many of the major changes and half of the deletions, were the result of the efforts of a small group to force the party to accept its view of the state of the economy, past as well as future.

Changes made at the full committee level are even more interesting to note. Those observing the process noted how democratic the entire process seemed. Any member of the full committee was able to amend the platform at any point. Those who had attended the Democratic Platform Committee's meeting in June saw a somewhat ironic contrast in that the Republican process appeared to be more open and more democratic than was that of the party renowned for opening its process to all comers. In point of fact, few of the changes made by the full committee were substantive at all. In fact, fewer than a fifth of the over one hundred amendments passed by the full committee could be deemed substantive. Most were stylistic, and nearly half were very minor in nature.

While observers were first impressed with the democratic nature of the Republican process, by the end of the two-day meeting, the most common remarks dealt with how amazing it was that so many people sat still for so long debating items of so little consequence. Virtually the entire Committee on Resolutions—senators, members of Congress, state legislators, as well as less prominent individuals—sat for hour after hour debating changes such as whether the words "the peace and security of the Middle East" should be added after "world peace" in the sentence, "Without the leadership of President Bush, Iraq would today threaten world peace and the very survival of Israel with a huge conventional army and nuclear weapons." Some important changes were made at the full committee meeting, for instance, the addition of a plank calling for the line item veto. However, the vast majority of the amendments, and the majority of the time debating the proposed amendments, addressed quite trivial matters, often a preference for one person's style and rhetoric over another's.

Nearly three-quarters of the paragraphs that the subcommittees submitted to the full committee emerged unchanged. Over 95 percent of the paragraphs did not change substantively. The only conclusion one can reach is that the full committee, despite its hours of work and the presence of a relatively large number of prominent Republicans, did very little. The staff draft, with some additions by the subcommittees but little change in the substance of the remaining paragraphs, became the Republican platform. Praise or blame should rest with the Bush-Quayle committee operatives who appointed the committee leadership, drafted the platform, and established subcommittee membership so that those with incentive to change the draft were not able to do so. The religious right and the economic conservatives might have dominated the Committee of Resolutions, but the platform they approved came from the presidential campaign, not from right-wing bastions.

The Democrats

Comparison with the Democrats is instructive. First, the Democratic platform in 1992—at every stage in the process—was much shorter than that of the Republicans. On the other hand, the 1992 Democratic platform was much longer than that in 1988. The goal was to strike a balance between offering something for everyone—and in so doing not really setting priorities—and saying so little that the platform did not appeal to those who need to hear its appeals.

Second, relatively little of the Democratic platform remained intact after the staff draft. Only twelve of the eighty-two paragraphs in the staff draft remained in the version that emerged from the Drafting Committee. But most of the changes, forty-six of the eighty-five, were stylistic, not substantive changes. That follows logically from the process. John Holum crafted the first draft and the second. In many ways the staff draft presented to the Drafting Committee was an unfinished product. Holum had another shot and edited and revised his own work. Unlike the Republican platform, which was amended only through the formal process of amendment proposing and votes, the Democratic platform was amended by its principal author and editor.

At the same time, five of the eighty-two paragraphs were substantively changed, nineteen were dropped, and fifteen new ones were added. That is a substantial amount of amendment by the Drafting Committee.

Again, examples are important. The Drafting Committee version included a long and detailed paragraph on "The Cities" that was absent in the staff working paper. Related to that were paragraphs on drug counseling and housing. The Drafting Committee document had a paragraph on immigration absent in the earlier version; under "National Security" a paragraph dealt with human rights, again missing from the earlier version. The paragraphs on industrial relations were substantially altered, again bringing in matters not previously included.

At the full committee the major additions dealt with agriculture and rural policies, a glaring omission from the earlier drafts, and with additional material on equal and civil rights. Also a number of environmental planks were altered or in one case added, but they generally dealt with noncontroversial, traditional Democratic positions that had previously been excluded, but probably assumed. Roughly two-thirds of the paragraphs remained intact when the full committee reviewed the Drafting Committee's version. Another quarter were changed stylistically, while only two paragraphs were altered substantively and five new ones were added.

The obvious conclusion from table 18.1 seems to be that the Democratic platform was a draft in progress before it went to Drafting Committee in Sante Fe. The members of the Drafting Committee had the opportunity for input and exercised that opportunity, but mainly to add material that had been missing, not to change that which was present. The clear impression from committee discussion was that much of the delegation and tightening was at the behest of the full committee chairs, who were of the opinion that the first document was too long and not focused enough.

Who Influenced the Process?

This analysis leads to naturally to a number of somewhat unexpected conclusions. First, conventional wisdom held that the religious right and, to a lesser extent, the economic conservatives, gained control of the Republican Committee on Resolutions and saddled President Bush with an extremist platform on which he had difficulty running. In fact, while those groups were present in large numbers and could have had control over the platform writing process had they exercised the power inherent in their numerical domination, the Bush-Quayle operatives who drafted the original version of the platform had the most influence. Their original draft survived in large part without amendment. When the economic conservatives sought to amend the draft, they were beaten back by the president's advisers pleading for party unity. In the Republican Party it is clear that the drafters had the most influence, not the vocal and visible representatives of the party's right wing.

While this conclusion flies in the face of the conventional journalistic wisdom regarding the 1992 Republican Convention and the role that the religious right played in Houston, it is not out of line with previous scholarly examinations of the platform process. In 1960, Paul David, Ralph Goldman, and Richard Bain commented on White House control of the process when an incumbent president was seeking reelection, "The actual drafting is performed by a relatively small group of leaders and specialists—in the case of the party in power usually with active White House participation. . . ."[10]

In both parties one is left to question the importance of the political struggles for seats on the platform committees. The members of the two full committees had relatively little to say about the substance of the documents that emerged from the two national conventions. In normal years this conclusion would not be surprising for the party that controls the White

House, especially with an incumbent president in power, can control his national committee and presumably his national convention. That conventional wisdom was challenged in the Republican Party in 1992 because many felt that the right wing had captured the organizational mechanisms of the party. That conclusion might well be valid if one looks at state committees and even at some state delegations of state after state. But if the platform represents a party's effort to define itself, to state what it stands for, then the conclusion has limited relevance. The 1992 Republican platform was a statement of what the Bush-Quayle committee, for political reasons that only the committee's strategist can explain, felt was best for their candidate. If the platform was a flawed document for political proposes, it was flawed because of miscalculation and/or neglect, not because of dominance by GOP extremists. Of course, one can only speculate whether the Committee on Resolutions would have played a more active role—moving the platform to the ideological right—had the Bush-Quayle campaign presented it with a more moderate draft. Surely in the past the committee members have played important roles on such controversial issues as civil rights in both parties in 1960.[11]

In normal years the conclusion that seats on the Platform Committee are not positions of any influence would seem surprising for the party out of power. Generally, one thinks of representatives of contenders for the party nomination fighting for symbolic victories in the platform long after they have lost their bids for nomination. "While incumbent presidents standing for election have dominated their conventions and obtained platforms that pledge to continue the policies of their administrations, other presidential candidates have not been in such a commanding position. . . ."[12] One thinks of fights for the soul of the party—battles between George McGovern's delegates and more traditional Democrats on 1972, between Jimmy Carter and Morris Udall delegates in 1976, between Carter and Ted Kennedy delegates in 1980, between Michael Dukakis and Jesse Jackson delegates in 1988. The examples in the Republican Party are less clear because the moderates have never had enough influence to effect platform change. However, the fight over the abortion plank in 1988 is a pertinent example, albeit one without a presidential contender as champion.

In 1992 the scenario was different for at least two reasons. Ron Brown's role and his influence deserve special attention. First, early in the process he sought to assure peace within the party. He brought the contenders together to set ground rules for the intraparty battle well before the first ballot was cast. He facilitated meetings between the defeated candidates and the eventual nominee. Bill Clinton was assured of the Democratic nomination relatively early in the process. Brown's efforts contributed to Clinton's ability to build a unified campaign for the future.[13] After the nomination was assured, but before either Sen. Paul Tsongas or Gov. Jerry Brown had officially dropped out, Ron Brown worked hard to make certain that the party

Table 18.1　Changes in the Drafts of the Party Platforms

Republicans	Paragraphs		Same	Minor Stylistic	Major Stylistic	Substantive	Deleted	Added
Changes by subcommittees								
Family values, education, and health care	64,	70	31	15	11	1	3	9
Individual rights, good homes, and safe streets	43,	40	31	5	4	0	3	0
Economy, trade, jobs, and the budget	65,	83	32	13	10	0	7	25
Reforming government and the legal system	45,	50	24	12	9	0	1	6
Our land, food, and resources	50,	59	30	4	16	0	0	9
Foreign policy, national defense, and intelligence	85,	91	56	13	14	0	0	6
Total	352,	394	204	62	67	1	14	55
Changes by full Committee								
Family values, education, and health care	70,	76	58	8	4	1	0	6
Individual rights, good homes, and safe streets	40,	43	32	2	4	0	1	4
Economy, trade, jobs, and the budget	83,	90	52	19	7	0	1	8
Reforming government and the legal system	59,	55	43	2	6	0	0	5
Our land, food, and resources	59,	65	51	3	5	0	0	6
Foreign policy, national defense, and intelligence	91,	92	72	8	10	1	0	1
Total	394,	421	308	42	36	1	2	30

Changes by Drafting Committee							
Opportunity	16, 17	0	4	8	1	3	4
Responsibility	16, 11	0	7	2	2	5	0
Community	20, 18	3	7	3	0	7	5
National security	30, 32	9	5	10	2	4	6
Total	82, 78	12	23	23	5	19	15
Changes by Full Committee							
Opportunity	17, 21	10	4	2	1	0	4
Responsibility	11, 11	5	4	2	0	0	0
Community	18, 18	13	2	3	0	0	0
National Security	32, 33	28	1	2	1	0	1
Total	78, 83	56	1	9	2	0	5

came together behind the Clinton candidacy and that the convention was a coronation, not a cat fight. Partially as a result of that effort, various elements of the Democratic Party worked together on platform, not in opposition to each other.

Second, the process stressed the importance of the Drafting Committee. Members were appointed by Chairman Brown either on the direct nomination of the Clinton camp, or in case of appointees who represented key components of the Democrats' camp. Drafting Committee members did have influence, and they did not carry their fights to the extreme of threatening to disrupt the unity behind that candidacy. Ron Brown's choices, his influence, and his firm commitment to work with Clinton all contributed to this harmony.

A third conclusion deals with informal as opposed to formal influence. In the Republican Party Vin Weber and his allies on the Subcommittee on the Economy could muster the requisite number of votes in the subcommittee to challenge the White House's view of past economic challenges. But they could not maintain their view in the face of pressure from Charles Black and Bush-Quayle campaign.

In the Democratic Party, Drafting Committee members worried that they might express their concerns but that changes would not be follow. However, a number of changes were indeed made; the careful observer can trace those changes to the influence of key participants: Mayor Kurt Schmoke of Baltimore, who worried that the cities' views were not adequately expressed; Congressman (and later Agriculture Secretary) Mike Espy of Mississippi, who had similar concerns on agriculture policy; County Supervisor (and later HUD Assistant Secretary) Roberta Achtenberg from San Francisco and Professor Mary Frances Berry, who fought for language on women's health care and on equal and civil rights; Ken Young of the AFL-CIO and the other labor representatives who were concerned about industrial relations. Membership on the Drafting Committee meant that individuals could have the shape of the final platform.

However, even that influence was at the margin. For more than anything else, the 1992 Democratic platform was a done deal. It was a meeting at Democratic Leadership Council headquarters on the eve of the full committee's deliberation, DLC president and executive director Al From polled DLC leaders on how they should react to all of the changes wrought in "their program" by the Drafting Committee. He worried that the changes had whittled away at DLC's coherent plan. One of those present pulled out a *New York Times* analysis of the platform, an examination that concluded that DLC fingerprints were scattered throughout the document. The conclusion of the assembled leaders? Declare victory. Let others have their small prizes, for the platform was a victory for moderate Democrats' view of how to capture the White House.

Conclusion

Finally, what does this analysis say about the roles of the platform in American political process? First, in 1992 at least, the platform writing process represented another example of the appearance but not the reality of democracy. Writing a platform was not a case of intraparty democracy. It was not a case of fighting for the soul of the party. It was not a case of intraparty battles over the direction the country will take. Someday those descriptions might be appropriate for a party not controlling the White House, if there is a pitched battle for the nomination. But platform fighting, indeed all platform drafting, is done in the context if the presidential election, not as an independent political process.

And that statement leads directly to the second conclusion. Under current practices, platforms really are not party platforms; rather, like the election process itself, they are now presidential candidate-centered platforms. They are the platforms on which the candidates feel comfortable running. They are platforms that party leaders allow, even encourage, the nominees' staff to write. In essence, they are the ultimate indication that the parties exist to win the presidential election, not to push policy agendas. The policy content of party in this is contained in the belief that the candidates of the party really are different in fundamental ways, but that the spectrum of issues on which a candidate runs is so broad that he or she ought to be able to define those due for emphasis. In today's political world that is perhaps how it should be, for the parties are seen in terms of their presidential candidates, not the other way around.

Of course, this conclusion does not seem surprising for the party of an incumbent president seeking reelection. Incumbents have always been able to control their conventions and to run on a platform of their choosing, emphasizing the accomplishments of their term of office. In 1992 the journalistic wisdom was that Bush did not exercise that kind of control. In fact, he did. If the platform and the convention hurt his campaign, the blow was self-inflicted.

The conclusion does seem somewhat odd for the nonincumbent candidate, especially for the nonincumbent candidate whose party does not control the White House. Lame duck presidents have been quite successful at having their parties draft platforms that support the accomplishments of their administration, even if some of those policies caused controversies. For example, Lyndon Johnson's Vietnam policy was endorsed, albeit with a floor fight on a minority plank, by the 1968 Democratic Convention. Remember other recent Democratic examples: George McGovern's nominating convention was dominated by platform fights, and similar battles were prominent features of Jimmy Carter's 1976 convention and Mike Dukakis's 1988 convention. But circumstances play important roles. According to Edward Sait, "Bryan dictated the 1908 platform over long-distance telephone."[14] And David, Goldman, and Bain remind us of the early years of platform writing: "The platform-drafting function had evolved out of the occasional efforts to prepare 'an address to the people,' and had become accepted as a normal part of the convention routine [by 1860]. Early platform drafting, when it occurred at all, was usually deferred until after the nomination had been made."[15] Thus, when we conclude that the platform-writing process has become candidate-centered, and if we believe that that seems innovative for the party out of power, we are well advised to remember that recent history is not all of party history, that common views of the process do not necessarily conform with more rigorous studies.[16]

The conclusion that platforms in 1992 were candidate, not party platforms in turn leads to another. If platforms are candidate platforms, then we should not be surprised that victorious candidates attempt to implement their platforms and that congressional parties of victorious candidates support major items in the platform. These issues define the winning candidate. The priority items in the platform are issues that the public, who voted for the winner, associates with the winner. And, despite the fact that neither the public nor the party regulars qua party activists determine how the platform's planks were drafted, it is totally appropriate that the victor and the victor's party be judged on their ability to implement their platform and on the extent to which the items called for in the platform address the problems confronting the nation.

Notes

1. American Political Science Association (APSA), Committee on Political Parties, *Toward a More Responsible Two-Party System* (New York: Rinehart, 1950).

2. See Gerald M. Pomper, "Controls and Influence in American Elections (Even 1968)," *American Behavioral Scientist* (November-December 1969): 215-28; Pomper, *Elections in America: Control and Influence in Democratic Politics* (New York: Dodd, Mead, 1970), 149-70; Pomper, "From Confusion to Clarity: Issues and American Voters, 1952-1968," *American Political Science Review* 66 (June 1972): 415; Pomper, *Party Renewal in America* (New York: Longman, 1980; and Jeff Fishel, *Presidential and Promises* (Washington, D.C.: Congressional Quarterly Press, 1985).

3. Morris P. Fiorina, *Retrospective Voting in American National Elections* (New Haven: Yale University Press, 1981); Fiorina, "Retrospective Voting" in L. Sandy Maisel, Ed., *Political Parties and Elections in the United States: An Encyclopedia* (New York: Garland Publishing Co., 1991).

4. See, as examples, Edward McCheney Sait, *American Parties and Elections*, rev. ed. (New York: D. Appleton-Century, 1939), 563-73; Paul T. David, Malcolm Moos, and Ralph M. Goldman, *Presidential Nominating Politics in 1952: Volume I: The National Story* (Baltimore: The Johns Hopkins Press, 1954); David Goldman and Richard C. Bain, *The Politics of National Party Conventions* (Washington, D.C.: Brookings Institution, 1960); and Judith H. Parris, *The Convention Problem: Issues in the Reform of Presidential Nominating Procedures* (Washington, D.C.: Brookings Institution, 1972), 109-41.

5. L. Sandy Maisel, *Parties and Elections in America: The Electoral Process*, 2nd ed. (New York: McGraw-Hill, 1993), 252–53.

6. Parris, *The Convention Problem*, 115.

7. See Jeanne J. Kirkpatrick, *Dismantling the Parties* (Washington, D.C.: American Enterprise Institute for Public Policy Research, 1978); Kirkpatrick, *The New Presidential Elite: Men and Women in National Politics* (New York: Russell Sage, 1976); Denis G. Sullivan, Robert T. Nakamura, Martha Wagner Weinberg, F. Christopher Arterton, and Jeffrey L. Pressman, "Exploring the 1976 Republican Convention," *Political Science Quarterly* 92 (winter 1977/1978): 531; Sullivan, Pressman, Arterton, Nakamura, and Weinberg, "Candidates, Caucuses, and Issues: The Democratic Convention, 1976" in Louis Maisel and Joseph Cooper, eds., *The Impact of the Electoral Process* (Beverly Hills, Calif.: Sage, 1977); Sullivan, Pressman, and Arterton, *Explorations in Convention Decisionmaking: The Democratic Party in the 1970s* (San Francisco: Freeman, 1976).

8. Republican Platform Committee press release, 17 August 1993. (Emphasis in original.)

9. Sait, *American Parties and Elections*, 566.

10. David, Goldman, and Bain, *The Politics of National Party Conventions*, 407; see also, Parris, *The Convention Problem*, 121.

11. See Parris, *The Convention Problem*, 126–28

12. Ibid., 123.

13. Martin P. Wattenberg, "The Republican Presidential Advantage in the Age of Party Disunity," in Gary W. Cox and Samuel Kernell, eds., *The Politics of Divided Government* (Boulder, Colo.: Westview Press, 1991).

14. Sait, *American Parties and Elections*, 564.

15. David, Goldman, and Bain, *The Politics of National Party Conventions*, 29.

16. See Mather D. McCubbins, "Party Decline and Presidential Campaigns in the Television Age" in Mathew D. McCubbins, ed., *Under the Watchful Eye: Managing Presidential Campaigns in the Television Era* (Washington, D.C.: CQ Press, 1992).

19

The Contract with America in the 104th Congress

Robin Kolodny

The 104th Congress has secured a place in political history because of the existence of a document known as the Contract with America. The Contract was devised as a campaign tool for Republican congressional candidates to use in the 1994 midterm congressional elections. What makes the Contract fundamentally different from other campaign tools is that Republican leaders in the House presented it as the governing document that the party would follow if the electorate made Republicans a majority party.

Thus, the Contract appears to be the sort of vehicle that advocates of responsible parties have long desired. Supporters of party government hold that a healthy democracy provides "coherent, unified set of rulers who will assume collective responsibility to the people for the manner in which the government is carried on" (Ranney 1962: 12). That such a "platform" should be produced by a congressional party in a midterm election is remarkable.

The problem, though, with viewing the Contract in these terms is that only a portion of the Republican Party embraced the party government idea, making the overall premise of collective responsibility unworkable. Russell Riley has recently argued that for advocates of responsible parties, it is hard to know "whether the midterm election results were a glass half empty or half full" (Riley 1995: 703). On the one hand, the Contract gave voters the opportunity to evaluate the desirability of a specific party program presented to them. On the other hand, to achieve true party government (like in the British parliament), one party would have to control all popularly elected branches of the government (Schattschneider 1942). The 1994 elections provided divided government all over again, though in a form not seen since the 1946 elections (that is, a Democratic president and a Republican Congress). In addition, it is widely believed that congressional party leaders do not possess sufficient inducements for allegiance by their average members. Though factors such as the direct primary, campaign finance system, and universal reward structure in Congress do deter strong party leadership, Beck and Sorauf declare, "Still, there is a possibility, albeit remote, that the increased resources of the national (and perhaps even state) party organizations might be employed to enforce some degree of ideological discipline." (Beck and Sorauf 1992: 433)

This chapter argues that the Contract was created by a subgroup of House Republicans who were committed to the notion of responsible party governance, but were naive about the chances for party government in the United States Congress. The House Republicans have been unable to advance many of their proposals in large measure because of opposition from fellow Republicans in the Senate. However, some of the more successful and lasting effects of the Contract are changes Republican leaders made in the institutional structure of the House to allow responsible parties to function more easily. The mixed success of the Contract also reveals the problems and limits of such a bold initiative.

The House Republicans before the Contract with America

One of the lamentable artifacts of the House Democrats' long majority rule (from 1955 to 1995) is the lack of understanding of the House Republicans during the last forty years. Only two books have been published on the topic during this time: Jones (1970) and Connelly and Pitney (1994).[1] The overwhelming bulk of scholarly literature on the House made little mention of the Republicans. Thus, their current majority status comes as more of a shock than perhaps it should. The common impression presented in the literature was of a homogeneous permanent minority that assumed the part of loyal opposition and played a peripheral role in policy debate. While this is normally the predicament of minority parties in legislatures, the House Republicans were in the unique situation of serving with Republican presidents throughout much of this period, and did not necessarily see themselves as passive receivers of a Republican president's wishes. Rather, they believed that they had the right to agree or differ with presidential proposals. When they did differ, the consequences could result in extreme partisan bickering and policy stalemates.[2]

Until the election of President Ronald Reagan in 1980, the Republican Party generally was perceived as economically conservative and socially moderate. After Reagan's nomination, it became clear that the party had taken a more conservative turn on social issues. The ideological changes in the House Republican Conference by the 1980s led to perceptible changes in their outlook and behavior. Instead of being conciliatory participants in the policy-making process, many House Republicans became confrontational, emphasizing their differences with moderates (of both parties). Eventually, some of the members who preferred confrontation to conciliation began to command more attention (Connelly and Pitney 1994: chap. 2). The most important subgroup, the Conservative Opportunity Society (COS), began to attract public attention by exposing a schism in the House Republican Conference.

The 1989 contest for Republican whip clearly reflected this division. After whip Dick Cheney (R-Wyo) resigned from the House of Representatives to accept the position of Secretary of Defense in the Bush administration, an open contest developed to fill his post. Two major candidates were Ed Madigan (R-Ill) and Newt Gingrich (R-Ga). Madigan was a member of the conciliatory school and a midwestern moderate. In contrast, Gingrich was the chief architect of the confrontational school (Connelly and Pitney 1994: 27). Gingrich won by a one-vote margin, 89–87. According to Koopman (1991), Gingrich owed his election not so much to conservative members, whose numbers were not sufficient to forge a majority within the Republican Conference, but to moderates who were growing weary of being ignored by the Democratic majority. Many in the ideological center of the Republican Conference felt that Gingrich's more aggressive style was the only way for House Republicans to become a majority party, or at the very least signal to presidents and Senate Republicans that they were not to be taken for granted.

Starting after the 1990 elections, there was much speculation over the retirement plans of House minority leader Robert Michel (R-Ill). The presumption was that Gingrich would become the new party leader upon Michel's departure. Anticipating Michel's retirement, Gingrich became heavily involved in the 1992 and 1994 elections with the hope that these years would see a significant increase in the number of Republican members who might support his leadership. Gingrich's substantial efforts formed the basis of his consideration as floor leader when Michel's retirement was announced at the end of the 103rd Congress—and for his ultimate acclamation as Speaker at the beginning of the 104th Congress.

House Republicans believed 1992 afforded significant possibilities: a near record number of members were slated to retire. Indeed, the mantra of the House Republicans became "one hundred open seats," and their electoral arm, the National Republican Congressional Committee (NRCC), was mobilized for the elections. Guy Vander Jagt (R-Mich), chair of the organization, had just survived a leadership challenge amidst allegations of sloppy management and poor strategic decision making and felt pressure to mount a major effort (Kolodny 1991). Despite considerable anticipation, the election was a near-bust for Republicans, netting them only a ten seat gain. However, there were signs of growing GOP strength in the House: it was the first time since 1882 that a president's party gained seats in the House while the president himself lost reelection (Herrnson 1995: 23).

Ironically, Vander Jagt was defeated in his own primary election in the summer of 1992. This created a vacancy at the NRCC and led to the selection of Rep. Bill Paxon (R-NY) as chair. When Paxon, a young and energetic

Gingrich protege, assumed control, he was confronted with a large debt left from the 1992 election cycle and held a more aggressive view of the role of the NRCC. In the recent past, members relied on the NRCC for a steady stream of cash and other resources for their own reelection campaigns, earning it a reputation as an "incumbent protection committee."[3]   Paxon sought and received assistance from the Republican National Committee (RNC) to alleviate the NRCC's debt and to assist in a successful electoral strategy for 1994. The reforms Paxon employed are too numerous to recount here, but one of the most noteworthy accomplishments was his insisting (together with Gingrich) that incumbent members contribute money out of their own campaign funds to challenger and open seat candidates. The argument was that the collective goal of winning the majority was more valuable than the extra few thousand dollars added to incumbent war chests. This became the basis for the 1994 electoral strategy and prompted the evolution of the Contract.[4]

The Origins of the Contract with America

Bill Paxon was not the only new Republican party leader after 1992. Haley Barbour was elected chair of the RNC at about the same time Paxon took over at the NRCC. Barbour inherited an organization bruised and battered by President George Bush's defeat. Since he did not have the White House to worry about in the immediate future, Barbour sought a working relationship with Republicans in Congress. There was resistance to these overtones at first. The RNC had more of a reputation for ignoring congressional Republicans than for helping them. But with a double change at both the NRCC and RNC, communications became easier and interactions more frequent. Barbour formed good working relationships with Gingrich as well. Together these three constructed an integrated party strategy for the 1994 election.

A critical move by Barbour was his creation of an office of congressional affairs at the RNC. Barbour intended this office to parallel the work of the Republican Governors' Association and to coordinate strategy and message with Republicans in Congress. The office was staffed with a House liaison and a Senate liaison, whose offices were located immediately adjacent to Barbour's, illustrating Barbour's commitment to work directly with the congressional Republicans. Indeed, Barbour stated in his 1993 report that "there is nothing we can do to help elect a Republican president in 1996 that is nearly as important as winning a big Republican victory in 1994" (Republican National Committee 1993: 12).

The RNC's commitment to the midterm congressional elections was also evident in the amounts of money raised and spent. The RNC lent the NRCC critical funds early in 1993 when debts threatened the organization with bankruptcy, and directly spending over $5.1 million on House elections. An additional $400,000 was spent on disseminating the Contract message alone (Barnes 1995: 474). Several key members of the RNC staff were involved in the development of the Contract document from the time it was formally initiated in the spring of 1994 through its debut in September of 1994.[5] The RNC also paid for the production of the paperback book version of the Contract with America.[6]

Part of the Gingrich/Paxon/Barbour strategy was to develop a common public agenda for challengers. Using an idea Gingrich had long espoused, the Republican Conference agreed to develop eleven task forces to flesh out legislative ideas on the theme of what the Republicans would do if they controlled the House. Gingrich believed they could enact a historic program in one hundred days, similar to Roosevelt's New Deal agenda. In July and August of 1994, the task forces went to work. They were aided by information gleaned from focus group studies conducted by the RNC and NRCC concerning the phrasing that should be used in various Contract items as well as reaction to the concept of the Contract as a whole. Some items were fairly simple to compose, being either straightforward ideas or based on bills previously introduced by Republican members. Other ideas, such as the proposal for welfare reform, were more difficult.[7] The members were under severe time constraints, and the particulars were glossed over. One of the more creative aspects of the Contract was the clause where members and candidates would promise to bring these proposals to the floor of the House and hold a vote on all of them, but it did not promise an affirmative vote on all the items in the agenda. This escape clause weakens claims to responsible party governance by stating up front that the party has no authority to issue sanctions for disloyalty to the Contract.

Gingrich had long envisioned such a scheme. When Gingrich became whip in 1989, he appointed two deputy whips, Bob Walker (R-Penn) and Steve Gunderson (R-Wis). Walker was assigned to the parliamentary details on the floor, while Gunderson was asked to create a strategic issue agenda for the House Republican Party. In fact, Gingrich specifically asked Gunderson to come up with ten items for a possible Republican agenda.[8] Gingrich was so interested in this concept that he also used the resources of GOPAC (G.O.P. Political Action Committee, a PAC designed to recruit Republican candidates at the state and local levels), which he chaired, to work on ideas for a potential campaign agenda and to hammer out a strategy to disseminate these ideas to future candidates (Seelye 1995: 26). This part of Gingrich's thinking explains much about the origins and effects of the Contract. Though there is no denying that the Contract was designed as part of an explicit campaign strategy, it is also true that it comes out of an ideological agenda.

Use of the Contract in the 1994 Elections

Once the Contract was completed, the NRCC and RNC arranged for an elaborate unveiling. On September 27, 1994, they assembled all the Republican candidates who agreed to sign the Contract[9] on the steps of the Capitol and invited the press to watch. Though the assembly made for an impressive media event, few observers (and even a good number of event participants) took the possibility of enacting the Contract seriously. News of its existence quickly died.

Another interesting question is how candidates used the Contract in their own campaigns. Most senior Republican House members made little use of the document or ignored it entirely.[10] Though they all hoped to move into the majority, it was deemed unlikely and continued their proven campaign strategies. The utility of the Contract for nonincumbent candidates was another matter. Without the benefit of previous electoral success in the House of Representatives (or in many cases any electoral experience whatsoever),[11] challenger and open seat candidates were more receptive to the idea of using the Contract as a campaign tool. However, few nonincumbents used the notion of a party agenda for a potential majority party in their campaigns. Instead, they used the Contract as a resource for campaign themes, choosing from the balanced budget amendment, welfare reform, legal reform, and so forth, as it suited their needs, particularly to localize national issues (Jacobson 1995).

Postelection Effects of the Contract

By now, the results of the 1994 election are well known. All Republican incumbents won reelection and thirty-four Democratic incumbents were defeated. Of the fifty-two open seats, Republicans won thirty-nine, and carried twenty-two of thirty-one previously Democratic open seats, while holding seventeen of twenty-one of their own. In all, the 104th Congress has two hundred and thirty-six Republicans, one hundred and ninety-eight Democrats and one Independent.

Virtually all Republican members, with the possible exception of Gingrich and his closest followers, were shocked (Abramowitz 1995: 874; Ornstein and Schenkenberg 1995: 184). The much-hyped majority had been achieved. Several factors help explain the Republican victory. In many areas of the South, a Republican-based realignment appears under way. Money also played an important role, with nonincumbent Republicans significantly better funded than they have been in the past. Republicans accounted for eighteen of the richest twenty-five challenger candidates in terms of cash received (*Roll Call*, October 27, 1994). Many believe that the election contained a significant element of white male backlash. Gary Jacobson (1995) argues that an unusually large portion of the electorate voted locally as they had been voting nationally; that is, Republicans gained seats in areas where they had done well in presidential races, but where Democratic incumbents held on in congressional and state-level elections. Overall, he reports that Republican gains were due in large measure to a strong crop with highly qualified candidates—something the Republicans had suffered from in the past. It seems clear that the Contract itself had little bearing on the outcome, with few voters knowing anything about it. Indeed, polls showed that only 28 percent of the electorate heard of the Contract before the election (Bardes 1996; see also Ladd 1995: 10).

Interestingly, the real impact of the Contract was not felt until the immediate postelection spin. Having ignored both the House Republicans and the Contract, the media scrambled to cover the Contract. Republican members who had not taken the idea of a Republican majority or the Contract seriously also scrambled to find answers to the question, What next? Consider their extraordinary situation: their previous leader had retired, they had few members and almost no staff who had served in a Republican majority, and they had promised to act upon a legislative agenda that included few details. Out of both convenience and necessity, the new Republican majority grasped the Contract as a starting point. Suddenly, Speaker-elect Gingrich and many from the Republican majority were talking about the "mandate" the voters had just given them. Not surprisingly, the new Republican majority began to act as though it believed it had been given a clear and undeniable message from the people.[12]

The new majority seized the moment and moved rapidly to prepare for the historic 104th Congress. November and December of 1994 were filled with frenetic activity. After all, the institution not only had to change partisan hands, but according to the Contract had to be reinvented as well. The Republicans selected their leaders committee and subcommittee chairs, hired more Republican staff while eliminating many Democratic staff positions, began to reallocate office space, and started laying plans for bringing all the items in the Contract to the floor in the first one hundred days of the session. In order to both consider the Contract and take care of all other necessary legislation business (the budget issues in particular), the Republican leadership decided to begin work on legislative business immediately upon swearing the new members in. In previous congresses, it was customary to swear members in on January 3 (the date required by the Constitution) and then recess to give new members time to move into their offices and hire staff. Not this time; the 104th Congress began with a whoosh.

It is hard to comprehend the tremendous repercussions the change in majority control had on the House. In addition to absorbing an unusually large freshman class (a total of 86, 73 of whom were Republicans), members of both parties had to adjust to tremendous changes in the organization and operation of the committee system and House rules. The congressional reforms passed on the first day of the 104th Congress bear this out. The Republicans approved a series of rules changes that included elimination of three full congressional committees; realignment or "tightening" of committee jurisdictions; a one-third reduction in the number of staff for committees; limiting the number of subcommittees per committee; restricting members to no more than two full standing committee memberships; eliminating proxy voting in committees; publishing of all committee votes; eliminating rolling quorums (chairmen of committees holding votes open indefinitely while waiting for members to arrive); term limits on the Speaker of the House (four) and committee chairs (three); consolidating administrative offices; commissioning a House audit by an outside auditor; and eliminating of all indirect support for legislative service organizations (*CQ Weekly Report*, 1995a). One outcome of this reorganization was to give an extraordinary amount of power to the Republican leadership to make order out of chaos. For example, Gingrich was permitted to violate seniority norms in naming committee chairs. This helped move items through committees quickly and bring them to the floor under favorable circumstances. Such allegiance to the leadership did not last in the post-Contract period the way it had during the Contract, but it is nonetheless still significant (Riley 1995: 705–6).

The new Democratic minority had many adjustments to make as well. They were not expecting the change and were utterly devastated. Their leader, Thomas Foley (D-Wash) was defeated for his own reelection. All the remaining incumbent leaders (including the de facto top leader Richard Gephardt) were challenged for their posts, an almost unheard-of situation for House Democrats, who usually reelect their leaders without contention. In addition, many southern Democrats were actively courted to switch over to the Republican ranks.[13] The biggest surprise was that the House Democrats had virtually nothing constructive to say in opposition to the Contract agenda. (Ornstein and Schenkenberg 1995: 202–3).

The House Republicans needed only ninety-three of their pledged one hundred days to bring all the Contract items to the floor for a vote. Table 19.1 lists the items in the Contract and recounts their fate. Several points are worth noting. First, though the Contract was constructed as a ten-item agenda, table 19.1 shows that many of the items had to be broken down into several subitems, while other pieces of legislation contained provisions called for in several different Contract items. This splintering results from the Contract's origins as a campaign document. Once it became clear that the Contract would become an operating agenda, committee jurisdictions and members' policy experiences came into play.

Second, of the twenty-two roll call votes on final passage of Contract legislation, only five were close victories or defeats for House Republicans. This may make it seem as though the Contract items were relatively uncontentious, but that is not quite true. The accounting does not include the myriad amendment votes that were held on the floor during this period. Also,

Table 19.1 Disposition of Items in the Contract with America

Contract item	House Vote	Day of Contract	Senate Action	Current Disposition
Congressional process				
End Congressional exemption From workplace laws (HR 1)	429-0	2	Passed parallel Bill S2	Signed into law
Revise house rules (H Res 6)		1	Not applicable	In force
1. The Fiscal Responsibility Act				
Balanced Budget Amendment (HJRes1)	300-132	23	Senate vote failed	Senate may hold future vote
Line item veto (HR 2)	294-134	34	Senate bill passed	Singed into law
2. The Taking Back of Our Streets				
Victim restitution (HR 665)	431-0	35	Senate bill passed	Now in Conference
Rules of evidence (HR 666)	289-142	36	No action	Stalled by Senate
Prison grants (HR 667)	265-156	38	No action	Stalled by Senate
Criminal aliens (HR 668)	380-20	38	No action	Stalled by Senate
Anticrime block grants (HR 728)	238-192	42	No action	Stalled by Senate
Death penalty appeals (HR 729)	297-132	36	No action	Stalled by Senate
3. The Personal Responsibility Act				
Welfare reform (HR 4)	234-199	80	Senate passed own bill Conference bill passed and sent to president	Vetoed by president
4. The Family Reinforcement Act				
Parental consent/surveys (HR 1271)	418-7	91	No action	Stalled by Senate
Increase sex crime penalties (HR 1240)	417-0	91	Senate approved	Signed into law
5. The American Dream Restoration Act				
Middle-class tax cut (HR 1215)	246-188	92	Senate passed own bill.	President vetoed

6. The National Security Restoration Act

	House vote		Senate action	Status
7. The Senior Citizens Fairness Act				
Increase S.S. earnings limit/ Long-term care (part of HR 1215)				
Senior housing policy (HR 660)	424-5	93	Senate passed amended version	Signed into law
8. Job Creation/Wage Enhancement Act				
Cut capital gains (part of HR 1215)				
Reduce unfunded mandates (HR 5)	360-74	29	Senate and conference bills passed	Signed into law
Reduce federal paperwork (HR 830)	418-0	50	Senate and conference bills passed	Signed into law
Regulatory review/"Takings" (HR 9)	277-141	59	Filibustered	Stalled in Senate
9. The Common Sense Legal Reform Act				
Product liability (HR 956)	265-161	66	Senate bill passed	In conference
Civil litigation overhaul (HR 988)	232-193	63	No action	Stalled in Senate
Shareholder lawsuits (HR 1058)	325-99	64	Senate and conference bills passed	Vetoed. Overridden by both Houses. Now law.
10. The Citizen Legislature Act				
Term limits amendment (HJRes 73)	227-204	85	Rejected-2/3 needed Under consideration in Senate	Stalled in both houses

those five votes that were contentious were very contentious and consumed much of the House's time. These more controversial votes occurred from the middle to the end of the one-hundred-day period, which shows that House Republican leaders needed the extra time to either allow committees to resolve their differences (as was the case with HR 4, the welfare reform bill) or to secure the votes of wavering Republicans or sympathetic Democrats. All items presented before day 40 passed with votes to spare. The only final passage vote to go down to defeat, the Term Limits Amendment, was held on day 85.

The workload figures for the first three months of the 104th Congress attest to the frantic pace of the new Republican majority. Between January 3 and March 31, the 104th Congress spent fifty-three days (for a total of 486 hours) in session and held 209 recorded votes. Statistics for the same period of the 103d Congress find the House in session for only thirty-five days (for a total of 189 hours) and holding only forty-two recorded votes. However, the difference in the number of measures passed is not that stark, with 111 passed during the 104th Congress and eighty-seven approved during the 103d.[14]

Third, only six provisions of the Contract became law as of this writing: the termination of the congressional exemption from workplace laws, the increase in sex crime penalties, the reduction of unfunded mandates, the reduction of federal paperwork, the elimination of discrimination in seniors' housing, the limitation of shareholder lawsuit proposals, and the line item veto. This amounts to only seven of the twenty-two roll calls held, with the shareholder lawsuits limitation becoming law over President Clinton's veto.

A final note concerns the real obstacles to enactment of Contract items: the Senate. Earlier, it was noted that Senate Republicans did not wish to be included in signing the Contract, and as table 19.1 shows, they continue to demonstrate their indifference to the House agenda. On eight of the twenty-two bills, the Senate has yet to take action. One bill (Regulatory Review or "Takings") was filibustered to death, one (the Balanced Budget Amendment) was defeated, and three are currently in conference. The Senate co-operated with the House on only eight bills.

This discussion obscures something else about the Contract: the extent to which many of these proposals were significantly transformed at the committee level. Senior members, now in charge of committees and subcommittees, took a hard look at the Contract items and decided to "make lemonade out of the lemons" they had been handed. Several items, especially regulatory and welfare reform, looked very different when passed by the House than they did when introduced. In fact, shortly after the 104th Congress began, senior Republicans expressed their uneasiness with the speed of the process, with some claiming that many items were not well developed and others citing the need to move matters through committee quickly because of extreme pressure from the leadership (*CQ Weekly Report* 1995b). Thus, the high party unity in this period must be interpreted cautiously.

As table 19.1 shows, the House Republicans were not ultimately effective at creating public laws from their Contract proposals. In their euphoria over majority status, House Republicans believed that their ability to control the agenda would be enduring. However, once the House finished its business of enacting Contract items, they had no standing to induce the Senate Republicans to follow through. After the Contract period, the House leadership did encounter some significant challenges, especially in the authorization and appropriation phases of the budget process. Legislators had the opportunity to work on pet projects (which in the case of House Republicans usually meant cutting rather than saving certain programs) because they were freed from a publicly agreed upon agenda. Though Republican unity was still relatively high, Gingrich experienced some surprise defeats (such as the rule on the Labor/HHS appropriations bill) and was kept busy talking members out of introducing controversial measures. The Republican leadership also found themselves invoking more restrictive rules for bill consideration because they were so far behind schedule on their budget work.

The remainder of the Republican agenda was overshadowed by the lack of a budget for fiscal year 1996. A permanent budget was passed on April 25, 1996 (FY 1996 began on October 1, 1995). Books will be written on the protracted budget debate between President Clinton and the Republican Congress, and it will take time to sort out the winners and losers. Yet it seems clear that the budget stalemate eclipsed the House Republican momentum. Though they have plans to tackle some significant issues in the second session of the 104th Congress (including reforms of Superfund, OSHA, and affirmative action), it is doubtful that they will regain the momentum they had in the first nine months of 1995.

The Contract's Role in the 1996 Election

One lasting effect of the Contract is that all House Republicans will share a collective campaign strategy: defending the Contract with America in 1996. Though few members used the document in their 1994 campaigns, all will have to defend their votes and the direction the agenda might have taken the country. Of course, the budget gridlock will serve as a major issue for both parties, but the Contract belongs wholly to the House Republicans—for better or worse. Polls still show that Contract items have great resonance with the public. The House Republicans, through the NRCC, are actively preparing their members for a dramatically different task in the 1996 elections: how to defend a governing position instead of attack one.

The ability of House Republicans to defend the Contract and retain their majority will say a good deal about whether parties can overcome the atomistic tendencies of congressional politics. If the Republicans remain in control, officeholders may attribute this success to the power of their agenda to focus choices for voters, and it may serve as a model for both parties for the future. If instead the Republicans return to minority status, officeholders will likely return to the candidate-centered campaigning they have practiced for the last thirty years.

The response to the Contract during the one-hundred-day period was clearly mixed. The Democrats may be able to regain their congressional majority by demonstrating that their policies are more in line with the American electorate. Significantly, the House Republicans have decided not to develop a new "contract" for the 1996 elections. Perhaps they have recognized that party government in the American context is not as workable as they earlier believed. Overall, the Contract demonstrates both a wistfulness and a naivete about the viability of party government in America. The House Republicans discovered that their ability to lead the party in the electorate or to unify the party in government is limited, at best.

Notes

1. Connelly and Pitney acknowledge that other works have included tangential discussion of the House Republicans in their larger analysis of the Republican Party. These include A. James Reichley's *Conservatives in an Era of Change* (Washington, D.C.: Brookings Institution Press, 1981) and Nicol Rae's *The Decline and Fall of the Liberal Republicans from 1952 to the Present* (New York: Oxford University Press, 1989). More recently, John B. Bader and Charles O. Jones have presented a late minority status view of the House Republicans in their chapter "The Republican Parties in Congress: Bicameral Differences," in *Congress Reconsidered*, Lawrence C. Dodd and Bruce I. Oppenheimer, 5th ed. (Washington, D.C.: CQ Press), 291–313.

2. The 1990 budget debacle between President Bush and House Republicans is the best example of this. See Connelly and Pitney 1994, pp. 120–21 and Kolodny 1991.

3. Information obtained through a personal interview with Maria Cino, executive director of the NRCC, November 13, 1995, in Washington, D.C.

4. This has been institutionalized for the 1996 cycle by requiring "dues" from all members for the NRCC's Incumbent Support Fund. The amounts required differ by the position held by House Republicans: 2500 = freshman, 5000 = regular, 6500 = subcommittee chairs, 7500 party leaders and committee chairs. (Cino interview)

5. Don Fierce, RNC communications director, and Cece Hall Boyer, hill liaison in the Office of Congressional Affairs, were both actively involved in the Contract's development.

6. Information obtained through a personal interview with Cece Hall Boyer, Congressional Liaison, Republican National Committee, October 4, 1995, in Washington, D.C.

7. Information from a telephone interview with Ed Gillespie, Communications Division, Republican National Committee, February 21, 1996. In fact, Gillespie reports that the welfare reform task force did not complete its work until the night before the Capitol Hill event.

8. Background interview with former whip office aide.

9. Three Republican incumbents, Lincoln Diaz-Balart (R-Fla), Ileana Ros-Lehtinen (R-Fla), and Don Young (R-Ark) did not sign the Contract or participate in the September event. Diaz-Balart and Ros-Lehtinen took issue with the anti-immigrant provisions in the proposals.

10. This observation is based on the author's experience as a 1995 APSA Congressional Fellow working in the office of a Republican member of the House of Representatives and reflects observations garnered through interactions with other members' staff.

11. According to Ornstein and Schenkenberg, only 53 percent of House freshmen previously held elective office.

12. Ornstein and Schenkenberg (1995: 205) state that the first 100 days resembled a parliamentary style of legislating rather than a transformative style of legislating. Also, they show that support for the Contract as a concept exceeds support for any of its individual items among the public.

13. Though most of these switches did not occur until after the Contract period, senator Richard Shelby of Alabama switched immediately after the election, giving House leaders a sound basis for alarm.

14. See "100 Days of Servitude," *Roll Call*, April 6, 1995, p. 4.

20

Leaders and Followers:
Major Party Elites, Identifiers, and Issues, 1980–92

John S. Jackson, III
Nancy L. Clayton

What do the major political parties stand for? Do their leaders offer distinct positions on public policy, or are they carbon copies of each other, hugging the middle ground? To what extent do party leaders represent the views of their followers, the members of the mass public who identify with the party? And what is the relationship over time between the policy views of party leaders and followers? The answers to these questions are important to understanding both the role of parties in a democratic government as well as present-day politics.

This chapter reports on the issue positions of major parties elites and their identifiers over twelve tumultuous years of recent history, 1980 to 1992. These data allow us to offer some tentative answers to the questions posed above. First, major party leaders have distinct positions on a host of issues, thus potentially giving American voters a real choice during elections. Second, these differences usually reflect similar, though weaker, divisions among party identifiers. At times party elites appear to represent the views of their followers quite well, at times, rather poorly. Thus, contrary to popular wisdom, there is a real contrast between the two parties, particularly at the elite level. Third, there is a more ambiguous relationship between party elites and identifiers over time. At some points leaders appear to lead their followers, and at other times they seem to follow.

Parties and Issues

Students of political parties have identified two opposite models of how parties approach issues: "responsible" and "pragmatic" parties. Responsible parties take distinct stands on public policy, offering clear alternatives, and then, if elected, govern accordingly (Schattschneider 1942; Ranney 1954;

White and Mileur 1992). As Wilson notes, "Instead of serving as neutral agents which mobilize majorities for whatever candidates and programs seem best suited to capturing the public fancy, the parties would become the source of programs and the agents of social change" (1962: 18-19). Pragmatic parties, on the other hand, take issue positions according to the electoral situation, thus representing the median voter in government if elected (Downs 1965; Schlesinger 1991). Wilson again notes, "Issues will be avoided except in the most general terms or if the party is confident that a majority supports its position. Should a contrary position on the same issue seem best suited for winning a majority at the next election, the party will try to change or at least mute its position" (1962: 17-18).

These two models suggest different postures between the major parties in a two-party system. The definition of responsible parties implies sharp differences between the major parties, at least on salient issues. The relationship of these stands to public opinion is a secondary consideration compared to programmatic consistency or ideological purity, since the aim of such parties is to make policy, not simply win elections. In contrast, the definition of pragmatic model parties implies that the major parties will closely resemble each other, at least on salient issues. The relationship of these stands to public opinion is a primary consideration compared to programmatic consistency or ideological purity, since the goal of pragmatic parties is to win elections, not to make policy.

These models also imply different relationships between party leaders and followers. In responsible parties, party leaders develop ideologically consistent programs from the general concerns of party followers, and then educate followers as to the specifics of policy. Thus, at any given moment, the views of elites may differ from their identifiers, within the same basic tendency. Pragmatic parties show an opposite pattern: leaders formulate programs that reflect the views of their followers, reflecting the nuances and inconsistencies in such opinion. Thus, at any given moment, the views of elites should closely match those of party identifiers, but not necessarily the same basic tendencies across issues.

Finally, each of these models suggests different sources of change. For responsible parties, change arises among party leaders: changes in the opinion of existing elites or the arrival of new elites alter the content of the party's program or ideology. Such changes are then presented to the followers, eventually leading them to new issue positions. But for pragmatic parties, leaders respond to the changes in the opinion or composition to party followers. Thus, party elites match or follow the identifiers.

The degree to which the responsible and pragmatic models fit the real world of American parties is, of course, an empirical question. The conventional wisdom is that American parties tend to be pragmatic, with a strong emphasis on winning elections and little interest in consistent policies

(Beck and Sorauf 1992). However, there is evidence that the major parties have moved toward the responsible model in recent times. Scholars have found considerable evidence that party elites have become increasingly polarized in ideological and policy terms (Stone, Abramowitz, and Rapoport 1989; Baer and Bositis 1988); other scholars have found a parallel but weaker shift among party identifiers (Page and Shapiro 1992). Here we offer an assessment of this question for major party elites and identifiers in recent times.

Data and Methods

This chapter is based on two sets of data collected during the last four presidential elections (1980–1992). The first set is for Democratic and Republican party elites, collected under the auspices of the Party Elite Study (PES) at Southern Illinois University at Carbondale. The PES is a national survey of delegates to the Democratic and Republican National Conventions in each presidential election year. These surveys were conducted by mail immediately after each convention, and involved systematic random samples drawn from lists provided by official party sources. In general, the response rate has been satisfactory, and few systematic differences between those who responded and those who did not respond have been identified. Overall, the PES produces an accurate portrait of these important party leaders who hold office every four years, with a particular emphasis on those active in presidential politics each election cycle (Jackson, Brown and Bositis 1982: 163; Baer and Bositis 1988)

The second data set is for the mass public in each presidential election: the National Elections Studies (NES) conducted by the Center for Political Studies at the University of Michigan. Identical or nearly identical questions were asked of both the PES and NES in each year, including self-identified ideology, and views on the level of government services, national health insurance, abortion, help to minorities, and defense spending.

In the tables that follow, we will use these data to make three comparisons. First, we will compare Democratic and Republican party elites to each other on these issue positions from 1980 to 1992. Then we will compare Democratic and Republican identifiers in the mass public to each other on the same issues and for the same years. Finally, we will compare party elites to their identifiers in the same way. In this manner, we can make *across party* and *within party* comparisons of party elites and identifiers over time.

Data Analysis

Ideology

Our comparisons begin with the self-identified ideology of the party elites, presented in table 20.1a.[1] These data are striking: a majority of the Democratic delegates called themselves "liberal" over this period, while a substantial majority of the Republican convention delegates label themselves as "conservative." It is on the Republican side that ideology has become most pronounced. In 1980, when Ronald Reagan was first nominated, a total of 63.8 percent of the Republican delegates identified themselves as conservatives. The growth in the conservatives at the Republican conventions has been steadily upward since 1980, with only a very minor downturn in 1988 when George Bush was first nominated. By 1992, when Bush was renominated, 71.3 percent of the delegates were conservatives.

The patterns are similar, although not quite so marked, on the Democratic side. When the Democrats renominated President Jimmy Carter in 1980, 52.9 percent of the delegates termed themselves as liberals. This distribution has remained fairly stable each succeeding year up to 1992, when 57 percent were liberals. Like liberals in the GOP, the conservatives in the Democratic Party are clearly an endangered species.

What about the Democratic and Republican identifiers in the mass public? Table 20.1b[2] shows that the party identifiers also differ on ideology, but not as much as the party elites. This pattern is particularly true for the Democratic party identifiers in 1992 where the distribution was fairly uniform one: 35.8 percent called themselves liberal, 37.7 percent moderate, and 26.5 percent conservative. The Republicans are more homogeneous, with 55.4 percent identifying as conservative, 30.7 percent as moderate, and 13.9 percent as liberal.

The longitudinal data for the Democrats show that these proportions in each of the three ideological categories hardly changed at all between 1980 and 1992. And it is interesting to note that the conservatives among Republican identifiers reached their apex in 1980 and then fell to their lowest level in 1992, with a decline of 12 percent across that twelve-year period. These data certainly fit with the popular view of the Democrats as a diverse party, but not with the common image of the Republicans as strictly right wing. Such an image may be driven by the more prominent components of GOP coalition, such as the Christian Right, and by the conservative leaders who get most of the attention.

In fact, a glance back at Table 20.1a shows that conservatives are heavily overrepresented among GOP elites compared to the Republican mass base.

Table 20.1a Democrat versus Republican Party Elites: Ideology

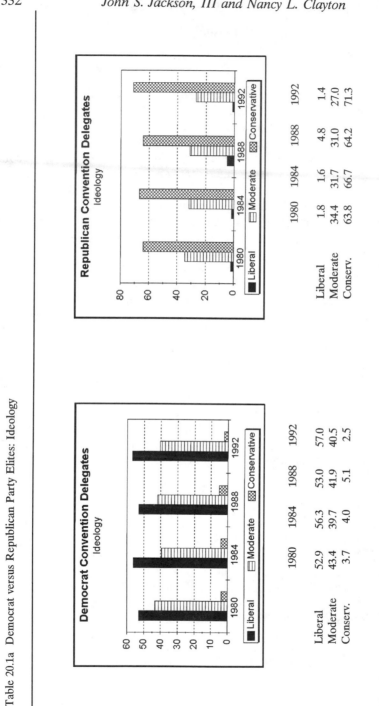

Republican Convention Delegates
Ideology

■ Liberal ▦ Moderate ▨ Conservative

	1980	1984	1988	1992
Liberal	1.8	1.6	4.8	1.4
Moderate	34.4	31.7	31.0	27.0
Conserv.	63.8	66.7	64.2	71.3

Democrat Convention Delegates
Ideology

■ Liberal ▦ Moderate ▨ Conservative

	1980	1984	1988	1992
Liberal	52.9	56.3	53.0	57.0
Moderate	43.4	39.7	41.9	40.5
Conserv.	3.7	4.0	5.1	2.5

Source: Party Elite Study 1980, 1984, 1988, and 1992.

Table 20.1b Democrat versus Republican Party Identifiers: Ideology

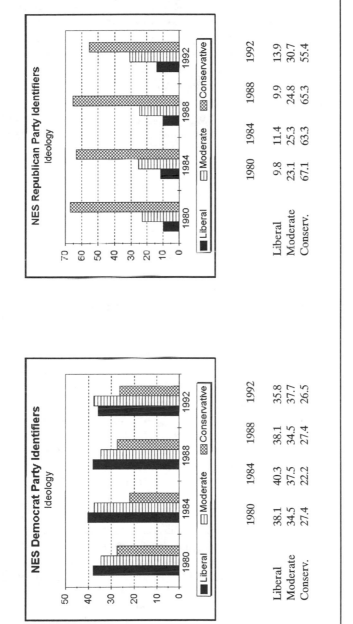

NES Republican Party Identifiers
Ideology

Liberal   Moderate   Conservative

	1980	1984	1988	1992
Liberal	9.8	11.4	9.9	13.9
Moderate	23.1	25.3	24.8	30.7
Conserv.	67.1	63.3	65.3	55.4

NES Democrat Party Identifiers
Ideology

Liberal   Moderate   Conservative

	1980	1984	1988	1992
Liberal	38.1	40.3	38.1	35.8
Moderate	34.5	37.5	34.5	37.7
Conserv.	27.4	22.2	27.4	26.5

Source: National Election Studies 1980, 1984, 1988, and 1992.

Thus, it is the liberal and moderate categories among the Republican base who are underrepresented in the ranks of the party leaders. On the Democratic side, it is clearly the conservative mass base that is not well represented among the party identifiers. It may be this disjuncture between these two components of the party that is causing the Democratic candidates to lose support—especially in the South. Overall, then, the leadership echelons of the two parties have polarized, but the mass base of each party has not followed suit. Clearly, the major parties are markedly different from one another in ideological identification, particularly at the elite level. It is certainly no longer accurate to charge that the parties occupy a bland middle ground. Throughout the period, the party elites were sort of an ideological vanguard for their respective parties.

Government Services

Do these ideological divisions carry over into specific policy areas? An important issue is whether governmental services should be continued at the same level or should be cut in order to balance the budget. Certainly the titanic struggle in Washington between President Clinton and the congressional Democratic minority on one side and the Republican majority in the House and Senate on the other is indicative of just how deeply divided the two parties have become on this issue, a division that was presaged among party elites and depicted in table 20.2a.[3]

The split between the two parties' elites on this issue was deep in 1980, and it remained a chasm in 1992. In 1980, 73.6 percent of the Democratic delegates wanted to continue governmental services compared to 83.3 percent of the Republican delegates who wanted fewer services. These results were almost exactly the same in the 1992 conventions, where 74.2 percent of the Democrats wanted to continue services, and 80.8 percent of the Republican delegates wanted to cut them. On this issue, there is almost no middle ground shared by the elites of the two parties. Thus, it should not be too surprising that the budget debate in Washington has proved to be so intractable as the 1996 elections approach.

Where are the party identifiers in this debate? As table 20.2b[4] reveals, party identifiers are also divided on this issue, but not nearly as sharply as party leaders. For the Democrats, the most popular option in 1992 was to continue services, with 53 percent; 27.3 percent were neutral, leaving 19.7 percent for fewer services. We do not have these data for 1980, but for 1984 and 1988 the data show a remarkably consistent pattern with support for continuing services hovering close to 50 percent both years. The Republican identifiers' show greater division: in 1992 only 38.8 percent wanted fewer services and 29.0 percent wanted to continue services. In fact, the fewer services option has declined steadily among GOP identifiers since 1984.

Thus, the Democratic Party elites are much more committed to the fight against service cuts than their mass identifiers, although that position receives substantial support among the followers. The Republicans show a remarkable division, with the elites far more committed to reducing the scope of government than their followers in the mass public. Unlike ideology, the party elites have maintained their relative positions on government services over the last twelve years, while their mass identifiers have moved in a liberal direction.

No doubt the 1992 Republican convention delegates were an advanced guard of the party, reflecting the views of GOP officials who took control of the majority in the Congress in 1994. It may be, however, that the ambivalence of the Republican identifiers coupled with the vehement opposition of the Democratic leadership is why the Republicans lost so much public support after 1994 as they tried to implement major reductions in government services.

Health Care

One of the most contentious issues of the first two years of President Clinton's administration was the fight over the health care plan crafted under the leadership of the First Lady, Hillary Rodham Clinton. It was a complicated plan that was characterized as "big government" by Republicans and defeated in Congress. However, the issue was then resurrected in the debate over what to do about Medicare and Medicaid in the 1995–96 budget fight. We have an item in our studies that is a surrogate for this debate, namely, public versus private health insurance plans; the results are presented in table 20.3a[5] for the party elites.

The partisan divisions have been fairly marked on this issue since 1980, especially because of the liberal stance of the Democratic elites. In 1980, 70.8 percent of the Democratic delegates wanted government-provided health insurance, compared to 91 percent of the Republican delegates who opted for the private insurance. By 1992, support among Democratic delegates for government health insurance plan had grown to 82.1 percent, while the support for private health insurance among Republicans declines to 77.5 percent in 1992.

Table 20.3b[6] provides comparative figures for the party identifiers. In 1992, the Democrats were clearly the most distinctive group on this question: 60 percent were in favor of government-provided health insurance. Once again, the Republican identifiers were much more evenly divided with 41 percent in the private health insurance category. On this issue, Democratic identifiers have moved sharply to the left, and Republicans have followed suit to a lesser extent.

Table 20.2a Democrat versus Republican Party Elites: Government Services

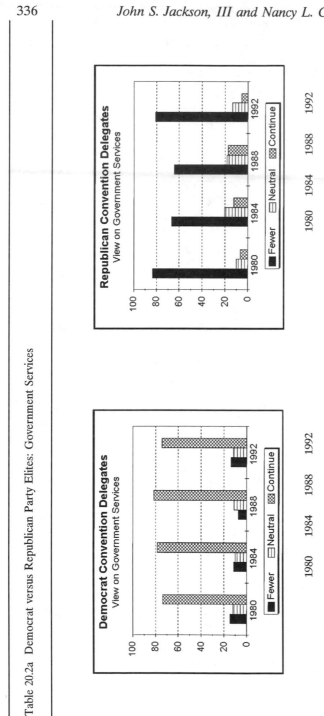

Republican Convention Delegates
View on Government Services

■ Fewer □ Neutral ▨ Continue

	1980	1984	1988	1992
Fewer	83.3	66.8	64.2	80.8
Neutral	10.1	20.6	18.4	13.7
Continue	6.6	12.6	17.4	5.5

Democrat Convention Delegates
View on Government Services

■ Fewer □ Neutral ▨ Continue

	1980	1984	1988	1992
Fewer	14.4	11.3	7.5	14.0
Neutral	12.0	10.2	11.0	11.8
Continue	73.6	78.6	81.5	74.2

Source: Party Elite Study 1980, 1984, 1988, and 1992.

Table 20.2b Democrat versus Republican Party Identifiers: Government Services

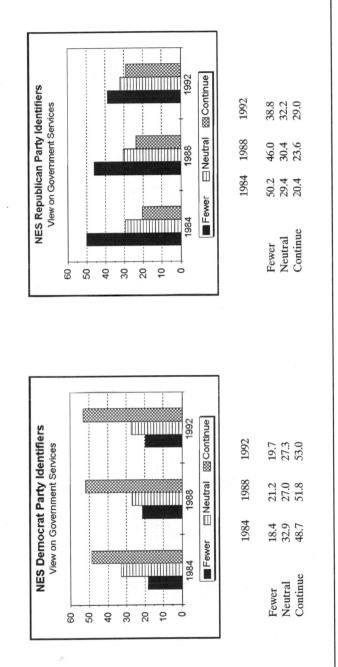

NES Republican Party Identifiers
View on Government Services

	1984	1988	1992
Fewer	50.2	46.0	38.8
Neutral	29.4	30.4	32.2
Continue	20.4	23.6	29.0

NES Democrat Party Identifiers
View on Government Services

	1984	1988	1992
Fewer	18.4	21.2	19.7
Neutral	32.9	27.0	27.3
Continue	48.7	51.8	53.0

Source: National Election Studies 1984, 1988, and 1992.

Table 20.3a Democrat versus Republican Party Elites: National Health Insurance

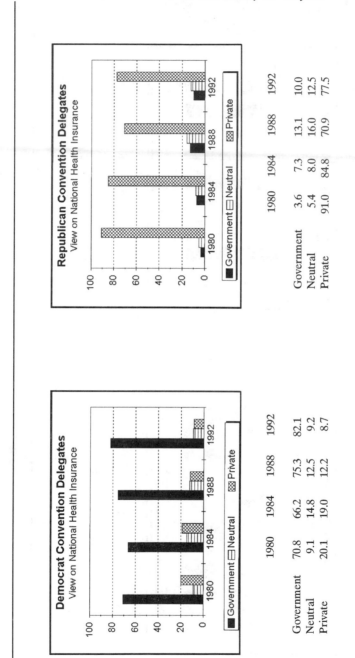

Republican Convention Delegates
View on National Health Insurance

	1980	1984	1988	1992
Government	3.6	7.3	13.1	10.0
Neutral	5.4	8.0	16.0	12.5
Private	91.0	84.8	70.9	77.5

Democrat Convention Delegates
View on National Health Insurance

	1980	1984	1988	1992
Government	70.8	66.2	75.3	82.1
Neutral	9.1	14.8	12.5	9.2
Private	20.1	19.0	12.2	8.7

Source: Party Elite Study 1980, 1984, 1988, and 1992.

Table 20.3b Democrat versus Republican Party Identifiers: National Health Insurance

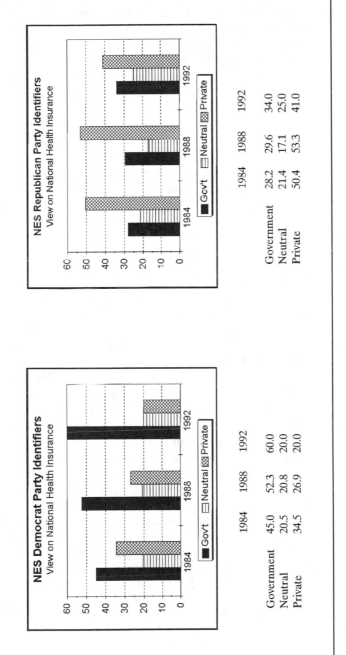

NES Democrat Party Identifiers
View on National Health Insurance

Gov't | Neutral | Private

	1984	1988	1992
Government	45.0	52.3	60.0
Neutral	20.5	20.8	20.0
Private	34.5	26.9	20.0

NES Republican Party Identifiers
View on National Health Insurance

Gov't | Neutral | Private

	1984	1988	1992
Government	28.2	29.6	34.0
Neutral	21.4	17.1	25.0
Private	50.4	53.3	41.0

Source: National Election Studies 1980, 1984, 1988, and 1992.

As before, the party elites hold more extreme views than their followers in the mass public, and the Democrats come somewhat closer to their identifiers than the Republicans do to theirs. Ironically, the advocates of national health insurance may have lost the battle in the Congress in 1993, but they may be winning the battle for public opinion. However, the Republican elites were much more united, and they were farther out in front of their partisans than the Democratic elites were in comparison to their identifiers.

Abortion

One of the most contentious issues in recent years has been abortion. At times there seems to be little middle ground between strongly held views. In addition, the two parties have staked out significantly different positions, with the Republicans clearly identified as the pro-life party and the Democrats strongly supporting the pro-choice position. These partisan divisions are evident among party elites and presented in table 20.4a.[7]

Although we did not ask this question in the 1980 PES, the results from the 1984 through 1992 studies document the deep partisan polarization on this difficult issue. In 1984, only 21.6 percent of the 1984 Democratic delegates took the two most pro-life positions and over 65 percent the pure pro-choice position. In contrast, 61.9% of the Republican delegates took one of the two most pro-life positions and just 22.0% were fully pro-choice. These patterns changed a little by 1992, but still showed considerable polarization: the pro-choice position had risen to 87.8 percent for Democratic elites, but the pro-life position had fallen to 53.6% among Republican elites. These data reveal that the 1992 Republican delegates may have been more divided on this issue than was popularly portrayed, although the 1992 convention took a pro-life stance. These data may have foreshadowed the revival of this debate with respect to the 1996 Republican platform.

Once again, the party identifiers are less polarized than the party elites, as demonstrated in table 20.4b.[8] From 1980 to 1992, pro-choice positions ranged from 33.8 to 45.0 percent of the Democratic and Republican party identifiers, with the two most pro-life positions ranging from 40.4 to 45.2%. In each year, the Democrats were modestly pro-choice and the Republicans modestly pro-life. In most instances, close to a majority of the identifiers of both parties are found in the two middle categories in every year.

As with other issues, the party elites are far more divided than their followers in the mass public. Here Republican elites are somewhat closer to the Republican identifiers than the Democrats were to theirs, something of a reversal of our findings for government services and health care. However, most identifiers of the two parties are in the middle and probably would welcome some sort of compromise between the extremes. It may not be accidental, then, that a moderate policy position seems to be emerging where officials from both parties try to discourage abortion and teenage pregnancies by both moral suasion and some publicly funded programs. It may be that this mixed and somewhat ambivalent total policy strategy is a reasonably accurate reflection of what a majority of Americans want on this divisive issue.

Helping Minorities

Another policy area where the two major parties have become deeply polarized over the past two decades is race relations. In the 1960s and 1970s the Democrats became advocates of civil rights, while the Republicans became increasingly skeptical of the use of national power for these purposes. As a result, most African-American voters came to support Democratic candidates, especially for president and for Congress. The Democrats paid a heavy price for this position as the Republican Party scored steady gains among white voters in the South. In fact, the realignment of the white South into one of the most dependable components of the Republican coalition is one of the great secular realignment events of modern American politics (Black and Black 1992, 1987), and it helped fuel the Republican Party's take-over of the majority in Congress in the 1994 elections. This division seems likely to continue into the 1996 campaign. Table 20.5a[9] presents data on this issue for the party elites.

On this dimension, too, there could hardly be a more clear indication of the issue polarization of the party elites. Beginning in 1980, well over 60 percent of the Democrats supported special governmental help for minorities, and over 50 percent of the Republican delegates opposed this position. Such polarization continued through each successive convention, so that by 1992, comparable figures were 74.5 percent for Democratic elites and 50.8 percent for the Republicans. Again, it is interesting to note that the Republican delegates who nominated Ronald Reagan (1980 and 1984) were slightly more conservative on this matter than George Bush's two conventions (1988 and 1992). With that slight exception aside, it is abundantly clear that the two major parties are offering the American voters "a choice; not an echo" on this policy matter.

The distinctions between the two parties' identifiers are quite interesting on this issue, as shown in table 20.5b.[10] The Democratic identifiers are fairly evenly divided, with the most popular category being support for helping minorities in 1984, but with the "no help" category most popular in 1980, 1988, and 1992. While the Republicans are also divided, the "no help" category is the largest, with a majority in every year except 1984.

It is on this issue that the Republican elites are more closely attuned to the views of their identifiers, while the Democratic elites do not do as well. Recent election results indicate that the Republicans have benefited from this harmony in the electoral arena. It has often been said that the American people believe in equality of opportunity but not equality of results, and one could find some support for that proposition in these data.

Table 20.4a   Democrat versus Republican Party Elites: Abortion

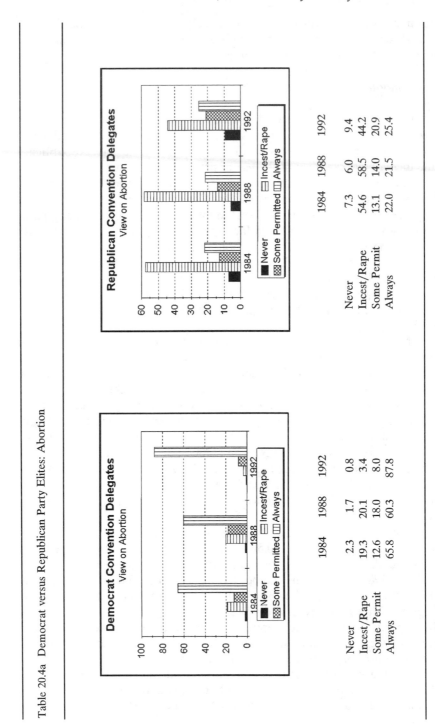

Democrat Convention Delegates
View on Abortion

	1984	1988	1992
Never	2.3	1.7	0.8
Incest/Rape	19.3	20.1	3.4
Some Permit	12.6	18.0	8.0
Always	65.8	60.3	87.8

Republican Convention Delegates
View on Abortion

	1984	1988	1992
Never	7.3	6.0	9.4
Incest/Rape	54.6	58.5	44.2
Some Permit	13.1	14.0	20.9
Always	22.0	21.5	25.4

Source: Party Elite Study 1984, 1988, and 1992.

Table 20.4b Democrat versus Republican Party Identifiers: Abortion

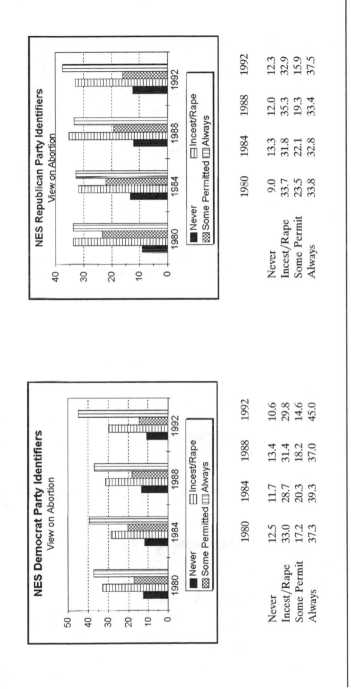

	1980	1984	1988	1992
Never	12.5	11.7	13.4	10.6
Incest/Rape	33.0	28.7	31.4	29.8
Some Permit	17.2	20.3	18.2	14.6
Always	37.3	39.3	37.0	45.0

	1980	1984	1988	1992
Never	9.0	13.3	12.0	12.3
Incest/Rape	33.7	31.8	35.3	32.9
Some Permit	23.5	22.1	19.3	15.9
Always	33.8	32.8	33.4	37.5

Source: National Election Studies 1984, 1988, and 1992.

Table 20.5a Democrat versus Republican Party Elites: Help to Minorities

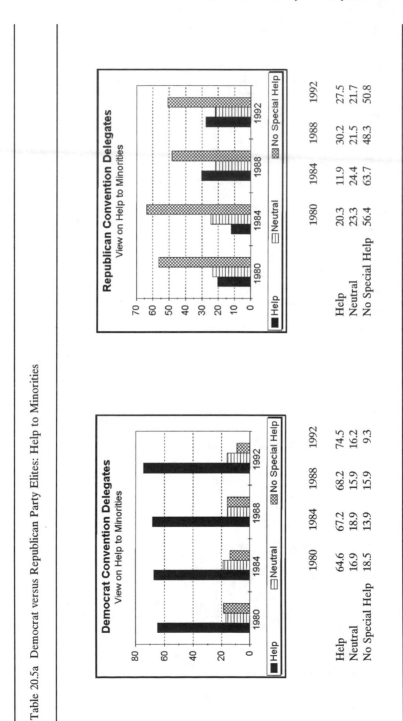

Source: Party Elite Study 1980, 1984, 1988, and 1992.

Table 20.5b Democrat versus Republican Party Identifiers: Help to Minorities

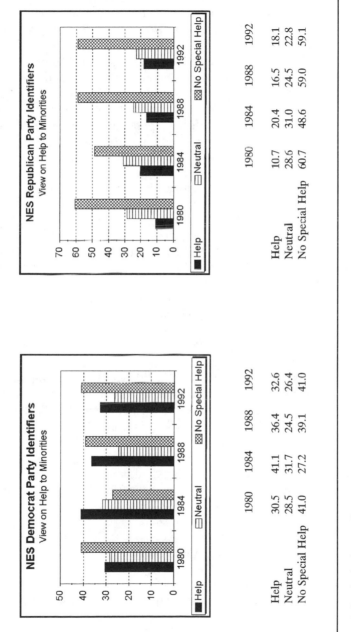

	1980	1984	1988	1992
Help	10.7	20.4	16.5	18.1
Neutral	28.6	31.0	24.5	22.8
No Special Help	60.7	48.6	59.0	59.1

	1980	1984	1988	1992
Help	30.5	41.1	36.4	32.6
Neutral	28.5	31.7	24.5	26.4
No Special Help	41.0	27.2	39.1	41.0

Source: National Election Studies 1980, 1984, 1988, and 1992.

Defense Spending

Finally, we turn to whether defense spending should be decreased or increased, another issue that has divided the two parties in Congress and the White House over most of the last two decades. Beginning with the first Reagan administration in 1981, the Republican leaders have consistently favored an increase in defense spending. The current Republican majority in Congress also seems to favor such an increase, although some are ambivalent about this goal versus cutting taxes and balancing the budget. The Democratic record is more mixed but generally critical of defense spending. For instance, President Clinton has cut defense spending below what the majority congressional Republicans wanted but less than what some congressional Democrats advocated. Table 20.6a[11] looks at this issue for party elites.

Here, too, one could hardly imagine a more graphic demonstration of the policy polarization which has developed between party leaders. In 1980, 37.5 percent of the Democratic delegates wanted to decrease defense spending, while 33.3 percent wanted to increase it—almost an equal split. But by 1992, a near consensus had developed among Democrats, with 82.2 percent wanting to decrease defense spending. The Republican elites moved in the opposite direction. In 1980, 88.8 percent of the Republican delegates wanted to increase defense spending, a figure that has declined steadily so that in 1992, only 23.8 percent supported an increase in defense spending.

Very similar patterns obtained for party identifiers in the mass public, shown in Table 20.6b.[12] In 1980, 64.5 percent of Democratic identifiers supported an increase in defense spending, while 81 percent of the Republican identifiers supported an increase compared to only 6.4 percent in opposition. It is little wonder, then, that the Reagan administration had so little trouble getting their massive defense build-up approved by the Congress in 1981–82. However, soon afterwards this consensus collapsed, so that by 1992, 50.2 percent of Democratic identifiers and 35.3 of their Republican counterparts favored decreasing defense spending. No doubt the end of the Cold War helps explain these numbers. By 1992, both party elites represent their identifiers fairly well on this issue, although the GOP may do a little better job. This issue appears to be an example of party elites responding to the opinion of their followers.

Conclusion

Overall, our findings indicate that the major parties do stand for something. First, the party elites are sharply divided on many important issues, offering meaningful alternatives to the electorate. In some cases this division has grown in recent times. Second, these divisions are also found among party identifiers in the mass public, although the differences are less clear and have in some cases declined. The party elites nearly always represent the basic tendencies of their mass followers, although sometimes they represent the followers' views more accurately than others. Finally, the relationship between party leaders and followers over time is more ambivalent. Sometimes the elites seem to serve as a vanguard leading the party faithful, and in others as a rear guard, following the lead of the public.

Thus, this research suggests that the American party system is perhaps more *internally* programmatic then previously envisioned. The major parties appear to be more "responsible" than is generally expected. This is not to suggest the absence of pragmatism: the major parties are clearly interested in winning elections and not above putting principle aside for the sake of victory. However, in this era of the "electoral connection," it is refreshing to find that American parties are not ideological voids, blindly following the whims of voters.

The concerns of party followers usually develop rather slowly, and public opinion is certainly not infinitely malleable in the hands of political leaders. Sometimes one hears so much about the power of the mass media and the wonders of the arts and crafts of the "spin meisters" that it becomes too easy to accept the proposition that voters are easily and often manipulated. For the sake of the viability of mass democracy, we have to believe that party followers have meaningful policy preferences (perhaps inchoate or "latent" in some areas) and that they react to the policy options presented to them by the party leaders. When time and circumstances change, followers are capable of learning, growing, and modifying their views. While the American public may not have in-depth knowledge of the finer points of public policy, the record indicates that a mass learning experience or a great civics lesson takes place in the conduct of our elections.

To be sure, the nexus between the concerns of party followers and the stands of party leaders is close at times, but at others it is broad. The latter could indicate that party leaders turn a blind eye to their followers, but we would like to believe it suggests a lag, where party leaders have not yet succeeded in developing broad support among followers for new policy stands. The education process is underway, but not complete. Where the gap is narrow, we suspect the task has already been accomplished.

The marketplace of ideas in the American polity is constantly changing and, of course, the voters are the ultimate judges and arbitrators of those changes. Nevertheless, political party elites drive much of that change also. The elites who make the presidential nominations official are constantly changing, and the turnover rate from convention to convention is very high. As we have seen from the data, the aggregate views of the convention delegates show elements of both continuity and change from election to election. One could do a lot worse in trying to create the conditions necessary to support a viable democracy late in the twentieth century.

Table 20.6a   Democrat versus Republican Party Elites: Defense Spending

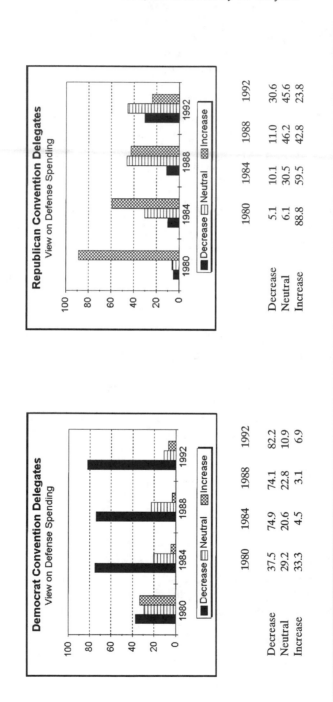

Democrat Convention Delegates
View on Defense Spending

■ Decrease ▥ Neutral ▨ Increase

	1980	1984	1988	1992
Decrease	37.5	74.9	74.1	82.2
Neutral	29.2	20.6	22.8	10.9
Increase	33.3	4.5	3.1	6.9

Republican Convention Delegates
View on Defense Spending

■ Decrease ▥ Neutral ▨ Increase

	1980	1984	1988	1992
Decrease	5.1	10.1	11.0	30.6
Neutral	6.1	30.5	46.2	45.6
Increase	88.8	59.5	42.8	23.8

Source: Party Elite Study 1980, 1984, 1988, and 1992.

Table 20.6b Democrat versus Republican Party Identifiers: Defense Spending

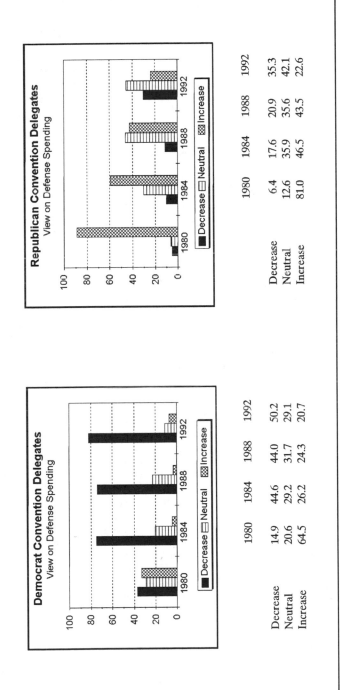

Republican Convention Delegates
View on Defense Spending

	1980	1984	1988	1992
Decrease	6.4	17.6	20.9	35.3
Neutral	12.6	35.9	35.6	42.1
Increase	81.0	46.5	43.5	22.6

Democrat Convention Delegates
View on Defense Spending

	1980	1984	1988	1992
Decrease	14.9	44.6	44.0	50.2
Neutral	20.6	29.2	31.7	29.1
Increase	64.5	26.2	24.3	20.7

Source: National Election Studies 1980, 1984, 1988, and 1992.

Notes

1. Respondents were asked the following question: We hear a lot of talk these days about liberals and conservatives. Here is a seven-point scale on which the political views that people might hold are arranged from extremely conservative. Where would you place yourself on this scale, or haven't you thought much about it? To facilitate the presentation of the data, the original seven-point scale for this question was recorded so that the variable values fell into three categories: liberal, moderate and conservative. Answers of 1, 2, and 3 were coded as "liberal"; an answer of 4 remained "moderate" and answers of 5, 6, and 7 were coded as a "conservative" response.

2. Footnote 1 also applies here.

3. Respondents were asked the following question: Some people think the government should provide fewer services, even in areas such as health and education, in order to reduce spending. Other people feel that it is important for the government to provide many more services even if it means an increase in spending. Where would you place yourself on this scale, or haven't you thought much about this? To facilitate the presentation of the data, the original seven-point scale for this question was recoded so that the variable values fell into three categories: fewer, neutral and continue. Answers of 1, 2, and 3 were coded as "fewer"; an answer of 4 remained "neutral"; and answers of 5, 6, and 7 were coded as a "continue" preference.

4. Footnote 3 also applies here.

5. Respondents were asked the following question: There is much concern about the rapid rise in medical and hospital costs. Some feel there should be a government insurance plan which would cover all medical and hospital expenses. Others feel that medical expenses should be paid by individuals, and through private insurance plans like Blue Cross or other company paid plans. Where would you place yourself on this scale, or haven't you thought much about it? To facilitate the presentation of the data, the original seven-point scale for this question was recoded so that the variable values fell into three categories: government, neutral and private. Answers of 1, 2, and 3 were coded as "government"; an answer of 4 remained "neutral" and answers of 5, 6, and 7 were coded as a "private" preference.

6. Footnote 5 also applies here.

7. Respondents were asked the following question: There has been some discussion about abortion during the recent years. Which one of the opinions on this page best agrees with your view? Answer choices for this question included (1) abortion should never be permitted; (2) the law should only permit abortion only in case of rape, incest, or when the woman's life is in danger; (3) the law should permit abortion for reasons other than rape, incest, or danger to the woman's life, but only after the need for the abortion has been clearly established; and (4) by law, a woman should always be able to obtain an abortion as a matter of personal choice.

8. Footnote 7 also applies here.

9. Respondents were asked the following question: Some people feel that the government in Washington should make every possible effort to improve the social and economic position of blacks and other minority groups. Others feel that the government should not make any special effort to help minorities because they should help themselves. Where would you place yourself on this scale, or haven't you thought much about it? To facilitate the presentation of the data, the original seven-point scale for this question was recoded so that the variable values fell into three categories: help, neutral, and no special help. Answers of 1, 2, and 3 were coded as "help"; an answer of 4 remained "neutral"; and answers of 5, 6, and 7 were coded as a "no special help" preference.

10. Footnote 9 also applies here.

11. Respondents were asked the following question: Some people believe that we should spend much less money for defense. Others feel that defense spending should be greatly increased. Where would you place yourself on this scale or haven't you thought much about this? To facilitate the presentation of the data, the original seven-point scale for this question was recoded so that the variable values fell into three categories: decrease, neutral, and increase. Answers of 1, 2, and 3 were coded as "decrease"; an answer of 4 remained "neutral"; and answers of 5, 6, and 7 were coded as an "increase" preference.

12. Footnote 11 also applies here.

21

Women's Political Leadership and the State of the Parties, 1992-94

Barbara C. Burrell
J. Cherie Strachan

What does the state of the parties have to do with women's political leadership in the United States? The women's movement has been one of the major social and political phenomena of the past quarter century. If the major parties were not to be marginalized, they would have to respond and adapt to feminism. But women have been vastly underrepresented as activists, leaders, nominees, and elected officials within the Democratic and Republican parties. Although the increase in the number of women candidates did not match that of 1992, record numbers of women ran for political office again in 1994. Yet even if every single one of these candidates had won, women would still only have made up 25 percent of the House of Representatives and 14 percent of the Senate (Rubin 1994: 2974).

Nevertheless, the parties have been affected by the revolution in women's roles in a number of ways. The difference in the voting behavior and attitudes of men and women in the 1980s, the so-called gender gap, stimulated a party response. The Republicans were especially driven to action, as they appeared to be on the wrong side of these issues. The importance of women as voters was clearly illustrated by the 1994 elections. Women's preferences for Democratic candidates declined enough to give Republicans an edge. Thus in a memo to women's leaders, Democratic consultant Celinda Lake said, "Democrats would have retained control over both the House and Senate if women were as excited about Democrats as men were about Republicans" (as cited by Feldman 1995). Second, the increasing presence of women as party leaders is an element in the transformation of the parties. As Burrell has stated elsewhere, women "may be leaders of organizations with little life or influence in the electoral process, or they may be catalysts in the revival of the parties" (1993). Third, women's campaigns for public office have received much attention, culminating in the 1992 "Year of the American Woman in Politics" and its aftermath in the 103rd Congress and the 1994 elections.

All of these features of women's political participation—electoral, organizational, and candidacies—are related to on the state of the parties. The gender gap has stimulated party efforts to recruit and promote women candidates and advance women in their organizations. The increased influence of women within the organizations has affected attitudes and party behavior toward women candidates. And partly as a result, increasing numbers of women have been major party nominees for national and statewide office.

This chapter outlines the development of these relationships in the contemporary party system. Major issues to be explored include the increased influence of women within the party organizations and the effect this change has had on the role of the parties in recruiting and supporting women candidates. Beyond description of these changes, there are theoretical questions concerning the importance of the state of the parties for those interested in women's political leadership. The conclusion argues that strengthened political parties, particularly their organizational capacity, would be a positive force in women's pursuit of political leadership in the United States.

Women and Party Organizations

As suffrage appeared imminent, Carrie Chapman Catt, an earlier leader of the women's suffrage movement, urged women to target their political energies on the parties. "The only way to get things done is to get them done on the inside of a political party. . . . You will see the real thing in the center with the door locked tight. You will have a long hard fight before you get inside . . . but you must move right up to the center" (Chafe 1972: 34). Although women achieved some sense of parity within the ranks of party activists early on, they did indeed have a long battle to gain influence.

Although contemporary feminists have often scorned the parties and party politics and have seen party organizations as something to be overcome, their activities suggest an acknowledgment of the importance of parties in the electoral process. The initial focus of the National Women's Political Caucus (NWPC) on gaining equality for women in the delegate selection process of the Democratic and Republican presidential nominations illustrates the significance of the parties to contemporary women's rights activists from their early years of organizing[1] (Shafer 1983; Baer and Bositis 1988). Since then the NWPC has established Democratic and Republican task forces to push for greater influence for women, to increase the number of women candidates each party nominates, and to promote women's issues within those organizations. In May 1976, for example, the two task forces held a joint press conference attacking the failure of both parties to achieve even the same number of women delegates they had in 1972 (Feit 1979). The Appointments and Elections Section of the 1976 Houston Women's Rights Convention adopted a plank which, among other things, called on the parties to "encourage and recruit women to run for office and adopt written plans to assure equal representation of women in all party activities, from the precinct to the national level, with special emphasis on equal representation on the delegations to all party conventions" (Bird 1977).

The parties thus have been targets of efforts by women activists during much of the contemporary era (Freeman 1987, 1988, 1993; Costain and Costain 1987). Within the organizations, staffers, professionals, strategists, managers, and even chairs and directors are more and more likely to be women (cf. Burrell 1994 for a more extended discussion of this "backstage revolution"). In 1988, Susan Estrich became the first woman to manage a presidential campaign when she took over the Dukakis race. Mary Matalin perhaps received the ultimate political insider compliment when in the 1992 presidential election she was referred to by the media as a "strategist" for the Bush campaign. Photos accompanying a *U.S. News and World Report* news story about the campaigns further illustrate the inroads women have made. The Bush campaign was represented by a picture of Mary Matalin in action, and the Clinton camp was captured by a photo of Betsy Wright at her desk—and the story was not about women in politics (Baer 1992).

The issue of the presence and influence of women in party organizations has achieved such prominence that the presidential candidates were quizzed about it in the third debate of the 1992 election. Susan Rook asked the candidates, "I acknowledge that all of you have women and ethnic minorities working for you and working with you, but when we look at the circle of the key people closest to you—your inner circle of advisors—we see white men only. Why, and when will that change?" President Bush, in response, cited Margaret Tutwiler as a key person and then listed his cabinet appointees and his appointment record in general. Mr. Perot emphasized his history of hiring women in his business and the presence of his wife and "four beautiful daughters." Governor Clinton responded that he disagreed "that there are no women and minorities in important positions in my campaign. There are many." He went on to talk about his appointment record in Arkansas.

In 1993, women were chairs of eight Democratic and seven Republican state party organizations. They were also executive directors of twenty-five Democratic and eight Republican state parties. Two former female state party chairs serve in the 103rd Congress.[2] In its June/July 1993 issue, *Campaigns & Elections* highlighted "74 Women Who Are Changing American Politics." Twenty-nine of those women either currently or formerly held positions in party organizations.[3]

Much of the campaign strategy adopted by Republican candidates in 1994 was crafted by a predominantly female staff at the National Republican Congressional Committee. Executive Director Maria Cino hired women to fill key positions such as finance director, political director, advertising director and political action committee coordinator. Representative Bill Paxon of New York, who hired Cino, acknowledges that the decision to hire a low-profile woman was controversial. Yet Cino and her staff proved themselves by eliminating a $4.5 million debt, by building support for the Contract with America, and by encouraging challengers to associate Democratic incumbents with President Clinton (Abramson 1995). Even though equality has yet to be achieved, a sea change has occurred within the parties regarding the role of women from a quarter of a century ago.

What accounts for this change? It is a confluence of factors. Women filled a vacuum as the parties became less central to the political lives of men. For example, Romney and Harrison describe the hiring of a group of women by the Republican National Committee in 1975. "There were about a dozen women who came in within six months or so of each other. There was no money and not much structure, and women were hired for jobs they might never have been offered if things had been more organized" (1987: 182). Thus, party decline provided opportunities for women. And as the parties became more professional, different skills became more valuable. With college educations increasingly common among women, they are more likely to have these important skills—media expertise, computer skills, writing ability, and especially public relations techniques. Feminists, too, played a role in promoting women within the parties. One prominent example has been Mary Louise Smith, who became the first female chair of the Republican National Committee in 1974. She had been a founder of the National Women's Political Caucus-Iowa in 1973, and has continued to fight for women's rights within the party.

The Parties and Women Candidates and Officials

Both conventional wisdom and empirical data suggest party support for female candidates prior to 1980 was limited primarily to hopeless races. With the transformation of party leadership, party organizations are less of a barrier to women candidates. In addition, the structure of the electoral process also has changed leaving the parties with less control over nominations.

Past Efforts

Initial party efforts to increase the pool of women candidates and to assist their nominees consisted primarily of conferences, workshops, and a few targeted fundraising efforts. As early as 1974, the Democratic Party sponsored a "Campaign Conference for Democratic Women." Twelve hundred women attended and passed resolutions urging the party to do more to encourage women candidates. The conference occurred primarily because women in the party demanded it (Freeman 1987). Similar conferences did not happen within the Republican Party until nearly a decade later to offset the perceived negative effects of the gender gap in the 1980 election. Sessions geared toward the particular problems of female candidates became part of both parties' regional and national candidate training workshops during the 1980s.

Perhaps the most significant party effort prior to 1992 aimed at women candidates was Senator Richard Lugar's plan, in his capacity as chair of the Republican Senatorial Campaign Committee, to provide special funds for female Republican senatorial candidates in the 1984 election. He issued a press statement declaring: "a concerted drive by the Republican Party to stamp itself as the party of the woman elected official would serve our nation as well as it served our own political interests. . . . The full political participation of women is a moral imperative for our society, and intelligent political goal for the Republican Party." Thus, he pledged to:

> commit the RSCC to the maximum legal funding and support for any Republican woman who is nominated next year, regardless of how Democratic the state or apparently formidable the Democratic candidate. I am prepared to consider direct assistance to women candidates even prior to their nomination, a sharp departure from our usual policy. (Lugar 1983)

The pledge to aid women in *primaries* was particularly significant. The parties traditionally do not get involved in primary elections because of the danger that the party-supported candidate might lose.

In 1988, for the first time, the national party platforms included statements endorsing "full and equal access of women and minorities to elective office and party endorsement" (Democrats) and "strong support for the efforts of women in seeking an equal role in government and [commitment] to the vigorous recruitment, training and campaign support for women candidates at all levels" (Republicans). These planks were symbolic statements and they were not substantive mandates to implement specific action. Their significance lies in the recognition of the problems women candidates face, and in the ability of influential party women to make that recognition explicit and public. However, no reference was made in either party's platform to women candidates in 1992. Indeed, conferences and workshops have become passe by the 1990s because women candidates have become more integrated into the parties.

The 1992 Election

The 1992 elections has been referred to as the "Year of the American Woman in Politics" after other years touted as such proved unworthy of the title. But Senator Bob Dole complained that it was the year of Democratic women in politics and that the media had been unfair to Republicans (Dole 1992). Yet, what made it a year of such prominence for women candidates was not a media bias against Republicans or for Democrats. It was the number of Democratic female nominees and the way in which they had obtained their party's nomination that attracted media attention. The

Democratic women achieved media attention early on because they defeated establishment candidates, not because they were part of the establishment. They were viewed as outsiders and that is what made it a story for the press. In the past, Republicans had nominated women for national office, but they had not received the same type of publicity in part because they were "establishment" candidates. Had Republican Jane Doe defeated Senator Robert Dole in the primary, female Republican candidates would have received much more media exposure. In addition, significantly fewer Republican women sought their party's nomination in 1992. In the primaries, 121 female nonincumbent Democrats and seventy nonincumbent Republicans ran. Fifty-seven female Democrats competed in open seat primaries compared with twenty-five Republicans. Seventy Democrats and thirty-six Republicans won party nominations (including incumbents).

Democratic women became political stars by capturing the imagination of the country through their upset victories in party primaries. It began with Carol Moseley Braun's win over Senator Alan Dixon in Illinois and was enhanced by Lynn Yeakel's defeat of the Democratic lieutenant governor in Pennsylvania. The momentum continued when both Barbara Boxer and Dianne Feinstein won their senate primaries in California. Never before had two women simultaneously won their party's nomination for U.S. Senate from the same state.[4] Some feminists complained that had Feinstein been a man she would not have had primary opposition, that the party would have discouraged any opponents. But party organizations were basically irrelevant to the nomination of these women. Once women achieved so much success, however, and grabbed media attention, the party capitalized on it. This was especially well illustrated at the 1992 Democratic National Convention.

The Women's Caucus of the Democratic National Committee consists of women members of the DNC, accounting for approximately one-half of the national committee women in 1992. The Caucus played a prominent role in the convention with its daily "theme" meeting hosted by DNC Vice Chair Lynn Cutler. The first day focused on "Issues Moving Women in '92." The second day highlighted women candidates, an event cosponsored by the Women's Campaign Fund, EMILY's List, and the National Women's Political Caucus. On the third day abortion was discussed, and the final day featured "A Call to Arms." These daily sessions came to be seen as "the place to be"; among other things, both Bill and Hillary Clinton appeared at them. In addition, the caucus produced a booklet to help all candidates deal with gender issues, and each day included campaign training sessions for women candidates.

Thanks to Harriett Woods, president of the National Women's Political Caucus, the Democrats featured their women senatorial candidates on the opening night of their convention, dubbed "Ladies Night." Those who had already won nominations for the Senate were given the chance to speak on prime time to a national audience. This event won much applause for the party. Building on the splash women candidates had made in the primaries, the Democratic Senatorial Campaign Committee initiated the "Women's Council" in May of that year. This council was touted as the "only official party organization dedicated to recruiting and supporting women candidates" in its fact sheet. However, it was created too late to be active in recruiting efforts and did not get involved in primaries. It did raise $1.5 million, which it allocated to ten Democratic women Senate nominees. In 1993, the Women's Campaign Council concentrated on expanding its female donor base and encouraging persons in that base to become more visible and involved in the party.

A much different situation existed for the Republicans in 1992. Although the Republican Party has historically received some praise for promoting women within the organization and as candidates (Freeman 1987), it has been criticized for holding seeming "antiwoman" public policy stands. Beginning in 1976, the Republican Party started to back away from its traditional support for the Equal Rights Amendment and began to take antiabortion stances in its platform. In 1980, the process was completed and has remained ever since. Thus, moderate women (and men) in the party have found themselves in battle with the party leadership. Energy devoted to overturning these planks has taken away from efforts to encourage and support women candidates. The primary activity of the Republican Task Force of the National Women's Political Caucus in 1992, for example, was an attempt to modify the Republican platform's antiabortion plank.

Indeed, it is widely felt that many potentially good female Republican candidates have not run because of the party's opposition to abortion rights and the difficulty of winning primaries against the right wing of the party. Those who have run and won have expressed dismay at the party for not championing them more (Schwartz 1992). This was especially notable at the 1992 Republican National Convention when GOP women candidates were not showcased as their counterparts had been at the Democratic Convention. Instead they chose to spotlight women in the administration and, of course, in a controversial speech, Vice President Dan Quayle's wife Marilyn delivered a keynote address stressing women's traditional roles. Barbara Bush also gave a prime-time talk focusing on her family. The problem for the Republicans was how to advance a more public role for women while at the same time advocating a conservative political philosophy.

This is not to say that the Republican Party has become entirely anti-feminist. At their 1992 convention, former Representative and Secretary of Labor Lynn Martin (who is pro-choice) nominated George Bush, while Kay Bailey Hutchinson was elected to the senate from Texas and Christine Todd Whitman as governor in New Jersey in 1993. Also, groups within the party are working on behalf of women candidates, including the WISH List, which held training sessions for female candidates in 1993, RENEW (Republican

Network to Elect Women), and the National Federation of Republican Women. Jeanie Austen, vice chair of the Republican National Committee is bringing this group together. Of no little consequence, a majority of GOP female candidates for high office in 1992 were pro-choice.[5]

The 103rd Congress

Despite their increased numbers after the 1992 elections, women still faced problems achieving influence within Congress. This lack of influence was exemplified by the Rose Garden signing ceremony of the family leave legislation. Although family leave was identified as a women's issue, the only members of Congress who spoke at the ceremony were male Democratic leaders and committee chairs. When describing women's position in Congress, the president of the National Women's Political Caucus, Harriett Woods, said, "the reality is they are the bottom of the heap and a decided minority" (Hook 1993: 2707).

Women face two obstacles within Congress. First, the seniority system prevents recently elected women from achieving powerful positions. This problem could be overcome by time, but women face a second obstacle of partisan and ideological differences. In the 103rd Congress, half of the Republican women did not vote for the family leave bill, and five refused to join the Congressional Caucus on Women's Issues, which was cochaired by Patricia Schroeder (D-Colo) and Olympia J. Snowe (R-Maine). Representative Barbara F. Vucanovich (R-Nev), for example, said, "I can't see spending money on a caucus to have Pat Schroeder out there representing me" (Hook 1993: 2709). As a result, women have less clout than the black and Hispanic caucuses, even though they now have comparable numbers in Congress (Hook 1993).

The 1994 Elections

The success of women candidates in 1992 raised expectations for the 1994 elections to unrealistic levels. In 1992, women candidates rallied around the Bush administration's threat to abortion rights and the Senate Judiciary Committee's treatment of Anita Hill. Such galvanizing issues were not present in 1994. The realization that 1994 would be different dawned when several promising female candidates lost primary races. For instance, the August 2 Michigan primary was billed as the "Day of the Woman in the Year of the Outsider" because three women vied for their party's nomination to run for statewide offices. Yet the day turned out to be "a romp for male insiders" (Connolly 1994b: 2274). Rona Romney, a former Republican radio talk show host, lost the Republican Senate primary to former state party chair Spencer Abraham, while Lana Pollock, a state senator, lost the Democratic Senate primary to nine-term U.S. Representative Bob Carr. Deborah Anne Stabenow, another state senator, lost the Democratic gubernatorial primary to former U.S. Representative Howard Wolpe. On the same day in Missouri, Jackson County Executive Marsha Murphy lost the Democratic Senate primary to U.S. Representative Alan Wheat (Groppe 1994).

Similar disappointments occurred in the Ohio primary elections. Bernadine Healy, the former head of the National Institutes of Health, lost the Republican Senate primary to insider Lt. Gov. Mike Dewine. Meanwhile, Cuyahoga county commissioner Mary Boyle lost the Democratic Senate nomination to Joel Hyatt, the son-in-law of retired Sen. Howard Metzenbaum.

Like 1992, voters in the 1994 general elections desired change. But women no longer symbolized the ideal alternative to Washington insiders. In 1994, "change" was associated with partisanship rather than gender. Thus, incumbent Democrats often faced difficult races regardless of their sex. Included in this category were first-term women members of the U.S. House, several of whom had won swing districts in 1992. Recognizing their vulnerability, these women held several joint fundraisers (Rubin 1994). Yet despite such efforts several succumbed to the Republican sweep in 1994. These included Karan English of Arizona, Lynn Schenk of California, Marjorie Margolies-Mezvinsky of Pennsylvania, Karen Shepherd of Utah and Leslie L. Byrd of Virginia. Four additional Democratic women incumbents were defeated. Other House losses included Olympia H. Snowe (R-Maine) who left to successfully pursue a seat in the Senate, and Helen Delich-Bently (R-Md) who was defeated in her state's gubernatorial election. In all, the House lost eleven female representatives in 1994.

Despite these losses, forty-seven House seats were held by women after the 1994 elections. While Democratic women won an historic number of races in 1992, women held on to these gains through Republican victories in 1994. Republicans elected seven new women representatives in 1994, while Democrats elected only three. In House races for open seats, Republican women won 67 percent of the time, while Democratic women won only 40 percent of the time (Mandel 1994). Snowe was the only 1994 addition to women in the Senate.

This string of successes for Republican women should probably be attributed to the political climate in 1994 rather than to GOP efforts to recruit and support women. Haley Barbour, chair of the Republican National Committee, admits that his party needs to be more aggressive in showcasing GOP women (Connolly 1994a: 1141). Barbour tried to address this flaw in 1994 with a monthly television show. The show, titled *Women Who Win*, spotlighted successful GOP women in politics and business. However, moderate women candidates still face challenges from the conservative wing of the GOP, particularly this new evangelical element. Former state Rep. Susan B. Stokes faced such opposition in the primary for Kentucky's Third District. Her opponent labeled her as "the evil of the national Republican Party" and the "Hillary Clinton" of the GOP (Connolly 1994a: 1141).

According to Amy S. Conroy, executive director of the nonpartisan Women's Campaign Fund, "The idea is if you are pro-choice, you are not pro-Christian" (Connolly 1994a: 1141). Even if moderate women candidates are supported by the Republican Party, they will still face conservative opponents and voters in elections.

The women candidates in the 1994 elections may not have met inflated expectations, but it should not be seen as a setback after 1992. Despite disappointments, a record number of women ran for office in 1994 with nine Senate candidates, one hundred and eleven candidates for U.S. House, ten gubernatorial candidates, twenty-nine candidates for lieutenant governor and nine for state attorney general (Rubin 1994: 2972). According to Ruth B. Mandel, director of the Center for the American Woman and politics at Rutgers University, "The epilogue for 1994 is that women returned to their familiar position—pushing forward here, stalling a bit there, chalking up firsts or near-firsts for gender politics." In short, neither 1992 nor 1994 dramatically altered the status of women in American politics. Such changes do not occur overnight, but are the result of long-term struggles. Women made progress in 1992 and 1994 because women with political ambitions had the experience and skill to take advantage of favorable political conditions. In 1992, these conditions favored Democratic women, while Republicans gained the advantage in 1994. Women's involvement within the party organizations and as elected officials at all levels of government continue to expand. This expansion suggests that more women will be capable of turning favorable political conditions to their advantage in the future.

Women's Political Leadership and Renewed Party Organizations

The women's movement of the second half of the twentieth century has profoundly altered American political and social life. Women's rights activists have adopted insider strategies to affect change in the party system. Making the parties more "women-friendly" has been one of those strategies. In response, the parties have acted to increase the presence of women in leadership positions. But American parties have been in a weak position to substantially affect the number of women in elective office. One weakness has been the single-member district structure of the electoral process:

> Generally the party list/proportional representation (PL/PR) system results in higher women's parliamentary representation than does the single member district system. . . . The single member district electoral system is a major cause of women's low representation in the U.S. House of Representatives and in the state legislatures. (Rule and Norris 1992: 44)

Another weakness is the inability of American parties to control nominations. As part of the Progressive movement at the turn of the century, and later the opening up of the system in the early 1970s, primary elections have become the means by which candidates are chosen to run under the party's label. Unlike other countries where the parties operate as private organizations, selecting their nominees and presenting them to the voters, American party nominees are chosen by voters. Thus, from a party organization perspective, the recruitment of different types of candidates is restricted.

This "fact of life" presents two possibilities. On the one hand, the entrepreneurial system allows individuals and groups historically shut out the opportunity to run. To be sure, much of the openness of the nomination system is a direct credit to the women's movement in the 1960s and 1970s. Candidates such as Lynn Yeakel, Carol Moseley Braun, and Dianne Feinstein need not seek the blessing of party organization officials—historically men—to launch their campaigns. Women might be hesitant to return to the smoke-filled rooms now that a bit of fresh air has been let in.

But on the other hand, the current system allows individuals to flood campaigns with personal funds and beat someone who may have labored within the party and developed responsible positions. Or it allows an extremely committed group, not necessarily representative of the majority of party adherents, to overwhelm the party structure in a primary election. Even if the parties encourage women to seek the nomination in winnable seats, there is no guarantee that they will get the nomination. Party organizations rarely get involved in primary elections, although they can, and do in some areas, operate under a system of preprimary endorsements. But these endorsements can be a negative asset; outsiders often use them to suggest the process is undemocratic. Thus, the idea that the parties can make greater efforts to run more women candidates rings hollow. In a sense, the success of early feminist activities—the opening up of the system—may now serve as golden handcuffs.

What role is left for the parties to increase the number of women in party affairs and elected office? We have seen that the organizational capacity of the party has increased over the last decade. Party units now represent the largest single source of contributions to congressional elections. As suggested in other chapters in this volume (chaps. 11 and 12), there is considerable variance as to which candidates are slated for assistance—the foremost criteria being the closeness of the race. Yet, if the parties wish to develop a competitive edge in the long run, and if they take the gender gap seriously, they should broaden their targeting criteria to heighten the importance of female candidates. Moreover, if Paul Herrnson (1986, 1988) is correct that party organizations have become "brokerage" units, they can narrow the historic distance between large, nonparty contributors (such as PACs) and women candidates. It would also be to the advantage of the parties to encourage *local* party organizations to support women candidates. They might draw up lists of potential candidates, aid their election efforts, and ultimately use these groups as "farm clubs" for higher level runs. After all, most of the successful women in congressional and senatorial elections in 1992 had considerable experience in governing and running for local office. Ultimately, the success of women in party politics will be judged by the number of female candidates the parties help get elected.

In recent times, women have become more prominent and skillful within the parties—both as insiders and as candidates. If parties continue to advance the cause of women it is likely they will remain viable instrument in the electoral process. If parties are primarily concerned with winning elections, this new direction simply makes good sense.

Notes

1. Anne and Douglas Costain have argued that the women's movement did not focus on the parties as a means to political power until the 1980s. They may have underestimated the extent to which transforming the parties was a tactic undertaken by elements of the women's rights community earlier (1987).

2. Nancy Pelosi (D-Calif) and Jennifer Dunn (R-Wash).

3. Many of the others had strong ties to one of the major parties, including such individuals as Hillary Clinton and Tipper Gore.

4. Of course it is an unusual set of circumstances when two Senate seats in one state are open at the same time.

5. In 1993, 50 percent of the female Republican members of the U.S. House of Representatives voted to repeal the Hyde Amendment, which prohibits federal financing of abortions, compared with only 4 percent of male Republicans.

PART FIVE

Reconceptualizing Parties

22

Resurgent or Just Busy?
Party Organizations in Contemporary America

John J. Coleman

Forty years ago, the American Political Science Association (APSA) Committee on Political Parties (1950) precipitated a storm of controversy with a critique of American parties. Many political scientists were sympathetic to the committee's call for responsible parties, but an equally sizable contingent agreed with Pendleton Herring's (1940) classic analysis: the United States had parties appropriate to its political culture and government structure, attempts to change these parties were probably futile, and any such changes would be dangerous for American democracy.

Twenty years ago, scholars began to diagnose the decline of American parties as central organizing structures in American politics.[1] Many writers pointed to decline stretching half a century or longer; others argued that the decline was particularly severe in the postwar period. In effect, these writers viewed even the parties criticized by the APSA party report to be preferable to the parties of the late 1960s.

Today, a new orthodoxy in party organization scholarship challenges the party decline analysis. With few exceptions, writers concentrating on party organizations argue that parties are more active and more significant than earlier literature implied. According to this view, the party decline school mistakenly assumed that problems in the electorate and in Congress indicated the decline of the party *system* and, by extension, party organizations. Although these scholars concede that the strength of the party system cannot be inferred from the strength of party organizations, they also argue that such an assessment has to include party organizations (Gibson, Cotter, Bibby, Huckshorn 1983: 194). The logical implication of this analysis is that the party system is stronger than the party decline model suggests. The irony is rich: the "revivalists," who usually express sympathy with the Herring view of parties, argue that some of what the APSA committee demanded has come to pass and the American political order is better for it (see inventory in Baer and Bositis 1993: appendix). But they challenge the "declinists" who grudgingly accepted the Herring-approved political parties of the early postwar period.

Once we move beyond the notion of increased party activity, several shortcomings in the recent party revival literature become clear. Here I address several of these deficiencies. Because it is done so well in many of the sources I cite, I will not provide an extensive review of the findings in the literature. Moreover, despite a critical tone, this chapter should not be construed as a wholesale indictment on an impressive body of research. Recent party organization research has filled a large gap in the study of parties, addressed with precision several anomalies in that larger literature, been innovative in measurement and research design, and proven remarkably cumulative. My objective is to point out research gaps and to encourage a more integrated analysis of the party system.

The New Orthodoxy

The past decade has seen a sea change among party scholars regarding the health of party organizations in the United States. Where fifteen years ago there was consensus that party organizations were weak, today the consensus argues that party organizations are revitalized, resurgent, and relevant. Scholars have conducted large-scale surveys of state and county party chairs and found that those organizations report performing more activities today than at any time since the second World War.[2] Campaign finance studies indicate that ever larger sums pass through the hands of various party committees on the national, state, and county (local) levels and that these funds, with some party differences, are generally targeted toward competitive races.[3] These scholars are enthused about what they see happening with the party organizations and are convinced that "parties matter" (Gibson and Scarrow 1993).

Virtually all party scholars agree that there has been real change in party activity on the national, state, and county levels. But there are some peculiarities in the data. Cotter, Gibson, Bibby, and Huckshorn (1984: 39, 54), for example, find that most of the increase in state and county party organizational strength occurred in the 1960s, which is not widely considered the heyday of party organizational resurgence. Indeed, Herrnson and Menefee-Libey (1990), *begin* their overview of party organizational change in the late 1960s, and many writers focus on changes in the late 1970s and early 1980s. A second disturbance in the claims about party organizations concerns the status of local parties. Most of the literature focuses on county party organizations, and here, as with the national and state parties, the consensus is that parties are doing more today than previously (cf. Lawson, Pomper, and Moakley 1986). Studies of cities, however, show a more mixed pattern, with the authors in Crotty (1986) generally encouraged by what they see while authors like Ware (1985) argue city party organizations have lost so many of their traditional functions, especially control of nominations, that they are but a shell of their former selves (Johnston 1979).

Despite these peculiarities in the data, the case that party organizations are performing more activities and raising more funds today is strong enough that one cannot get very far arguing that it is not so. But armed with this data, the party organization literature has leapt too quickly to words like "resurgence" and "revitalization." Increased activity should only be the *start* of a conception of resurgent parties. That conception also needs to account for the party organizations' relations with other actors and institutions in the political universe. To make a business analogy, over the past few years there has been much speculation in the business press about the troubles afflicting the International Business Machines Corporation (IBM). Suppose that with new leadership, IBM were to begin restructuring and reallocating organizational responsibilities, changing prices, and introducing new product lines. It is difficult to imagine that we would hear much about IBM being "resurgent" and "revitalized" unless customers returned to IBM products and IBM's profitability improved, even if analysts admired IBM's efforts. Even praising the company's ability to hold its market share steady would be considered at best a backhanded compliment. We should ask the same questions of parties: are the customers returning and are the parties increasing their "market" share? One might argue that if market share is measured as the percentage of offices held by the two major parties or by candidates' use of party services, then indeed market share is high and perhaps growing. But if market share is measured in other ways—such as the percentage of voters given enough incentive to turn out to vote—a different picture might well emerge. However one measures the benchmarks, the point is that resurgence is indicated not by organizational restructuring alone but by the *effects* of restructuring.

Bringing the Voters Back In

One striking anomaly in the contemporary party system is that at the same time scholars argue that party organizations are reviving, the public has become increasingly skeptical about the relevance of political parties to governing and the desirability of partisan activity in general (Fiorina 1980; Burnham 1982; Brady 1990; Milkis 1993). More citizens say that interest groups better represent them than do political parties, and the interest group advantage is particularly heavy among the young (Advisory Commission on Intergovernmental Relations 1986: 52). Record numbers of voters split their tickets and record numbers of districts have split outcomes—that is, supporting a president of one party and a member of Congress from another. Voting patterns are increasingly inconsistent: it is harder to predict what will happen in one race by knowing the outcome in another and it is harder to predict voting patterns two years hence based on voting patterns today. Only half the electorate bothers to vote in presidential elections and about one-third votes in off-year congressional elections. Electoral turnout varies substantially across states and across offices; in the absence of a gubernatorial campaign, turnout is low. Local turnout is usually low as well. In 1992, nineteen percent of the voting public supported an independent candidate for president who had held no political office, was all but unknown seven months before the election, did almost no campaigning in the traditional sense, and spoke a harshly antiparty message.

It is difficult to understand any of these developments through the lenses provided by party organization theory. Perhaps one could argue that decreasing party loyalty is a sign of party organizational strength: that is, the organizations have become so effective at campaigning that they uproot traditional voter loyalties (Cotter, Gibson, Bibby, and Huckshorn 1984: 103). Perhaps organizational strength would explain the phenomenon of segmented or dual partisanship—identifying oneself with one major party for federal offices and the other major party for state offices—but segmented partisanship is difficult to correlate with the data indicating that party organizations are also becoming more integrated, unless national-state-local party integration is devoid of substantive policy content. But we know that this is certainly not true for the Republicans and their widely praised service-provision activities for candidates at all levels. These arguments also reverse the causation in Schlesinger's (1991) much cited formulation that decreased voter loyalty *led* to increased party organizational efforts (it is not clear in Schlesinger what led to the decreased loyalties). In short, no compelling case has been made within the organizational framework to explain increasingly variable voting patterns across offices and years.

Thus, widespread lack of trust in parties and the increasing tendency for voters to view parties as unnecessary and perhaps unhelpful appendages to the political system pose a large puzzle for the new orthodoxy (Wattenberg 1990). Now, this is not to argue that antipartisan attitudes are unique to the present period; they have to one extent or another been a common part of American political culture (Epstein 1986). But the level of disgust and bitterness with "politics as usual" is now exceptionally high—and political parties are surely part of "politics as usual." Though today many political scientists do indeed scoff at the public's discontent, suggesting that the public is either spoiled, ignorant, manipulated by demagogues, or all three,[4] the negative public mood is reflected in turnout, voting behavior, and attitudes toward parties. Party organizations have increased their activity levels; voters are unimpressed. Ross Perot may not be easy to explain in any context, but within the celebration of party "resurgence" and "revitalization" in the party organization literature he becomes an enormous enigma. If the dominance of offices and votes by the two major parties is a measure of party strength, then it is hard to understand why one-fifth of the electorate abandoned the parties' presidential candidates *after* a sustained period of party "resurgence." [5]

One might argue that this discontent is a result of particularly effective campaign tactics spearheaded by party strategists. In this reading, discontent is actually a result of party organizational strength. Certainly many post-mortem analyses of the 1988 Bush campaign reached such a conclusion. But for the party organizations, such a resolution is hardly satisfactory because it suggests one of two things: (1) party organizations help candidates whip up discontent about real issues to win office, but along with party-in-government they are unable to do anything to restore public confidence once in office—that is, the problems are real but the parties are unable to effect any change; or (2) party organizations help whip up discontent about nonexistent or irrelevant problems. The first alternative suggests a collapse of account-ability in the political system, at least accountability oriented around political parties; the second suggests that party organizations willingly debase public discourse to win office, which raises disturbing normative issues (see below).

The striking contrast between the literature on party organizations and observations on partisanship in the electorate results from the dominance of supply-side analysis in the party organization literature, namely, examining what parties are doing (or say they are doing). From such analysis it is easy to conclude that parties are resurgent—parties must be stronger if they are doing more rather than less.[6] But what this literature has ignored is the demand-side represented by the electorate. Where studies of late nineteenth and early twentieth century party organizations place a great deal of emphasis on the interaction between party officials and the citizenry (McGerr 1986; Bridges 1986; Shefter 1976, 1994: chap. 4; cf. Brown and Halaby 1987), studies of recent party organization stress what the party is supplying and de-emphasize how the public is responding. The emerging "truncated" or service-provider model of the party teaches us about changes in modern campaigning, but not about the broader place of party in American politics. How much must public discontent with the parties grow before organizational studies recognize the implications of those negative signs for party "revitalization" or "resurgence"? Is it more important that targeted party activity might raise turnout two or three percentage points in a given election *or* that turnout has dropped steadily over time and is lower now than when the party organizations were "weak"? Only an unduly narrow view of party organization can suggest our primary interest is whether candidates think party assistance is helpful.

A handful of studies do look closely at the link between party organization (or party competition, which is not necessarily the same thing) and public response. These studies stress primarily the parties' direct and indirect influence on turnout; they usually find that party activities indeed have some impact.[7] But if public response to turnout efforts is a valid part of party organization scholarship, why not public views or behavior toward party?

One argument might be party organizations see voter turnout as one of their functions, but public attitudes toward parties are not in their purview. This argument misses the point. Intended or not, party behavior through campaigning and governing are public acts and may produce public discontent. Parties ignoring this discontent because "it's not our problem" have a history of being deformed through reforms. Public opinion matters.

What about linkage at the other end? Although my focus is on the linkage between party organizations and voters, studies of the connection between party organizations and party-in-government have been similarly limited. Two strong supporters of contemporary party organizations acknowledge that "much less is known about how party organizations affect public policy" (Gibson and Scarrow 1993: 245) than about how they affect elections. They note there is some possibility that these organizations can affect policy direction. On the whole, however, it is "highly doubtful that [they] have much of an ideological effect" (1993: 245) once public officials take office. But, they point out, there is some possibility for affecting party policy at the margin through the recruitment and nomination process (Gibson, Frendreis, and Vertz 1989). Although Republican National Committee chairman Haley Barbour's involvement in congressional party strategy in 1994 and 1995 was notable, it is unclear whether this is an institutional relationship between the organizational and legislative branches of the party or a personal relationship between particular individuals that may fade as these individuals depart the scene. It is also unclear whether Barbour was a leading, influential policy player or primarily carrying water for the Republican leadership. One small group of recent studies does attempt to discern whether party organization activity has any influence on elected officials' policy decisions; the influence is at best slight (Cotter et al. 1984; Leyden and Borrelli 1990; Dwyre 1992, 1993; cf. Wright 1994). As Lawson, Pomper, and Moakley (1986: 368, 369) point out, our knowledge about the parties' performance as linkages between citizens and the state "remain[s] fragmentary and inconclusive."

Methodological obstacles have surely been one hindrance to examining the linkage between party organizations and party-in-government. In their discussion of party organization relationships with elected officeholders, Cotter, Gibson, Bibby, and Huckshorn warn that "these interpretations must be treated as only suggestive because of the small number of cases, the lack of control variables, and uncertainty about the appropriateness of generalizing from the high and low strength ranges that are actually party-specific" (1984: 118). This cautionary note provides a good sense of the difficulties. Similar complexities face the analyst examining whether party organizations influence election results.

Linkage at both ends—citizen to party organization and organization to elected officeholder—is strained. Because I believe the problems with voters deserve special attention, I have placed extra emphasis on the former. If parties' "raison d'être is to create a substantive connection between rulers and ruled" (Lawson 1980: 3),[8] then we have a problem if voters pay little attention to party efforts or their antipathy to party grows. It is misleading to cast stepped-up party activity as yet another indication of party "resurgence." Before drawing such conclusions, we need to look beyond party intentions to their results, and these results must encompass the behavior and perceptions of the public as well as candidates.

Accentuate the Positive, Ignore the Normative

Part of the reason that party organization scholars have been eager to move the discipline away from the notion of party decline is that these scholars tend to believe deeply in the positive contributions parties make to the American political system. Even though many if not most disagree passionately with E. E. Schattschneider's vision of the ideal political party for the United States, they typically endorse Schattschneider's frequently noted contention that "modern democracy is unthinkable save in terms of the parties" (1942: 1). When party organization students contend that "parties matter," they are making both an empirical and normative statement.[9]

Despite this normative endorsement of parties, the organization literature has been surprisingly quiet about key features of American politics during the era of resurgent party organizations. Beyond the problem of the electorate's response to party organizational changes are questions concerning practices in American politics that are directly related to the parties' service-provider activities. The results of these activities have not always been pretty. Yet the party organization literature has said little about their normative implications.

Our interest in the health of political parties should not be divorced from our interest in the health of politics or the political system. For example, the new orthodoxy is generally very positive about the efforts of the parties to raise and distribute more campaign funds and their efforts to coexist peacefully with interest groups and political action committees. Yet other studies raise troubling questions about the parties' increasing reliance on raising huge sums of money from special interests (Edsall 1984; Ferguson and Rogers 1986; Ferguson 1995). The implicit stance of organization theorists is that the parties' *ability* to raise this money is more significant than the *effects* of this reliance on massive fundraising. Are party organizations part of the problem with money in politics or part of the solution? Are they making a bad situation—the intersection of money and politics—worse? Indeed, the intersection of money and politics is a significant aspect of the public discontent mentioned above. It is one thing to note that a party committee is holding a "breakfast" for important contributors; it is quite another to ignore that these activities may resonate very poorly within the public at large and may, in the long run, be harmful for the credibility and legitimacy of political parties. The party organizations' tremendous "success" at funneling "soft money" into campaigns raises similar problems. Although some studies make the plausible argument that parties make the situation less distasteful than it might be by serving as an intermediary of funds for candidates—and as the largest single provider for most candidates (Herrnson 1988, 1990)—these important normative questions are discussed infrequently.

Another normative issue concerns voter turnout. As I mentioned above, several studies indicate that party mobilization efforts can have a positive impact on voter turnout. But studies of organization tend to ignore the flip side—parties can and do effectively demobilize as well (Shefter 1984; Piven and Cloward 1989). This is certainly not news, as the trajectory of Southern and Progressive politics after the turn of the century makes clear. Rosenstone and Hansen (1993: 162–77, 215) attribute the bulk of the decline in turnout since the early 1960s to decreasing efforts to mobilize voters by various organizations, including, most prominently, the political parties. One explanation is that the parties have chosen to de-emphasize labor-intensive mobilization in the new capital-and-technology-intensive electoral system (Frantzich 1989). Officials and workers in party organizations may not have the luxury to contemplate the participatory implications of this kind of shift; it is incumbent upon party organization scholars to do so. Organizational adaptation that is rational in the short term may not prove to be so in the long term.

The point here is simple: we either believe that declining turnout is bad for the political system or we do not. If we do, we need to be clear about the parties' contribution to something we consider corrosive to democracy. Without denying the need for technological adaptation and sophistication, we can question whether the extent of the move *away* from labor-intensive mobilization is as inevitable as it is normally portrayed. It may be the case that county chairs see their efforts as most significant in "grass-roots activity emphasizing ties to local people," such as organizing campaign events and get-out-the-vote drives (Frendreis, Gitelson, Flemming, and Layzell 1993: 10), but the dismal state of turnout (especially in local races) has to lead one to question how effective or extensive these activities are. What do we want from parties? A party organization and party system that I would label "resurgent" or "revitalized" would not be one that witnesses sustained declining participation or one with participation levels as low as at present.

A third normative issue concerns the quality of modern campaigns. As party organizations claim increasing involvement in recruiting candidates, assisting the strategy and conduct of campaigns, and acting as intermediaries between the candidates and the private market of campaign services (Maisel, Fowler, Jones, and Stone 1990; Kazee and Thornberry 1990; Frendreis, Gibson, and Vertz 1990), they should be judged on the quality of these campaigns. I do not want to overstate this point. The organization literature is, it seems to me, very careful to avoid projecting party organizations as the lead institutions in contemporary campaigns but rather as the supporting cast for candidate organizations (which some students might, of course, reasonably note as a sign of party decline). Again, although party organizations do not have the luxury of stepping back to analyze the quality of campaigns, political scientists, even those enthused about the changes in party organizations, should. There are plausible arguments on each side of this issue—some argue that modern campaigns are informative (Popkin 1991), others assert that campaigns have become shrill, uninformative, divisive, and unrelated to the real tasks of governance that follow the election (Blumenthal 1990; Dionne 1991; Bennett 1992). Are the resurgent party organizations helping corrode the discourse of American campaigns? If campaigning is increasingly divorced from governing, we should question the contributions of institutions intimately involved in campaigns and campaign strategy.

The point of these examples is that such normative issues should not be ignored by the proponents of party organizational resurgence. The literature lacks a critical appraisal of the content of the activities the parties perform. By way of contrast, analyses of interest groups often manage to merge support of interest group involvement in the political process with critical assessments of the impact of interest groups on the political system. This omission is important, for as Lawson, Pomper, and Moakley (1986: 369) note, "the parties, including their hard-working activists, may be willing to endure public contempt so long as they win elections, but how long will the public tolerate such parties?"

Successful at What?

One message found throughout the party organization literature is that party organizations play an important role in American politics. Surprisingly, however, the exact nature of the success achieved by these organizations is often left vague. And measures of success that appear obvious are overlooked. This problem is related to the more general tendency to focus on activities and pay less attention to effects.

Most studies on party organization are particularly impressed with the efforts of the Republican Party to restructure its organizational apparatus, upgrade its service capacities, and improve the product it offers candidates and potential candidates. What is surprising, however, is the lack of hard data in the literature showing that the Republican efforts have made much difference in the electoral landscape. Republican organizational efforts have probably boosted the party's fortunes in the South, though certainly the internal collapse of the Democrats was also a factor. But more generally one can ask: where is the evidence that Republicans have received much of a return on the massive amounts of money they have spent on organizational enhancement over the past two decades? Perhaps the Republican capture of the Senate in 1980 was due in part to Republican organizational efforts, with the cooperation of sympathetic groups like the National Conservative Political Action Committee. Some scholars (e.g., Jacobson 1985–86) argue plausibly that Republican losses might have been much more severe in the deep recession of 1982 if not for the efforts of the Republican campaign committees, but the data is not hard.[10] And one can expect similar contentions about Republican prowess to be made in the wake of the massive Republican success in the 1994 elections. Party organization efforts, however, must compete with other significant explanatory factors. General approval of the Reagan/Republican governmental reduction agenda, skepticism about Democratic competence, lack of a Democratic program, a perception of tremendous economic and social insecurity, the inexorable waning of the Democratic New Deal regime; the efforts of Republican leadership PACs, the widespread funding of conservative think tanks and ideas, and the gradual withdrawal of lower-income individuals from the electorate are a few of the more prominent possibilities for explaining these recent events. I make these points not to suggest that the Republican organizational efforts have been for naught; at the very least, the Republicans' ability to compete for more offices has been a great boon to the party. Even here, however, ambition theory suggests that an ambitious politician would find the Republican label attractive not because of the Republican organization per se but because the long-term implosion and dissolution of the Democratic Party made it an increasingly questionable strategic career choice (Aldrich 1995; Schlesinger 1991). If the Democrats do not seem to be the road to political security and success, and certainly they looked less and less like that road over the last two to three decades, then the Republicans are the only other significant game in town. Republican organizations can assist these putative candidates; they are less likely to create the conditions that produce these candidates. My point is simply that for all the apparent Republican advantages in party organization, both at the national and state level, one might have expected some clearer demonstrated payoff over and above the success produced by the other forces listed above.

Beyond the question of recent Republican "success," evidence is mixed regarding the effect of party organizations on election outcomes. Gibson and Scarrow (1993: 242–43) note that evidence suggests party organizations made a difference in election outcomes in specific cases. Cotter et al. (1984), on the other hand, found that over time a party's relative electoral success (measured by the Ranney index) bore little relationship to the strength of its state party organizations. A mild to moderate relationship was, however, uncovered for nonsouth gubernatorial elections. Both studies properly note the methodological difficulties inherent in teasing out the effect of party organizations on election results.

Success is also related to what writers believe the important role of the parties to be. As mentioned above, the service-provider and party-as-broker views have clearly gained ground in recent years, but it is not generally acknowledged that we should consider the set of tasks confronting parties—or that they choose to confront—when we estimate whether party organizations are resurgent and revitalized. In other words, what are we expecting parties to do? The more limited our expectations, the more likely we see success and resurgence. Ware perhaps puts this point most clearly when he observes that

> A strong party organization is one which, at the very least, can determine who will be the party's candidates, can decide (broadly) the issues on which electoral campaigns will be fought by its candidates, contributes the "lion's share" of resources to the candidates' elections campaigns, and has influence over appointments made by elected public officials. (1988: x)

For scholars the question must be whether the "successes" garnered by the truncated party are as significant as the "successes" of past parties as depicted by Ware.

An increasing party role in campaign finance is seen by many as a key success of modern party organizations. Although it is true that the parties raise more money than previously and that they use that money more carefully, it is also the case that legislative campaign committees have become dominant in the funding of legislative races. Rather than increasing the influence of party or working to pull parts of the party together, Sorauf and Wilson (1990) argue that the dominance of the legislative campaign committees reflects an effort by legislators to remain autonomous from the wider party (see also chap. 11 in this volume). Therefore the increasing role for the parties in this aspect of campaign finance may increase the likelihood of party members winning but it does not, as Sorauf and Wilson suggest, increase the integration of the party.

Another irony regarding success is that as party organizations became more efficient in campaign finance and campaign assistance, fewer members of the parties in Congress needed the services as incumbency reelection rates and margins increased. When one-half of the challenger party's adherents are willing to abandon their party identification in order to support the incumbent member of Congress (Abramson, Aldrich, and Rohde 1994), the incumbent's party organization needs to play a truly relevant role in fewer contests. This is useful, because it allows parties to concentrate their resources, but it does suggest how much of the electoral universe is largely beyond the influence of party organizations.

As noted above, organization scholars are careful to avoid attributing too much influence or strength to party organizations. In campaigns, for example, the party is clearly seen as a supporting institution to the candidate. Yet the line between success and failure is perilously close. To take the most recent data as an example, Frendreis, Gitelson, Flemming and Layzell (1993) report that state legislative candidates rate county party organizations as "slightly" effective only in recruiting campaign volunteers and getting out the vote. On organizing campaign events, fundraising, and campaign management and development of strategy, the county parties rate somewhere between "not important" to "slightly important." Even discounting for candidate hubris, this evidence suggests the parties are of rather minimal importance. It is difficult to imagine that someone attracted to the party decline idea would find this evidence particularly challenging. The literature needs to provide a better sense of why *this level* of influence matters. Party organization students clearly want to believe that parties are an important and necessary part of modern campaigns and elections, even if idealistic, responsible parties are implausible: "While adaptive brokerage parties may be less than perfect vehicles for the organization of political debate and the development of public policy, the alternative—electorally irrelevant parties—are wholly inadequate to the requirements of American politics" (Frendreis et al. 1993: 14). But scholars need to spell out *why* these parties would be wholly inadequate. Indeed, Bledsoe and Welch suggest that this electoral role may be the *least* significant one parties perform and not one they need perform alone: "Though these other agents [interest groups, political action committees, consultants] can replace the party organization as an election vehicle, they contribute nothing to the process of governing: the coalition building, political accountability, and policy coherence that may be offered by a healthy party system" (1987: 265).

Fighting the Last Battle

One reason for the shortcomings in the party organization literature, I believe, is an ongoing interest in challenging the thesis of party decline. The argument between these schools is remarkably reminiscent of the responsible parties vs. functional (or "indigenous") parties dispute that swept the field forty years ago. But like that dispute, today's debate has become unproductive.

First, there has been a tendency in the organization literature to overstate the central thrust of the decline argument. Some decline analysts certainly projected an extremely dim view of party prospects. Most, however, were making the simple point that the contemporary parties were in several respects less central to the political process than they were previously. It is correct to note that they usually overlooked party organizations. But it seems to me unhelpful to caricature the party decline approach with terms like "demise," "prophets," "strident," "impressionistic," "exaggerate," "swamped," or "decimated," or to suggest that party decline theorists yearned only for the "golden age" of party modeled on a "few" urban political machines or "disciplined, socialist" parties as found in Europe (all in Patterson 1989).[11] It would also be fair to suggest that these strident prophets have so far given us more leverage to understand contemporary political discontent in the United States than have the apostles of adaptation and resurgence.

For many decline writers it was difficult to imagine the trends changing dramatically. As we know, however, the trends did partially change: parties in the Congress and party organizations both showed new signs of life in the 1980s. But when most of the decline arguments were being written, it was indeed difficult to see signs of renewal. This was especially true because of the lack of any overarching theory of party that integrated the developments at each geographic level of party and for each of the three major party components. Yet far from falsely assuming party decline, the decline theorists did not typically make arguments that were incompatible with "the facts" as presented in the party organization literature. One major study in the party organization school, for example, accepts that the party organizations from World War II to the mid-1970s were clearly inferior to and of lesser significance than the party organizations before the war (Herrnson 1988). For a decline writer to *assume* weak party organizations was not advisable, but apparently not incorrect. Herrnson argues that the party organizations adapted and took on new roles after the mid-1970s and that the party organizations now fit their environment well (Herrnson 1988: 30). But he does acknowledge that they may not be needed to the same degree they were in the environment of the late nineteenth century—that is, the "constituent" nature of and demands on parties had shrunk (Lowi 1975 and also chap. 4 in this volume).

Intent on demonstrating that at least part of the party system was not declining, a second problem in the party organization literature is an insufficient emphasis on integrating party theory. As I stated above, this relative neglect has meant turning a blind eye to the response of the public to the improvements in party organizational strength. Cotter et al. (1984: 167), for example, who *are* interested in integrating party organizations into the bigger party picture, devote but one paragraph to the relations between party organizations and the public, and that one paragraph seems to dismiss the reality or significance of negative public perceptions.[12] I would suggest that the failure to deal with normative questions also stems from this desire to demonstrate that not all of the party system has declined. This approach was perhaps warranted at the outset; it has now become counter- productive.

Third, there is a real risk of walking into the same analytical trap that ensnared writers on party decline: if one builds ones theory on a single part of the data trend one finds it very difficult to explain how that trend might stop. The variables examined by party decline analyses pointed in the direction of future decline; by limiting the dependent variable to periods of decline, declinists overlooked independent variables that might alter the trend. Today, the party organization literature faces the same problem. To build more theory into these studies, revivalists need to consider seriously what could disrupt the projected trajectory of ever more involved, ever more relevant party organizations.

Finally, this concern with fighting the last battle leads to the use of a "counteracting" party model (see Cotter and Bibby 1980: 26–27 for an early example; see Frendreis, Gibson, and Vertz 1990 for a recent treatment). This model suggests that even if there is some sign of decline elsewhere in the party system, say among voters, the revival in party organization "counteracts" that decline. Unfortunately, it is not clear what is entailed in counteracting other parts of the political system. What would be different if this counteraction did not occur? How do we know? How does this counteraction affect what happens in those areas that might indeed be in decline; that is, what does this mean for the "counteractee"? How are party organizations different because they play a counteracting rather than parallel role with other party elements? A stronger version of the counteracting model argues that party organizational resurgence *depended* on party decline among voters (Schlesinger 1991). Although perhaps consistent with recent American politics, a look back to the late nineteenth century suggests that this pattern is not a general principle of party development. A more modest version asserts that strong party organizations have counteracted party decline elsewhere in the system, "thus making the party system more resilient to anti-party and dealigning influences" (Bibby et al. 1983: 26). But how do we know if these organizations have indeed made the system more resilient—what is the null expectation? Looking at the recent developments in public opinion and behavior makes one wonder just how effective these counteractive party organizations have been in resisting these influences, or whether counteraction is likely only under certain conditions (Coleman 1996b).

Searching for Integration: "The State of the Parties"

I have suggested in this chapter some reasons to question the new orthodoxy that party organizations are "resurgent" or "revitalized." In conclusion I want to focus less on the organizations per se and more on the political science analysis of these organizations.

Party scholars need to take seriously the goal of integrating party theory and probing the relationships between different parts of the party system. Herrnson reports:

> Some analysts have questioned the propriety of using evidence about the party-in-the-electorate and the party-in-government to support the hypothesis that political parties in general, and especially party organizations, are in decline. Blurring the distinctions between the three dimensions of the political party may lead to a misunderstanding of the nature of party development and result in faulty conclusions about the condition of party organizations. (1988: 5)

I am not arguing that the distinctions be blurred, only that we understand better how these aspects of party fit together. Indeed, many party organization studies touch on these connections. I am not arguing that we aim for faulty conclusions, only that we recognize that because the party system fits together it is misleading to ignore the other components when studying any one of the three. If there is finally something called "party" that exists beyond these individual components, it is at least partially defined as the centrality of party organizations, party-in-government, and party-in-the-electorate to the way in which the business of democracy gets done: selecting candidates and running campaigns, deciding how to vote, designing and implementing public policy, and so on. If voters were exceptionally loyal to parties and thought they mattered greatly, but parties in Congress were hardly cohesive and party organizations did next to nothing, I would be uncomfortable talking about parties being healthy. Similarly, when assessing the health of the party system it is a mistake to overlook party-in-government and especially unwise to overlook public opinion, voting turnout, and political behavior, even if the party system has active party organizations. When party organizations begin to pull the electorate along as they perform their activities, my enthusiasm about the revitalization of American party organizations and the party system will increase.

Though there are good reasons to begin integrating party theory, less clear is how one goes about this (Epstein 1986; Schlesinger 1991). Elsewhere I make the argument that party decline—*and* party improvement—can be understood only if parties are analyzed within their structural and policy settings (Coleman 1994, 1996a). For the postwar period, this means tying party decline to the construction of a "fiscal state" in the 1930s and 1940s that oriented party competition around macroeconomic management issues on which the parties in Congress tended to converge at crucial moments (e.g., recessions). At the same time, this fiscal state structurally limited party responsibility for the economy. Voters, sensibly, paid decreasing attention to parties, and either exited the electorate or focused on individual candidates. When this macroeconomic system began to crumble in the stagflation of the 1970s, the collapse of the Keynesian consensus created an opening for improvement in the status of political parties.[13] Increased party cohesiveness in Congress and new attempts to enhance the capacities of party organizations reflected this improvement. But enough of the fiscal state remained intact that these changes did not filter down to the electorate. Because elites and voters can restructure the state, especially at crisis points, the decline of party need not be inevitable or irreversible. To this approach, "the state of the parties" is a phrase rich in meaning.

There are three important points here. First, this kind of approach suggests that party organizational resurgence occurred when it did for some concrete reasons. Herrnson and Menefee-Libey's (1990) outline of the development of party organization since 1968 is a necessary but not sufficient explanation of what happened because it overlooks the success of the parties' fundraising efforts from the donors' perspective. To understand the changes in party organization over the past twenty-five years, we need to know why donors were particularly willing to give in the late 1970s. With the collapse of the postwar macroeconomic governing consensus and dramatic changes emerging in the global economy, it is not surprising that concerned elites and members of the middle class would find Republican appeals to be particularly attractive. That is, Republican organizational improvement depended crucially on the availability of a large body of willing givers, and a model of party development needs to explain why those givers were available at that particular time. Organizational and technological changes may have helped locate these donors, but it was less responsible for creating the incentives to contribute than were the events in the political economy. In this vein, one might say that the difference between Barry Goldwater in 1964, Ronald Reagan in 1980, and Newt Gingrich in 1994 was not that the Republicans' party organization had become so much more proficient, but that Goldwater was running in 1964, Reagan in 1980, and Gingrich in 1994—years that were worlds apart politically and economically.

Second, political scientists have learned a significant amount by analyzing the components of political parties in isolation from each other, but in a period of transition such as the present this tripartite model of parties obscures our understanding (Baer and Bositis 1988: chaps. 1–2; Aldrich 1995). We cannot understand what has happened with party organizations or, more importantly, the significance of any changes that have occurred, unless we demonstrate concretely how party activity affects citizens, public officials, and elections.

The final point is that in a democratic polity the status of political parties ultimately boils down to the public. Despite the enthusiasm in the party organization literature, *party* decline does not end until the voters return to party. The public's beliefs and behavior regarding the salience and relevance of party has to be an important standard of party decline or resurgence. Not just changes in party activities, but also changes in the state—the structural settings of parties—are required before the voters return. Voters (and nonvoters) must believe parties control policy areas, that these policy areas are important, and that the parties differ in significant ways before we can expect any resurgence at the voter level. Short of this change, the plausibility of parties as grassroots, representative institutions comes under serious strain. The meaningfulness of party organizational "resurgence" in such a system is dubious.

Notes

1. The literature is enormous. A representative sample includes Burnham 1982; Clubb and Traugott 1977; Cooper and Hurley 1977; Brady, Cooper, and Hurley 1979; Collie and Brady 1985; Brady 1990; Nie, Verba, and Petrocik 1979; Lipset and Schneider 1987; Crotty 1984; Fiorina 1980, 1987, 1990; Kirkpatrick 1979; Ranney 1975; Polsby 1983; Shefter 1994: chap. 3; Silbey 1990.

2. Cotter and Bibby 1980; Bibby, Gibson, Cotter, and Huckshorn 1983; Gibson, Cotter, Bibby, and Huckshorn 1983; Cotter, Gibson, Bibby, and Huckshorn 1984; Gibson, Cotter, Bibby, and Huckshorn 1985; Reichley 1985; Huckshorn, Gibson, Cotter, and Bibby 1986; Kayden and Mahe 1985; Sabato 1988; Gibson, Frendreis, and Vertz 1989; Bibby 1990; Frendreis, Gibson, and Vertz 1990; Frantzich 1989; Crotty 1991b; Longley 1992; Jackson 1992; and Frendreis, Gitelson, Flemming, and Layzell 1993.

3. Herrnson 1986, 1988, 1990; Jacobson 1985–86; Wilcox 1989; Sorauf and Wilson 1990; and Dwyre 1992.

4. "When levels of trust in government plummet, our finest students of public opinion say, 'it does not matter.' When divided government becomes the norm on every level of government and threatens civic accountability, our wisest scholars show us why it does not matter. When discontent with politics causes party identification to crumble, participation to fall, and younger Americans to disengage from public affairs, political scientists just repeat, 'it does not matter.' And when a remarkable mobilization of middle America is aborted by Ross Perot's personal idiosyncrasies, we sigh with relief. It didn't really matter after all . . . [The] discussion can be summarized in three aphorisms: There is nothing wrong. If there is, we don't know how to fix it. If we do, it's politically impractical, anyway" (Putnam 1993).

5. Two-party dominance is not in fact a compelling measure of party strength. One can have three parties competing because people have indeed *greater* faith in the potentialities of political parties; i.e., it's worth the effort to create and support a third party. Such an interpretation of the People's Party, for example, would not do great violence to history (Goodwyn 1978). But this observation does not get us far with Perot because his was so strongly an antiparty appeal.

6. Interestingly, McGlennon (1993) finds that there is no clear relationship between the extent of activities performed by a state political party in the South and the perception of the party's organizational strength held by grassroots party activists. Note also that for reasons of space I focus here on activities as a measure of strength rather than devote attention to changing organizational complexity, i.e., bureaucratization. Cotter, Gibson, Bibby, and Huckshorn (1984: 44–45) point out that one should not dismiss party significance simply because of the lack of organizational complexity.

7. Caldeira, Patterson, and Markko 1985; Lawson, Pomper, and Moakley 1986; Bledsoe and Welch 1987; Caldeira, Clausen, and Patterson 1990; Frendreis, Gibson, and Vertz 1990; Rosenstone and Hansen 1993; and Huckfeldt and Sprague 1992. In some cases, however, party activities and campaign activities are lumped together. See, for example, Caldeira, Clausen, and Patterson (1990). This study also provides a unique measure of turnout as the number of offices for which a voter recalls voting. The respondents' ability to recall this information might be questioned, but this novel attempt to view voting as a continuous rather than a dichotomous variable deserves testing elsewhere.

8. Lawson's (1980) elegant essay acknowledges the difficulties inherent in such a seemingly simple statement.

9. To avert misunderstanding, I will simply state here that I believe that parties can and have made important contributions to American democracy and that they are crucial agents of representation. For an elegant discussion of the strengths and weaknesses of party organizations in pursuit of these functions, see Pomper (1992: 20–34).

10. On the other side, one might suggest that the improvement in Democratic fortunes in the late 1980s and 1992 were a result of organizational efforts, but one would need to contend with the argument that a fundamental fissure in the Democratic Party organization exploited by the Democratic Leadership Council was *just* as responsible for this renewed party success (see Rae 1991 and Hale, chap. 16 in this volume, for overviews of the development of the DLC).

11. The notion of a "few" political machines is particularly misleading. Brown and Halaby (1987) show that from 1870 to 1945 at least 50 percent of all middle and major sized U.S. cities featured machine politics, from the mid-1870s to the mid-1930s the figures were above 60 percent, and in the early 1890s the figures were at least 80 percent of all cities.

12. Baer and Bositis's (1988) excellent study of how social movements revitalized party organizations runs into similar difficulties, especially when attempting to explain low voter turnout (118-19). This is an important problem for their approach because it is never very clear why, if social movements infused the political parties with new life and new representativeness, the impact in the public was rather muted. If social movements were sweeping through party organizations, as the authors argue, then where were the followers of these movements? Why did movement elites fail to bring their adherents into the party system? Why is voting turnout stagnant or declining during most of the period they study?

13. Though with a different interpretation than the suggested here, Cotter and Bibby (1980) also link changing national party organization to the evolution of the New Deal political settlement.

23

Voters, Government Officials, and Party Organizations: Connections and Distinctions

John Frendreis

This chapter provides a response to the essay by Coleman in this volume (chapter 22). Coleman addresses a significant issue: are American political parties of genuine relevance to the outcomes of American electoral politics? His answer is guarded, but negative. In particular, he takes aim at what he describes as "the new orthodoxy in party scholarship," which he feels has declared American political parties to be resurgent. He argues that this conclusion is overstated, arising from a misplaced emphasis upon party organizations and a failure of contemporary party scholars to take into account evidence of continued decline of party among voters and in government. Since I was asked to respond in part because I am a contributor to the new orthodoxy (e.g., Gibson, Frendreis, and Vertz 1989; Frendreis, Gibson, and Vertz 1990; Frendreis and Gitelson, 1993), I will not disappoint either the editors or readers by failing to disagree with this assessment.[1]

In the grand tradition of such responses, I agree with much that Coleman says, but I also disagree with him on a fundamental point. My agreement is with what he identifies as weaknesses in our current state of knowledge, particularly with regard to the relationship between party organizational activity and what happens in the electorate and in government. My disagreement, however, is over what constitutes party activity, or, more precisely, what constitutes our objects of inquiry—American political parties. With apologies to Frank Sorauf, V. O. Key, and Ralph Goldman, I suggest that it is time to bid farewell to the idea that parties have three components—parties-as-organizations, parties-in-the-electorate, and parties-in-government—whose joint condition defines the form and function of American political parties. Instead, it is only the first of these that comprises "political parties" and recognition of this offers the best hope for the advancement of our knowledge about the place of parties in American politics. Before presenting this model of American political parties, however, I will first address directly the arguments advanced by Coleman.

The State of Research on Political Parties

Coleman notes that a steady stream of work over the past fifteen years has found party organizations to be active, and to the extent that trends are apparent, becoming more, rather than less, active (see Cotter et al. 1984; Gibson, Frendreis, and Vertz 1989; Frendreis et al. 1993, 1994). This is especially true of national (Longley 1992; Herrnson 1990; Bibby 1986) and state (Bibby 1990; Patterson 1989) party organizations, but also extends to local parties (Gibson et al. 1985). Increasing levels of activity are found in a variety of areas, including the bureaucratization of party organizations, the variety and level of campaign activities, and the amounts of campaign money raised and distributed (Herrnson 1993; Dwyre 1993).

Coleman does not dispute the substance of these studies; rather, he argues that the implications which are drawn from them are flawed. In his view, "the party organization literature has leapt too quickly to words like 'resurgence' and 'revitalization.' Increased activity should only be the *start* of a conception of resurgent parties" (chap. 22: 369 in this volume, emphasis in original). Coleman goes on to argue that the behavior of the party-in-the-electorate is key to assessing the vibrancy of American parties and that the new orthodoxy has failed to uncover evidence of resurgence or revitalization in this area. Later in his essay, he extends this argument to include the party-in-government, and he concludes "because the party system fits together it is misleading to ignore the other components when studying any one of the three" (chap. 22: 380 in this volume).

It is here that Coleman and I part company. I believe his account of recent scholarship is accurate. And his identification of a key problem—the apparent lack of parallel trends in party activity, mass partisanship, and party government—accurately identifies what should be the target of the next wave of party research. My main problem with his argument, however, lies in the implications of his phrases, "party system" and "one of the three [components]" in describing the familiar three-part formulation of parties—party organizations, party-in-the-electorate, and party-in-government. In the remainder of this chapter, I will argue that only the first of these—the party organizations—should be properly thought of as the political party, and I will suggest how the acceptance of this perspective defines how research aimed at understanding the problems Coleman has identified should be oriented. Before turning to this task, however, I must respectfully disagree with a few of the specific positions advanced by Coleman.

While I am flattered to be listed among the creators of a new orthodoxy, I must confess that such an orthodoxy is based upon a fairly small amount of research. Particularly with respect to state and local party organizations, there has been one major study, the Party Transformation Study (Cotter et al. 1984), two partial follow-up studies (Gibson et al. 1989; and Frendreis et al.

1994), and an unrelated comparative analysis of party organizations in several major American cities (Crotty 1986). Aside from this, there have been only scattered studies of organizations at one point in time in a few locales (e.g., Lawson, Pomper, and Moakley 1986; Pomper 1990). Alan Gitelson and I have discussed this problem at length elsewhere (Frendreis and Gitelson 1993); I will simply note briefly that—despite the presumed importance of political parties to the American polity—we have relatively little contemporary data on parties, compared with other political phenomena, such as the behavior of voters, legislators, or candidates. This is especially true with regard to the functioning of state and local parties in state and local politics and government. While I agree that the central focus for our research should shift from documenting what parties do toward understanding what difference parties make, we should recognize that there continues to be an urgent need for more complete cross-sectional and longitudinal data on party activity.

In a similar vein, I would also disagree that this research suffers from a mind set based upon "fighting the last battle." The original Party Transformation Study was conceived at a time when Broder's view that *The Party's Over* (1971) really *was* orthodox. The research I did with Gibson and Vertz followed fast upon Wattenberg's documentation of what he felt was *The Decline of American Political Parties 1952–1980* (1984). In our 1990 article (Frendreis, Gibson, and Vertz 1990), we described the lack of correspondence between organizational and mass partisanship trends as paradoxical, an observation that still holds true. Rather than being consumed by a desire to further dispute Broder's twenty-year-old position, however, I see this work as an ongoing attempt to make sense of what *continues* to be a paradox.

Finally, I would dispute that this research suffers from a misplaced emphasis upon party organizations, rather than the really important things like mass political behavior or governance. First, it should be evident from my comments thus far that I believe we still lack a clear understanding of what *contemporary* parties actually do. Second, it is not exactly the case that research has ignored the relationship between party activity and other electoral phenomena. In addition to my own work cited above, this question has attracted the attention of a number of other scholars, including Herrnson (1986, 1988), Gibson and Smith (1984), and Huckfeldt and Sprague (1992). (For an extension of this work to a comparative setting, see Whitely and Seyd 1994). Indeed, this represents the latest wave in a line of research that stretches back to Eldersveld (1956), Katz and Eldersveld (1961), Cutright (1963), Kramer (1970–71), and Crotty (1971). To me, the problem is not that previous research suffers from a misplaced emphasis upon uninteresting or well-worn organizational phenomena; rather, it is that there has been too little research to confidently describe contemporary parties in very much detail. Our lack of understanding of the electoral relevance of contemporary parties is merely one symptom of this broader problem.

A Model of American Political Parties

My basic disagreement with Coleman is with his implicit assumption that the three component model of political parties is the appropriate basis for future research. Following Schlesinger (1984), I would argue that the party should be conceived as consisting of those individuals and institutions whose manifest purpose is the contesting of elections with a goal of winning the elections. Obviously, this is hardly a novel conception of party. It corresponds closely to the "minimal definition" presented by Sartori: "A party is any political group identified by an official label that presents at elections, and is capable of placing through election (free or nonfree), candidates for public office" (1976: 63). Even Key, it should be noted, stressed the importance of focusing on those who "carry on the routine work in the winning and maintenance of power," a group termed the "party organization" or "inner core" (Key 1947: 247, quoting Gosnell's entry in volume 11 of the *Encyclopedia of the Social Sciences*). Key concludes that: "Nevertheless, in the examination of political party activities it is well to concentrate attention on the inner core or the organization, for that really is 'the party'" (Key 1947: 247).

Beyond this point, party scholars need to take seriously the word "organization" in the phrase "party organization." Organizational theory is well-developed, yet insights from this field are only beginning to be adapted to the study of party organizations. Identifying the degree of bureaucratization of state and local parties and assessing its connection with programmatic activity (e.g., Cotter et al. 1984; Gibson, Frendreis, and Vertz 1989) represents one step in this direction. Another recent example is Baer's (1993) discussion of the role of the "integrative community life" of parties, a concept she draws from March and Olsen (1989).

Although analogies are imperfect, I would link organizational theory with the definition of party I have set forth above as follows. In the electoral setting, the Democratic and Republican parties in the United States can be considered to be two firms, competing for customers in such a way that a vote for the party's candidates represents a purchase of the firm's product. Currently, the two parties collectively dominate the market, essentially because of the high cost of entry into the market. For a number of reasons, particularly favorable state laws and the absence of proportional representation, it is difficult for a new firm (i.e., a new party) to successfully enter the market. As a result, the two parties operate as a duopoly, dominating the market, as Schlesinger (1991) has noted.

Furthermore, these two firms operate in an atmosphere of declining brand loyalty, i.e., a weakening of partisanship. This means that the reliability of consumers' purchasing decisions is declining, as is apparent in the increase in independence, split-ticket voting, and defection by party voters. However, this decline in partisanship should be seen for what it is—a change in the marketplace in which the firms compete rather than a direct symptom of organizational decline by the firm. As I note in the next section, a methodological decision not to view mass partisanship as a component of the political party has important consequences in a search for connections between party activity and mass political behavior.

At the same time, while the structure of the electoral market has insulated the two parties from ready competition, the declining brand loyalty means that the system is potentially unstable. This insight has a number of implications. First, it would suggest that, ceteris paribus, greater than average swings in outcomes from election to election are possible. Recent electoral history, which has featured the first Democratic presidential victory in sixteen years in tandem with the strongest third party candidacy since 1912, followed only two years later by a smashing Republican victory in the congressional and state elections, would seem to bear this out. Second, there should be a drop-off in purchases based solely upon brand loyalty, e.g., an increase over time in ballot roll-off for minor offices. Third, if a new firm *is* capable of absorbing the costs of entry into the market, it has the potential for significant market penetration. From this perspective, the 1992 presidential campaign of Ross Perot is less a sign of the further decline of the two parties than it is the exception that proves the rule: a "third party" candidate threatens the recent dominance of the two parties described by Schlesinger (1991) only when he or she is backed by the considerable resources necessary to overcome the high costs of market entry. Furthermore, the inability of either Perot or his organization (United We Stand or the New Reform Party) to field candidates in the 1994 election again highlights the high barriers to entering the market, even with the large decline in brand loyalty for the two major parties.

In the next two sections, I describe the implications for further research of this model of American parties as firms operating in an electoral marketplace. In particular, I discuss how this might guide our research into the two critical linkages highlighted by Coleman: the linkages between parties and voters, and between parties and government officeholders.

Parties and Voters

Coleman's essay identifies two central questions that must be answered about voters: "What has caused decreased partisanship?" "What has caused declines in voter trust of political parties as institutions?" At first glance, it would seem that these two questions are linked and, moreover, that the answers must focus at least in part upon the behavior of parties themselves. Wattenberg's decision to title his studies of declining voter loyalty as portraits of declining political *parties* rather than declining political *partisanship* clearly implies such linkage (Wattenberg 1984, 1990).

The methodological peril of trying to consider trends in mass political behavior as an attribute of parties becomes readily apparent when one adopts the perspective that parties and voters are as distinct as firms and their customers. What causes changes in consumer tastes? To be sure, the experience of U.S. automakers in the last twenty years suggests that brand loyalty may break down in the face of poor product quality or bad service. Yet economic history is full of examples of firms losing customer support because of exogenous factors, such as technological change or changes in customer needs and wants.

Considered in this light, the behavior of the parties becomes only one of several possible causal agents which might influence trends in partisanship. An example of another potential culprit is the rising level of education and middle-class sensibilities among the American electorate. Coleman notes the breakdown in the apparently strong linkage between party machines and voters that existed in the late nineteenth century. Accounts of this breakdown generally stress the role of rising education and the bureaucratization of the welfare function as causes. Neither of these factors could be regarded as evidence of poor performance on the part of the parties, behavior which might induce a turning away on the part of voters.

If we only take the period for which we have reliable time series data on mass political attitudes and behaviors—roughly the last fifty years—it is difficult to identify any long term trend in the behavior of parties which correlates with the decline in mass partisanship. Consider the products that the parties have to offer to the voters: candidates and party platforms. With the possible exception of presidential nominees, any analysis of today's candidates with those of the 1950s would show today's to be better educated and more knowledgeable about policy problems and the powers of the offices they are seeking (Ehrenhalt 1991). One of the effects of the decline in political machines was the elimination of offices awarded to party regulars who were unprepared for and uninterested in them. Similarly, it is not at all clear that the quality of party platforms has declined over this period. On the other hand, it is certain that other trends, many of them long-term, underlying demographic changes, can be discerned over the same time period, and some of these may be substantially correlated with changes in mass partisanship.

None of this is meant to indicate that there is no connection between party activity and the attitudes of voters. Yet, it is a very different proposition to regard party activity as one of many potential factors which might influence consumer preferences rather than to see these preferences as direct reflections of party failure or irrelevance. Coleman is correct in asserting that we do not understand the decline in partisanship, but this assertion cuts both ways. His skepticism of a "counteracting party model," in which party organizational strength may be offsetting the effects of these broader social trends, is equally unwarranted. If it turns out that the widespread and well-documented decline in partisanship during the 1960s and 1970s slowed or even stopped during the 1980s, it may yet support the view that party activity has altered an otherwise exogenously determined decline in partisanship. Coleman's dismissal of what was never more than a hypothesis is premature; more appropriately, the "counteracting party model" needs to be tested.

Parties and Government Officials

The view of American political parties as two firms competing in a duopolistic electoral marketplace marked by declining brand loyalty addresses most directly the relationship between the parties and the voters. However, with some modifications, this model can be extended to address the relationship between the parties and government officeholders. Before directly addressing this linkage, it is necessary to briefly discuss the relationship between parties and public policy.

The conception of political party I am arguing for does not make direct reference to parties as agents of policy formation and enactment. If one focuses on parties as purely electoral actors, policy is relevant only to the extent that it enhances or retards the ability of the parties to attract voters. Clearly, neither voters nor normative treatments of democracy view public policy in this way. For example, it is likely that at least some of the current voter distrust of political parties is part of a general lack of regard for government institutions, a sentiment based at least partially upon the performance of these institutions in enacting policy.

At the same time, to consider the behavior of Congress as a manifestation of the activities of the political parties—of the parties-in-government—just as surely does violence to the truth. Congress and the parties are separate institutions; as a result, they must be kept analytically and methodologically distinct. However, members of Congress are part of both of these institutions. How is their behavior to be understood? Using the market model I have proposed, they are either the product being marketed, or the sales force, or both; perhaps the best analogy is that they operate as independent franchise holders.

The logic of this argument is that the behavior of legislators and executives should not be seen as *the* behavior of parties, but as a *function* of the behavior of parties. Legislatures and executive agencies are not a component of the parties, but rather the institutions which the parties seek to control. Considered from this perspective, two questions emerge as being critical. In what way do parties control the behavior of governmental officeholders? What is the relationship between the behavior of governmental officeholders, and the linkage between parties and the voters?

The first of these two questions is the most accessible and is indirectly the subject of a substantial body of recent research, especially with respect to Congress (e.g., Little and Patterson 1993; Rohde 1991; Huitt 1990; Sinclair 1983; Jones 1970; Ripley 1969). However, in general this work approaches the relationship of party to Congress from the congressional perspective. As a result, it focuses less on the means by which the parties control legislators and more on the mechanisms of partisan influence that exist internal to the legislature.

From the perspective of the party organizations, a somewhat different set of questions emerges. To the extent that the organization (the party) has a set of institutional goals regarding the behavior of legislators, (e.g., that the legislators seek to enact a specific set of policies), the problem for the party is insuring that the individuals making up the organization (i.e., party members) behave properly, that is, in concert with the organizational goals. The problem of American parties is immediately apparent: unlike many other organizations, American parties cannot usually replace recalcitrant members, at least the members who hold elective office. The direct primary, more than any other factor, is responsible for the weak hold of American parties over government institutions. Although this situation is fundamental to understanding the operation of American parties in a comparative perspective, the diffusion of the direct primary is essentially a historical fact. The question for scholars now is how the party exerts control over its officeholders in the absence of the ability to readily replace them.

Here, organizational theory offers some clues. Perrow (1979) observes that the surest means of organizational control is the inculcation of the organization's norms in its members. Baer's (1993) discussion of the integrative community life of parties suggests that parties do indeed attempt to do this. In addition, like all organizations, parties seeking to structure their members' attitudes should utilize recruitment and socialization as means to this end. Finally, even though parties cannot definitively eliminate deviant members, they still can seek to influence these members via the offering of selective incentives, such as funding and support by other group members.

Seen in this light, many of the organizational developments over the last two decades documented by party scholars may be seen as manifestations of the efforts of parties to achieve greater control over their officeholders—assuming they wish to do so. Still unclear is the relationship between achieving such control and the manifest purpose of parties, to contest and win elections. More important, however, is the fact that in this area of party life, we also possess little systematic evidence assessing the linkage between party activities and manifestations of partisan control over the party's officeholders. It is clear that parties are weaker in this area than a century ago; however, there is no real data to support Coleman's assertion that recent efforts toward strengthening party organizations bear no relationship toward *recent* trends in parties' influence over officeholders.

Party Organizations, Voters, and Governmental Officials

It is easy for someone whose vision is narrowed by their own research agenda to construct a party-centered vision of American political life. Coleman raises the question: Is such a perspective justified? This question might be approached in two ways, normatively and empirically. From a normative perspective, the answer is surely yes. Although the U.S. Constitution is silent on the subject of political parties, it is virtually impossible to discuss the operation of American democracy without reference to parties. Technological change may eventually foster the creation of governing mechanisms embodying direct democracy, but for the near future, it is likely that most of our vehicles for self-governance will embody representative democracy. Given this, it seems likely that political parties—even weakened ones—will remain central components of discussions of the linkage between voters and governmental officials, between the public will and public policy.

The empirical basis for seeing political parties as central to the workings of a democratic American polity are less clear. Coleman is skeptical of the relevance of parties to either voters or government, although he tempers his concern with a desire for more research. Obviously, on this latter point we are in agreement. A general theme throughout this chapter is that we actually know very little about the relationships among parties, voters, and government. To say that parties are not moribund—as might be expected if trends in mass partisanship were closely tied to the internal vitality of the parties—is not to say that they exert a powerful hold over both voters and officeholders. The "new orthodoxy" that Coleman claims to see is based on a few summary speculations rather than upon the main substance of what party organizational scholars have said.

Throughout this chapter I have identified a number of significant questions which should be the target of the next generation of party scholarship. What has caused decreased partisanship? What has caused the declines in voter trust of political parties? In what way do parties control the behavior of governmental officeholders? What is the relationship between the behavior of government officeholders and the linkage between parties and the voters? That these questions can be deduced from the old three component model of American parties does not mean that this is simply "old wine in new wineskins." The conceptualization of parties as having three components confuses the objects of party activity with the party itself. This point is more readily apparent with regard to the voters, but is true nonetheless for government as well. That parties seek to control government does not mean that party members within the government are acting upon the shared organizational norms that define their party when they exercise authority as officeholders. Conceiving of the officeholders as a "party-in-government" has diverted attention away from the very real question of how the institution of the party seeks to influence and control the institutions of government.

It bears repeating that Coleman and I are in complete agreement on a basic point: There is a need for a great deal more careful research on the activities of political parties and their relevance to both elections and governance. To cite one more example of what we do not know about contemporary American parties, the general view of much of the recent party research is that party organizational behavior conforms to what might be termed an *adaptive brokerage* model (Frendreis and Gitelson 1993; also see chap. 10 in this volume). In this view, party organizations respond to changes in their environment—legal, technological, and organizational—by developing new capacities and by altering the electoral roles they perform. Whereas general party organizations once were the main electoral organizations for the campaigns of many candidates, these organizations now serve as support organizations for candidate-centered organizations. Within this changed electoral environment, party organizations often serve as brokers, facilitating the connection between candidate organizations and pools of necessary resources, such as money, expertise, and volunteers.

While this description of parties as adaptive organizations is a powerful image, it has yet to be subjected to extensive empirical examination. The "new orthodoxy" cited by Coleman has provided a reasonably clear picture of what party organizations do and, to a lesser extent, what some of the electoral effects of this activity are. Still needed is research that extends our empirical understanding beyond this static portrait into the dynamic realm implied by the adaptive brokerage image. Such research would take as its starting point the idea that the contemporary electoral world includes a number of distinct actors, including candidates (and their organizations), general party organizations (i.e., geographically defined organizations that perform multiple activities), other party organizations (principally, finance committees), campaign consultants, political action committees (PACs), and voters. Ultimately, electoral outcomes are a function of the attributes and activities of all of these actors. To some extent, all of these actors are interconnected, but some linkages are more direct than others.

A number of hypotheses could be developed and tested that describe the interrelationships among these various electoral actors, given the general outlines of an adaptive brokerage model of party behavior. The following list of hypotheses is illustrative, rather than exhaustive.

A. Candidate-Party Relationships
    1. Candidates of lesser quality will be more dependent upon party organizations for campaign assistance than higher quality candidates.
    2. Candidates will substitute consultants for assistance from the general party organizations, i.e., the importance of consultants and party organizations to candidates will be inverse.

3. General party organizations will not withhold campaign assistance from candidates whose issue positions or voting records as officeholders deviate from party positions.

B. General Party Organization-Other Organization Relationships
   1. General party organizations will be less likely to coordinate their activities with legislative party caucus campaign committees when these caucus committees are controlled by a single caucus leader.[2]
   2. General party organizations will concentrate their direct campaign efforts in activities in which competing electoral actors are not well equipped to act.
   3. Over a number of elections, candidates will become less dependent upon party organizations for assistance.

C. Contextual Factors Relating to Party and Candidate Behavior
   1. Party organizations will be more organizationally developed and electorally active in states with "party-supportive" statutory environments.
   2. Strong state party organizations are a necessary but not sufficient condition for state and local party integration.
   3. State and local party systems which are more integrated will be more efficient in their allocation of campaign resources.
   4. Over time, overall levels of party strength and activity between competing parties within a state will converge.

D. Electoral Outcomes
   1. Electoral gains and losses are a function of both candidate- and party-related factors.
   2. Electoral activity by parties will be indirectly rather than directly linked to voter outcomes, i.e., party activity will be directly related to candidate activity, while candidate activity will be directly related to electoral outcomes.
   3. Party organizations will respond to electoral setbacks with increased activity and innovation.[3]

The most significant observation about this list of hypotheses is that, with some limited exceptions, they are essentially untested in the current literature. Perhaps it seems unexceptional to argue for a continued and expanded research agenda for the study of American political parties. To avoid appearing pedestrian, I will offer a somewhat bolder suggestion. I believe that it is time for scholars of American politics to come together to support a substantial data collection effort, which will provide a basis for extensive analysis of American political parties in the same way that the National Election Studies surveys have created a foundation for work in electoral behavior. At a minimum, the scholarly community should systematically collect data on party activity, electoral behavior, and governmental policy making for a broad cross-section of political systems and over an extended period of time. Such a database would permit the testing not only of the adaptive brokerage model hypotheses identified above, but of the many other unanswered questions identified by Coleman. An obvious setting for such research would be the states, which would permit some variation in significant social, political, and legal variables to be manifested in the data. Even focusing on the states, though, we know that data on both local and national party activity (and probably electoral and governmental activity) also need to be incorporated into such a research effort. As Alan Gitelson and I have suggested elsewhere, such an effort argues strongly for the development of a consortium of scholars who will bring diverse concerns and perspectives to a common effort to raise our understanding of parties to the level already enjoyed by other key aspects of American politics, such as voting or the operation of Congress (Frendreis and Gitelson 1993).

Throughout this chapter I have argued for the adoption of a perspective that sees the party organizations *as* the party. One formulation that I have offered is to conceive of the Democratic and Republican parties as two firms competing in a duopolistic marketplace marked in recent years by declining brand loyalty among consumers. Further, these firms can be seen to face unique problems of internal cohesion in that some of their key members, candidates/officeholders, cannot be controlled via replacement. I have tried to indicate how adoption of this perspective might focus subsequent scholarship on the beckoning research frontier. Whatever perspective is adopted, however, one thing is clear: without additional research, future volumes on the "state of the parties" will continue to substitute discussions based upon a clear understanding of the actual relationships among parties, voters, and officeholders with ones driven by speculation, skepticism, and hope.

Notes

1. I wish to thank Laura Vertz and Alan Gitelson for their comments on this chapter.
2. As Shea (1995) notes, there is considerable variation in the control of legislative campaign committees, with many operating as extensions of the legislative leaders and as potential competitors with other party actors.
3. This relationship between electoral setbacks and party innovation has been proposed and partially tested for state party organizations in two states by Appleton and Ward (1994).

References

Abramowitz, Alan I. 1995. "The End of the Democratic Era? 1994 and the Future of Congressional Election Research." *Political Research Quarterly* 48: 873–89.

Abramowitz, Alan I., John McGlennon, and Ronald B. Rapoport. 1983. "An Analysis of State Party Activists," in Ronald B. Rapoport et al., eds., *The Life of the Parties*. Pp. 44–58. Lexington, Ky.: Kentucky University Press.

Abramson, Jeffrey, F. Christopher Arterton, and Gary R. Orren, 1988. *The Electronic Commonwealth: The Impact of New Media Technologies on Democratic Politics*. New York: Basic Books.

Abramson, Paul R., John H. Aldrich, and David W. Rohde. 1994. *Change and Continuity in the 1992 Elections*. Washington, D.C.: CQ Press.

Advisory Commission on Intergovernmental Relations.1986. *The Transformation of American Politics: Implications for Federalism*. Washington, D.C.: Advisory Commission on Intergovernmental Relations.

Aldrich, John H. 1995. *Why Parties? The Origins and Transformation of Party Politics in America*. Chicago: University of Chicago Press.

Alexander, Herbert E. 1992. *Financing Politics*. 4th ed. Washington, D.C.: CQ Press.

Alexander, Herbert, and Monica Bauer. 1991. *Financing the 1988 Election*. Boulder, Colo.: Westview Press.

American Political Science Association Committee on Political Parties. 1950. "Toward a More Responsible Two-Party System." *American Political Science Review* 44: Supplement.

Anderson, Jack, and Michael Binstein. 1993. "Democrats: Playing Not to Lose." *The Washington Post* July 11.

Appleton, Andrew, and Daniel S. Ward. 1994. "Party Organizational Response to Electoral Change: Texas and Arkansas."*American Review of Politics* 15: 1191–212.

Argersinger, Peter H. 1980. "A Place on the Ballot: Fusion Politics and Antifusion Laws." *American Historical Review* 85:287.

———. 1992. *Structure, Process, and Party-Essays in American Political History*. Armonk, N.Y.: M. E. Sharpe, Inc.

Arterton, F. Christopher. 1982. "Political Money and Political Strength," in Joel L. Fleishman, ed. *The Future of American Political Parties*. Englewood Cliffs, N.J.: Prentice-Hall.

Atkeson, Lonna Rae, James A. McCann, Ronald B. Rapoport, and Walter J. Stone. 1994. "Citizens for Perot: Activists and Voters in the 1992 Presidential Campaign," in Stephen C. Craig, ed., *Broken Contract? Changing Relationships between Citizens and Their Government in the United States*. Boulder, Colo.: Westview Press.

Ayres, B. Drummond. 1992. "Man Behind Convention Emerges as Major Force." *The New York Times* July 20.

Bachrach, Peter. 1967. *The Theory of Democratic Elitism*. Boston: Little, Brown.

Bader, John, and Charles O. Jones. 1993. "The Republican Parties in Congress: Bicameral Differences," in Lawrence Dodd and Bruce Oppenheimer, eds., *Congress Reconsidered*. Pp. 291–314. 5th ed. Washington, D.C.: CQ Press.

Baer, Donald. 1992. "The Race." *U.S. News & World Report* August 31.

Baer, Denise L. 1993. "Who Has the Body? Party Institutionalization and Theories of Party Organization." *American Review of Politics* 14: 1–38.

Baer, Denise L., and David Bositis. 1988. *Elite Cadres and Party Coalitions.* Westport, Conn.: Greenwood Press.

———. 1993. *Politics and Linkage in a Democratic Society.* Englewood Cliffs, N.J.: Prentice-Hall.

Balz, Dan. 1991. "Democrats' Perennial Rising Star Wants to Put New Face on Party." *The Washington Post* June 25.

———. 1993. "Clinton, Centrist Democrats Avoid Rift on Overhaul of Health Care." *The Washington Post* December 4.

———. 1994a. "DNC Ready to Give up Grass-Roots Health Lobby in Favor of Media Blitz." *Washington Post* March 19.

———. 1994b. "DNC Chairman Restructures Senior Staff." *Washington Post* June 9, AL.

———. 1994c. "New DNC Health Ads Wind Up Offending Senate Democrats." *Washington Post* July 15, A4.

———. 1995. "Senator Mack Buys TV Ads." *Washington Post* December 31, All.

Balz, Dan, and Ronald Brownstein. 1995. *Storming the Gates: Protest Politics and the Republican Revival.* Boston: Little Brown.

Barbour, Haley. 1993a. "RNC Chairmanship Campaign Manifesto." Republican National Committee. January.

———. 1993b. "The Barbour Plan." Washington, D.C: Republican National Committee.

———. 1996. "Statement by RNC Chairman Haley Barbour." RNC News Release. April 19.

Bardes, Barbara A., Mack C. Shelley II, and Steffen W. Schmidt. 1996. *American Government and Politics Today: The Essentials 1996–1997 Edition.* St. Paul, Minn.: West Publishing.

Barnes, Fred. 1986. "Flying Nunn." *The New Republic* April 28.

Barnes, James A. 1989a. "Reinventing the RNC." *National Journal* January 14.

———. 1989b. "Ron Brown's Fast Start." *National Journal* May 5.

———. 1993a. "Regrouping." *National Journal* June 12.

———. 1993b. "Double Identity." *National Journal* November 11.

———. 1995. "Haley's Comet." *National Journal,* February 25. Pp. 474–78.

Barone, Michael, and Grant Ujifusa. 1995. *The Almanac of American Politics 1996.* Washington, D.C.: National Journal.

Beck, Paul Allen. 1974a. "A Socialization Theory of Partisan Realignment," in Richard G. Niemi, ed., *The Politics of Future Citizens.* Pp. 199–219. San Francisco: Josey-Bass.

———. 1974b. "Environment and Party: The Impact of Political and Demographic County Characteristics on Party Behavior." *American Political Science Review* 68: 1229–44.

———. 1979. "The Electoral Cycle and Patterns of American Politics," *British Journal of Political Science* 9: 129–56.

Beck, Paul Allen, and M. Kent Jennings. 1982. "Pathways to Participation." *American Political Science Review* 76: 94–108.

Beck, Paul Allen, and Frank J. Sorauf. 1992. *Party Politics in America.* 7th ed. New York: Harper Collins.

Beck, Paul Allen, and Audrey Haynes. 1994. "Party Effort at the Grassroots: Local Presidential Campaigning in 1992." Paper presented at the Midwest Political Science Association, Chicago, Ill. April 14–16.

Bennett, W. Lance. 1992. *The Governing Crisis: Media, Money, and Marketing in American Elections.* New York: St. Martin's Press.

Berke, Richard L. 1992. "After Party Rebuke, Brown Says Leadership Is Protecting Clinton." *The New York Times* March 28.

———. 1993. "Shades of Perot: Parties Go for the Grass Roots." *The New York Times* June 21.

Bibby, John F. 1986. "Political Party Trends in 1985: The Continuing but Constrained Advance of the National Party." *Publius* 16: 90.

———. 1987. *Politics, Parties, and Elections in America.* Chicago: Nelson-Hall.

———. 1990. "Party Organization at the State Level," in L. Sandy Maisel, ed., *The Parties Respond.* Pp. 21–40. Boulder, Colo.: Westview Press.

———. 1992. *Politics, Parties, and Elections in America.* 2d ed. Chicago: Nelson-Hall.

———. 1994. "Party Leadership, the Bliss Model, and the Development of the Republican National Committee," in John C. Green, ed., *Politics, Professionalism, and Power.* Pp. 19–33. Lanham, Md.: University Press of America.

Bibby, John F., James L. Gibson, Cornelius P. Cotter, and Robert J. Huckshorn. 1983. "Trends in Party Organizational Strength, 1960–1980." *International Political Science Review* 4: 21–27.

Biersack, Robert. 1994. Introduction to Robert Biersack, Paul S. Herrnson, and Clyde Wilcox, eds., *PAC Decision Making and Strategy in Congressional Elections.* Armonk, N.Y.: M. E. Sharpe.

Biersack, Robert, and Paul S. Herrnson. 1994. "Helping to Put Women in Their Places—the House and the Senate: Political Parties and the 1992 Congressional Elections," in Elizabeth Adell Cook, Sue Thomas, and Clyde Wilcox, eds., *The Year of the Woman: Myth or Reality.* Pp. 61–80. Boulder, Colo.: Westview Press.

Binning, William C., Melanie L. Blumberg, and John C. Green. 1995. "Change Comes to Steeltown: Local Parties as Instruments of Power." Paper prepared for the 1995 annual meeting of the American Political Science Association, Chicago.

Bird, Caroline. 1977. *What Women Want.* New York: Simon and Schuster.

Black, Earl, and Merle Black. 1987. *Politics and Society in the South.* Cambridge, Mass.: Harvard University Press.

———. 1992. *The Vital South: How Presidents Are Elected.* Cambridge, Mass.: Harvard University Press.

Black, Gordon S., and Benjamin D. Black. 1994. *The Politics of American Discontent.* New York: John Wiley.

Bledsoe, Timothy, and Susan Welch. 1987. "Patterns of Political Party Activity among U.S. Cities." *Urban Affairs Quarterly* 23: 249–69.

Blumenthal, Sidney. 1990. *Pledging Allegiance: The Last Campaign of the Cold War.* New York: HarperCollins.

Bolingbroke, Henry St. John. 1982. *Contributions to the Craftsman.* Ed. Simon Versey. New York: Oxford University Press.

Boyer, Cece Hall. Congressional Liaison, RNC. Personal Interview. October 4, 1995. Washington, D.C.

Brady, David W. 1990. "Coalitions in the U.S. Congress," in L. Sandy Maisel, ed., *The Parties Respond: Changes in the American Party System.* Pp. 249–66. Boulder, Colo.: Westview Press.

Brady, David W., Joseph Cooper, and Patricia A. Hurley. 1979. "The Decline of Party in the U.S. House of Representatives, 1887-1968." *Legislative Studies Quarterly* 4: 381–407.

Bridges, Amy. 1986. "Becoming American: The Working Classes in the United States before the Civil War," in Ira Katznelson and Aristide R. Zolberg, eds., *Working-Class Formation.* Pp. 157–96. Princeton: Princeton University Press.

Broder, David S. 1971. *The Party's Over: The Failure of American Parties.* New York: Harper and Row.

———. 1992. "The Decline of Jesse Jackson." *The Washington Post* July 14.

———. 1993. "Politics without Parties." *The Washington Post* January 5.

———. 1995. "Uphill with Dodd." *Washington Post.* January 18, A17.

———. 1996. "Ideology at a Safe Distance," *Washington Post National Weekly Edition*, February 26–March 3, 1996, 4.

Brown, M. Craig, and Charles N. Halaby. 1987. "Machine Politics in America, 1870–1945." *Journal of Interdisciplinary History* 17: 587–612.

400 *References*

Brown, Courtney. 1991. *Ballots of Tumult*. Ann Arbor: University of Michigan Press.

Brownstein, Ronald. 1996. "Buoyed by Polls, Democrats Work on Blueprint for Recaptured House." *Los Angeles Times* April 22, A5.

Buell, Emmett H., Jr. 1986. "Divisive Primaries and Participation in Fall Presidential Campaigns: A Study of 1984 New Hampshire Primary Activists." *American Politics Quarterly* 14: 376–90.

Burnham, Walter Dean. 1970. *Critical Elections and the Mainsprings of American Politics*. New York: Norton.

———. 1982. *The Current Crisis in American Politics*. New York: Oxford University Press.

———. 1995. "Critical Realignment Lives: The 1994 Earthquake," in *The Clinton Presidency: First Appraisals*, ed. Colin Campbell and Bert A. Rockman. Chatham, N.J.: Chatham House.

Burrell, Barbara. 1993. "John Bailey's Legacy: Political Parties and Women's Candidacies for Public Office," in Lois Duke Lovelace, ed., *Women in Politics*. Pp. 123–34. Englewood Cliffs, N.J.: Prentice-Hall.

———. 1994. *A Woman's Place Is in the House: Campaigning for Congress in the Feminist Era*. Ann Arbor: University of Michigan Press.

Calhoun, Jim. 1993. "OKI Plan Rapped." *Cincinnati Enquirer* September 15.

Caldeira, Gregory A., Aage R. Clausen, and Samuel C. Patterson. 1990. "Partisan Mobilization and Electoral Participation." *Electoral Studies* 9: 191–204.

Caldeira, Gregory A., Samuel C. Patterson, and Gregory A. Markus. 1985. "The Mobilization of Voters in Congressional Elections." *Journal of Politics* 47: 490–509.

Canfield, James Lewis. 1984. *A Case of Third Party Activism: The George Wallace Campaign Worker and the American Independent Party*. Lanham, Md.: University Press of America.

Carlson, Jody. 1981. *George C. Wallace and the Politics of Powerlessness*. New Brunswick, N.J.: Transaction Books.

Carmines, Edward G., and James A. Stimson. 1989. *Race and the Transformation of American Politics*. Princeton: Princeton University Press.

Ceasar, James. 1982. *Reforming the Reforms*. Cambridge, Mass.: Ballinger.

Ceasar, James, and Andrew Busch. 1993. *Upside Down and Inside Out: The 1992 Elections and American Politics*. Lanham, Md.: Rowman & Littlefield.

Center for Party Development. 1993. *Former Members of Congress View the Role of Political Parties in the U.S. Congress*. Washington, D.C.: Center for Party Development.

Chafe, William. 1972. *The American Woman: Her Changing Social, Economic, and Political Roles, 1920–1970*. New York: Oxford University Press.

Charter Committee. 1988. "Draft 4/88." Mimeo: Charter Committee of Greater Cincinnati.

Charter Research Institute. 1991. *Queen City Almanac: A Practical Guide to Cincinnati Government and Services*. Cincinnati, Ohio: Charter Research Institute.

Cincinnati Enquirer. 1993. "Queen City at a Crossroads," an eight part series, July 25–August 1.

Cino, Maria. Executive Director, NRCC. Personal Interview. November 13, 1995. Washington, D.C.

Clubb, Jerome M., and Santa A. Traugott. 1977. "Partisan Cleavage and Cohesion in the House of Representatives, 1861-1974." *Journal of Interdisciplinary History* 7: 375–401.

Cole, Richard L. 1974. "The Urban Policy Process: A Note on Structural and Regional Influences," in Samuel A. Kirkpatrick, ed., *Quantitative Analysis of Political Data*. Columbus, Ohio: Charles E. Merrill.

Coleman, John J. 1994. "State Formation and the Decline of Political Parties: American Parties in the Fiscal State," in *Studies in American Political Development*. New Haven: Yale University Press. 8: 195–230.

———. 1996a. *Party Decline in America: Policy, Politics, and the Fiscal State*. Princeton: Princeton University Press.

———. 1996b. "Party Organizational Strength and Public Support for Parties." *American Journal of Political Science.* 40: 805–24.

Collie, Melissa P., and David W. Brady. 1985. "The Decline of Partisan Voting Coalitions in the House of Representatives," in Lawrence C. Dodd and Bruce I. Oppenheimer, eds., *Congress Reconsidered.* 3d ed. Pp. 272–87. Washington, DC: CQ Press.

Congressional Quarterly Weekly Report. 1992. "Democratic Endorsements." 50: 485.

Connelly, William F., Jr., and John J. Pitney, Jr. 1994. *Congress' Permanent Minority? Republicans in the U.S. House.* Lanham, Md.: Rowman & Littlefield.

Converse, Philip E., Warren E. Miller, Jerrold G. Rusk, and Arthur C. Wolfe. 1969. "Continuity and Change in American Politics: Parties and Issues in the 1968 Election." *American Political Science Review* 63: 1083–105.

Conway, M. Margaret. 1983. "Republican Political Party Nationalization, Campaign Activities, and Their Implications for the Political System." *Publius* 13: 1–17.

Cook, Rhodes. 1991. "Cuomo Says 'No' to Candidacy at Last Possible Moment." *Congressional Quarterly Weekly Report* 49: 3734–36.

———. 1992. "Candidate Field Shapes up as Primaries Approach." *Congressional Quarterly Weekly Report* 50: 28.

———. 1993. "DNC under Wilhelm: Seeking a New Role." *Congressional Quarterly Weekly Report* 50: 939.

Cooper, Joseph, and Patricia Hurley. 1977. "The Electoral Basis of Party Voting: Patterns and Trends in the U.S. House of Representatives, 1887-1969," in Louis Maisel and Joseph Cooper, eds., *The Impact of the Electoral Process.* Pp. 133–65. Beverly Hills, Calif.: Sage Publications.

Corrado, Anthony. 1991. "Party Rules Reform and Candidate Nomination Strategies: Consequences for the 1990s." Presented at the annual meeting of the American Political Science Association, Washington, D.C.

———. 1993. *Paying for Presidents.* New York: Twentieth Century Fund Press.

Costain, Anne, and W. Douglas Costain. 1987. "Strategy and Tactics of the Women's Movement in the United States: The Role of Political Parties," in Mary Katzenstein and Carol McClurg Mueller, eds., *The Women's Movements of the United States and Western Europe.* Pp. 196–214. Philadelphia: Temple University Press.

Cotter, Cornelius, P., and John F. Bibby. 1980. "Institutional Development of the Parties and the Thesis of Party Decline." *Political Science Quarterly* 95: 1–27

Cotter, Cornelius, P., James L. Gibson, John F. Bibby, and Robert J. Huckshorn. 1984. *Party Organizations in American Politics.* New York: Praeger.

Cotter, Cornelius, P., and Bernard C. Hennessey. 1964. *Politics Without Power: The National Party Committees.* New York: Atherton Press.

Crotty, William J. 1971. "Party Effort and Its Impact on the Vote." *American Political Science Review* 65: 439–50.

———. 1978. *Decision for the Democrats.* Baltimore: Johns Hopkins University Press.

———. 1984. *American Parties in Decline.* Boston: Little, Brown.

———, ed. 1986. *Political Parties in Local Areas.* Knoxville, Tenn.: University of Tennessee Press.

———. 1991a. "Urban Political Machines," in L. Sandy Maisel, ed., *Political Parties and Elections in the United States: An Encyclopedia.* Vol. 2. Pp. 1154–163. New York: Garland Press.

———. 1991b. "Political Parties: Issues and Trends," in William Crotty, ed., *Political Science: Looking to the Future.* Vol. 4. Pp. 137–201. Evanston, Ill.: Northwestern University Press.

Cutler, Lynn. 1993. "Comments," in Michael Margolis and John C. Green, eds., *Machine Politics, Sound Bites and Nostalgia: On Studying Political Parties.* Pp. 52–54. Lanham, Md.: University Press of America.

Cutright, Phillips. 1963. "Measuring the Impact of Local Party Activity on the General Election Vote." *Public Opinion Quarterly* 27: 372–86.

———. 1964. "Activities of Precinct Committeemen in Partisan and Non-Partisan Communities." *Western Political Quarterly* 17: 93–108.

Cutright, Phillips, and Peter Rossi. 1958. "Grass Roots Politicians and the Vote." *American Sociological Review* 63: 171–179.

Dahl, Robert A. 1967. "The City in the Future of Democracy." *American Political Science Review* 61: 953–70.

Daley, Steve. 1991a. "Democratic Chief Sets Up Meeting between Donors, '92 Hopefuls." *The Chicago Tribune* May 18.

———. 1991b. "Democrats Plan Early, United Fight for '92." *The Chicago Tribune* June 14.

Davidson, Roger, ed. 1992. *The Post Reform Congress.* New York: St. Martin's.

Davis, James W. 1983. *National Conventions in an Age of Party Reform.* Westport, Conn.: Greenwood Press.

———. 1992. *The President as Party Leader.* New York: Praeger.

Democratic Congressional Campaign Committee. 1992. DCCC Mid-Year Report. Washington, D.C.: Democratic Congressional Campaign Committee.

Democratic Leadership Council. 1988. "The Democratic Leadership Council." Pamphlet.

———. 1990. "The New Orleans Declaration." Pamphlet.

———. 1991a. "Convention Program." Pamphlet.

———. 1991b. "The New Choice Resolutions." Mimeo.

———. 1992. "The New Choice: Draft for a Democratic Platform." Mimeo.

Dillin, John. 1991. "Democrats Unite to Map Presidential Strategy." *Christian Science Monitor* May 21.

Dionne, E. J., Jr. 1991. *Why Americans Hate Politics.* New York: Simon and Schuster.

———. 1993. "The Politics of Nastiness." *The Washington Post* July 22.

Dionne, E. J., Jr., and Ann Devroy. 1992. "Bush-Buchanan Clash Could Soften in Tone." *The Washington Post* March 15.

Dole, Robert. 1992. "Is America Ignoring GOP Women?" *The Washington Post* May 31.

Dorsey, Robert W. 1993. "The Last True Government." *Cincinnati Magazine* August.

Downs, Anthony. 1957. *An Economic Theory of Democracy.* New York: Harper and Row.

———. 1965. *An Economic Theory of Democracy.* New York: Harper and Row.

Downtown Cincinnati Incorportated (DCI). 1995. *Program of Work for Year Two.* Cincinnati, Ohio: DCI.

Duffy, Michael, and Dan Goodgame. 1992. *Marching in Place: The Status Quo Presidency of George Bush.* New York: Simon and Schuster.

Duverger, Maurice. 1954. *Political Parties.* New York: Wiley.

Drew, Elizabeth. 1983. *Politics and Money: The New Road to Corruption.* New York: Macmillan.

———. 1993. "Watch Them Squirm." *The New York Times Magazine* March 14.

Dwyre, Diana. 1992. "Is Winning Everything? Party Strategies for the U.S. House of Representatives." Presented at the annual meeting of the American Political Science Association, Chicago.

———. 1993. "The Complete Congressional Party, Governing and Electing: The Congressional Campaign Committees and Responsible Party Government During Realignments." Paper presented at the annual meeting of the American Political Science Association, Washington, D.C.

———. 1994. "Party Strategy and Political Reality: The Distribution of Congressional Campaign Committee Resources," in Daniel M. Shea and John C. Green, eds., *The State of the Parties: The Changing Role of Contemporary American Parties.* Pp. 175–89.

Dwyre, Diana, and Jeffrey M. Stonecash. 1992. "Where's the Party? Changing State Party Organizations." *American Politics Quarterly* 20: 326–44.

Elden, James M., and David R. Schweitzer. 1971. "New Third Party Radicalism: The Case of the California Peace and Freedom Party." *Western Politics Quarterly* 24: 761–74.

Edsall, Thomas Byrne. 1984. *The New Politics of Inequality.* New York: Norton.

Edsall, Thomas Byrne, with Mary Edsall. 1991. *Chain Reaction.* Boston: Norton.

Edsall, Thomas Byrne, and Dan Balz. 1991. "DNC Poised to Play Role in Late-Starting Campaign." *The Washington Post* September 23.

Ehrenhalt, Alan. 1991. *The United States of Ambition.* New York: Random House.

Eldersveld, Samuel J. 1956. "Experimental Propaganda Techniques and Voting Behavior." *American Political Science Review* 50: 154–65.

——. 1964. *Political Parties: A Behavioral Analysis.* Chicago: Rand McNally.

——. 1982. *Political Parties in American Society.* New York: Basic Books.

Engler, David L. 1993. "Youngstown Is a Ruin No Longer: Bit by Bit, the Mahoning Valley Has Emerged from the Rust." *Cleveland Plain Dealer* December 29, 11B.

Erie, Steven P. 1988. *Rainbow's End: Irish Americans and the Dilemmas of Urban Machine Politics, 1840–1985.* Berkeley: University of California Press.

Epstein, Leon D. 1986. *Political Parties in the American Mold.* Madison: University of Wisconsin Press.

——. 1989. "Will American Political Parties Be Privatized?" *Journal of Law and Politics* 5: 239.

Federal Election Commission. 1992a. "Spending Jumped to $504 Million by '92 Congressional Candidates: FEC Finds Spending in House Races Grew 41 Percent." Press Release. December 30.

——. 1992b. *Federal Elections 92: Election Results for the U.S. President, the U.S. Senate and the U.S. House of Representatives.* Washington, D.C.: Federal Election Commission.

——. 1993a. "1992 Congressional Spending Jumps 52 Percent to $678 Million." Press Release. March 4.

——. 1993b. "Democrats Narrow Financial Gap in 1991–92." Press Release. March 11.

Feit, Rona. 1979. "Organizing for Political Power: The National Women's Political Caucus," in Bernice Cummings and Victoria Schuck, eds., *Women Organizing.* Pp. 184–208. Metuchen, N.J.: Scarecrow Press, Inc.

Fenno, Richard. 1975. "If, as Ralph Nader says, Congress is 'the Broken Branch,' How Come We Love our Congressmen so Much?" in Norman J. Ornstein, ed., *Congress in Change: Evolution and Reform.* Pp. 277–87. New York: Praeger Publishers.

——. 1978. *Home Style.* Boston: Little, Brown.

Ferguson, Thomas. 1995. *Golden Rule: The Investment Theory of Party Competition and the Logic of Money-Driven Political Systems.* Chicago: University of Chicago Press.

Ferguson, Thomas, and Joel Rogers. 1986. *Right Turn: The Decline of the Democrats and the Future of American Politics.* New York: Hill and Wang.

Fiorina, Morris P. 1980. "The Decline of Collective Responsibility in American Politics." *Daedalus* 109: 25–45.

——. 1987. "Party Government in the United States: Diagnosis and Prognosis," in Richard S. Katz, ed., *Party Governments: European and American Experiences.* Pp. 270–300. New York: Walter de Gruyter.

——. 1990. "The Electorate in the Voting Booth," in L. Sandy Maisel, ed., *The Parties Respond: Changes in the American Party System.* Pp. 116–36. Boulder, Colo.: Westview Press.

Fisher, Bonnie, Michael Margolis, and David Resnick. 1996. "Surveying the Internet: Democratic Theory and Civic Life in Cyberspace," *Southeastern Political Review.*

Fishman, Robert. 1992. "Megalopolis Unbound: America's New City," in *The Best of the Wilson Quarterly.* Pp. 9–25. Washington, D.C.: Woodrow Wilson International Center.

Frankovic, Kathleen A. 1993. "Public Opinion in the 1992 Campaign," in Gerald M. Pomper, ed., *The Elections of 1992.* Pp. 74–109. Chatham, N.J.: Chatham House.

Frantzich, Stephen E. 1989. *Political Parties in the Technological Age.* New York: Longman.

Freeman, Jo. 1987. "Whom You Know versus Whom You Represent: Feminist Influence in the Democratic and Republican Parties," in Mary Katzenstein and Carol McClurg Mueller, eds., *The Women's Movements of the United States and Western Europe*. Pp. 215–44. Philadelphia: Temple University Press.

———. 1988. "Women at the 1988 Democratic Convention." *PS* 21: 875–81.

———. 1988. "Feminist Activities at the 1988 Republican Convention." *PS* 22: 39–46.

———. 1993. "Feminism vs. Family Values: Women at the 1992 Democratic and Republican Conventions." *PS* 26: 21–27.

Frendreis, John P., James L. Gibson, and Laura L. Vertz. 1990. "The Electoral Relevance of Local Party Organizations." *American Political Science Review* 84: 226–35.

Frendreis, John P., and Alan R. Gitelson. 1993. "Local Parties in an Age of Change." *American Review of Politics* 14: 533–47.

Frendreis, John P., Alan R. Gitelson, Gregory Flemming, and Anne Layzell. 1993. "Local Political Parties and the 1992 Campaign for the State Legislature." Paper presented at the annual meeting of the American Political Science Association, Washington, D.C.

———. 1994. "Local Political Parties and Legislative Races in 1992." Pp. 133–46 in D. Shea and J. Green, eds., *The State of the Parties*. Lanham, Md.: Rowman & Littlefield.

Frisby, Michael K. 1992. "A Spending Problem for the GOP." *The Boston Globe* November 2.

From, Al, and Will Marshall. 1993a. "The First 100 Days." *The New Democrat* May.

Galston, William, and Elaine Kamarck. 1989. *The Politics of Evasion: Democrats and the Presidency*. Washington, D.C.: Progressive Policy Institute.

Germond, Jack W., and Jules Witcover. 1985. *Wake Us When It's Over*. New York: Macmillan.

———. 1993. *Mad as Hell: Revolt at the Ballot Box, 1992*. New York: Warner Books.

Gibson, James L., Cornelius P. Cotter, John F. Bibby, and Robert J. Huckshorn. 1983. "Assessing Party Organizational Strength." *American Journal of Political Science* 27: 193–222.

———. 1985. "Whither the Local Parties? A Cross-Sectional and Longitudinal Analysis of the Strength of Party Organizations." *American Journal of Political Science* 29: 139–60

Gibson, James L., John P. Frendreis, and Laura L. Vertz. 1989. "Party Dynamics in the 1980s: Change in County Party Organizational Strength, 1980–1984." *American Journal of Political Science* 33: 67–90.

Gibson, James L., and Susan E. Scarrow. 1993. "State and Local Party Organizations in American Politics," in Eric M. Uslaner, ed., *American Political Parties*. Pp. 232–62. Itasca, Ill.: Peacock.

Gibson, James L., and Gregg Smith. 1984. "Local Party Organizations and Electoral Outcomes: Linkages Between Parties and Elections." Paper presented at the annual meeting of the American Political Science Association, Washington, D.C.

Gierzynski, Anthony. 1992. *Legislative Party Campaign Committees in the American States*. Lexington: University Press of Kentucky.

Gierzynski, Anthony, and David Breaux. 1991. "Money and Votes in State Legislative Elections." *Legislative Studies Quarterly* 16: 203–17.

———. 1994. "The Role of Parties in Legislative Campaign Financing." *American Review of Politics* 15: 171–89.

Giles, Michael W., and Anita Pritchard. 1985. "Campaign Expenditures and Legislative Elections in Florida." *Legislative Studies Quarterly* 10: 71–88.

Gillespie, Ed. Communications Division, RNC. Telephone Interview. February 21, 1996.

Gillespie, J. David. 1993. *Politics at the Periphery: Third Parties in Two-Party America*. Columbia: University of South Carolina Press.

Ginsberg, Benjamin. 1986. *The Captive Public: How Mass Opinion Promotes State Power*. New York: Basic Books.

Ginsberg, Benjamin, and Martin Shefter. 1990. *Politics by Other Means*. New York: Basic Books.

Gitelson, Alan R., M. Margaret Conway, and Frank B. Feigert. 1984. *American Political Parties: Stability and Change*. Boston: Houghton Mifflin.

Goldman, Peter, and Tom Mathews. 1992a. "How He Won." *Newsweek Special Election Issue* November/December. New York: M. Evans.

Goldman, Ralph M. 1983. *Transnational Parties: Organizing the World's Precincts*. Lanham, Md.: University Press of America.

———. 1990. *From Warfare to Party Politics*. Syracuse: Syracuse University Press.

Goldstein, Joshua. 1991. *The $43 Million Loophole: Soft Money in the 1990 Congressional Elections*. Washington, D.C.: Center for Responsive Politics.

Goodin, Robert E. 1992. *Green Political Theory*. Cambridge: Polity Press.

Goodwyn, Lawrence. 1978. *The Populist Moment*. New York: Oxford University Press.

Green, John C., and James L. Guth. 1986. "Big Bucks and Petty Cash: Party and Interest Group Activists in American Politics," in *Interest Group Politics*. Ed. Allan Cigler and Burdett Loomis. (2d ed.), Washington, D.C.: CQ Press.

———. 1991. "Who Is Right and Who Is Left? Activist Coalitions in the Reagan Era," in *Do Elections Matter?* Ed. Benjamin Ginsberg and Alan Stone. Armonk, N.Y.: M. E. Sharpe.

———. 1994. "Controlling the Mischief of Faction: Support for Party among Party Activists," in John C. Green, ed., *Politics, Professionalism, and Power*. Lanham, Md.: University Press of America.

Greider, William. 1992. Who Will Tell the People: The Betrayal of American Democracy. New York: Simon and Schuster.

Gross, Bertram M. 1980. *Friendly Fascism: The New Face of Power in America*. New York: M. Evans.

Grove, Lloyd. 1994. "Man on a Tightrope." *The Washington Post* April 20.

Hames, Tim. 1994. "Strengths and Limitations: The Republican Committee from Bliss to Brock to Barbour," in John C. Green, ed., *Politics, Professionalism and Power*. Pp. 149–66. Lanham, Md.: University Press of America.

Hamilton, Alexander. 1851. "Letter to Bayard, April 1802," in John C. Hamilton, ed., *The Works of Alexander Hamilton*. Vol. 6. Pp. 540–43. New York: John F. Trow.

Harmel, Robert, and Kenneth Janda. 1982. *Parties and Their Environments: Limits to Reform?* New York: Longman.

———. 1994. "An Integrated Theory of Party Goals and Party Change." *Journal of Theoretical Politics* 6: 259–87.

Hazlitt, Joseph M. II. 1992. *The Libertarians and Other Minor Political Parties in the United States*. Jefferson and London: McFarland.

Herbst, Susan. 1994. *Politics at Margin: Historical Studies of Public Expression Outside the Mainstream*. New York: Cambridge University Press.

Herson, Lawrence J. R., and John M. Boland. 1990. *The Urban Web: Politics, Policy and Theory*. Chicago: Nelson-Hall.

Herring, E. Pendleton. 1940. *The Politics of Democracy: American Parties in Action*. New York: Norton.

Herrnson, Paul S. 1986. "Do Parties Make a Difference? The Role of Party Organizations in Congressional Elections." *Journal of Politics* 48: 589–615.

———. 1988. *Party Campaigning in the 1980s*. Cambridge: Harvard University Press.

———. 1989. "National Party Decision Making, Strategies, and Resource Distribution in Congressional Elections." *Western Political Quarterly* 42: 301–23.

———. 1990. "Reemergent National Party Organizations," in L. Sandy Maisel, ed., *The Parties Respond: Changes in the American Party System*. Pp. 41–66. Boulder, Colo.: Westview Press.

——. 1993. "Political Parties and Congressional Elections: Out of the Eighties and into the Nineties," in Michael Margolis and John C. Green, eds., *Machine Politics, Sound Bites, and Nostalgia: On Studying Political Parties*. Pp. 7–19. Lanham, Md.: University Press of America.

——. 1994a. "The Revitalization of National Party Organizations," in L. Sandy Maisel, ed., *The Parties Respond*. 2d ed. Pp. 45–68. Boulder, Colo.: Westview Press.

——. 1994b. "The National Committee for an Effective Congress: Ideology, Partisanship, and Electoral Innovation," in Robert Biersack, Paul S. Herrnson, and Clyde Wilcox, eds., *PAC Decision Making and Strategy in Congressional Elections*. Armonk, N.Y.: M. E. Sharpe.

——. 1994c. *Congressional Elections: Campaigning at Home and in Washington*. Washington, D.C. CQ Press.

——. 1995. *Congressional Elections: Campaigning at Home and in Washington*. Washington, D.C.: Congressional Quarterly.

Herrnson, Paul S., and David Menefee-Libey. 1990. "The Dynamics of Party Organizational Development." *Midsouth Political Science Journal* 11: 3–30.

Hershey, Marjorie Randon. 1984. *Running for Office*. Chatham, N.J.: Chatham House.

Hewitt, Don. 1992. "How About We Chuck the Parties?" *The Washington Post* November 12.

House Republican Conference. "Update on the Bills of the Contract with America," January 3, 1996.

Huckfeldt, Robert, and John Sprague. 1992. "Political Parties and Electoral Mobilization: Political Structure, Social Structure, and the Party Canvass." *American Political Science Review* 86: 70–86.

Huckshorn, Robert J. 1976. *Party Leadership in the States*. Amherst: University of Massachusetts Press.

Huckshorn, Robert J., James L. Gibson, Cornelius P. Cotter, and John F. Bibby. 1986. "Party Integration and Party Organizational Strength." *Journal of Politics* 48: 976–91.

Huitt, Ralph K. 1990. "Democratic Party Leadership in the U. S. Senate," in R. Huitt, ed., *Working Within the System*. Berkeley, Calif.: Institute of Governmental Studies Press.

Ideas Matter. 1995. Agenda for America Update. July: 4.

Ifill, Gwen. 1992a. "At Jackson's Behest, Clinton Kicks Off Voter Drive." *The New York Times* September 13.

——. 1992b. "Keeper of Democratic Flame Applies Heat as Necessary." *The New York Times* April 19.

Inglehart, Ronald. 1987. "Changing Values in Industrial Societies Revisited." *American Political Science Review* 81: 1298–303.

——. 1990. *Culture Shift in Advanced Industrial Society*. Princeton, N.J.: Princeton University Press.

Isikoff, Michael. 1992. "Democrats Hire Firms to Investigate Bush." *The Washington Post* July 2.

Jackson, Brooks. 1988. *Honest Graft*. New York: Knopf.

Jackson, John S. 1992. "The Party-as-Organization: Party Elites and Party Reforms in Presidential Nominations and Conventions," in John Kenneth White and Jerome M. Mileur, eds., *Challengers to Party Government*. Pp. 63–83. Carbondale: Southern Illinois University Press.

Jackson, John S. III, Barbara L. Brown, and David Bositis. 1982. "Herbert McClosky and Friends Revisited." *American Politics Quarterly*. 158–80.

Jacobson, Gary C. 1980. *Money in Congressional Elections*. New Haven: Yale University Press.

——. 1986. "Party Organization and Campaign Resources in 1982." *Political Science Quarterly* 100: 604–25.

———. 1985. "The Republican Advantage in Campaign Finance," in John Chubb and Paul Peterson, eds., *The New Direction in American Politics*. Pp. 143–73. Washington, D.C.: Brookings Institution.

———. 1992. *The Politics of Congressional Elections*. New York: HarperCollins.

———. 1996. "The 1994 House Elections in Perspective," in Philip A. Klinkner, ed., *Midterm: Elections of 1994 in Context*. Boulder, Colo.: Westview Press.

Jacobson, Gary C., and Samuel Kernell. 1983. *Strategy and Choice in Congressional Elections*. New Haven: Yale University Press.

Jehl, Douglas. 1992. "Buchanan Seeks GOP Chairman's Ouster." *The Los Angeles Times* March 11.

Jewell, Malcolm E., and David Olson. 1988. *Political Parties and Elections in American States*. 3d ed. Chicago: Dorsey Press.

Johnson, Richard R. 1987. "Partisan Legislative Campaign Committees: New Power, New Problems." *Illinois Issues* July.

Johnston, Michael. 1979. "Patrons and Clients, Jobs and Machines: A Case Study of the Uses of Patronage." *American Political Science Review* 73: 385–98.

Jones, Charles O. 1970. *The Minority Party in Congress*. Boston: Little, Brown.

Kamarck, Elaine Ciulla. 1990. "Structure as Strategy: Presidential Nominating Politics in the Post-Reform Era," in L. Sandy Maisel, ed., *The Parties Respond*. Pp. 160–86. Boulder, Colo.: Westview Press.

Katz, Daniel, and Samuel Eldersveld. 1961. "The Impact of Local Party Activity upon the Electorate." *Public Opinion Quarterly* 25: 1–24.

Kayden, Xandra, and Eddie Mahe, Jr. 1985. *The Party Goes On*. New York: Basic Books.

Kazee, Thomas A., and Mary C. Thornberry. 1990. "Where's the Party? Congressional Candidate Recruitment and American Party Organizations." *Western Political Quarterly* 43: 61–80.

Keefe, William J. 1994. *Parties, Politics and Public Policy in America*. 7th ed. Washington, D.C.: CQ Press.

Keith, Bruce E., David B. Magleby, Candice J. Nelson, Elizabeth Orr, Mark C. Westlye, and Raymond E. Wolfinger. 1992. *The Myth of the Independent Voter*. Berkeley: University of California Press.

Kelly, Michael. 1992. "The Making of a First Family: A Blueprint." *The New York Times* November 14.

Key, V. O., Jr. 1947. *Politics, Parties, and Pressure Groups*. New York: Thomas Y. Crowell.

———. 1955. "A Theory of Critical Elections." *Journal of Politics* 18: 3–18.

———. 1956. *American State Politics: An Introduction*. New York: Knopf.

———. 1964. *Politics, Parties, and Pressure Groups*. (5th ed.) New York: Thomas Y. Crowell.

Kirkpatrick, Jeane J. 1976. *The New Presidential Elite: Men and Women in National Politics*. New York: Russell Sage Foundation.

———. 1979. *Dismantling the Parties*. Washington, D.C.: American Enterprise Institute.

Klinkner, Philip A. 1994. *The Losing Parties: Out-Party National Committees, 1956–1993*. New Haven: Yale University Press.

Kolodny, Robin. 1991. "Congressional Party Politics and the Congressional Campaign Committees: The 1990 Leadership Challenge to Rep. Guy Vander Jaft." Paper presented at the annual meeting of the American Political Science Association, Washington, D.C., August 19–September 1, 1991.

Kondracke, Morton. 1996. "Political Imagery to the Forefront." *The Washington Times* April 20, C4.

Kondratieff, Nikolai. 1984. *The Long Wave Cycle*. New York: Richardson and Snyder.

Koopman, Douglas L. 1991. "The House Divided: House Republican Party Factions Revealed in the 1989 Gingrich-Madigan Whip Race." Paper presented at the annual meeting of the Midwest Political Science Association, Chicago, Illinois, April 18–20, 1991.

Kosova, Weston. 1994. "Party Pooper." *The New Republic* June 20.

Knaggs, John R. 1986. *Two-Party Texas*. 2d ed. New York: Oxford University Press.

Kramer, Gerald. 1971. "The Effects of Precinct-Level Canvassing on Voter Behavior." *Public Opinion Quarterly* 34: 560–72.

Kurtz, Karl T. 1996. "Party Spends $15 Million on Ads to Burnish Clinton." *Washington Post* February 7, A8.

Labaton, Stephen. 1992. "Despite Economy, Clinton Sets Record for Funds." *The New York Times* October 24.

Ladd, Everett Carll. 1991. "On the Uselessness of 'Realignment' for Understanding Changes in American Politics," in Byron E. Shafer, ed., *The End of Realignment*? Pp. 24–36. Madison, Wis.: University of Wisconsin Press.

———. 1995. "The 1994 Congressional Elections: The Postindustrial Realignment Continues." *Political Science Quarterly* 110: 1–24.

Lambrecht, William. 1994. "It Is the Future: GOP Marshals 3 New Television Ventures." *The St. Louis Post-Dispatch* January 30.

Lambro, Donald. 1994. "President's Team on the Lookout for Potential Primary Challengers." *The Washington Times* May 10.

Lawson, Kay. 1980. "Political Parties and Linkage," in Kay Lawson, ed., *Political Parties and Linkage: A Comparative Perspective*. Pp. 3–24. New Haven: Yale University Press.

Lawson, Kay, Gerald Pomper, and Maureen Moakley. 1986. "Local Party Activists and Electoral Linkage: Middlesex County, N.J." *American Politics Quarterly* 14: 345–75.

Leyden, Kevin M., and Stephen A. Borrelli. 1990. "Party Contributions and Party Unity: Can Loyalty Be Bought?" *Western Political Quarterly* 43: 343–65.

Lind, Michael. 1995. *The Next American Nation*. New York: The Free Press.

Lipset, Seymour Martin, and William Schneider. 1987. "The Confidence Gap during the Reagan Years, 1981–1987." *Political Science Quarterly* 102: 1–23.

Little, Thomas H. 1996. "On the Coattails of a Contract: RNC Activities and Republican Gains in the 1995 State Legislative Elections." Paper presented at the annual meeting of the midwest Political Science Association, Chicago.

Little, Thomas H., and Samuel C. Patterson. 1993. "The Organizational Life of the Congressional Parties." *American Review of Politics* 14: 39–70.

Loftus, Tom. 1985. "The New 'Political Parties' in State Legislatures." *State Government* 58: 108.

Longley, Lawrence D. 1992. "The Institutionalization of the National Democratic Party: A Process Stymied, Then Revitalized." *Wisconsin Political Scientist* 7: 9–15.

Lowi, Theodore J. 1975. "Party, Policy, and Constitution in America," in William N. Chambers and Walter Dean Burnham, eds., *The American Party Systems: Stages of Political Development*. 2d ed. Pp. 238–76. New York: Oxford University Press.

Lugar, Richard. 1983. "A Plan to Elect More GOP Women." *The Washington Post* August 21.

Luttner, Steve. 1993. "The Voice of Ohio's Last Party Machine." *The Cleveland Plain Dealer* November 21: 3.

Maisel, L. Sandy. 1993. *Parties and Elections Process*. 2d ed. New York: McGraw Hill, 252–53.

———. 1994. "The Platform-Writing Process: Candidate-Centered Platforms in 1992." *Political Science Quarterly* 108: 671–98.

Maisel, L. Sandy, Linda L. Fowler, Ruth S. Jones, and Walter J. Stone. 1990. "The Naming of Candidates: Recruitment or Emergence?" in L. Sandy Maisel, ed., *The Parties Respond: Changes in the American Party System*. Pp. 137–59. Boulder, Colo.: Westview Press.

Maisel, L. Sandy, Elizabeth J. Ivry, Benjamin D. Ling, and Stephanie G. Penniz. 1996. "Re-exploring the Weak Challenger Hypothesis: The 1994 Candidate Pools." in Philip A. Klinkner. ed., *Midterm: Elections of 1994 in Context*. Boulder, Colo.: Westview Press.

March, James G., and Herbert Simon, and Johan P. Olsen. 1984. "The New Institutionalism: Organizational Factors in Political Life." *American Political Science Review* 78: 334–49.

March, James G., and Johan P. Olsen. 1989. *Rediscovering Institutions: The Organizational Basis of Politics*. New York: Free Press.

Margolis, Michael, and John C. Green, eds. 1992. *Machine Politics, Sound Bites, and Nostalgia*. Lanham, Md.: University Press of America.

———. 1993. "The Importance of Local Parties for Democratic Governance," in Michael Margolis and John C. Green, eds., *Machine Politics, Sound Bites, and Nostalgia*. Pp. 29–37. Lanham, Md.: University Press of America.

Margolis, Michael, Robert Burtt, and Jeffrey McLaughlin. 1986. "The Impact of Industrial Decline: Braddock, North Braddock, and Rankin," in Jim Cunningham and Pamela Martz, eds., *Steel People: Survival and Resilience in Pittsburgh's Mon Valley*. Pp. 9–32. Pittsburgh: River Communities Project, University of Pittsburgh, School of Social Work.

Margolis, Michael, and Raymond E. Owen. 1985. "From Organization to Personalism: A Note on the Transmogrification of the Local Party Organization." *Polity* 18: 313–28.

May, A. L., and Joe Drape. 1991. "Democrats Make Pitch to Middle America, Seek to Blame Bush for Economic Squeeze." *The Atlanta Constitution* June 23.

Mayhew, David R. 1986. *Placing Parties in American Politics*. Princeton: Princeton University Press.

———. 1991. *Divided We Govern: Party Control, Lawmaking, and Investigations, 1946–1990*. New Haven: Yale University Press.

Mazmanian, Daniel A. 1974. *Third Parties in Presidential Elections*. Washington, D.C.: Brookings.

McCann, James A., Randall W. Partin, Ronald B. Rapoport, Walter J. Stone. 1996. "Presidential Nomination Campaign Participation and Party Mobilization: An Assessment of Spillover Effects." *American Journal of Political Science*.

McGlennon, John. 1993. "Party Activity and Party Success: Southern Precinct Leaders and the Evaluation of Party Strength." Paper presented at the annual meeting of the American Political Science Association, Washington, D.C.

McGeer, Michael E. 1986. *The Decline of Popular Politics: The American North, 1865–1928*. New York: Oxford University Press.

Menefee-Libey, David. 1994. "Embracing Campaign-Centered Politics at the Democratic Headquarters: Charles Manatt and Paul Kirk," in John C. Green, ed., *Politics, Professionalism, and Power*. Pp. 167–85. Lanham, Md.: University Press of America.

Mileur, Jerome M. 1989. "In the Polity." *Polity* 22: 1–3.

Milkis, Sidney M. 1993. "The New Deal, Party Politics, and the Administrative State," in Peter W. Schramm and Bradford P. Wilson, eds., *American Political Parties and Constitutional Politics*. Pp. 141–80. Lanham, Md.: Rowman & Littlefield.

Miller, Zane L. 1993. "The Rules of the Game (Changing) at City Hall, 1893–1993," in *Cincinnati: Rededication of City Hall, May 13, 1993*. Cincinnati: Berman Printing Company.

Morin, Richard, and E. J. Dionne, Jr. 1992. "Public Takes Dim View of Political Parties." *The Washington Post* July 8.

Nagourney, Adam. 1991. "Select Democrats Try to Regroup at '92 'Summit'." *USA Today* June 13.

National-House Democratic Caucus. 1984. *Renewing America's Promise: A Democratic Blueprint for Our Nation's Future*. Washington, D.C.: National-House Democratic Caucus.

National Republican Congressional Committee. 1992. *NRCC Report '92: A Report Outlining Services and Activities of 1992.* Washington, D.C.: National Republican Congressional Committee.

New York Democratic State Committee. 1994. *Rules of the Democratic Party of the State of New York.* Albany, N.Y.: New York State Board of Elections.

New York Republican State Committee. 1993. *Rules of the New York Republican State Committee.* Albany, N.Y.: New York State Board of Elections.

New York State Board of Election. 1992. *Reports on Financial Disclosure Data*, 1984–1995. Albany, N.Y.: New York State Board of Elections.

New York State Board of Election 1993. *Reports on Financial Activity*, 1990–1992. Albany, N.Y.: The State of New York.

Nie, Norman H., Sidney Verba, and John R. Petrocik. 1979. *The Changing American Voter.* 2d ed. Cambridge: Harvard University Press.

Niquette, Mark. 1992. "City Sues to Get Payments on Loans." *The Vindicator.* September 4, A1.

———. 1993. "Hanni and Engler Tangle over Comments." *The Vindicator.* December 31, B1.

———. 1994a. "Battle Heats up for Party Leader." *The Vindicator.* February 14, A1.

———. 1994b. "Breakaway Dem Group to Run Its Own Slate." *The Vindicator.* February 17, A1, A3.

———. 1994c. "Write-ins File to Fill Party Slots in May Primary." *The Vindicator.* March 25, B1.

———. 1994d. "In the Leadership Race, Proof Is in the Precincts." *The Vindicator.* April 26, A1, A4.

———. 1995a. "Group to Plan Cargo Hub at Airport." *The Vindicator.* February 20, B1.

———. 1995b. "It's Time for Change, Victor Levy Says." *The Vindicator.* May 3, A1, A3.

———. 1995c. "Clinton Is Working for Valley, Aide Says." *The Vindicator.* June 29, A1, A3.

OKI Regional Council of Governments. 1993. *State of the Region: Committee Report on Transportation, the Economy, and the Environment.* Cincinnati: OKI Regional Council of Governments.

Oldfield, Duane M. 1992. "The Christian Right in the 1992 Campaign." Paper presented at the annual meeting of the Northeastern Political Science Association, Providence, R.I.

Ornstein, Norman J., Thomas E. Mann, and Michael J. Malbin. 1992. *Vital Statistics on Congress, 1991–1992.* Washington, D.C.: CQ Press.

Ornstein, Norman J. and Amy L. Schenkenberg. 1995. "The 1995 Congress: The First Hundred Days and Beyond." *Political Science Quarterly* 110: 183–206.

Orren, Gary R. 1982. "The Changing Styles of American Party Politics," in Joel L. Fleishman, ed., *The Future of American Political Parties.* Englewood, Cliffs, N.J.: Prentice Hall.

Ott, J. Steven. 1994. "Boss Democrat: Mahoning County's Old-Style Chairman Fights Young, Reform-Minded Opponents Who Seek an End to His Abrasive Reign." *The Cleveland Plain Dealer* April 25, 1A, 8A.

Paddock, Joel. 1990. "Beyond the New Deal: Ideological Differences Between 11 State Democratic Parties, 1956–1980." *Western Political Quarterly* 43: 181–90.

Page, Benjamin I., and Robert V. Shapiro. 1992. *The Rational Public: Fifty Years of Trends in Americans' Policy Preferences.* Chicago: University of Chicago Press.

Pannebianco, Angelo. 1988. *Political Parties: Organization and Power.* Cambridge: Cambridge University Press.

Partin, Randall W., Lori M. Weber, Robert B. Rapoport, and Walter J. Stone. 1994. "Sources of Activism in the 1992 Perot Campaign," in Shea and Green, eds., *The State of the Parties: The Changing Role of Contemporary American Parties.* Lanham, Md.: Rowman & Littlefield.

Patterson, Samuel C. 1990. "State Legislators and the Legislatures," in Virgina Gray, Herbert Jacob, and Robert Albitton, eds., *Politics in the American States*. 5th ed. Glenview, Ill.: Scott, Foresman/Little.

Pendleton, Scott. 1994. "Perot Backers Urge GOP to Act Fast or Face Possible Third-Party Music." *The Christian Science Monitor*. November 18, 3.

Perot, Ross. 1992. *United We Stand: How We Can Take Back Our Country*. New York: Hyperion.

Perrow, Charles. 1979. *Complex Organizations*. 2d ed. Glenview, Ill.: Scott, Foresman.

Phillips, Kevin P. 1982. *Post-Conservative America*. New York: Vintage Books.

———. 1993. *Post-Conservative America*. New York: Vintage.

Pitney, John. 1993. "Comments," in Michael Margolis and John C. Green, eds., *Machine Politics, Sound Bites, and Nostalgia*. Pp. 49–52. Lanham, Md.: University Press of America.

Pitney, John, and William F. Connelly. 1996. "Permanent Minority No More: House Republicans in 1994," in Philip A. Klinkner, ed., *Midterm: Elections of 1994 in Context*. Boulder, Colo.: Westview Press.

Piven, Frances Fox, and Richard A. Cloward. 1989. *Why Americans Don't Vote*. New York: Pantheon Books.

Polsby, Nelson W. 1963. "Two Strategies of Influence: Choosing a Majority Leader 1962," in Robert Peabody and Nelson Polsby, eds., *New Perspectives on the House of Representatives*. Pp. 237–70. Chicago: Rand McNally.

———. 1983. *Consequences of Party Reform*. New York: Oxford University Press.

Polsby, Nelson W., and Aaron Wildavsky. 1984. *Presidential Elections*. 6th ed. New York: Scribner's.

Pomper, Gerald M. 1970. *Elections in America*. New York: Dodd, Mead.

Pomper, Gerald M., ed. 1981. *Party Renewal in America*. New York: Praeger.

Pomper, Gerald M. 1985. "The Nominations," in Gerald Pomper, ed., *The Election of 1984*. Pp. 1–34. Chatham, N.J.: Chatham House.

———. 1990. "Party Organization and Electoral Success." *Polity* 23: 187–206.

———. 1992. *Passions and Interests: Political Party Concepts of American Democracy*. Lawrence, Kans.: University Press of Kansas.

Popkin, Samuel L. 1991. *The Reasoning Voter*. Chicago: University of Chicago Press.

Price, David E. 1984. *Bringing Back the Parties*. Washington, D.C.: CQ Press.

Priest Dan. 1994. "New DNC Health Ads Wind Up Offending Senate D's." *Washington Post* July 15, A4.

Putnam, Robert. 1992–93. "Celebrators of the Status Quo: Reflections on the Study of Politics in the 1990s." *Clio Newsletter of Politics and History* 3: 1ff.

Pyle, Arthur. 1993. "Big Help Wanted." *Cincinnati Magazine* August.

Quirk, Paul J., and Jon K. Dalager. 1993. "The Election: A 'New Democrat'," in Michael Nelson, ed., *The Elections of 1992*. Pp. 57–88. Washington, D.C.: CQ Press.

Rae, Nicol C. 1991. "The Problem of Centrist Politics in an Ideological Age: The Case of the DLC." Paper presented at the annual meeting of the American Political Science Association, Washington, D.C.

Ranney, Austin. 1954. *The Doctrine of Responsible Party Government*. Urbana, Ill.: University of Illinois Press.

———. 1962. *The Doctrine of Responsible Party Government*. Urbana, Ill.: University of Illinois Press.

———. 1975. *Curing the Mischiefs of Faction*. Berkeley: University of California Press.

Rapoport, Ronald B., Walter J. Stone, Randall W. Partin, and James A. McCann. 1992. "Spillover and Carryover: Nomination Involvement and General Election Success." Presented at the annual meeting of the American Political Science Association, Chicago.

Rapoport, Ronald B., and Walter J. Stone. 1995. Candidate-Centered Sources of Party Change: Perot Activists in 1995. Presented at the annual meeting of the American Political Science Association, Chicago.

Redfield, Kent D. and Jack Van Der Slik. 1992. "The Circulation of Political Money in Illinois Elections." Paper delivered at the 1992 Midwest Political Science Association, Chicago.

Reichley, A. James. 1985. "The Rise of National Parties," in John Chubb and Paul Peterson, eds., *The New Direction in American Politics*. Pp. 175–200. Washington, D.C.: Brookings Institution.

——. 1992. *The Life of the Parties: A History of American Political Parties*. New York: Free Press.

Republican National Committee, 1993. *1993 Chairman's Report to the Members of the Republican National Committee*. Washington, D.C.: Republican National Committee.

Riker, William H. 1982. *Liberalism Against Populism*. New York: W. H. Freeman.

Riley, Russell L. 1995. "Party Government and the Contract with America." *PS: Political Science and Politics* 28: 703–7.

Ripley, Randall B. 1969. *Majority Party Leadership in Congress*. Boston: Little, Brown.

Roberts, George C. 1994. "Paul Butler and the Democratic Party: Leadership and New Directions in Party Building," in John C. Green, ed., *Politics, Professionalism, and Power*. Pp. 93–104. Lanham, Md.: University Press of America.

Rohde, David W. 1991. *Parties and Leaders in the Postreform House*. Chicago: University of Chicago Press.

Roll Call. 1995. "100 Days of Servitude." April 6, 4.

Roll Call. 1994. "Republicans Now Dominate Ranks of Best-Funded House Challengers." October 27, 1, 14.

Romney, Ronna, and Beppie Harrison. 1987. *Momentum: Women in American Politics Now*. New York: Crown Publishers.

Rosenstone, Steven J., Roy L. Behr, and Edward H. Lazarus. 1984. *Third Parties in America: Citizen Response to Major Party Failure*. Princeton, N.J.: Princeton University Press.

Rosenstone, Steven J., and John Mark Hanson. 1993. *Mobilization, Participation, and Democracy in America*. New York: Macmillan.

Rosenthal, Alan. 1990. *Governors and Legislatures: Contending Powers*. Washington, D.C.: CQ Press.

Ross, Bernard H. and Myron A. Levine. 1996. *Urban Politics: Power in Metropolitan America*. 5th ed. Itasca, Ill.: F. E. Peacock.

Rozell, Mark J., and Clyde Wilcox. 1995. *God at the Grassroots*. Lanham, Md.: Rowman & Littlefield.

Rule, Wilma, and Pippa Norris. 1992. "Anglo and Minority Women's Underrepresentation in the Congress: Is the Electoral System the Culprit?" in Joseph F. Zimmerman and Wilma Rule, eds., *United States Electoral Systems: Their Impact of U.S. Electoral Systems on Minorities and Women*. Pp. 41–54. Westport, Conn.: Greenwood Press.

Rusk, David. 1993. *Cities without Suburbs*. Washington, D.C.: Woodrow Wilson Center.

Sabato, Larry J. 1981. *The Rise of the Political Consultants*. New York: Basic Books.

——. 1984. *PAC Power: Inside the World of Political Action Committees*. New York: W. W. Norton.

——. 1988. *The Party's Just Begun*. Glenview, Ill.: Scott, Foresman.

Salmore, Barbara G., and Stephen A. Salmore. 1989. *Candidates, Parties, and Campaigns: Electoral Politics in America*. Washington, D.C.: CQ Press.

Sartori, Giovanni. 1976. *Parties and Party Systems: A Framework for Analysis*. Cambridge: Cambridge University Press.

Scarrow, Howard A. 1983. *Parties, Elections, and Representation in the State of New York*. New York: New York University Press.

Schattschneider, E. E. 1942. *Party Government.* New York: Rinehart.

Schlesinger, Arthur M. 1986. *The Cycles of American History.* Boston: Houghton Mifflin.

Schlesinger, Joseph A. 1984. "On the Theory of Party Organization." *Journal of Politics* 46: 369–400.

———. 1985. "The New American Political Party." *American Political Science Review* 79: 1152–69.

———. 1991. *Political Parties and the Winning of Office.* Ann Arbor: University of Michigan Press.

Schwartz, Maralee. 1992. "GOP Women Complain About Role in Shadows." *The Washington Post* August 19.

Scott, William. 1961. "Organization Theory: An Overview and Appraisal." *Journal of the Academy of Management* 4: 1.

Seasongood, Murray. 1954. "The Triumph of Good Government in Cincinnati," in Robert Loren Morlan, ed., *Capitol, Courthouse, and City Hall.* Boston: Houghton-Mifflin.

Seib, Gerald F. 1994. "Modem Operandi." *The Wall Street Journal* March 16.

Seplow, Stephen. 1996. "Clinton's PA Ad Strategy: Get a Jump on November." *Philadelphia Inquirer* April 21, A.

Shafer, Byron E. 1983. *Quiet Revolution: The Struggle for the Democratic Party and the Shaping of Post-Reform Politics.* New York: Russell Sage.

———. 1988. *Bifurcated Politics: Evolution and Reform in the National Nominating Convention.* Cambridge: Harvard University Press.

———. 1991. "The Nature of an Electoral Order," in Byron E. Shafer, ed., *The End of Realignment?* Pp. 37–84. Madison: University of Wisconsin Press.

Shea, Daniel M. 1995. *Transforming Democracy: State Legislative Campaign Committees and Political Parties.* Albany, N.Y.: State University of New York Press in cooperation with the Center for Party Developments, Washington, D.C.

Shefter, Martin. 1976. "The Emergence of the Political Machine: An Alternative View," in Willis Hawley, ed., *Theoretical Perspectives on Urban Politics.* Pp. 14–44. Englewood Cliffs, N.J.: Prentice-Hall.

———. 1984. "Political Parties, Political Mobilization, and Political Demobilization," in Thomas Ferguson and Joel Rogers, eds., *The Political Economy: Readings in the Politics and Economics of American Public Policy.* Pp. 140–48. Armonk, N.Y.: M. E. Sharpe.

———. 1986. "Trade Unions and Political Machines: The Organization and Disorganization of the American Working Class in the Late Nineteenth Century," in Ira Katznelson and Aristide R. Zolberg, eds., *Working-Class Formation.* Pp. 197–276. Princeton: Princeton University Press.

———. 1994. *Political Parties and the State, the American Historical Experience.* Princeton, N.J.: Princeton University Press.

Shogan, Robert. 1991. "Democrats Map a Strategy for '92 Comeback." *The Los Angeles Times* March 24.

Silbey, Joel H. 1990. "The Rise and Fall of American Political Parties, 1790–1990," in L. Sandy Maisel, ed., *The Parties Respond: Changes in the American Party System.* Pp. 3–20. Boulder, Colo.: Westview Press.

Simon-Rosenthal, Cindy. 1993. "Partners or Solo Players: Legislative Campaign Committees and State Parties." Paper delivered at the State of the Parties: 1992 and Beyond, sponsored by the Bliss Institute of Applied Politics, University of Akron, September 23–24, 1993.

Sinclair, Barbara. 1983. *Majority Leadership in the U. S. House.* Baltimore: Johns Hopkins University Press.

Smallwood, Frank. 1983. *The Other Candidates.* Hanover, N.H.: University Press of New England.

Smith, Ben. 1991. "GOP Working to Keep Duke Off State Ballots." *The Atlanta Constitution* December 21.

Smith, Larry David, and Dan Nimmo. 1991. *Cordial Concurrence: Orchestrating National Party Conventions in the Telepolitical Age.* New York: Praeger.

Sorauf, Frank J. 1980. "Political Parties and Political Action Committees: Two Life Cycles." *Arizona Law Review* 22: 445–64.

———. 1988. *Money in American Elections.* Glenview: Scott, Foresman/Little, Brown.

———. 1992. *Inside Campaign Finance: Myths and Realities.* New Haven: Yale University Press.

Sorauf, Frank J., and Scott A. Wilson. 1990. "Campaigns and Money: A Changing Role for the Political Parties?" in L. Sandy Maisel, ed., *The Parties Respond: Changes in the American Party System.* Pp. 187–203. Boulder, Colo.: Westview Press.

The Speed of Sound. 1994. "Running the Race: Ten Questions You Should Always Ask a Candidate." April.

Spitzer, Robert J. 1987. *The Right to Life Movement and Third Party Politics.* New York: Greenwood.

Stone, Walter J. 1984. "Prenomination Candidate Choice and General Election Behavior: Iowa Presidential Activists in 1980." *American Journal of Political Science* 28: 361–78.

———. 1993. "Asymetrics in the Electoral Bases of Representation, Nomination Politics, and Partisan Change," in Lawrence Dodd and Calvin Jillons, eds., *New Perspectives on American Politics.* Pp. 98–117. Washington, D.C.: Congressional Quarterly Press.

Stone, Walter J., Alan Abramowitz, and Ronald B. Rapoport. 1989. "How Representative Are the Iowa Caucuses?" in Peverill Squire, ed., *The Iowa Caucuses and the Presidential Nominating Process.* Pp. 19–49. Boulder: Westview Press.

Stone, Walter J., Lonna Rae Atkeson, and Ronald B. Rapoport. 1992. "Turning On or Turning Off? Mobilization and Demobilization Effects of Participation in Presidential Nomination Campaigns." *American Journal of Political Science* 36: 665–91.

Strom, Kaare. 1990. "A Behavioral Theory of Competitive Political Parties." *American Journal of Political Science* 34: 565–98.

Sturrock, David E., Michael Margolis, John C. Green, and Dick Kimmins. 1994. "Ohio Political Parties and Elections in the 1990s," in Alexander P. Lamis and Mary Anne Sharkey, eds., *Ohio Politics.* Kent, Ohio: Kent State University Press. Forthcoming.

Sullivan, Denis G., Jeffrey L. Pressman, and F. Christopher Arterton. 1976. *Explorations in Convention Decision Making: The Democratic Party in the 1970s.* San Francisco: Freeman.

Sundquist, James L. 1981. *The Decline and Resurgence of Congress.* Washington, D.C.: Brookings Institution.

———. 1982. "Party Decay and the Capacity to Govern," in Joel Fleishman, ed., *The Future of American Political Parties.* Englewood Cliffs, N.J.: Prentice-Hall.

———. 1983. *Dynamics of the Party System: Alignments and Realignments of the Political Parties in the United States.* Washington, D.C.: The Brookings Institution.

Tashjian v. Republican Party of Connecticut. 479 U.S. 209 [1986] 210–11.

Tisinger, Russell. 1993. "Keeping Clinton Politically Correct." *National Journal* December 4.

Toner, Robin. 1991b. "Despite Bleak Polls, Democrats Insist They Aren't a War Casualty." *The New York Times* March 23.

———. 1991c. "Democrats Review Presidential Bids, Vowing to Avoid the Losers' Mistakes." *The New York Times* September 23.

U.S. Department of Commerce. 1992. *1990 Census of Population: General Characteristics of Ohio.* Washington, D.C.: U.S. Government Printing Office.

Van Buren, Martin. 1967. *Inquiry into the Origins and Course of Political Parties in the United States.* New York: Kelley.

Verba, Sidney, and Norman H. Nie. 1971. *Participation in America.* Chicago: University of Chicago Press.

Verba, Sidney, Kay Lehman Schlozman, Henry Brady, and Norman H. Nie. 1993. "Citizen Activity: Who Participates? What Do They Say?" *American Political Science Review* 87: 303–18.

The Vindicator. 1994a. "The Hanni Influence." A4.

———. 1994b. "Time to Move Forward." May 1, C2.

———. 1995. "The Change One Year Later." June 14, A10.

The Washington Post. 1992. "RNC Chairman Scores Buchanan." April 16.

Ware, Alan. 1985, 1988. *The Breakdown of Democratic Party Organization, 1940–1980.* New York: Oxford University Press.

Wattenberg, Martin P. 1984. *The Decline of American Political Parties, 1952–1980.* Cambridge, Mass.: Harvard University Press.

———. 1990. *The Decline of American Political Parties, 1952–1988.* Cambridge, Mass.: Harvard University Press.

———. 1991b. "The Republican Presidential Advantage in the Age of Party Disunity," in Gary W. Cox and Samuel Kernell, eds., *The Politics of Divided Government.* Boulder, Colo.: Westview Press.

Wekkin, Gary D. 1984. "National-State Party Relations: The Democrats' New Federal Structure." *Political Science Quarterly* 99: 45–72.

Whitely, Paul F., and Patrick Seyd. 1994. "Local Party Campaigning and Electoral Mobilization in Britain." *Journal of Politics* 56: 242–52.

Wickham, DeWayne. 1992. "If Clinton Wins, Credit Brown." *USA Today* October 14.

Wilcox, Clyde. 1989. "Share the Wealth: Contributions by Congressional Incumbents to the Campaigns of Other Candidates." *American Politics Quarterly* 17: 386–408.

Wilson, James Q. 1960. *The Amateur Democrat.* Chicago: University of Chicago Press.

Wines, Michael. 1992. "Crippled by Chaos and Lack of Strategy, Bush Campaign Stumbled to Defeat." *The New York Times* November 29.

The Wisconsin State Journal. 1992. "GOP Video Town Meeting." September 24.

Wolfinger, Raymond E. 1963. "The Influence of Precinct Work on Voting Behavior." *Public Opinion Quarterly* 27: 387–98.

Wright, Gerald C. 1994. "The Meaning of 'Party' in Congressional Roll Call Voting." Paper presented at the annual meeting of the Midwest Political Science Association, Chicago.

Wright, Quincy. 1942. *A Study of War.* Chicago: University of Chicago Press.

Index

About the Contributors

Andrew M. Appleton is an assistant professor of political science and associate director of the Division of Governmental Studies and Service (DGSS) at Washington State University in Pullman. He is coauthor of *State Party Portraits* (CQ Press, forthcoming).

Laura Berkowitz is an instructor of political science at the University of Akron.

Robert Biersack is supervisory statistician at the Federal Election Commission. He has written on congressional elections and campaign finance.

William C. Binning is professor and chair of political science at Youngstown State University. His most recent writing has been on Ohio politics.

Melanie J. Blumberg is a visiting assistant professor of political science at Kent State University and writes on political parties and congressional elections.

Barbara C. Burrell is a researcher with the Wisconsin Research Laboratory at the University of Wisconsin–Madison. She has published extensively on parties and elections, and women and politics.

Nancy L. Clayton is a Ph.D. candidate in the department of political science at Southern Illinois University at Carbondale.

John J. Coleman is assistant professor of political science at the University of Wisconsin–Madison. He has written on party organizations and political economy, and he is the author of *Party Decline in America: Policy, Politics, and the Fiscal State* (1996).

Christian Collet is a graduate student in the Department of Politics and Society at University of California, Irvine.

Anthony Corrado is associate professor of government at Colby College in Waterville, Maine. Most recently, he is the author of *Let America Decide* (1996) and coauthor of *Financing the 1992 Election* (1995).

Gregory Flemming is a graduate student in political science at the University of Wisconsin–Madison.

John Frendreis is professor and chair of political science at Loyola University of Chicago. He has published extensively on political parties, elections, and urban politics.

Alan R. Gitelson is professor of political science at Loyola University of Chicago. In addition to numerous articles on political parties and elections, he is coauthor of *American Political Parties: Stability and Change* (1984).

Ralph M. Goldman is president of the Center for Party Development, Washington, D.C. Among his most recent books are *The National Party Chairmen and Committees: Factionalism at the Top* (1990) and *From Warfare to Party Politics* (1990).

John C. Green is professor of political science and director of the Ray C. Bliss Institute of Applied Politics at the University of Akron. His most recent publication is the edited volume *Religion and the Culture Wars* (1996).

James L. Guth is professor of political science at Furman University. He is coeditor of *The Bible and the Ballot Box: Religion and Politics in the 1988 Election* (1991) and has published extensively on religion and politics, campaign finance, and interest groups.

Jerrold Hansen is a graduate student in politics and society at University of California, Irvine.

Paul S. Herrnson is associate professor of government and politics at the University of Maryland at College Park. His most recent book is *Congressional Elections: Campaigning at Home and in Washington* (1995).

Anne Hildreth is assistant professor of political science at the University of Albany, State University of New York. Her research interests include public attitudes about polling and the way polls are used to influence the policy environment.

John S. Jackson, III is dean of the liberal arts college and professor of political science at Southern Illinois University at Carbondale. His most recent book, *The Politics of Presidential Elections,* was coauthored with William Crotty.

Robin Kolodny is assistant professor of political science at Temple University and was an APSA congressional fellow during the first session of the 104th Congress. She is the author of a forthcoming book on the congressional campaign committees and other works on American parties in comparative perspective.

Anne Layzell is a graduate student in political science at Loyola University of Chicago.

Steve Lilienthal is a writer and journalist living in Washington, D.C.

Theodore J. Lowi is the John L. Senior Professor of American Institutions at Cornell University.

L. Sandy Maisel is the William R. Kenan, Jr., Professor of Government at Colby College. His most recent books are *The Parties Respond* and *Parties and Elections in America* (1994).

Michael Margolis is professor of political science at the University of Cincinnati. His publications include *Manipulating Public Opinion* (1989) and *Machine Politics, Sound Bites, and Nostalgia* (1993).

Randall W. Partin is a Ph.D. candidate in political science at the University of Colorado.

Ronald B. Rapoport is the John Marshall Professor of Government at the College of William & Mary. He is coeditor of *The Life of the Parties: A Study of Presidential Activists* (1993).

A. James Reichley is a visiting senior fellow in the graduate public policy program at Georgetown University. His most recent book is *The Life of the Parties* (1992).

David Resnick is associate professor of political science and director of the Center for the Study of Democratic Citizenship at the University of Cincinnati. He has written on democratic theory and political philosophy.

Daniel M. Shea is assistant professor of political science and Bliss Institute fellow at the University of Akron. He is the author of *Transforming Democracy* (1995).

Walter J. Stone is professor of political science at the University of Colorado. He is the author of *Republic at Risk: Self-Interest in American Politics* (1992).

J. Cherie Strachan is a Ph.D. candidate in political science at the State University of New York at Albany.

Daniel S. Ward is assistant professor of political science at Rice University. He has published on the role of parties in Congress and party organizational change. He is coeditor of *State Party Profiles* (CQ Press, forthcoming).

Lori M. Weber is a graduate student in political science at the University of Colorado.